CHRISTIAN DISCOURSES

THE CRISIS AND A CRISIS IN
THE LIFE OF AN ACTRESS

KIERKEGAARD'S WRITINGS, XVII

CHRISTIAN DISCOURSES

THE CRISIS AND A CRISIS IN THE LIFE OF AN ACTRESS

by Søren Kierkegaard

Edited and Translated
with Introduction and Notes by

Howard V. Hong and
Edna H. Hong

PRINCETON UNIVERSITY PRESS
PRINCETON, NEW JERSEY

BV
4505
.K3413
1997

Library of Congress Cataloging-in-Publication Data

Kierkegaard, Søren, 1813–1855.
[Christelige taler. English]
Christian Discourses ; The Crisis and a crisis in the
life of an actress / by Søren Kierkegaard ;
edited and translated with introduction and notes by
Howard V. Hong and Edna H. Hong.
p. cm. — (Kierkegaard's writings ; 17)
Includes bibliographical references (p.   ) and index.
ISBN 0-691-01649-6 (cloth : alk. paper)
1. Christian life—Lutheran authors.   2. Theater.
3. Heiberg, Johanne Luise, 1812–1890.
I. Hong, Howard Vincent, 1912–.
II. Hong, Edna Hatlestad, 1913–.
III. Kierkegaard, Søren, 1813–1855. Krisen og en
krise in en skuespillerindes liv. English.   IV. Title.
V. Title: Crisis and a crisis in the life of an actress.
VI. Series: Kierkegaard, Søren, 1813–1855.
Works. English. 1978 ; 17.
BV4505.K3413   1997
248.4—dc21   96-49099

Preparation of the volume has been made possible in part by a grant from
the Division of Research Programs of the National Endowment
for the Humanities, an independent federal agency

CONTENTS

Part Two
States of Mind in the Strife of Suffering
93

Part Three
Thoughts That Wound from Behind—for Upbuilding
161

IV. I Corinthians 11:23
275

V. II Timothy 2:12-13
282

VI. I John 3:20
289

VII. Luke 24:51
296

The Crisis and a Crisis in the Life of an Actress
301

ADDENDUM
Phister as Captain Scipio
327

Contents

HISTORICAL INTRODUCTION

The year 1848 was a momentous time for Denmark, as for all of Europe, and also for Søren Kierkegaard. Internally, the crucial event for the country was the termination of absolute monarchy and the establishment of a constitutional monarchy. Externally, there was the open collision with Prussia over the duchies of Slesvig and Holsten.[1] For Kierkegaard, it was on the one hand the year of his "richest productivity"[2] in a direct, intensified Christian mode. On the other hand, it marked the beginning of an open collision with the established order of Christendom, and during that time he wrestled with the question of publishing the finished works, which in most cases contained an explicit critique of the established order. Of the many completed works, only *Christian Discourses* (April 26) and *The Crisis and a Crisis in the Life of an Actress* (July 24–27) were published that year. Kierkegaard intended to terminate his writing with them,[3] just as he had planned to end with *Concluding Unscientific Postscript* in 1845. But then "it was the tension of actuality that put a new string in my instrument. . . .. And so again in 1848."[4]

During the first eight months of 1847, Kierkegaard was immersed in the writing of *Works of Love*. The manuscript was delivered to the printer on August 17 and the volume published on September 29, 1847. Early in June 1847, a sketch of Part Two[5] of *Christian Discourses* was written, and elements of Part Four[6]

---

[1] See Supplement, p. 402 (*Pap.* VIII[1] A 602) and note 36.

[2] *JP* VI 6356 (*Pap.* X[1] A 138). See also, for example, *JP* 6370, 6418, 6438, 6444, 6501, 6511, 6721, 6801 (*Pap.* X[1] A 167, 424, 529, 541; X[2] A 66, 106; X[4] A 6, 545). During 1848 Kierkegaard began and/or completed the writing of *Christian Discourses, A Cycle of Ethical-Religious Essays, The Lily in the Field and the Bird of the Air, Armed Neutrality, The Point of View for My Work as an Author, The Sickness unto Death, Practice in Christianity*, and a piece on the actor Joachim Ludvig Phister as Captain Scipio.

[3] See *JP* VI 6356 (*Pap.* X[1] A 138).

[4] Ibid.

[5] See Supplement, pp. 367–68 (*Pap.* VIII[1] A 180–84).

[6] See Supplement, pp. 393, 396, 397 (*Pap.* VIII[1] A 265, 266, 260).

were entered in the journals of August-September 1847. Thereafter, the various parts were substantially written in quick succession: Part Four by the end of October 1847, Part Two in November, Part One by New Year's Day 1848, and Part Three in
January-February 1848. At the same time, work was being done
on *Practice in Christianity*.

From the very beginning of his authorship, when *Two Upbuilding Discourses* was published within a few weeks of *Either/Or*,
discourses under Kierkegaard's name constituted a series of
signed works parallel to the series of pseudonymous works. After
Postscript and the review of Thomasine Gyllembourg's *Two Ages*,
Kierkegaard wrote only discourses (*Upbuilding Discourses in Various Spirits*, *Works of Love*, and *Christian Discourses*). In the substance and emphasis of the whole series of discourses, there is
movement in continuity. The substance of the six volumes of
1843–1844 that make up *Eighteen Upbuilding Discourses* is within
the ethical-religious categories of immanence, what Climacus in
Postscript calls Religiousness *A*. The three discourses in *Upbuilding Discourses in Various Spirits* (March 13, 1847) Kierkegaard
characterizes as "related to one another esthetically, ethically, religiously."[7] Part Three, "The Gospel of Sufferings," has the subtitle "Christian Discourses," a designation that is here used for
the first time. This is in accord with a journal entry from August,
a few months after the volume was published. "From now on the
thrust should be into the specifically Christian."[8] Accordingly,
Works of Love (September 29, 1847) has the subtitle "Some
Christian Deliberations in the Form of Discourses," and the next
publication has as its main title *Christian Discourses*. The term
discourse is used rather than *sermon* because a sermon presupposes
authority and does not deal with doubt.[9]

The temporal order of the writing of the four parts of *Christian
Discourses* is consonant with the changes in tone and intention.
Parts Four and Two, written first, are a reassuring affirmation of
the joy and blessedness of the Christian life in a world of adversity
and tribulation. In Parts One and Three, there is a polemical

[7] *JP* V 5975 (*Pap.* VIII[1] A 15).
[8] *JP* V 6037 (*Pap.* VIII[1] A 229).
[9] See Supplement, p. 359 (*Pap.* VIII[1] A 6).

tone. In fact, Part Three, the more polemical, was not intended for *Christian Discourses* and was included in the manuscript at the last minute. Originally it was to be the first section of a three-part volume, "Thoughts That Cure Radically, Christian Healing," which was also to include *Sickness unto Death* and what eventually became *Practice*. "First comes: (1) Thoughts that wound from behind—for upbuilding. This will be the polemical element, something like 'The Cares of the Pagans,'[10] but somewhat stronger than that, since Christian discourses should be given in an altogether milder tone."[11] The polemical character of Part Three is epitomized in an early subtitle: "Christian Attack."[12] Because of its polemical character, Kierkegaard had some misgivings about having included Part Three in the final manuscript of *Christian Discourses*,[13] but subsequently he regarded the contrasting Parts Three and Four as being first "a temple-cleansing celebration—and then the quiet and most intimate of all worship services—the Communion service on Fridays."[14]

The presence of Part Three in *Christian Discourses* gave rise also to misgivings about the intended dedication of Part Four to Bishop Mynster.[15] But since Part Three was the overture to Kierkegaard's collision with the established order of Christendom and because he did not want to attack Mynster, whom he both admired and criticized and from whom he still hoped for an admission of the misrepresentation of Christianity,[16] he withdrew the dedication.[17]

The contemporary reception of *Christian Discourses* was very quiet. Apparently there were no reviews of the volume.[18] Three

---

[10] Pp. 3–91.

[11] See Supplement, p. 399 (*Pap.* VIII[1] A 558).

[12] See Supplement, p. 377 (*Pap.* VIII[2] B 101).

[13] See Supplement, p. 399 (*Pap.* VIII[1] A 559) and pp. 402–03 (*Pap.* VIII[1] A 602).

[14] See Supplement, p. 402 (*Pap.* VIII[1] A 590) and pp. 400–01, 402–03 (*Pap.* VIII[1] A 560, 602).

[15] See Supplement, p. 384 (*Pap.* VIII[2] B 116, 118).

[16] See, for example, Supplement, pp. 384–87, 405–06 (*Pap.* VIII[1] A 414, 415; X[4] A 511) and *JP* I 376 (*Pap.* IX A 60).

[17] See Supplement, pp. 387–88, 400–01 (*Pap.* VIII[1] A 438, 560).

[18] None is listed in the copious volume edited by Jens Himmelstrup, *Søren*

appreciative letters from readers are extant, including one in which attention is called to a care of poverty not mentioned in the book, "a care not about what one is going to eat, but about what one *has* eaten and—*not paid for.*"[19] The second edition of the discourses was published in 1862. The contemporary silence notwithstanding, a twentieth-century translator and critic sees in *Christian Discourses* a work in which Kierkegaard writes in ordinary language a devotional book that combines simplicity and inwardness with reflection and presents crucial Christian concepts and presuppositions with unusual clarity. And among the discourses are some of Kierkegaard's masterpieces.[20]

Kierkegaard had always been very interested in drama and opera as well as in literature. In the published works there are, for example, insightful discussions of *Don Giovanni*, ancient and modern tragedy, and Scribe's *First Love* in *Either/Or*,[21] of drama, farce in particular, in *Repetition*;[22] and of Hamlet in *Stages on Life's Way*.[23] It is not surprising, therefore, that this interest in drama, particularized in his admiration of Johanne Luise Heiberg[24] and J. Ludvig Phister,[25] eventuated in appreciative writing about them.

The piece on Mrs. Heiberg was completed before the summer of 1847[26] and was not published until over a year later. In October of that year, Kierkegaard contemplated a pseudonymous volume to include *Crisis* with a special purpose that eventually was fulfilled in published form by *Crisis* alone.

Kierkegaard International Bibliografi (Copenhagen: Nyt Nordisk Forlag Arnold Busck, 1962).

[19] *Kierkegaard: Letters and Documents, KW* XXV, Letter 174. See also Letters 277 and 280.

[20] Emanuel Hirsch (ed.), *Sören Kierkegaard: Christliche Reden* (Düsseldorf, Cologne: Diederichs Verlag, 1959), pp. viii-ix.

[21] *Either/Or*, I, *KW* III, pp. 45–135, 137–64, 231–79 (*SV* I 29–113, 115–41, 205–51).

[22] *Repetition, KW* VI, pp. 156–69 (*SV* III 196–207).

[23] *Stages on Life's Way, KW* XI, pp. 452–54 (*SV* VI 421–23).

[24] See pp. 455–56, note to overleaf of *Crisis*.

[25] See note 27 below.

[26] See Supplement, p. 415 (*Pap.* VIII[2] B 90:26).

I would like to create a little literary mystification by, for example, publishing something I would call "The Writings of a Young Man"; in the preface I would appear as a young author publishing his first book.
I would call myself Felix de St. Vincent. The contents would include:
1. The Crisis in the Life of an Actress
2. A Eulogy on Autumn
3. Rosenkilde as Hummer
4. Writing Sampler[27]

The "mystification" Kierkegaard had in mind was the same mystification initiated by the appearance of two series of publications, the signed *Two Upbuilding Discourses* and the pseudonymous *Either/Or*, both published in the first half of 1843. Now in 1848, when he intended to terminate his writing[28] after a series of religious discourses, the publication of a pseudonymous esthetic work would be appropriate. At one point he even considered as a subtitle "From the Papers of One Dead,"[29] a variation of the title of his first publication, *From the Papers of One Still Living* (1838). Inasmuch, however, as he regarded *Either/Or* as the beginning of the authorship proper, he dropped the subtitle and used a pseudonym, Inter et Inter.

The pseudonym itself is mystifying. The phrase had been used earlier as the heading of a proposed section of a work[30] that ulti-

[27] *JP* V 6060 (*Pap.* VIII¹ A 339). Although the book was never written and the pseudonym was never used, no. 1 appeared separately in *Fædrelandet*, 188–91, July 24–27, 1848, under the title *The Crisis and a Crisis in the Life of an Actress*. At least parts of no. 2 (*Pap.* VII¹ B 205–10) were completed but remained unpublished. Work on no. 3 (*Pap.* VIII² B 172–74) on the Danish actor Christen Niemann Rosenkilde (1786–1861) in the part of Hummer in Johan Ludvig Heiberg's *De Uadskillelige* was begun, but after writing little more than one draft page, Kierkegaard turned to another Danish actor, Joachim Ludvig Phister (1807–1896). If the projected volume had been published in its entirety, the final copy of the piece on Phister (*Pap.* IX B 67–68) would most likely have been no. 3. Therefore it has been included in the present volume as an addendum to the published section no. 1 on Johanne Luise Heiberg.
[28] See Supplement, pp. 420–21 (*Pap.* IX A 227).
[29] See Supplement, p. 412 (*Pap.* VIII² B 90:1).
[30] "New Year's Gift," ed. Nicolaus Notabene. See *JP* V 5708 (*Pap.* IV B 126). See also *Pap.* VIII² B 77.

mately became *Prefaces*. *Inter* as a Latin word simply means "between"—between what? Work on a new pseudonymous series
(by Anti-Climacus, author of *Sickness unto Death* and *Practice*) had
been initiated before the publication of *Crisis*, which would then
be a pseudonymous work between the first pseudonymous series
concluding with *Postscript* and the new Anti-Climacus works, a
point between the two sections of a discontinuous linear series.
Why, then, *Inter et* [and] *Inter?* The second "between" may refer
laterally to the relation between the entire twofold pseudonymous series and the parallel series under Kierkegaard's own
name. The first pseudonymous series needed to be "terminated
in the normal dialectical structure"[31] with a pseudonymous work
as the companion piece to what was planned as the terminating
religious work (*Christian Discourses*).[32] In the journals there are
repeated references to how good it was, how right and fitting, to
have published "that little article" at that particular juncture.[33]

It was not, however, simply for the sake of literary mystification in itself, in order to maintain the dialectical structure of the
dual authorship, that the publication of *Crisis* was important to
Kierkegaard. The important thing was his conception of the religious life, that it is not a substitute satisfaction for those who have
grown old and that the entire complicated authorship was an
expression of that view.

> Yes, it was a good thing to publish that little article. I began
> with *Either/Or* and two upbuilding discourses; now it ends,
> after the whole upbuilding series—with a little esthetic essay.
> It expresses: that it was the upbuilding—the religious—that
> should advance, and that now the esthetic has been traversed;
> they are inversely related, or it is something of an inverse con-
> frontation, to show that the writer was not an esthetic author
> who in the course of time grew older and for that reason be-
> came religious.[34]

[31] See Supplement, pp. 424–25 (*Pap.* IX A 263).
[32] See *JP* VI 6356 (*Pap.* X¹ A 138).
[33] See Supplement, pp. 417–18, 418–23, 424–25 (*Pap.* IX A 181, 189, 205, 216, 218, 227, 228, 234, 241, 263).
[34] See Supplement, p. 420 (*Pap.* IX A 227, p. 124). See *On My Work as an Author*, with *The Point of View, KW* XXII (*SV* XIII 522).

How *Crisis* was received by Danish readers is not known. Mrs. Heiberg's husband, the leading literary figure of that time, thought well of it.[35] In that single individual to whom *Crisis* was addressed, Kierkegaard definitely found an appreciative reader. Mrs. Heiberg may or may not have guessed the author of the piece before he wrote to her three years later, but she did discern that it must be about her.

> Upon reading this in more than one respect remarkable piece, I had to believe that he had made me and my artistic work the subject of his thinking, of his psychological reflections. It could not be anything but reassuring and pleasing for me to read the judgment of me in a type of role that people would have liked to insist lay outside my sphere. . . .
>
> Before Kierkegaard himself had sent this essay, I had, of course, read it again and again and felt happy and was encouraged by it. . . .
>
> For a working artist it is a wonderful surprise to read what the inspired theoretician manages to express clearly and unambiguously, what one to a high degree has *felt* without being able to find the words to clarify and illustrate this feeling. Thus I have always been surprised by what Kierkegaard says on page 162 in this piece. . . .
>
> These remarks from a nonactor were what surprised me. They are altogether correct. I have many times felt precisely as it is described here.[36]

When Laurence Olivier received the Sønning Prize (the highest Danish honor given to authors, artists, and actors), Professor F. J. Billeskov Jansen presented him also "an intellectual gift," a translation of *Crisis*. For Kierkegaard, *Crisis* was his gift of appreciation to Mrs. Heiberg and at the same time a crucial element in the "dialectical structure" of the authorship. To readers over a century later, "that little article" is a valuable contribution to an understanding of Kierkegaard's esthetics and of his complex authorship.

[35] See p. 456, note on overleaf.

[36] Johanne Luise Heiberg, *Et Liv gjenoplevet Erindringen*, I–IV, ed. Aage Friis (Copenhagen: Gyldendal, 1944), II, pp. 134–37 (ed. tr.).

CHRISTIAN DISCOURSES

by Søren Kierkegaard

Part One

THE CARES OF THE PAGANS

CHRISTIAN DISCOURSES[1]

[2]PRAYER X 13

Father in heaven! In springtime everything in nature comes back again with new freshness and beauty. The bird and the lily have lost nothing since last year—would that we, too, might come back unaltered to the instruction of these teachers! But if, alas, our health has been damaged in times past, would that we might recover it by learning again from the lilies in the field and from the birds of the air!

No one can serve two masters, for he must either hate the one and love the other or be devoted to the one and despise the other. You cannot serve God and mammon.

Therefore I say to you, do not worry about your life, what you will eat and what you will drink, nor about your body, what you will wear. Is not life more than food, and the body more than clothing? Look at the birds of the air; they sow not and reap not and gather not into barns, and your heavenly Father feeds them. Are you not much more than they? But who among you can add one foot to his growth even though he worries about it? And why do you worry about clothing? Look at the lilies in the field, how they grow; they do not work, they do not spin. But I say to you that not even Solomon in all his glory was clothed as one of them. If, then, God so clothes the grass of the field, which today is and tomorrow is cast into the stove, would he not much more clothe you, you of little faith? Therefore you should not worry and say, "What shall we eat?" or "What shall we drink?" or "What shall we wear?" The pagans seek all these things; your heavenly Father knows that you need all these things. But seek first God's kingdom and his righteousness; then all these things will be added to you. Therefore do not worry about tomorrow; tomorrow will worry about itself. Each day has enough trouble of its own.

It was on top of Mt. Sinai that the Law was given, during the thundering of heaven; every animal that, alas, innocently and inadvertently, approached the holy mountain had to be put to death—according to the Law.[5] It is at the foot of the mountain that the Sermon on the Mount is preached. This is the way the Law relates to the Gospel, which is: the heavenly down on earth. It is at the foot of the mountain; so mollified is the Gospel, so close is the heavenly that comes down, now on earth and yet even more heavenly. It is at the foot of the mountain; indeed, what is more, the bird and the lily have also come—that they are there almost sounds as if it ends up jesting . . . . . in a game. Although the earnestness becomes all the more holy just because the bird and the lily are there, it becomes that by way of the jest, and it still remains a jest that the lily and the bird are there. They are there; indeed, what is more, they are not merely there, they are there as instructors. The Gospel itself is certainly the actual teacher, he[6] *the Teacher*—and the Way and the Truth and the Life—as the instructor, but the bird and the lily are still there as a kind of assistant teachers.

How is this possible? Well, the matter is not so difficult. Neither the lily nor the bird is a *pagan*, but the lily and the bird are not *Christians* either, and for that very reason they are able to succeed in being helpful with the instruction in Christianity. Pay attention to the lily and the bird; then you will discover how pagans live, because they do not live in exactly the same way as do the bird and the lily. If you live as the lily and the bird live, then you are a Christian—which the lily and the bird neither are nor can become. Paganism forms the opposition to Christianity, but the lily and the bird form no opposition to either of these contending parties—they play outside, if one may put it this way, and shrewdly keep out of all oppositions. In order, then, not to judge and condemn, the Gospel uses the lily and the bird to make clear what paganism is, but thereby in turn in order to make clear what is required of the Christian. The lily and the bird are slipped in to prevent judging, because the lily and the bird judge no one—and you, you are certainly not to judge the pagan; you are to learn from the lily and the bird. Yes, it is a difficult task, a difficult position that the lily and the bird have in the instruction; neither could anyone else do it; anyone else would very likely indict and judge the pagan and eulogize (rather than instruct) the Christian or sneeringly denounce the so-called Christian who does not live this way.

But the lily and the bird, who are solely occupied with and absorbed in instructing, appear totally unconcerned, look neither to the right nor to the left. They neither praise nor scold as a teacher ordinarily does; just like him, *the Teacher*, of whom it is said, "He gives heed to no one" (Mark 12:14), they give heed to no one or they give heed to themselves. And yet, yet it is almost an impossibility not to learn something from them if one pays attention to them. Ah, a person may do everything he is capable of, and yet at times it can be doubtful whether the learner learns anything from him; but the bird and the lily do nothing at all, and yet it is almost an impossibility not to learn something from them. Cannot a person already learn from them what it is to instruct, what it is to instruct Christianly, learn the great art of instruction: to go on as usual, to give heed to oneself, and yet to do it in such a stirring, gripping, charming, also in cost very inexpensive, and moving way that it is impossible not to learn something from it!

It is quite true that when a human teacher has done everything and the learner has still not learned anything, the teacher can say, "It is not my fault." Ah, but when you have learned so very much from the lily and the bird, does it not seem as if they said, "It is not our fault!" So kind are these teachers to the learner, so kind, so humane, so worthy of their divine appointment. If you have forgotten something, they are promptly willing to repeat it for you and repeat and repeat until you finally must know it; if you do not learn anything from them, they do not reproach you but with rare zeal only go on with the instruction, solely concerned with teaching; and if you learn something from them, they give you all the credit, pretend that they had no part what-

ever in it, that it was not to them that you owed it. They give no
one up, no matter how unwilling he is to be taught, and they
demand no dependency, not even the dependency of the one
who learned most from them. O you wonderful teachers, if one
learned nothing else from you, if one learned to instruct, how
much one would have learned! It is already a great thing if a
human teacher does some of what he himself says, since most
often one says much and does only little of it—ah, but even this
comment about others the bird or the lily would never have
made! But you—well, in a certain sense you are not really doing
what you say either; you do it without saying anything. But this
reticent silence of yours and this fidelity of yours to yourselves in
doing the same thing, all day long year in and year out, appreciated or unappreciated, understood or misunderstood, seen or un-
seen—what wonderful mastery in instructing!

Thus with the help of the lily and the bird we get to know the
pagans' cares, what they are, namely, those that the bird and the
lily do not have, although they do have comparable necessities.
But we could, of course, also get to know these cares in another
way: by traveling to a pagan country and seeing how people live
there, what cares they have. Finally, in a third way: by traveling
to —but what am I saying, by traveling—after all, we are living
in the place, in a Christian country where there are only Christians. Therefore one must be able to draw the conclusion: the
cares that are not found here with us, although the comparable
necessities and pressures are present, must be the cares of the
pagans. One could draw this conclusion if, alas, another observa-
tion did not perhaps deprive us of the power to draw the conclusion by removing the presupposition, and now one would draw
another conclusion: these cares are found among people in this
country; ergo, this Christian country is pagan. In that case the
discourse about the cares of the pagans would come to sound like
subtle mockery. Yet we would not dare allow ourselves to take
such a harsh view of Christendom or allow ourselves this almost
cruel mockery, a cruelty that would, note well, backfire on the
speaker himself, who certainly is not such a perfect Christian
either. But let us not forget that the discourse could have this up
its sleeve, as it were, that if an angel were to speak, he could in

this way carry out his mockery of us, who call ourselves Christians, by turning the matter in this way, that instead of censuring us for our mediocre Christianity he would describe the pagan cares and then always add, "But here in this country, which is Christian, no such cares are, of course, to be found." Drawing his conclusion from the assumption that the cares are indeed the cares of the pagans, or, conversely, from the assumption that the country is indeed Christian, he could draw the conclusion that such cares have no doubt unjustly been called the pagans'; or he could imagine a Christian country where there actually are only Christians, pretend that this country is our country, and draw the conclusion: since these cares are not found there, they must be the pagans'. Let us not forget this, and let us never forget either that the pagans who are found in Christendom have sunk the lowest. Those in the pagan countries have not as yet been lifted up to Christianity; the pagans in Christendom have sunk below paganism. The former belong to the fallen race; the latter, after having been lifted up, have fallen once again and have fallen even lower.

Thus the upbuilding address is fighting in many ways for the eternal to be victorious in a person, but in the appropriate place and with the aid of the lily and the bird, it does not forget first and foremost to relax into a smile. Relax, you struggling one! One can forget how to laugh, but God keep a person from ever forgetting how to smile! A person can forget much without any harm and in his old age certainly has to put up with forgetting a lot that he could wish to remember, but God forbid that a person would forget the lily and the bird before his final blessed end!

I

The Care of Poverty[7]

Therefore you should not worry and say, "What shall
we eat?" or "What shall we drink?"—the pagans seek
all these things.

[8]*This care the bird does not have.* What does the bird live on? At this
point we shall not speak about the lily; it is easy for the lily—it
lives on air—but what does the bird live on? The public authority, as everyone knows, has much to care for. At times it has the
concern that there are some who have nothing to live on, but
then, in turn, at other times it is not satisfied that a person has
something to live on and he is summoned and asked what he is
living on. What, then, does the bird live on? Certainly not on
what it gathers into barns, since it does not gather into barns—
and actually one never does live on what one has lying in the
barn. But what, then, does the bird live on? The bird cannot
explain itself. If it is summoned, it presumably would have to
answer as did the man blind from birth who was asked about the
one who had given him his sight, "I do not know, but this I do
know, that I, who was born blind, now see."[9] Likewise the bird
presumably would have to answer, "I do not know, but this I do
know—I live." What, then, does it live on? The bird lives on the
daily bread, this heavenly food that is never stale, this enormous
supply that is kept so well that no one can steal it, because the
thief can steal only what "is saved over night"—what is used
during the day no one can steal.

Thus the daily bread [*Brød*] is the bird's livelihood [*Levebrød*].
The daily bread is the most scantily measured supply; it is just
exactly enough but not one bit more; it is the little that poverty
needs. But then is the bird indeed poor? Instead of answering we

shall ask: Is the bird poor? No, the bird is not poor. See, here it
is evident that the bird is the teacher. Its state is such that if one
is to judge according to its external condition one must call it
poor, and yet it is not poor; it would not occur to anybody to call
the bird poor. What does this mean? It means that its condition
is poverty, but it does not have the care of poverty. If it were
summoned, there can be no doubt that the public authority
would find that in the strictest sense it would qualify for public
welfare, but if one just lets it fly again, it is not poor. Indeed, if the
welfare department had its say, the bird would certainly become
poor, because it would be badgered with so many questions
about its livelihood that it would see for itself that it is poor.

Therefore you should not worry and say, "What will we eat?" or
"What will we drink?"—the pagans seek all these things—*because
the Christian does not have this care*. Is the Christian then rich? Well,
it can perhaps happen that there is a Christian who is rich, but of
course we are not speaking about that—we are speaking about a
Christian who is poor, about the poor Christian. He is poor, but
he does not have this care; therefore he is poor and yet not poor.
In other words, if one in poverty is without the care of poverty,
one is poor and yet not poor, and then if one is not a bird but a
human being and yet like the bird, then one is a Christian.

What, then, does the poor Christian live on? On the *daily
bread*. In that he resembles the bird. But the bird, which certainly
is not a pagan, is not a Christian either—because the Christian
prays for the daily bread. But then is he even poorer than the bird,
since he even has to pray for it, whereas the bird receives it without praying? Yes, the pagan is of that opinion. The Christian
prays for the daily bread; by praying for it he receives it, yet
without having something to save over night; he prays for it and
by praying for it he dismisses the care for the night, sleeps soundly
in order to wake up the next day to the daily bread for which he
prays. Therefore the Christian does not live on the daily bread as
the bird does or as the adventurer, who takes it where he finds it,
because the Christian finds it where he seeks it and seeks it by
praying. But for this reason the Christian, however poor he is,
also has more to live on than the daily bread, which for him has

X
21

something added, a worth and a sufficiency that it cannot have for the bird, because the Christian indeed prays for it and thus knows that the daily bread is *from God.* Does not even an otherwise humble gift, an insignificant little something, have infinite worth for the lover when it is from the beloved! Therefore the Christian does not merely say that the daily bread is enough for him, insofar as he thinks of his earthly wants and necessities, but he also speaks about something else (and no bird and no pagan knows what it is he is talking about) when he says, "It is enough for me that it comes from him," that is, from God. Just as that simple wise man, although he continually spoke about food and drink,[10] still spoke profoundly about the highest things, so also the poor Christian, when he speaks about food, speaks simply about what is highest, because when he says "the daily bread" he is not thinking so much about food as about his receiving it from God's table. The bird does not live on the daily bread in this way. It certainly does not, like a pagan, live in order to eat; it eats in order to live—but then is it really *living*?

The Christian lives on the daily bread; there is no question that he lives on that, but neither is there any question about what he will eat or what he will drink. In this regard he knows himself to be understood by the heavenly Father, who knows that he has need of all these things. The poor Christian does not ask about all such things, which the pagans seek. There is, however, something else that he seeks, and therefore he *lives* (for it was, after all, doubtful to what extent it can really be said that the bird *lives*), therefore he lives, or it is for this that he lives, and therefore one can say that he lives. He believes that he has a Father in heaven, who every day opens his benign hand and satisfies everything that lives[11]—also him—with his blessing; yet what he seeks is not to become satisfied, but the heavenly Father. He believes that a human being is not differentiated from the bird by his inability to live on just as little but by his inability to live "on bread alone."[12] He believes that it is the blessing that satisfies; yet what he seeks is not to become satisfied, but the blessing. He believes that no sparrow falls to the ground without the heavenly Father's will[13] (something no sparrow knows anything about, and of what help would it actually be to the sparrow that it is so!). He believes that,

just as he will certainly receive the daily bread as long as he has
to live here on earth, he will some day live blessed in the hereafter. This is how he explains the passage "that life is more than
food," since even temporal life is surely more than food, but an
eternal life is nevertheless certainly beyond all comparison with
food and drink, in which the *life of a human being* does not consist
any more than does the kingdom of God! He always bears in
mind that the life of holiness is lived here on earth in poverty,
that *he* hungered in the desert and thirsted on the cross; thus
not only can one live in poverty, but in poverty one can *live*.
—Therefore he does indeed pray for the daily bread and gives
thanks for it, something the bird does not do. But to pray and to
give thanks are more important to him than meat and drink and
for him are indeed his food, just as it was Christ's "food to do the
Father's will."[14]

But then is the poor Christian indeed rich? Yes, he is indeed
rich. The bird, which in poverty is without the care of poverty,
the poor bird is admittedly no pagan and therefore not poor either; although poor, it is not poor. But it is no Christian either,
and therefore it is still poor—the poor bird, oh, indescribably
poor! How poor not to be able to pray, how poor not to be able
to give thanks, how poor to have to receive everything as if in
ingratitude, how poor not to exist, as it were, for the benefactor
to whom it owes its life! To be able to pray and to be able to give
thanks—that, of course, is to exist for him, and to do that is to
live. The poor Christian's wealth is precisely to exist for the God
who certainly did not once and for all give him earthly wealth—
oh, no, who every day gives him the daily bread. Every day! Yes,
every day the poor Christian has occasion to become aware of his
benefactor, to pray and to give thanks. Indeed, his wealth increases each time he prays and gives thanks, and each time it
becomes clearer to him that he exists for God and God for him,
whereas earthly wealth becomes poorer and poorer each time
the rich man forgets to pray and to give thanks. Ah, how poor to
have received once and for all one's share for one's whole life,
but what wealth to receive one's share "every day!" How dubious to have occasion almost every day to forget that one has
received what one has; how blessed to be reminded of it every

day—that is, be reminded of one's Benefactor, that is, of one's God, one's Creator, one's Provider, one's Father in heaven, thus of the love for which alone it is worth living and which alone is worth living for!

But then is the poor Christian indeed rich? Yes, he certainly is rich, and in fact you will recognize him by this: he does not want to speak about his earthly poverty but rather about his heavenly wealth. Therefore at times his words sound very strange. While everything around him reminds of his poverty, he speaks about his wealth—ah, and this is why no one but a Christian can understand him. It is told of a pious hermit, who had lived, dead to the world, for many, many years strictly observing the vow of poverty, that he had won the friendship and devotion of a rich man. Then the rich man died and bequeathed his whole fortune to the hermit, who for so long a time now had lived on the daily bread. But when someone came and told the hermit this, he answered, "There must be a mistake. How can he make me his heir when I was dead long before him!"[15] Ah, how poor wealth looks alongside of—wealth! Earthly wealth always looks poor in relation to death. But the Christian, who in poverty is without the care of poverty, is also dead to the world and from the world. Therefore he *lives*. By dying the bird ceases to live, but the Christian lives by dying. This is why the wealth of the whole world, which one can have the use of as long as one lives, looks so poor in comparison with his—poverty, yes, or his wealth. That a dead person does not need money, we all know, but the living person who actually has no use for it—well, he must either be very rich, and in that case it can very well be that he needs more—or he must be a poor Christian.

Inasmuch, then, as the poor Christian is rich, he does not resemble the bird. The bird is poor and yet not poor, but the Christian is poor, yet not poor but rich. The bird is without care for the lower, which it does not seek, but neither does it seek the higher. The bird itself is without care, but to the bird it is also as if its life were not the object of anyone else's care. The Christian shares, as it were, with God; he lets God take care of food and drink and all such things, while he seeks God's kingdom and his righteousness."[16] The poor bird rises high into the clouds

X
24

without being weighed down by the care of poverty, but the Christian rises even higher. It is as if the bird were seeking God in its flight toward heaven, but the Christian finds him; it is as if the bird flew far, far away seeking for God, but the Christian finds him, and finds him (what heavenly bliss!) down on the earth; it is as if the bird flew into heaven but heaven still remains closed—only for the Christian is it opened!

Therefore you should not worry and say: What will we eat or what will we drink?—for all such things the pagans seek. Yes, *the pagans worry about such things*.

   The bird is in poverty without the care of poverty—it is silent. The Christian is in poverty without the care of poverty, but he does not speak of the poverty but instead of his riches. [17]The pagan has the care of poverty. Instead of being in poverty without care, he is "without God in the world"[18] (the one corresponds completely to the other). See, that is why he has the care. He is not silent like the carefree bird; he does not speak like a Christian, who speaks of his riches; he has and knows really nothing else to talk about than poverty and its care. He asks: What will I eat, what will I drink, today, tomorrow, the day after tomorrow, this winter, next spring, when I have become old, I and my family and the whole country—what will we eat and drink? Alas, he does not ask this question only in a troubled moment and then repent of it; he does not ask it in a time of hardship and then pray to God for forgiveness. No, he is without God in the world and makes himself important—by means of the question, which he calls the proper life-question; he becomes significant to himself by means of the thought that he is exclusively occupying himself with this life-question. He finds it indefensible on the part of the public authorities (since he has nothing to do with God) if he should lack something, he who is living solely for this life-question. Anyone who does not occupy himself with it, or at least with supporting him, he regards as a dreamer; in comparison with this most profound life-question, he regards even the highest and the holiest as vanity and delusion. He finds it fatuous to refer an adult person to the bird and the lily. Indeed, what would

there be to see, and what would one learn from them! If someone, like him, is a man who has learned what the earnestness of
life is, if he is a man, citizen, and father, it is a rather silly joke and
a childish caprice to send him to contemplate the lilies and the
birds, as if he had nothing else to attend to. "If it were not out of
a sense of decency," he says, "and out of respect for my children,
whom according to custom one has of course had instructed in
religion, I would bluntly say that there is very little to be found
in Holy Scripture that answers this most important question, and
very little at all that is of any benefit, with the exception of an
occasional splendid maxim. We read about Christ and the apostles but find not the slightest contribution to an answer to the
proper life-question, the primary question: what they lived on,
what they did in order to give everyone his due and to pay taxes
and fees. To solve the problem of a time of scarcity by a miracle
is a very meaningless answer to this question—even if it is true,
what does it demonstrate! Not to give any advance thought at all
to any solution and when the settlement time comes and taxes
are due, then to have a disciple pull out of the water a fish in
whose mouth is a coin[19] that one uses to make payment—even
if that is true, what does it demonstrate! On the whole, I miss
earnestness in Holy Scripture, an earnest answer to the earnest
question; an earnest man does not want to be taken for a fool, as
if one were at a comedy. Let the preachers prattle about such
things to women and children; yet every earnest and enlightened
man secretly agrees with me, and where the earnest people come
together, in public meetings, there they honor only the sagacity
that has an understanding of reality."

So it is with the pagan, for paganism is without God in the
world, but Christianity makes it quite evident that paganism is
ungodliness. The ungodliness is not so much being worried, although it certainly is not Christian to be that; the ungodliness is
to be totally unwilling to know anything else, to be totally unwilling to know that this care is sinful, that Scripture therefore
says that a person can burden his heart with worry about his
livelihood in the same sense as he can burden it with gluttony
and drunkenness (Luke 21:34). Everywhere in life there are

crossroads. Every human being at some time, at the beginning, stands at the crossroads—this is his perfection and not his merit. Where he stands at the end (at the end it is not possible to stand at the crossroads) is his choice and his responsibility. For the one who is in poverty and who then cannot turn away from poverty, the crossroads are: either Christianly to turn away from the care of poverty by turning onto *the Way*[20] upward, or in ungodliness to abandon oneself to the care of poverty by turning onto the wrong way downward. From the point of view of the eternal, there are never two ways; although there are the crossroads, there is only one Way—the other way is the wrong way. The deeper he sinks down into the care of poverty, the more he distances himself from God and the essentially Christian. He has sunk the deepest when he *wills* not to know anything higher but instead wills that this care be not only the heaviest (something it in fact is not, because that is the pain of repentance), no, that it be the highest.

But those who want to be rich fall into many temptations and snares,[21] and what is the care of poverty but wanting to be rich! Perhaps the care does not demand riches immediately; forced by hard necessity and facing impossibility, it perhaps is satisfied with less for the time being. Yet this same care, if it were to have its present wish fulfilled, if the prospect of more opened up, would continually crave more and more. It is an illusion if someone thinks that the care of poverty, when it has been unwilling to let itself be spiritually healed (and in that case the healing can just as well begin with a little less as with a little more), would find any condition whereby it would be satisfied before it had attained riches, with which it would not be satisfied anyway. Oh, what a long road lies ahead of the care of poverty, and what is most terrible is that this road is everywhere crisscrossed with temptations! We all walk in danger wherever we go,[22] but the one who wants to be rich walks in temptation everywhere, and it is inevitable that he will fall into this temptation, into which God has not led him but into which he has plunged himself. The one who is in poverty is already placed in a difficult position but is by no means abandoned by God; the deliverance is what is *commanded*: to be without care—that the deliverance commanded by God is the only true deliverance is recognized precisely by its being deliverance and is that because it is what is "commanded."

To be without care—indeed, it is a difficult walk, almost like walking on water, but if you are able to have faith, then it can be done.[23] In connection with all danger, the main thing is to be able to get away from the thought of it. Now, you cannot get away from poverty, but you can get away from the thought of it by continually thinking about God: this is how the Christian walks *his* course. He turns his gaze upward and looks away from the danger; in his poverty, he is without the care of poverty. But the thoughts of the one who wants to be rich are continually on the earth; in his care he is on the earth, with his care is on the earth; he walks bowed down, continually looking ahead to see if he might be able to find riches. He is continually looking ahead—alas, ordinarily this is the best way to avoid temptation, but for him, yes, he does not know it, for him looking ahead is the very way to walk into the pitfall, the way to finding the temptation greater and greater and to sinking deeper and deeper into it. He is already in the power of the temptation, because the care is the temptation's most ingenious servant. And the temptation is down on the earth, there where "all such things are what the pagans seek"; the temptation is down on the earth—the more it gets a person to look downward, the more certain is his downfall. What is *the temptation* that in itself is many temptations? Certainly it is not the glutton's temptation to live in order to eat; no (what rebellion against the divine order!), it is to live *in order to slave.* The temptation is this, to lose oneself, to lose one's soul, to cease to be a human being and live as a human being instead of being freer than the bird, and godforsaken to slave more wretchedly than the animal. Yes, to slave! Instead of *working* for the daily bread, which every human being is commanded to do, to *slave* for it—and yet not be satisfied by it, because the care is to become rich. Instead of *praying* for the daily bread, to *slave* for it—because one became a slave of people and of one's care and forgot that it is to God one must pray for it. Instead of being willing to be what one is, poor, but also loved by God, which one certainly is, never happy in oneself, never happy in God, to damn oneself and one's life to this slaving in despondent grief

day and night, in dark and brooding dejection, in spiritless busyness, with the heart burdened by worry about making a living—
smitten with avarice although in poverty!

Consider now, in conclusion, the bird, which is, after all, there
in the Gospel and must be here in the discourse. Compared with
the pagan's ungodly depression, the bird, which in poverty is
without the care of poverty, is carefreeness; compared with the
Christian's devout faith, the carefreeness of the bird is light-
mindedness. Compared with the bird's lightness, the pagan is
heavily burdened like a stone; compared with the Christian's
freedom, the bird is still subject to the law of gravity. Compared
with the bird, who lives, the pagan is dead; compared with the
Christian, one still cannot really say that the bird lives. Compared
with the bird that is silent, the pagan is talkative. Compared with
the Christian, the pagan is indeed an inarticulate being; he neither prays nor gives thanks, which is human language in the most
profound sense; everything else, everything the pagan says, is
related to it as a bird that has learned to talk is related to a human
being. The bird is poor and yet not poor; the Christian is poor,
yet not poor but rich; the pagan is poor, poor, poor—poorer
than the poorest bird. Who is *the* poor one who is so poor that
this is the only thing to be said about him, just as it is the only
thing he himself can talk about? It is the pagan. According to
Christianity's doctrine, no one else is poor, no one, neither the
bird nor the Christian. It is a long road, in poverty to want to be
rich; the bird's shortcut is the shortest, the Christian's the most
blessed.

X
28

II

The Care of Abundance

Therefore you should not worry and say, "What shall we eat?" or "What shall we drink?"—the pagans seek all these things.

This care the bird does not have. But is, then, abundance a care? Perhaps it is only subtle sarcasm to speak so similarly about things so different, about poverty and abundance, so similarly as the Gospel does—alas, almost as if instead abundance were simply care in abundance. After all, a person thinks that wealth and abundance would keep him free from cares—perhaps also from the care of wealth? Wealth and abundance come hypocritically in sheep's clothing[24] under the guise of safeguarding against cares and then themselves become the object of care, become *the care.* They safeguard a person against cares just as well as the wolf assigned to look after the sheep safeguards these against—the wolf.

The bird, however, does not have this care. Is the bird poor? No, this we made clear in the previous discourse. Is, then, the bird rich? Well, if it is, it must not know about it; if it is, it is ignorant of it. Or where has the bird hidden its store? If each of all the lords of estates and of all the farmers stood by his barn and said, "No, stop, this is mine," where, then, is the barn belonging to the bird? [25]Thus the bird does not have the care of possessing abundance, does not have the care of abundance, that others own more, or, alas, that others own less or nothing at all.

How, then, does the bird live? Indeed, it is God who measures out the definite portion to the bird every day—enough. But it never occurs to the bird that it has more or to want to have more, to want to have in abundance. What God gives every day is—

enough. But the bird wants to have neither more nor less than—
enough. [26]The measure with which God each day measures out
to the bird, that same measure, if I may put it this way, the bird
has in its mouth. It measures with the same measure as God measures: he gives the bird *enough*; so the bird measures and says, "It
is enough." Whether the little bird quenches its thirst with a drop
of dew, which is just enough, or drinks from the biggest lake, it
takes just as much; it does not insist on having everything it sees,
the whole lake because it drinks from it, does not insist on taking
the lake with it in order to be safeguarded for all its life. If at
harvest time the bird comes to the richest supply, it does not
know what abundance [*Overflod*] is, what superfluous [*overflødig*]
knowledge that is. If out in the forest where the bird builds and
lives with its family, there is the greatest possible abundance of
everything that it and its family need, even if they were to live
ever so long, it does not know what abundance is, neither it nor
its mate nor their young. But if one, even if one has abundance,
does not know what abundance is, then it is impossible for abundance to become a care. When the bird has eaten and drunk, it
never occurs to it to think: How shall I get something next
time—therefore the poor bird is nevertheless not poor. But neither does it ever occur to it to think: What am I going to do with
the remainder, with the whole lake, with the enormous supply
of grain that was left over when it had taken the three kernels of
grain that were *enough*; it does not have, it does not possess an
abundance, and it does not have its care. And when the time
comes and the longing awakens and it must be off, it abandons
house and home, everything it possesses and has, the nest built so
diligently and skillfully, the perhaps most favorable spot so fortunately chosen, the likes of which it will never find. The bird
thinks: There is no point in looking ahead for trouble[27]—and
flies away. The bird is a traveler, even the one that does not travel
is still a traveler; therefore it wants to have nothing to do with
abundance and nothing with its care.

Thus it is indeed intrinsic to the bird that it does not have
abundance, that it does not have the care of abundance. The first
barrel of gold, say the financiers, is the most difficult to acquire;

when one has that, the rest comes by itself. But the first penny
acquired with the idea that one is beginning to accumulate in
abundance is in fact an advance payment—the bird wants nothing, wants not a penny in abundance, in order to avoid the rest
(which of course comes by itself): the care. With the most punc-
tilious accuracy it always takes just exactly *enough*, every time,
not the least bit more—lest it come in the remotest contact with
the ambiguous knowledge about what abundance is. In poverty,
the bird is without the care of poverty; against the care of abundance it has carefully safeguarded itself.

But how is the bird a teacher; where is the contact point of the
instruction? Well, of course it teaches us the surest way to avoid
the care of wealth and abundance—not to gather riches and
abundance, bearing in mind that one is a traveler. And next it
teaches us—something that is a particular point of this discourse—in abundance to be ignorant that one has abundance,
bearing in mind that one is a traveler. The bird, like that simple
wise man of antiquity,[28] is a teacher in ignorance. How difficult
even to be beautiful and not know it (yet something of which
both the bird and the lily are capable); how much more difficult not to know it when one has abundance! But in its abundance the bird is as ignorant of having abundance as if it did not
have it.

The Christian does not have the care of abundance. Is, then, the Christian poor; is every Christian poor? Certainly there are Christians
who are poor, but we are not speaking of them now; we are
speaking of the rich Christian who has riches and abundance, and
we are speaking about his still not having this care. If, namely,
someone in abundance is without its care—through ignorance—
then one is either a bird, or if one is a human being and yet like
the bird, then one is a Christian.

So the rich Christian *does have* abundance but is ignorant of it,
and therefore he must *have become* ignorant. To be ignorant is no
art, but to *become* ignorant and to be ignorant by having become
ignorant—that is the art. To that extent the Christian is different
from the bird, because the bird is ignorant, but the Christian

becomes ignorant; the bird begins with ignorance and ends with it; the Christian ends with being ignorant—and Christianly the question is never asked about what a person was but about what he became, not about what he was like, but about what sort of person he became, not about the beginning but about the end.

Yet to become ignorant in this way can take a long time, and it is a difficult task before he succeeds, little by little, and before he finally succeeds in really becoming ignorant of what he knows, and then in remaining ignorant, in continuing to be that, so he does not sink back again, trapped in the snare of knowledge. The Christian, when he has abundance, is as one who does not have abundance;[29] so, then, he is ignorant, and thus he indeed does not have it if in other respects he actually is as one who does not have abundance. But originally the Christian is a human being, and as such he is not like this; he becomes this as a Christian, and the more he becomes a Christian, the more he who has is as one who does not have.

What, specifically, can take wealth and abundance away from a person? Need and destitution can do it, or the God who gave can also take away. When this happens, the formerly rich become actually poor. But about that we do not speak, nor about the rich man's being able to give away all his wealth and abundance, because then, after all, he becomes one of the formerly rich. But is there not something that can take wealth and abundance away from him so that it is taken away without his becoming one of the formerly rich? Yes, there is such a thing! What power is it, then? It is thought and the power of thought. Can, then, thought take the abundance away from the rich in any external way? No, thought cannot do that. With regard to abundance, thought can take the *thought of possession* away from the rich person, the thought that he possesses and owns this wealth and abundance as *his*. Yet in the external sense thought allows him to keep it all; no one else acquires his riches and abundance; everyone else must say that it belongs to the rich person. This is the way thought goes about it; if it succeeds in this, if the rich person complies with it, if he totally submits himself and his abundance to the power of thought, then he who has is as one who does not have. And this is what the Christian does.

Yes, it is a sly power, the power of thought! In this way no
thief can steal, in this way no assailant can rob. In this way not
even God can take away, not even when he takes the power of
thought and reason away from the rich man; and yet no thief and
no robber can so totally take everything away from the rich man
as thought can when it is allowed to rule. But how does this
happen? When I do not know what I am going to live on tomorrow, then is it not true that I do not own anything? But when I
think that I can perhaps die tonight, "this very night,"[30] then,
however rich I am, I do not own anything either. In order to be
rich, I must own something for tomorrow etc., I must be secure
for tomorrow; but in order to be rich, I must also be sure *of* tomorrow. Take the riches away, then I can no longer be called
rich; but take tomorrow away—alas, then I can no longer be
called rich either. In order to be rich, I must possess something;
but in order to be rich, I certainly must also still exist. And this
the rich Christian does not know, whether he will be alive tomorrow, or he knows that he does not know it. Basically everyone knows that, but the Christian bears it in mind "this very day"
and every day bears in mind that he does not know it, does not
know whether he perhaps will die "this very night."

Furthermore, if I own nothing and therefore can lose nothing,
then I am not rich. But when I unfortunately own something
that can be lost and can be lost at any moment, am I then rich?
When I have nothing in my hands, then I do not clutch anything
either; but when I hold in my hands something that slips away
through the fingers, something losable, what then am I clutch-
ing? Riches are indeed a possession, but actually or essentially to
possess something of which the essential feature is losableness or
that it can be lost is just as impossible as to sit down and yet
walk—at least thought cannot get anything in its head except
that this must be a delusion. If, namely, losability is an essential
feature of riches, then it is obvious that no essential change has
occurred in it when it is lost, no essential change occurs in it by
being lost. Therefore, it is essentially the same, but then it is
indeed also essentially the same while I possess it—it is lost—
because it must indeed be essentially the same at every moment.
Lost, it is essentially the same; possessed, it is essentially the same,

x
33

is lost; that is, in the deeper sense it cannot be possessed—this matter of possessing is a delusion. In its own way the thought of justice can take the thought of possession away from all unlawful goods and take it by force or by foul means; but the thought of eternity takes the thought of possession away from wealth and abundance, even if it is lawfully possessed—by fair means, without using any force other than the power of thought, provided the person is willing to submit himself to the power of thought or wills his own welfare.

Yes, it is a sly power, the power of thought. If people are not safeguarded or have not safeguarded themselves in so many ways against this power, they would admit that it is sly, but they would also sense that it is in the service of truth that it is so sly. The sharp eye of the bird of prey does not discover its quarry as swiftly and as surely as the saving thought discovers what it has to hurl itself upon. It does not take a false aim at the quibbling about what should be called riches, prosperity, wealth, etc.—it takes aim at the thought of possession. The Christian does not evade having the aim directed at him but even cooperates in making the healing wound as deep as possible.

X
34

Then also in another way thought takes aim at the thought of possession. If I am to be rich, I must indeed own something, and thus what I own is mine. But now if I own something that is not mine! See, here is the contradiction, and this battle of contradiction cannot be fought out within the relationships between persons. Insofar as it is not mine, I of course do not own it; but yet if there is no other human being who owns it, then humanly speaking it is mine; but if it is mine, then I indeed own it. But this is meaningless. Therefore, there must be (for the sake of meaning and of thought) a third party who is involved wherever in these innumerable human relationships there is a question of "mine"—a third party who says, "It is mine." It is like an echo; every time someone says "mine," the recurring "mine" sounds. "It is mine," you say; "It is mine," he says, he, the third party; "It is all mine," says he who is all. Everyone really knows well enough that in the more profound sense no human being owns anything, that no one has anything except what is given to him—

basically everyone knows this. But the rich Christian bears in mind that he knows it; every day he renders to himself an account of his knowing it and an account of his responsibility if he does not know it; this belongs to his accounting of mine and yours. He bears in mind that he owns nothing except what is given to him and owns what is given to him not for him to keep but only on loan, as a loan, as entrusted property. Basically everyone knows that when all is said and done a person certainly cannot keep the riches he has, but the rich Christian bears in mind that he has not received it *in order to* keep it but as entrusted property. [31]Thus he manages it in the best manner on behalf of the owner, shuddering only at the thought of something false in mine and yours. But the owner is God. And God, if he is to be satisfied, does not want his assets increased by ingenious transactions, as if he were a financier, but in a totally different way.

The rich Christian, who is the steward, understands this perfectly—and therefore he cannot understand why explaining the parable of the unfaithful steward[32] has caused such great difficulty for the interpreters. Suppose, he says, that it had been that steward's lawful possession; if this is assumed, then God has no objection to your sitting down and writing—false receipts, writing receipts for one-half less. That is, God has no objection to your releasing *your* debtors from one-half of the claim; if you like, you may release them from the whole debt and in this way gain for yourself friends who can greet you in the hereafter. The unfaithfulness was that the steward dealt with someone else's property in this way. That was why it was sagacious, and that is why the children of the world, who understand the things of this world, praise his sagacity. If he had not been the steward but the master and then had managed the property the way the steward managed the master's, it would have been noble, magnanimous, and Christian—and then the children of the world would not only not have found it sagacious but would have found it stupid and fatuous and would have laughed him to scorn. The parable actually wants to teach that in this world the noble act is regarded as stupidity, the evil act as sagacity. To cancel the debt, to steal from one's own pocket—how stupid; but adroitly to steal from

X
35

someone else's pocket—how sagacious! The parable, however, recommends the nobility of acting in the same way as the steward—but, but with one's own property.

But what am I saying, "one's own property"—the rich Christian indeed realizes that in the highest sense the wealth is not his own property. Are we back to the same place again? Oh no, the owner is God, who expressly wants it administered in this way. That is how far it is from the rich Christian's being able to call the earthly wealth "mine"—it is God's property; and as far as possible it is to be managed according to the owner's wishes, managed with the owner's indifference to money and monetary value, managed by being given away at the right time and place.

Yet if the goods of this world are to be managed in this way, they are best managed by a *traveler*—indeed, as soon as the steward had made that most sagacious maneuver, he thought of something equally sagacious—to clear out. And we—we certainly are not to be like the steward but rather to learn from him. But every Christian, like the bird, is a traveler; so also is the rich Christian. As a traveler he is a Christian, and as a Christian he is a traveler who knows exactly what he should take with him and what he should not take with him, what is his and what is not his. For everyday use we perhaps at times have something lying around that does not belong to us; but the moment we think of going on a journey, we check very carefully to see what is ours and what belongs to others. This is the way the rich Christian, who at every moment is a traveler, thinks and speaks at every moment about his earthly riches. He who has something altogether different to think about does not wish right now, at the last moment, to be reminded of what he is not to have with him and what is not his. Do you perhaps find it more difficult to understand him? Well, he understands it, and he understands himself. At one time he may have had difficulty understanding it, but now he does understand it. Perhaps at times it is difficult for the rich Christian's wife and children to understand him; they are so eager to press upon him an awareness of his wealth, to make him believe that he has abundance, but then he says reprimandingly: "I do not want to hear such talk, and I do not wish to hear it from you, especially now at the last moment." Alas, and in turn no one but a Christian can understand him, since he is neither sick nor, as the passport clerk knows, is he going on a journey tomorrow. That is how ignorant he is of his earthly wealth—he became and remains ignorant [*uvidend*] by having become aware [*vidend*] of something else totally different (because by becoming aware of something else one *becomes* ignorant of what one knew), namely, that he could die this very night, that wealth essentially cannot be possessed, that it is entrusted property, that he himself is a traveler—that is how ignorant the rich Christian is of his earthly wealth, yes, just like an absent-minded person.

Now, if the rich Christian is in this way ignorant of the abundance he has, he cannot possibly have the care of abundance. Nor does he have it. In abundance, he is without the care of abundance; he has no care about what ordinarily, according to a fine saying,[33] is gathered with uneasiness, about what ordinarily is possessed with uneasiness, about what ordinarily is lost with uneasiness, about what ordinarily is given up with uneasiness—and yet he has abundance. He has no care [*Bekymring*] in gathering abundance, because he does not care [*bryde sig*] about gathering abundance; he has no care about keeping it, because it is easy enough to keep what one does not have, and he is indeed like one who does not have; he has no care about losing it, that is, losing what one does not have, because he is indeed like one who does not have; he has no care about others' owning more, because he is like one who owns nothing; he knows not the care about others' owning less, because he is like one who owns nothing; and he has no care about what he is going to leave to his family. Thus he has no care from his abundance, but, on the other hand, every time he uses some of it to do good, he has a surprise such as one has in finding something, because, since he who has is like one who does not have, he indeed finds what he does not have.

But then, when all is said and done, is the *rich* Christian basically *just as poor* as the poor Christian? Yes, that he certainly is. But as a Christian he is rich. He is just as ignorant of his earthly wealth as the poor Christian is of his earthly poverty. Just as the latter does not talk about his earthly poverty, he does not talk about his earthly wealth; they both talk about the very same thing, about the heavenly wealth, about existing before God as one who prays and gives thanks for the daily bread, as one who is God's steward.

In this sense, only in this sense, the rich Christian has joy from his earthly wealth. But is it not remarkable how much more quickly the move was made from poverty to joy and, on the other hand, how many difficulties were attached to moving from earthly wealth to joy, and yet we cannot be said to have made unnecessary difficulties! Thus, as a Christian, the rich Christian has joy from his earthly wealth. As a Christian he believes that he has a father in heaven and that this is the father who gives him the earthly wealth. Yet for him the giver is infinitely more than the gift; therefore he does not seek the gift but the giver; he does not take the gift but receives it from the giver's hand. He believes (what every Christian believes but what is very necessary for the rich Christian in particular) that a Christian's wealth is in heaven; therefore his heart turns there where his treasure must be.[34] He always bears in mind that *he* who possessed all the world's wealth gave up everything he possessed and lived in poverty,[35] that consequently the life of holiness is lived in poverty, and thus in turn in ignorance of all the wealth that is possessed.

This is why the rich Christian is able to have joy from his earthly wealth, joy every time he is granted opportunity to do something good with his wealth, that he can do another person a service and that he at the same time can serve his God. Oh, it is of course difficult to do two things at the same time, but it certainly would be difficult to find a more blessed twofold thing to do at the same time than to do another person a service and at the same time to serve God! It is difficult to remember two things at the same time; it is difficult enough for many a person to remember the words "Remember to do good and to share";[36] yet the rich Christian remembers one thing more, "Do not forget God when you do good and share." Therefore the rich Christian

X
38

has double joy from doing good because he also comes to think of God. The rich Christian believes that all good and perfect gifts come from above[37] (something that seems to pertain more particularly to the receiver but, Christianly, pertains just as much to the giver); therefore if the gift he gives is to be good and perfect, it must be God who gives it through him. Therefore he has joy from his wealth, because they give him the occasion and the opportunity to learn to know God, who is indeed the actual, the hidden benefactor, and the rich Christian is his confidant, who is used in these blessed errands. Therefore the rich Christian has joy from his earthly wealth in helping others to thank and praise God, while in turn he himself also gains friends, who no doubt will be unable to repay him, but who still (ah, is this not almost usury!) will in return greet him in the hereafter.

Thus the rich Christian in the state of abundance is without the care of abundance, is ignorant as the bird, and to that extent poor as the poor Christian, is rich as a Christian, and thus at last has joy from his earthly wealth. He has this advantage over the bird, to be rich as a Christian and, in turn, when it is understood in this way, to have joy from his earthly wealth—he is not merely like the bird without care.

Therefore you should not ask, "What will we eat?" or "What will we drink?"—the pagans seek all these things. *The rich pagan does have this care.*

The rich pagan is as far as possible from being ignorant of his wealth and abundance. In other words, the one who has wealth and abundance can *become* ignorant only by becoming aware of something else, but the rich pagan neither knows nor wants to know about anything else. Indeed, it is a difficult matter for a person who has wealth and abundance to become ignorant of what day in and day out thrusts itself upon one in so many ways, but always ensnaringly. Yet it can be done by becoming Christianly aware of God. This knowledge totally engages the Christian's mind and thought, blots out everything else from his memory, captures his heart forever, and thus he becomes absolutely ignorant. The rich pagan, however, also has only one thought: riches. All his thoughts revolve around that—yet he is anything but a thinker. Not only is he without God in the world,[38] but wealth is his god, which attracts to itself his every thought. He has only one need, wealth, the one thing needful[39]—therefore he does not even need God. But where one's treasure is, there is one's heart also,[40] and the rich pagan's heart is with wealth, on the earth—he is no traveler; he is enslaved to the earth. If the rich Christian who has wealth is as one who does not have, then the rich pagan is as one who has nothing else—nothing else to think about, nothing else in which to put his trust, nothing else in which to find joy, nothing else about which to be concerned, nothing else to talk about. He is capable of disregarding everything else, everything that is lofty and noble and holy and lovely, but it has become impossible for him to disregard his wealth at any moment.

Yes, the rich pagan has knowledge about his wealth and abundance, and with increased knowledge increased care. He knows what causes care, and since it is the only thing he knows, he has nothing but care. Indeed, you can see it on him when you look at him: him, the sallow money-grubber who accumulates and accumulates for himself—care—him, the starved glutton who starves in abundance, who also says: What will I eat? What will I drink? How will it be possible tomorrow (today it is still tolerable) to find a repast so delectable that it could please me?—him, the sleepless skinflint whom money, more cruel than the cruelest executioner, keeps more sleepless than the most abominable criminal—him, the squint-eyed miser who never looks up from his money except to see enviously that someone else owns more—him, this dried-up, stingy wretch who is starving himself to death for money (something ordinarily unheard of, that anyone has done this for money). Look at them—and listen to what they say; they all say it, and this is the only thing they talk about; basically they all are saying: What will we eat and what will we drink? The more wealth and abundance they acquire, the more knowledge they also acquire; and this knowledge, which is the care, does not satisfy the hunger, does not quench the thirst—no, it stimulates the hunger and intensifies the thirst.

Indeed, those who want to be rich fall into many temptations and snares that corrupt a person[41]—and what is the care of wealth but wanting to be rich, wanting, entirely secured, to continue to be rich, wanting to be richer? It is an illusion that the care of wealth that is not religiously healed (and then the beginning can occur just as well whether one owns more or owns less) would find any condition whereby it would be satisfied. Just as there has never lived a bird that has ever taken more than *enough*, so there has never lived a rich pagan who has obtained *enough*. No, there is no hunger as insatiable as abundance's unnatural hunger, no knowledge so unsatisfiable as the defiling knowledge about wealth and abundance.

What, then, is *the temptation* that in itself embraces the many temptations? It is the temptation, by doing away with God, to cease to be a human being: instead of being purer than the innocent bird, to sink, godforsaken and worse than the animal, below the animal; to slave away, poorer than the slavish mind of the poorest pagan, in that most wretched slavery of madness, in abundance to slave for food and drink, in wealth to slave for money, to oneself a curse, to nature an abomination, to the human race a defilement.

Let us now in conclusion consider the bird, which, after all, was there in the Gospel and must be here in the discourse. The bird, well, if it is rich, it *is* ignorant of being rich. The rich Christian *became* ignorant of it; he is rich, poor, rich. The rich pagan is poor, poor, poor. The bird keeps silent, which is easy for it to do; it keeps silent about what it does not know. The rich Christian does not talk about his earthly wealth at all but only about the wealth. The rich pagan knows nothing else to talk about except his mammon. Compared with the ignorant bird, the rich Christian in ignorance is a wise person; but the pagan is a fool, one who knows much of the knowledge that is folly. Compared with the Christian, the ignorant bird is a little simpleton; compared with the pagan, it is like a wise man. The ignorant bird is innocently aware of nothing; the rich pagan is guiltily aware of and only aware of what is defiling. The ignorant bird lives like a sleepwalker in the power of sleep; it sees nothing. The rich Christian who became ignorant of his earthly wealth can, as in blindman's buff, see nothing—because eternity blinds him, he cannot see by this earthly daylight. The rich pagan somberly sees only in darkness—he cannot see by the light of eternity. The bird is the light, the transient traveler. The rich Christian who became ignorant traveled ceaselessly and further away. The rich pagan remained heavy, like a stone, upon the earth, even heavier

X
40

because of the defilement. When one is rich, there is only one way to become rich: to become ignorant of one's wealth, to become poor. The bird's way is the shortest, the Christian's way the most blessed. According to Christianity's doctrine, there is only one rich person: the Christian; everyone else is poor, the poor and the rich. A person is most healthy when he does not notice his body at all or does not know he has a body, and the rich person is healthy when, healthy like the bird, he is not aware of his earthly wealth; but when he is aware of it, when it is the only thing he knows, then he is lost. When the rich Christian became totally ignorant of his earthly wealth, he gained more than the bird that soars up toward heaven; he gained heaven. When the rich pagan became totally and solely aware of his wealth, he lost what no bird loses when it falls to the earth—he lost heaven!

X
41

III

The Care of Lowliness

Do not worry about what you will wear—the pagans
seek all these things.

This care the bird does not have. Sparrows [*Spurve*[42]] are divided into
grey sparrows and yellow—or, if you please, gold sparrows, but
this distinction, this classification "lowly/eminent" does not exist
for them or for any one of them. The other birds do indeed
follow the bird that flies at the head of the flock or to the right;
there is the distinction first and last, to the right and the left. But
the distinction lowly/eminent does not exist; in their bold
wheeling flight when the flock is soaring lovely and free in aerial
formations, first and last, right and left also change. And when the
thousand voices sing in chorus, there certainly is one that strikes
the note; there is this distinction. But lowly/eminent, this distinction does not exist, and joy lives freely in the alternating of
voices. It gratifies "the single individual" so indescribably to
sing in chorus with the others; yet it does not sing to gratify the
others. It is gratified by its singing and the singing of the others;
therefore it stops quite abruptly, pauses for a moment, until it is
again inclined to join in—and to hear itself.

The bird, then, does not have this care. Why is this so? It is
because the bird is what it is, is itself, is satisfied with being itself,
is contented with itself. It hardly knows distinctly or realizes
clearly what it is, even less that it should know something about
others. But it is contented with itself and with what it is, whatever that happens to be. It does not have time to ponder or even
merely to begin to ponder—so contented is it with being what
it is. In order to be, in order to have the joy of being, it does not
have to walk the long road of first learning to know something
about the others in order by that to find out what it is itself. No,

it has its knowledge firsthand; it takes the more pleasurable short-cut: it is what it is. For the bird there is no question of to be or not to be;[43] by way of the shortcut it slips past all the cares of dis-similarity. Whether it is a bird just like all other birds, whether it is "just as good a bird" as the others of the same species, indeed, even whether it is just like its mate—of all such things it does not think at all, so impatient it is in its joy of being. No young girl on the point of leaving for a dance can be as impatient to leave as the bird is to set about being what it is. It has not a moment, not the briefest, to give away if this would delay it from being; the brief-est moment would be a fatally long time for it if at that moment it was not allowed to be what it is; it would die of impatience at the least little objection to being summarily allowed to be. It is what it is, but it *is*. It lets things take their course, and so it is. This is indeed the way it is.

Even if you did not see the proud flight of the royal bird—when you see the little bird that is sitting and swinging on a spike of wheat and amusing itself by singing, is there the slightest trace of the care of lowliness? You certainly will not object to what is indeed the lesson: that it is someone of consequence [*høit paa Straa*]. If you want to do that, then take the straw [*Straa*] upon which it is sitting. In its joy over being, the bird is more animated than the lily, but it is just like the lily in its innocent self-satisfac-tion. Even if you did not see the magnificent lily that humbly holds its head high in all its loveliness, when you see the unim-pressive lily that grows in a ditch and is teased by the wind as if the two were equals, when you see it after the storm has done everything to make it feel its insignificance—when you look at it as it again tosses its head to see if there will soon be fair weather again, does it seem to you that there is the slightest care of lowli-ness? Or when it stands at the foot of the mighty tree and looks up at it in wonder, does it seem to you that there is the least little trace of the care of lowliness in this, the amazed lily; or do you believe that it would feel itself to be less if the tree were even twice as large? Or is it not rather as if in all innocence it were under the delusion that everything exists for its sake?

So easy is it for the bird and the lily with being; so easily do they go about living; so natural is the beginning for them or their coming to begin. It is the lily's and the bird's fortunate privilege that it is made so easy for them to begin to be, that once they have come into existence they have begun at once, they are immediately at full speed in being and there is no need at all for any preliminaries to the beginning, and they are not at all tested in that difficulty much discussed among people and portrayed as very perilous—the difficulty of beginning.

How, then, is the bird the teacher; where is the contact point of the instruction? I wonder if it is not in making the detour after the beginning, that is, after finding the beginning, to make this detour, which can become so very long, as short as possible in order as quickly as possible to come to oneself, to be oneself.

This care the lowly Christian does not have. But he is different from the bird in having to be tested in this difficulty of the beginning, because he is aware of the distinction, lowly/eminent. He knows, and he knows that others know the same about him, that he is a lowly human being, and he knows what this means. He knows also what is understood by the advantages of earthly life, how very diverse they are, and alas, that they are all denied to him, that while they otherwise exist to manifest what the others are in these advantages, in his case they seem to be for the purpose of indicating how lowly he is. With every advantage the eminent individual adds, the more eminent he becomes, and with every advantage the lowly individual must confess has been denied him he in a way becomes more lowly. What exists to indicate how the greatness of the eminent seems from the other side to exist to indicate how very little the lowly one is. Oh, what a difficult beginning to existing or for coming to exist: to exist, then to come into existence in order first to exist. Oh, what a slyly concealed snare, one that is not set for any bird! It indeed seems as if in order to begin to be oneself, a human being first of all must be finished with what the others are and by that find out then what he himself is—in order to be that. But if he falls into the snare of this optical illusion, he will never become himself. He walks on and on like the person who walks along a road that the passersby tell him definitely leads to the city but forget to tell him that if he wants to go to the city he must turn around; he is walking along the road that leads to the city, is walking along the road—away from the city.

But the lowly Christian does not fall into the snare of this optical illusion. He sees with the eyes of faith; with the speed of faith that seeks God, he is at the beginning, is himself before God, is contented with being himself. He has found out from the world or from the others that he is a lowly person, but he does not abandon himself to this knowledge; he does not lose himself in it in a worldly way, does not become totally engrossed in it; by holding fast to God with the reservedness of eternity, he has become himself. He is like someone who has two names, one for all the others, another for his nearest and dearest ones; in the world, in his association with the others, he is the lowly person. He does not pretend to be anything else, and neither is he taken to be anything else, but before God he is himself. In his contacts with others, it seems as if at every moment he must wait in order to find out from the others what he is now at this moment. But he does not wait; he is in a hurry to be before God, contented with being himself before God. He is a lowly human being in the crowd of human beings, and what he is in this way depends on the relationship, but in being himself he is not dependent on the crowd; before God he is himself. From "the others" a person of course actually finds out only what the others are—it is in this way that the world wants to deceive a person out of becoming himself. "The others" in turn do not know what they themselves are either but continually know only what "the others" are. There is only one who completely knows himself, who in himself knows what he himself is—that is God. And he also knows what each human being is in himself, because he is that only by being before God. The person who is not before God is not himself either, which one can be only by being in the one who is in himself. If one is oneself by being in the one who is in himself, one can be in others or before others, but one cannot be oneself merely by being before others.

The lowly Christian is himself *before God*. The bird is not itself in this way, because the bird *is* what it is. By means of this being, it has at every moment escaped the difficulty of the beginning; but then neither did it attain to the glorious conclusion of the difficult beginning: in redoubling [*Fordoblelse*] to be itself. The bird is like a number one; the person who is himself is more than a ten. The bird fortunately escapes the difficulty of the beginning and therefore acquires no conception of how lowly it is; but then, of course, it is incomparably more lowly than the lowly Christian who knows how lowly he is. The *idea* of lowliness *does not exist* for the bird, but the lowly Christian *does not exist essentially for this idea.* He does not want to exist essentially for it, because essentially he is and wants to be himself before God. Thus the bird actually is the lowly one. *In contrast* to his lowliness, the lowly Christian is himself but without fatuously wanting to cease being the lowly person he is in relation to others; in *lowliness* he is himself. This is how the lowly Christian in lowliness is without the care of lowliness. In what does the lowliness consist? In the relation to "the others." But on what is its care based? On existing only for the others, on not knowing anything but the relation to the others. The bird does not know anything at all about the relation to the others and to that extent is not lowly and to that extent in turn does not have the care of lowliness, but neither does it know, of course, that it has a higher relation.

What, then, is the lowly Christian who before God is himself? He is a *human being.* Inasmuch as he is a human being, he in a certain sense is like the bird, which is what it is. But we shall not dwell further on this here.

But he is also a *Christian,* which is indeed implied in the question about what the lowly *Christian* is. To that extent he is not like the bird, because the bird *is* what it is. But one cannot be a Christian in this way; if one is a Christian, one must *have become* that. Consequently the lowly Christian has become something in the world; the bird, alas, cannot become something—it is what it is. The lowly Christian was a human being, just as the bird was a bird, but then he became a Christian; he became something in the world. And he can continually become more and more, because he can continually become more and more Christian. As a *human being* he was created in *God's image* [*Billede*],[44] but as a *Christian* he has God as the *prototype* [*Forbillede*]. This unsettling thought that incessantly calls to one, a prototype, the bird does not know. It is what it is; nothing, nothing disturbs this, its being.

It is indeed true, nothing disturbs it—not even the blessed thought of having God for its prototype. A prototype is certainly a summons, but what a blessing! We even speak of good fortune when we say that there is something in the poet that summons him to write lyrics, but the prototype is an even more rigorous requirement, is an incentive for everyone who sees it, everyone for whom it exists. The prototype is a promise; no other promise is so reliable, because the prototype is indeed the fulfillment.— There is no prototype before the bird, but the prototype exists before the lowly Christian, and he exists before his prototype— he can continually grow to resemble it more and more.

X
47

The lowly Christian, who before God is himself, *exists* as a Christian *before his prototype*. He believes that God has lived on earth, that he has allowed himself to be born in lowly and poor circumstances, yes, in ignominy, and then as a child lived together with the ordinary man who was called his father and the despised virgin who was his mother. After that he wandered about in the lowly form of a servant, not distinguishable from other lowly persons even by his conspicuous lowliness, until he ended in the most extreme wretchedness, crucified as a criminal—and then, it is true, left behind a name. But the lowly Christian's aspiration is only to dare in life and in death to appropriate his name or to be named after him. The lowly Christian believes, as it is told, that he chose as his disciples lowly persons of the simplest class and that for company he sought those whom the world rejected and scorned. He believes that in all the various vicissitudes of his life, when people wanted to elevate him and then wanted to lower him even lower, if possible, than he had lowered himself, in all this he remained faithful to the lowly persons to whom he was linked by more intimate connections, faithful to the lowly persons whom he had linked to himself, faithful to the despised people who had been expelled from the synagogue for the very reason that he had helped them. The lowly Christian believes that this lowly person or that his life in lowliness has shown what significance a lowly person has and, alas, what significance, humanly speaking, an eminent person really has, how infinitely much it can signify to be a lowly person, and how infinitely little it can signify to be an eminent person, if one is not anything else. The lowly Christian believes that this prototype exists right before him, him who, after all, is a lowly person, perhaps struggling with poverty and straitened circumstances, or the even more lowly circumstance of being scorned and repudiated. He certainly admits that he is not in the situation of having himself chosen this slighted or despised lowliness and to that extent does not resemble the prototype. But he still trusts that the prototype exists before him, the prototype who by means of lowliness compassionately imposes himself on him, as it were, as if he would say, "Poor man, can you not see that this prototype is before you?" To be sure, he has not seen the prototype with his own eyes, but he believes that he has existed. In a certain sense, of course, there had not been anything to *see*—except the lowliness (because the glory must *be believed*), and of the lowliness he can very well form an idea. He has not seen the prototype with his own eyes; neither does he make any attempt to have his senses form such a picture. Yet he often sees the prototype. Every time he totally forgets his poverty, his lowliness, his being disdained, forgets it in faith's joy over the glory of this prototype, then he does see the prototype—and then he himself looks more or less like the prototype. If, namely, at such a blessed moment when he is absorbed in his prototype, someone else looks at him, the other person sees only a lowly person before him; it was just the same with the prototype—people saw only the lowly person. He believes and hopes he will ever more and more approach a likeness to this prototype, who will only in the next life manifest himself in his glory, since here on earth he can only be in lowliness and can be seen only in lowliness. He believes that this prototype, if he continually struggles to resemble him, will bring him again, and in an even more intimate way, into kinship with God, that he does not have God only as a creator, as all creatures do, but has God as his brother.

But then is this lowly Christian nevertheless something very lofty? Yes, he certainly is, something so lofty that one completely loses sight of the bird. Like the bird, he is lowly without the care of lowliness, weighed down in a certain sense by the consciousness of his lowliness as the bird is not—yet he is highly elevated. Nor does he speak of the lowliness, and if he does, it is never

X
48

sadly; indeed, it only reminds him of the prototype while he
thinks about the loftiness of the prototype—and when he does
that, he himself more or less resembles the prototype.

The lowly pagan, however, does have this care. The lowly pagan, he
is without God in the world and therefore is never essentially
himself (which one is only by being before God) and therefore is
never satisfied with being himself, which one certainly is not if
one is not oneself. He is not himself, is not satisfied with being
himself, nor, like the bird, satisfied with what he is: he is dissatis-
fied with what he is; detesting himself, he groans over and la-
ments his fate.

What, then, is he? He is the lowly one, nothing else at all—
that is, he is what "the others" make of him and what he makes
of himself by being only before others. His care is: *being nothing*—
indeed, not being at all. Thus he is a long way from being like the
bird, which is what it is. Therefore, in turn, his concern is: *to
become something* in the world. To exist before God—that is not
anything, he thinks—neither does it make a good showing in the
world in contrast to or in comparison with others. To be a
human being—that is not anything to be, he thinks—after all,
that is to be nothing, because in that there is no distinction from
or advantage over all other human beings. To be a Christian—
that is not anything to be, he thinks—we all, of course, are that.
But to become a councilor of justice—to be that would be something, and he must above all become something in the world; to
be nothing at all is something to despair over.

"This is something to despair over." He speaks as if he were
not already in despair; yet he is in despair, and despair is his care.
It is assumed that in every nation the lowly are generally exempt
from bearing the burdens the more favored must bear. But the
pagan, the despairing lowly one, even if he is that, will not be
exempt; he bears the heaviest of all burdens. We say that the king
bears the weight of the crown, the high official the weight of the
responsibility of administration, the one to whom much is entrusted the weight of custody; but whereas the king is after all
indeed the king, the person of high rank the person of high rank,
the trusted one the trusted one, the pagan, the despairing lowly

one, slaves himself to death under the weight of what he is not—
he, yes, it is indeed insanity, he overstrains himself on what he
does not bear. Whether it is the king who as the base bears all the
others or whether it is all the others who bear the king as the one
on top, we shall not investigate here, but the pagan, the despairing lowly one, bears all the others. This enormous weight, "all
the others," weighs upon him, and with the doubled weight of
despair; it does not weigh upon him by dint of the idea that he
is something—no, it weighs upon him by dint of the idea that
he is nothing. Truly, no nation or society has ever treated any
human being so inhumanly that on the condition of being nothing one has to bear the burden of all; only the pagan, the despairing lowly one, treats himself so inhumanly. He sinks deeper and
deeper into desperate care, but he finds no footing for bearing his
burden—after all, he is nothing, of which he becomes conscious
to his own torment by dint of the idea of what the others are.
More and more ludicrous—oh no, he becomes more and more
pitiable or, rather, more and more ungodly, more and more
nonhuman in his foolish striving to become at least something,
something, even if it is ever so little, but something that in his
opinion is worth being.

In this way the despairing lowly one, the pagan, sinks under
comparison's enormous weight, which he himself lays upon
himself. This, to be a lowly person, which for the lowly Christian
belongs to him together with being a Christian as the scarcely
audible slight aspiration before the letter belongs to the letter that
actually is heard (and this is the way the lowly Christian speaks
about his earthly lowliness; he speaks of it only in declaring that
he is a Christian)—this for the pagan is his care night and day; all
his endeavors are occupied with this. Without the prospect of
eternity, never strengthened by the hope of heaven, never
himself, abandoned by God, he lives in despair, as if for punishment he were condemned to live these seventy years tortured
by the thought of being nothing, tortured by the futility of his
efforts to become something. For him the bird has nothing consoling, heaven no consolation—and it goes without saying that
earthly life has no consolation for him either. Of him it cannot
be said that he remains enslaved on the earth, persuaded by the

X
50

enchantment of earthly life that led him to forget heaven—no, instead it is as if temporality did everything to push him away from itself by making him nothing. And yet he wants to belong to temporality on the most wretched conditions; he does not want to escape it. He clings tightly to being nothing, more and more tightly, because in a worldly way, and futilely, he tries to become something; with despair he clings more and more tightly to that—which to the point of despair he does not want to be. In this way he lives, not on the earth, but as if he were hurled down into the underworld. See, that king[45] whom the gods punished suffered the dreadful punishment that every time he was hungry luscious fruits appeared, but when he reached for them they vanished; the despairing lowly one, the pagan, suffers even more agonizingly in self-contradiction. While he, tortured by being nothing, futilely tries to become something, he really is not only something but is much. It is not the fruits that withdraw themselves from him; it is he himself who withdraws himself even from being what he is. For he is not a human being—and he cannot become a Christian!

Let us then in conclusion consider the bird; it is there in the Gospel and must be here in the discourse. The lowly bird is without the care of lowliness. In lowliness the lowly Christian is without the care of lowliness and then—is elevated high above all earthly loftiness. The lowly pagan in his care, even if he were the most lowly of all, is far beneath himself. The bird does not look closely at what it is; the lowly Christian looks closely at what he is as a Christian; the lowly pagan stares, to the point of despair, at his being lowly. "What . . . . . lowly?" says the bird. "Let us never think about such things; one flies away from that!" "What . . . . . lowly?" says the Christian. "I am a Christian!" "Alas, lowly!" says the pagan. "I am what I am," says the bird; "What I shall become has not yet been disclosed," says the lowly Christian; "I am nothing and will never become anything," says the lowly pagan. "I exist," says the bird; "Life begins in death," says the lowly Christian; "I am nothing, and in death I remain nothing," says the lowly pagan. Compared with the lowly Christian, the bird is a child; compared with the lowly pagan, it is a fortunate child. Like the free bird when it soars highest in its joy over existing, just so does the lowly Christian soar even higher; like the trapped bird when it hopelessly and fearfully struggles to its death in the net, just so the lowly pagan, even more pitiable, desouls himself in the captivity of nothingness. According to Christian doctrine, there is only one loftiness, that of being a Christian; everything else is lowly, lowliness and loftiness. If one is lowly, there is only one way to loftiness—to become a Christian. The bird does not know this way; it remains what it is. But then there is also another way that the bird does not know— along this way the pagan walks. The bird's way of being is enigmatic and has never been found; the Christian's way has been found by him who is the Way, and it is blessed to find it; the pagan's way ends in darkness and no one has found the way back by it. The bird slips past that devious way and fortunately past all dangers; the lowly Christian does not walk along that devious way and is blessedly saved unto glory; the lowly pagan chooses the devious way and "walks his own way"[46] to perdition.

IV

The Care of Loftiness

Do not worry about what you will wear—the pagans seek all these things.

This care the bird does not have. —But then is loftiness a care? After all, one would think that the higher a person stands the more free he would be from all cares, the more he would be surrounded by people who are concerned and occupied solely with keeping all cares away from him. Alas, there is probably no mendacious sarcasm in speaking, as the Gospel does, altogether impartially about the care of loftiness and the care of lowliness. Loftiness and power and honor and prestige offer their faithful service like security guards who are supposed to protect the person of high standing so that no care presses close to him; they pledge him their loyalty, as it were, on bended knee. Ah, but this very bodyguard, with which the person of high standing does not have the courage to break, this very bodyguard, which for the sake of security is so close to him, it is precisely this that costs him his night's sleep. Something that has in fact been seen can serve as a symbol: an emperor who rules over the whole world but is surrounded by his loyal bodyguard[47] who rule over the emperor, an emperor who makes the whole world tremble but is surrounded by his gallant bodyguard, behind whom and before whom the emperor trembles.

But the bird, which is indeed always lofty, does not have the care of loftiness—*neither* the care that cannot be discussed here, that which is an honor for the person of high standing, that he is solicitous for the welfare of those entrusted to him (because in this little book we are continually speaking only of the care a person can be without, yes, should be without, and not about the care without which a person cannot possibly be a Christian), *nor* the care [*Bekymring*] of loftiness that is the subject of the discourse. It scarcely occurs to the bird that it is to take care of [*sørge for*] itself, even less that it is appointed to take care of others. In all innocence of its relation to others, the bird says, "Am I my brother's keeper?"[48] It does not occur to any bird, not even the bird that flies highest, that it is so highly placed that it would have to rule over others. But then neither does it have the care about whether the others show him dutiful attention or deny it to him, or whether they perhaps would even consider toppling him from loftiness—no bird is so highly placed.

And yet every bird is lofty, but it seems as if every bird is essentially placed equally high. This heavenly equality among birds, or their equal loftiness under heaven, has something in common with the loftiness of eternal life—where there likewise is neither high nor low and yet there is loftiness. All birds are lofty, but among themselves none of them is lofty. Under the arch of heaven there is ample space for each one to soar as high as it wishes, but also the bird that walks on the ground is essentially lofty. The bird understands it in no other way. If someone says to it, "But you actually are not lofty if you are not *loftier* than the others," the bird would answer, "How so? Am I not lofty?"—and then the bird flies high or it remains on the ground, but where it is still lofty, aware of its loftiness. Therefore it is lofty without the care of loftiness, lofty without being elevated above anyone—under the arch of heaven there is too much room—or there is no room for pettiness.

Just look at that solitary bird, how high up it stands highly elevated in the sky, so serene, so proud, without a single movement; it does not support itself with even a wing stroke. If you perhaps have gone about your business and returned to the same place after a few hours—look, it stands unchanged up in the air; it proudly rests on its outspread wings, which do not move, while it surveys the earth. Yes, it is difficult for the unpracticed eye to measure distance in the air and on the water, but it perhaps has not changed its position one foot. It is standing, without any

X
54

footing, because it is standing in the air, so serene standing there loftily—may I now say, like a ruler, or was any ruler indeed so serene? It fears nothing, sees no danger, no abyss beneath it; it never gets dizzy in this loftiness, its eyes never dim. Ah, but no human being was ever as clear- and sharp-sighted as this bird, not even the one who in lowliness envies loftiness. But what is it, then, that loftily holds it there, so serene? It is loftiness. In loftiness itself there is no danger, and beneath it there is no abyss. Only when beneath it there is a loftiness that is lowlier than it and so on and on—in short, when there is someone beneath it, then there is something beneath it, and then there is also the abyss beneath it. But for the bird there is no one lowlier; therefore it is lofty without having the abyss beneath it, and therefore it is without the care that comes with and from the abyss.

The bird is lofty without being higher than anyone else and therefore is without the care of loftiness. In this way it is the teacher, and this is the contact point of the instruction. To be lofty in this way can be done without care. If someone were to say, "To be lofty in this way is not being lofty at all, and to speak of the bird's loftiness is merely a play on words," this shows that he is unwilling to be taught, is a naughty child who does not want to sit quiet in class but disturbs the instruction. Certainly, if he is unwilling to take the trouble to understand the bird, if instead of learning to change his idea in conformity with the bird's instruction he wants to take the bird to task and to insist on his own idea of it and therefore repudiates the bird as teacher, then it is of course impossible to learn anything from the bird—and, to the bird's honor, it must be said that this is indeed the only way in which one cannot learn anything from the bird. But the person who wants to learn learns that with regard to loftiness the only way one can truly be without care is in loftiness not to be higher than anyone else.

The eminent Christian does not have this care.

What, then, is the eminent Christian? Well, if you ask in a worldly way whether he is a king or an emperor or his lord-

ship or his grace, etc., it is, of course, generally an impossibility
to answer. But if you ask in the Christian sense, the answer is
easy: He is a Christian. As a Christian, he knows about shutting
his door when he is to speak with God[49]—not so that no one
will find out that he is speaking with God but so that no one will
disturb him. When he speaks with God, he discards all earthly,
all sham pomp and glory, but also all the untruth of illusion.

He believes that there is a God in heaven who is not a respecter of persons;[50] he believes that the person who ruled over
all of humanity, if we will imagine such a one, is not the least bit
more important to God than the lowliest—yes, than the sparrow
that falls to the ground.[51] Therefore he understands that it is an
illusion to think that because at every moment of his life and in
countless ways he feels his sense of life continually strengthened
by his being important to all or to countless people, and directly
important to many people for their lives, and that because in his
lifetime he enjoys the heightening of life by being indispensable
and the exuberant presentiment of being missed in death—that
therefore his life would also be more important to God. To God
he is not more important than the sparrow that falls to the
ground—neither he, this most powerful person who has ever
lived, nor the wisest person who ever lived, nor any person. He
believes (instead of paying attention to all the talk about the
many who cannot live without him) that it is he who, in order to
live, is in need at all times, indeed, every minute, of this God,
without whose will certainly no sparrow falls to the ground, but
without whom no sparrow comes into existence or exists either.
If the rest of us understand it differently, that the reason we pray
for him[52] is that we are in need of him, are in need of his continuing to live, with God he understands it differently, that just
because his task is the incomparably greatest, he, more than anyone else, needs to be prayed for. He believes that it is a changeless
God who lives in heaven, who wills his will—even if everything
were to rise up against him, which means nothing to him—a
changeless God who wants obedience, the same in the greatest as
in the least, in the slightest triviality of the widest ranging world-
historical enterprise as in the most common everyday under-

taking, the same from the most powerful person who has ever lived as from the most powerless, and the same as from all nature, which allows itself nothing, nothing, without his will.

Therefore he understands that it is an illusion—if someone wants to make him believe, because a word of authority from him is sufficient to set thousands in motion, indeed, almost to transform the shape of the world, because thousands crowd around him and court a smile of authority—that God would therefore also be different toward him, this powerful authority, different than toward every other, unconditionally every other human being, that toward him the unchanged God would not be the same unchanged one, unchanged as the eternal, more changeless than the rock—but certainly able omnipotently to change everything even more terribly by his omnipotent word, to change both thrones and governments, both heaven and earth. He believes that before this God he is a sinner and that this God is equally zealous against sin, whoever the sinner is. He understands that it is an illusion—if someone wanted to make him fancy that, because scarcely any human being is able to make a survey of his management of affairs, of what he did wrong and what he left undone, because no human being dares to sit in judgment on him—that therefore the righteous God (for whom it is not more important that the most powerful one sins than that the lowliest does, however different, humanly speaking, the magnitude of the consequences, and for whom it is not more forgivable that the most powerful one sins than that the lowliest does), amazed at human power, would also not be able or would not dare to judge him according to the strictness of the Law. He believes that he stands in need of the gracious God's forgiveness at every moment. Therefore he believes that God has walked in lowliness on earth and in this way has judged all such worldly power and might to be nothing. He believes that just as no one enters into the kingdom of heaven without becoming *like* a child again,[53] so no one comes to Christ except *as* a lowly person, as someone who by himself and by what he is by himself is nothing. He believes that even if Christ had chosen not lowly, but eminent, persons to be his disciples, those he chose first would have had to become lowly persons in order to be his disciples. He believes that Christ is not a respecter of persons, because for Christ there is only lowliness, that just as surely as no healthy person[54] has ever been or can ever be saved by Christ, so also no eminent person as such can be saved by him but only as a lowly person. No one can become or be a Christian except in the character of or as a lowly person.

"But then is the eminent Christian basically just as lowly as the lowly Christian?" Certainly, that he is indeed. "But then does not the eminent Christian really know how eminent he is?" No, basically he does not know that. "But then the discourse has actually deceived the reader by not talking about earthly loftiness, about titles and ranks and their care!" Well, yes—and yet no. The discourse has not deceived, because the eminent Christian does not have this care—and the discourse is about that very subject, about his not having this care. And which discourse expresses this more truthfully, the one that gives assurances and assurances that he does not have this care, or the one that by speaking about what actually occupies the eminent Christian, namely, *lowliness*, implies by its very silence that he does not at all have the care of that *loftiness*.

One can become and be a Christian only as or in the capacity of a lowly person. To become (and in this way also to be) a Christian is admittedly one thought, but it is a twofold thought that consequently is double-visioned. Thus it is one and the same thought that makes the lowly Christian understand his loftiness and the eminent Christian his lowliness. The eminent Christian allows the conception (the Christian conception) to take away from him the power and the loftiness (the earthly), or he surrenders to the power of the conception; he thereby becomes the lowly person one must be in order to become and to be a Christian. If an actor wanted to walk around the streets and be king because he played a king the evening before, we would all laugh at him. If a child who was "the emperor" in a game with his peers were to go to adults and pretend to be the emperor, we would all laugh at the child. And why? Because the play and the child's game are a nonreality. But neither is it reality, in the Christian sense, to be eminent in actuality; the real is the eternal, the essentially Christian. True loftiness is Christian loftiness, but in true

x
57

Christian loftiness no one is higher than others. Therefore, to be eminent is a nonreality compared with true loftiness. In the Christian sense, then, it is proper when the eminent Christian *himself* smiles (that others do it has neither place nor support in Christianity, but only in the abominable insolence of ungodly worldliness) at his earthly loftiness, at his so-called real loftiness, because only Christian loftiness is real loftiness.

But then has it not been more difficult for the eminent person to become a Christian (we are, after all, speaking about the eminent Christian) than for the lowly person? To this question Holy Scripture answers yes.[55] To be sure, people think it must be just as easy and just as difficult for the lowly one to become a Christian as for the eminent, because, so they say, the lowliness under discussion is not the external but the internal, a feeling of one's own lowliness, which the eminent can have just as well as the lowly; the essentially Christian is a much too spiritual power to speak about external lowliness. Well, so it is. Scripture, however, perhaps out of circumspection and in its knowledge of the human heart, also speaks about it in another way, speaks about literally being a lowly person, and this is indeed also the way the prototype speaks, who witnesses more powerfully than all words or all expressions. *He* lived in actual earthly lowliness; therefore, when he resolved to be the prototype, he did not choose to be an eminent person and yet a lowly person in his innermost being. No, he literally was the lowly person, and in earnest in an entirely different way than when a king momentarily sets aside his rank and is known by the courtiers, consequently all the more honored—for his humility.[56]

See, in the life of the spirit there is something that corresponds to what spelling out is in relation to reading whole words and phrases. One spells it out, proceeds slowly, distinctly and perceptibly separates the particulars from each other lest in the end one make the whole content of life into "annulled elements" and life into an empty annulment. So also with possessing external advantages in relation to becoming a Christian. Christianity has never taught that literally to be a lowly person is synonymous with being a Christian, nor that there is a direct and inevitable

x
58

transition from literally being a lowly person to becoming a Christian; neither has it taught that if the worldly eminent person relinquished all his power he therefore was a Christian. But from literal lowliness to becoming a Christian there is still only one course. Literally to be a lowly person is no unfortunate introduction to becoming a Christian; to be in the possession of external advantages is a detour that makes a double introduction necessary for the more apprehensive. In that strict science,[57] we speak of a construction line or help-line [*Hjælpelinie*]; one draws, as it is called, a help-line. One can indeed also demonstrate the theorem without the help-line, but one does not do it for the sake of the demonstration but in order to give oneself help. It is not the demonstration that needs the help-line, but one needs it oneself. So it is also when the one who is in possession of external advantages helps himself by literally becoming poor, scorned, lowly. If he does not do that, he must watch himself all the more scrupulously so that he dares to trust himself, so that he is convinced that nothing, nothing of all this external eminence and loftiness, has blinded him in such a way that he could not easily become reconciled to being the lowly person among the people.

It can undeniably also be done in this manner. Christianity has never unconditionally required of anyone that he must literally give up external advantages; it has rather proposed to him a little precautionary measure. Does he think he does not need it, as people once thought they did in those ages when one apprehensively spelled one's way forward? Oh, what a strenuous life, in loftiness, surrounded by everything that beguiles, to be so completely sure of oneself in this way, so that a person could easily reconcile himself to being a simple laborer—because to be a Christian is so infinitely important to him that he naturally has made sure through the most rigorous self-examination that none of this beguiles him in the slightest! What extreme circumspection with fire and candles when one lives in a powder depot, but what strenuous circumspection in order to be a Christian in this environment!

What a difficult life to live in this way! It is only a faint intimation of the daily difficulty of this life when you consider how

much more easily it went in the previous discourse to reach
Christian loftiness from lowliness than it does here to reach
Christian loftiness from earthly loftiness through lowliness. Yet
this is how the eminent Christian lives. He has power and honor
and prestige, is in possession of the advantages of earthly life, but
he is as one who does not have anything; he sees all this around
him, how just as in an enchantment only a hint from him is
awaited, only his wish, but he, in the power of an even higher
enchantment, is as one who does not see it. He hears all this,
perhaps almost always flattery, but his ears are plugged—to him
all this is like being king in the play, and like the child's being
emperor in the game—because he is a Christian.

And as a Christian he is in the condition of real loftiness, because, in the Christian sense, in God's kingdom it is just as it is
under the sky; there all are lofty without being higher than anyone else. The bird is lofty without being higher than anyone else;
the eminent Christian, although in earthly loftiness elevated
above others, is lofty without being higher than anyone else.
Therefore, he is without the care of loftiness, because, as stated,
in this way one can be that. When one is lofty in this way, then
one is either a bird or, if one is a human being and yet like the
bird, then one is a Christian, no matter whether or not one
otherwise is high or low in the worldly sense.

X
60

The eminent pagan, however, does have this care.

The eminent pagan is without God in the world; if the eminent Christian is ignorant of his earthly loftiness, the pagan is
ignorant of the nature of true loftiness. He knows no other loftiness than this earthly kind—and it is impossible to come to know
what it truly is, since it is in itself untruth, miasma, delusion—
which provides no knowledge of truth except the truth that it is
this. He is thoroughly informed about the high, higher, highest,
utterly highest, but he does not realize that at the base of all this
lies nothing, so that all that he knows is nothing. In this nothing
he now has his place. Where it is, he determines with the help of
the determinants within nothingness. We speak of a nightmare

ride in one's sleep—the sleeper pants and groans but does not move from the spot—so also with the eminent pagan. Now he ascends loftily, now he descends; he shouts with joy, he sighs, he pants, he groans, but he never moves from the spot. Now there is another who loftily ascends above him, now one who plunges down from loftiness—yet nothing, nothing, not even the latter can arouse him from sleep, tear him out of his delusion, open his eyes to the fact that the whole thing is nothing. But would this indeed be nothing? Is any better evidence needed that it is not nothing than just to look at him, how he fights and struggles and hankers and aspires and never allows himself a moment's rest, how many he keeps in his service through bribery, how many he associates with so that they might be helpful to him in grasping the sought-after? Would this still be nothing; would "nothing" be able to set so much in motion? Then that busy man must also be wrong, the one who concludes that he has a big business because he keeps four clerks and has no time either to eat or to drink.[58]

X
61

This is the way the eminent pagan lives in loftiness. That there are many below him in loftiness, he knows full well, but what he does not know is that below him—it is still below him—there is the abyss. In other words, when, as stated, someone is higher in loftiness than others or has others below him, he also has the abyss below him, because only in earthly loftiness can one be lofty in this way. The eminent pagan who knows nothing else and thinks of nothing else but his earthly loftiness lacks knowledge of the true loftiness, which could keep him hovering in ignorance of earthly loftiness. No, he has the abyss below him, and out of it the care rises, or he sinks in the care.

What is the care? A craving to become more and more—for nothing, since the whole thing is indeed nothing; a craving to rise higher and higher in loftiness—that is, to sink lower and lower in the care of the abyss—for what else is the care of worldly loftiness than the care of the abyss! What is the care? It is the care lest someone by slyness, by force, by lies, or by truth will take away his delusion. Therefore he secures himself in every way, since he sees danger everywhere, everywhere covetousness, everywhere envy, everywhere ghosts—as is natural, because for an anxious person not even in the darkest night is there as much to horrify the delusion as there are horrors in a delusion.

Finally the care swallows its prey. Just as pithless rotten wood glows in the dark, just as the nebulous will-o'-the-wisp of miasma tricks the senses in the fog, so in this glittering of his earthly loftiness he exists before others. But his self does not exist; his innermost being has been consumed and depthed in the service of nothingness; slave of futility, with no control over himself, in the power of giddy worldliness, godforsaken, he ceases to be a human being; in his innermost being he is as dead, but his loftiness walks ghostlike among us—it lives. When you speak with him, you do not speak with a human being; in his hankering after loftiness, he has himself become what was coveted: a title regarded as a human being. Within there is sheer emptiness and trumpery—indeed, there is nothing. But the appearance is there, the vain appearance that bears the marks of worldly loftiness that command the deference of the passersby—while he bears all this loftiness somewhat as the cushions that bear his medals at the funeral. Oh, how terrible it can be to see a human being almost unrecognizable in lowliness and wretchedness, to see such wretchedness that one can scarcely discern the human being; but to see human loftiness and, look, it is no human being—that is dreadful. It can be terrible to see a person walking around as a shadow of his former loftiness, but to see worldly loftiness and scarcely the shadow of a human being within—that is dreadful. Death will not make him into nothing; he does not need to be buried; while he is still living, it can already be said of him, as is otherwise said at the grave: Here see earthly loftiness!

Let us then in conclusion consider the bird, which was there in the Gospel and must be here in the discourse. In its loftiness the bird is without the care of loftiness. In his earthly loftiness elevated above others, the eminent Christian is lofty without the care of loftiness. The eminent pagan with his care belongs in the abyss; he actually is not lofty but is in the abyss. The bird is lofty, the eminent Christian is lofty, the eminent pagan is in the abyss. The bird's loftiness is a symbol of the Christian's loftiness, which

X
62

in turn is a counterpart to the bird's loftiness. For the understanding the two correspond, with the difference of infinity, to each other. You understand the bird's loftiness by understanding the Christian's, and by understanding the bird's you understand the Christian's. The pagan's loftiness belongs nowhere, neither under heaven nor in heaven. The bird's loftiness is the shadow, the Christian's the reality, the pagan's the nothingness. The bird has air within itself, and therefore it can hold itself up in loftiness; the eminent pagan has emptiness within himself, and therefore his loftiness is a delusion; the eminent Christian has faith within himself, and therefore he hovers in loftiness above the abyss of earthly loftiness. In his loftiness the Christian never forgets the bird; to him it is more than what the beacon is to the sailor. It is the teacher, and yet in turn, alas, the one that the pupil left far behind when it called to him, "Remember me in your loftiness." The eminent pagan never saw the bird. The bird is in loftiness and yet actually on the way toward loftiness. If it could understand this, it would have to sink. The Christian understands this and through this very understanding attains loftiness. According to the doctrine of Christianity, however, there is only one loftiness: to be a Christian—and one abyss: paganism. No bird ever attained the former nor ever flew over the latter. Over this abyss no bird can fly; it would have to perish on the way. To this loftiness no bird can attain—it is only on the way. Thus the bird is fortunate in its loftiness, ignorant of the abyss, but also ignorant of the blessedness; the Christian is blessed in his loftiness; the eminent pagan, unblessed, is lost in the abyss.

X
63

V

The Care of Presumptuousness

No one can add one foot to his growth—[59]the pagans seek all these things.

This care the lily and the bird do not have, because neither the lily nor the bird is presumptuous. With presumptuousness it is not the same as with poverty and abundance, with lowliness and loftiness. There the given, to mention a particular point, was to be in poverty, the task to be in poverty without the care of poverty. But here it is not as if the given were that after all one is presumptuous and that the task is to be presumptuous without the care of presumptuousness. No, there is no given here; the task is: not to be presumptuous—and this is the only way in which one can be without the care of presumptuousness. That is, poverty and abundance, lowliness and loftiness are in themselves matters of indifference, of innocence, that which one has not given oneself or made oneself into, that which, Christianly, does not matter at all. Therefore the discourse begins at once with the care; it does not speak against poverty or abundance, lowliness or loftiness, but against the care. Being presumptuous is a different matter; no one is ever innocent in being presumptuous, and thus the discourse aims at that and not so much at the care. Indeed, if it were possible, this impossibility, to take away the care without taking away the presumptuousness, the discourse would by no means do this; here the care must be just like a curse upon the presumptuous person.

But the lily and the bird do not have this care. Even if a particular lily, straight in stem, shoots up to almost human height—it does not crave to add either a foot or an inch to its stature, it does not crave the least bit more. Nor is there any presumptuousness in its height compared with the other lilies, which do not crave it—*that* would indeed be presumptuousness. That the yellow bunting[60] wears all its finery and the grey sparrow is poorly dressed is not presumptuousness on the part of the yellow bunting; the grey sparrow does not crave this—*that* would indeed be presumptuousness. And when the bird hurtles down from dizzying heights, there is no presumptuousness in that, nor is the bird tempting God—who is indeed also the One who holds it up more securely than if all the angels were holding it up lest it bruise its foot upon some stone.[61] Even if the bird sees so clearly that it sees the grass grow, there is no presumptuousness in that; with its sharp sight it does not force its way into what is forbidden, nor when it sees clearly in the darkness of night, since it is not by inadmissible means. Although the bird is ignorant of God, there is no presumptuousness in that, because it is innocently ignorant, not spiritlessly ignorant.

Thus neither the bird nor the lily is guilty of any presumptuousness and obviously does not have the care of presumptuousness. Why is this? It is because the bird and the lily *continually will as God wills and continually do as God wills.* —Because the bird continually wills as God wills and continually does what God wills, it enjoys all its freedom without care. And when, while it is superbly flying in the air, it gets a sudden notion that it would like to set itself down, it sets itself down on a branch, and that—this is indeed curious—that was exactly what God wanted it to do. When upon awakening some morning it decides, "Today you must leave," and then it travels the hundreds and hundreds of miles, that—this is indeed curious—that was exactly what God wanted it to do. Although the stork makes the long journey to and fro ever so often, it never does it otherwise than as it does at this particular time; it knows no other way than the particular way it travels at this time; it notes no mark on the route for the sake of next time, no sign of the time for the sake of next time; it ponders nothing beforehand, nothing afterward. But then when it awakens some morning, it leaves the same morning, and that was exactly what God wanted it to do.

A human being ordinarily plans and prepares a long time for a journey, and yet perhaps rarely has anyone ever started a

journey with such assurance that this journey was God's will as
the bird does when it leaves. A pleasant journey, then, you fleeting traveler—that is, if you need any such wish for you! People
have envied you, envied you your easy passage through the air.
If I were to envy you, I would envy you the sureness with which
you always do exactly what is God's will for you! You have your
sustenance only from hand to mouth, it is true, but then in turn
you have an even shorter way from thought to accomplishment,
from intention to decision! No doubt on account of your inexplicable assurance you are fortunately prevented from being able
to be presumptuous.

Because the lily continually wills as God wills and continually
does as God wills, it enjoys without care its fortunate existence of
being lovely without the knowledge that disfigures loveliness.
Then one day, when it thinks that it has stood long enough looking like a scarecrow, it throws off all its outer garments and now
stands in all its loveliness, and then—this is indeed curious—then
it was exactly this that God wanted it to do. It never occurs to the
lily to want to wear its finery at any other time or on any other
day than exactly when God wills.

Because this is the way it is with the lily and the bird, it seems
as if God, if he were to speak about them, might say, "The lily
and the bird are indeed the children who give me the most joy
and are the easiest to bring up; they are good by nature and are
never naughty at all; they continually will only what I will and
continually do what I will; from them I have sheer enjoyment."
He has no need to add, as parents ordinarily do, "Let this be said
while it lasts."

But how, then, are the lily and the bird teachers? That is easy
to see. It is clear enough that neither the bird nor the lily permits
itself the slightest presumptuousness; so, then, be like the lily and
the bird. In their relation to God, the lily and the bird are like a
baby when it is still as good as one with its mother. But when the
child has grown older, even though it is in the parents' house and
ever so close to them, never out of their sight, there still is an
infinite distance between it and the parents; and in this distance
lies the possibility of being able to presume. If the mother clasps
the child, if she hugs it close in her arms in order in her closeness

to protect it completely against every danger, in the possibility of being able to presume it is still infinitely far away from her. It is an enormous distance, an enormous remoteness. Is it not true also that the person who lives on his old place but far from his only wish nevertheless lives at a distance? In the same way also the child, although at home with the parents, is at a distance through this possibility of being able to presume. In the same way a person, in the possibility of being able to presume, is infinitely far from God, in whom he nevertheless lives and moves and has his being.[62] But if he returns from this distance and in this distance is at any time just as close to God as the lily and the bird are by continually willing and doing only as God wills, then he has become a Christian.

The Christian does not have this care. But what is presumptuousness, for that, of course, is what we are speaking about, about not being presumptuous. What presumptuousness is, that is, what the particular manifestations are, we get to know best when we speak about the pagans, who certainly do have this care. But we must also provisionally know what presumptuousness is in order to see that the Christian is not presumptuous, or that he, by never presuming, not even in the least thing, is a Christian. Presumptuousness pertains essentially to a person's relationship to God; and this is why it is inconsequential whether a person presumes in the least or in the greatest matters, because even the least presumptuousness is the greatest, is toward God. Presumptuousness is essentially toward God; it is only a subsequently formed, a derived but correct language usage to say that a child is presumptuous toward its parents, a subject toward the king, a pupil toward the teacher. Between God and a human being, there is the eternal essential difference of infinity;[63] and when this difference is in any way encroached upon even in the slightest, we have presumptuousness. Presumptuousness therefore is *either* in a forbidden, a rebellious, an ungodly way *to want to have God's help, or,* in a forbidden, a rebellious, an ungodly way *to want to do without God's help.*

Therefore it is first and foremost presumptuousness to be spiritlessly ignorant of how a person needs God's help at every moment and that without God he is nothing. Perhaps many people, lost in the worldly and the sensate, live this way. They think they understand life and themselves, yet they have left God out completely. But they are secure enough, they are just like the others—they are, if one may put it this way, pirated editions, because every human being is an original edition from God's hand. If one were to charge them with being presumptuous toward God, they would no doubt answer, "That really never occurred to us." But precisely this is the presumptuousness, that it never occurred to them—to think about God. Or if they had ever been enjoined in their youth to think about the Creator, this is the presumptuousness, that since then they have completely forgotten him—worse than the beasts, because the beasts have *forgotten* nothing.

X
68

But the Christian knows that to need God is a human being's perfection.[64] Thus the Christian is once and for all aware of God and is saved from the presumptuousness that could be called ungodly unawareness. The Christian is not aware of God at some particular time in his life, on the occasion of great events and the like—no, in his daily perseverance he is aware that he at no time can do without God. Thus the Christian is wide awake, which neither the innocently ignorant bird nor the spiritlessly ignorant human being is; he is wide awake, awake to God.

The Christian is on the watch, and without ceasing he is on the watch for God's will. He craves only to be *satisfied with God's grace*;[65] he does not insist on helping himself but prays for God's grace. He does not insist that God shall help him in any other way than God wills; he prays only to be satisfied with his grace. The Christian has no self-will whatever; he surrenders himself unconditionally. But with regard to God's grace he again has no self-will; he is satisfied with God's grace. He accepts everything by God's grace—grace also. He understands that even in order to pray for his grace he cannot do without God's grace. So diminished is the Christian with regard to self-will that in relation to God's grace he is weaker than the bird in relation to instinct, which has it completely in its power, is weaker than the bird is strong in relation to its instinct, which is its power.

But then is the Christian basically even further from presumptuousness toward God than the bird is? Yes, that he is, although in the possibility of being able to presume he would be infinitely closer to it than the bird. But therefore the Christian also must slowly *learn*, something the bird, which finds it easy enough continually to will only as God wills, does not need to do. The Christian must learn to be satisfied with God's grace; for that purpose an angel of Satan[66] may sometimes be necessary to slap his mouth lest he behave with arrogance. The first thing he must learn is to be satisfied with God's grace; but when he is in the process of learning this, the final difficulty comes along. Yet to be satisfied with God's grace, which at first glance seems so meager and humiliating, is indeed the highest and most blessed good—or is there any higher good than God's grace! Therefore he must learn not to behave with arrogance, not to presume—to be satisfied with God's grace.

Thus the Christian, educated from the ground up, is much further from presumptuousness toward God than the bird— indeed, how would it be possible for him to be able to want to be presumptuous toward the one whose will is grace? But only the Christian knows that God's will is grace; at most the bird knows that his will is his will. The Christian is much further from presumptuousness and in that very way much closer to God than the bird. That there is a God in heaven without whose will no sparrow falls to the ground pertains indeed to the sparrow, but that there is a gracious God in heaven pertains only to the Christian. The bird keeps close to God by willing as he wills; but the Christian keeps even closer to him by keeping to his grace, just as the older but obedient child who wants to please its parents has and exists for the parents' love in a still more inward sense than the infant, who is one with the mother. In its need, the bird is as close as possible to God; it cannot do without him at all. The Christian is in even greater need; he *knows* that he cannot do without him. The bird is as close as possible to God; it cannot do without him at all. The Christian is even closer to him; he cannot do without—his grace. God encompasses the bird on every side but still holds back. To the Christian he opens himself, and on every side his *grace* encompasses the Christian, who is presumptuous in nothing, who wants nothing but his grace and never wants anything but his grace. Thus God's grace encompasses the

x
69

Christian in blessed closeness and keeps away every, even the slightest, expression of presumptuousness. "His grace *comes* to the Christian *beforehand*" (Psalm 59:10), so that he may will to be satisfied with God's grace, and *"comes afterward"* (Psalm 23:6), so that he may not have willed in vain and may blessedly never regret that he was satisfied with God's grace.

The pagan, however, does have this care, since paganism is actually presumptuousness and rebellion against God. First and foremost we cite the presumptuousness of *spiritlessness* in being ignorant of God, this presumptuousness that actually appears only in Christendom. Quite possibly such a pagan, lost in the worldly and the sensate, considers himself to be without care, especially without the many useless cares the God-fearing person has. But this is not true. It may well be true that he is without those cares that the God-fearing person has and from which he has benefit both for this life and the next, but it is not true that the pagan in his apathetic security is without care. On the contrary, he is in the power of anxiety, is anxious about living—and anxious about dying. Every time some event or the expectation of it tears him out of his beast-metamorphosis, the anxiety that lives in his innermost being awakens and casts him into despair, in which he indeed already was.

The presumptuousness, then, is spiritless ignorance of God. What is told in the parable fits such a pagan, the parable about the vineyard workers who misappropriated the vineyard and acted as if the owner did not exist; and insofar as he is brought up in Christianity, what they are reported to have said also fits him: "Let us kill the son, and the vineyard is ours."[67] The life [*Liv*] of every human being is God's possession; the human being is his bond servant [*Livegne*]. But one cannot kill God; on the other hand, as is said, one certainly can kill the thought of him. The spiritless ignorant person at one time has been conscious of God; therefore, as is also said with particular emphasis, he has parted from this thought, has slain it. When a person has succeeded in killing the thought of God and every feeling and mood that like his emissaries bring him to mind, then that person lives on as if he were his own master, himself the architect of his fortune, himself the one who must take care of everything but also the one who is entitled to everything—that is, he cheats God of what is due him. Is not this indeed wanting to add one foot to his growth—by having the owner killed, or the thought of him, by becoming the owner oneself, becoming the master instead of the bond servant? Then in his spiritless ignorance of God and in his vain knowledge about the world, the pagan sinks below the beast. To slay God is the most dreadful suicide; utterly to forget God is a human being's deepest fall—a beast cannot fall that deep.

The second form of presumptuousness is the one that in a forbidden, a rebellious, an ungodly way wants to do without God. This is *disbelief.* Disbelief is not spiritless ignorance; disbelief wants to deny God and is therefore in a way involved with God.

Perhaps such a pagan does say that he is without care. But this is not so, just as on the whole it is impossible to be presumptuous and then to be without the care of presumptuousness. However much he hardens himself, he nevertheless carries in his innermost being the mark that God is the strongest, the mark that he *wills* to have God against himself. If the God-fearing person limps after having wrestled with God,[68] then truly the disbeliever is annihilated in his innermost being. And his care is precisely to add one foot to his growth, for it certainly would be an enormous foot to add to his growth if a person directly before God were capable of denying God, or if it should even be the case that it is God who is in need of human beings, perhaps, as the wisdom of this age has understood it (if it is at all understandable), in order to understand himself. But if it is certain that no blessing accompanies stolen goods and no title to them is acquired, so also does the presumptuous person have the care that God will take everything away from him, has this care at every moment. Furthermore, if it is easy to work when one has the help of God, this truly is the hardest work one can lay upon oneself, the work of *willing* to do without God.

Therefore the pagan is in a very real way in the power of anxiety, since he never really knows in whose power he is—is this not fearful! Although disbelieving, he scarcely knows whether he is in the power of disbelief [*Vantro*] or of superstition [*Overtro*], and truly it is very difficult even for someone else to

X
71

know that. Abandoned by God, whom he wants to deny, overwhelmed by God, whom he wants to do without, he is—with no
stronghold [*Tilhold*] either in God or in himself (a person cannot have a stronghold in himself without God's agreement
[*Medhold*])—in the power of evil forces, the sport of disbelief and
superstition. No bird is tossed about in this manner, not even in
the worst weather!

Finally, this is a form of the presumptuousness: wanting to
have God's help in a forbidden, a rebellious, an ungodly way.
This is *superstition*.

So the presumptuous pagan insanely wants to add a foot to his
stature, insanely wants what was denied, in blind confidence
wants to venture the foolhardiness of plunging down from the
peak of the temple[69]—and what is even more presumptuous,
wants God to help him do it. Abandoning himself more and
more to this unholy game, he wants by inadmissible means to
penetrate the forbidden, discover the hidden, discern the future.
Like that Simon of whom the Scripture speaks,[70] he perhaps
wants insanely to buy the Holy Spirit with money or wants to
make money with the help of the Holy Spirit. He wants to force
himself on God, to force his help and support on God, wants to
make himself, him the uncalled, into what only God's call can
make a person. The disbeliever presumptuously wants to do
without God, does not want to let God help him, and presumptuously lets God know it; but the superstitious person wants God
to serve him. What else is it, even if the superstitious person
declares that it is God's help that he wants to have—when he
arbitrarily wants to have it, what else is it but wanting God to
serve him? Truly, this also would add one foot to his growth if
someone carried it to the point of being something so extraordinary that he had God as his servant. —But God does not let
himself be mocked.[71] Indeed, where are care and anxiety, pale
fear, and dreadful shuddering more at home than in the captious
kingdom of superstition! This anxiety no bird has known, not
even the fearful, panic-stricken bird.

So it is with the presumptuous pagan. He does not (like the
bird) will as God wills; even less does he (like the Christian) will
to be satisfied with God's grace; "the wrath of God rests upon

him."[72] If the bird does not even have God's grace, which only
the Christian has, then it really does not have God's wrath either,
which only the pagan has. However far the bird flies, it never
loses its connection with God; but however far the pagan would
flee, and however far he fled, it would be futile for the escaping
of God's wrath, however far he fled—if he did not flee to God's
grace. If anxiety and hardship will be upon the one who does
evil,[73] then first and foremost upon the presumptuous person.
Just as grace comes through God to each person who as a Christian draws nearer to him, so anxiety comes through himself to the
person who presumptuously withdraws from God or presumptuously draws near to him.

Let us in conclusion consider the bird, which was there in the
Gospel and must be here in the discourse. May there, then, be
joy on earth over the lily and the bird who will as God wills and
do as God wills; in heaven there is joy over the Christian who is
satisfied with God's grace, but there is anxiety both here and in
the next world over the pagan who is presumptuous. As much
closer to God as the Christian is than the bird, so much further
away from God the pagan is than the bird. The greatest distance,
greater than from the most distant star to the earth, greater than
any human skill can measure, is the distance from God's grace to
God's wrath, from the Christian to the pagan, from being
blessedly saved in grace to "eternal perdition [*Fortabelse*] away
from the face of God,"[74] from seeing God to seeing from the
abyss that one has lost [*tabt*] God. It would be a senseless jest if
one were seriously to use the position of the bird to help measure
this distance. The Christian can use that as the mark only with
the bird, but if the distance is Christian/pagan, then the bird
determines nothing, because here the discourse is not about poverty and abundance, about lowliness and loftiness, but about
presumptuousness.

X
73

VI

The Care of Self-Torment

Therefore do not worry about tomorrow—the pagans seek all these things.

This care the bird does not have. From however high up the bird looked out over the whole world, in whatever it saw, it never saw "the next day"; whatever it saw on its long journey, it never saw "the next day." And even if we say of the lily, "It stands today; tomorrow it is cast into the stove"[75]—oh, this noble, simple wise one, the lily, it is as one to whom this does not pertain at all. However much and however particularly it pertains to the lily, it is occupied solely with what pertains to it more particularly—that it stands today! However many days the bird saw come and go, it never saw "the next day." The bird does not see visions—but the next day is seen only in the mind; and the bird is not tormented by dreams—but the next day is an obstinate dream that returns; and the bird is never troubled—but the next day is each day's trouble. When the bird flies the long way to the far-off place, it seems to the bird as if it arrived at its destination the same day it started from home. We ride so fast on trains that we arrive at a distant place the same day, but the bird is more ingenious or swifter; it travels many, many days and arrives the same day. We cannot travel that fast by train if we are to travel
just as far. No, no one can make time go as fast as the bird can, and no one can go as far as the bird in such a short time. For the bird there is no yesterday and no tomorrow; it lives only one day, and the lily blossoms only one day.

Of course, the bird has no care about the next day. But care about the next day is precisely self-torment [*Selvplagelse*], and therefore the bird does not have the care of self-torment. What exactly is self-torment? It is the trouble [*Plage*] that today (which has enough trouble of its own) does not have. And what is self-torment? It is to cause this trouble oneself. The bird can also have trouble the day it lives, the day can also have enough trouble for it, but the next day's trouble the bird does not have—because it lives only one day, something we can also express in another way: because it has no self. Trouble and today correspond to each other; self-torment and the next day also go together.

But how, then, is the bird the teacher? Quite simply. That the bird has no "next day" is certain enough. Therefore be like the bird: remove the next day and then you are without the care of self-torment—and this can be done just because the next day lies in the self. On the other hand, let today drop away almost entirely in comparison with the next day's trouble, and then you are deepest in self-torment. It all is the difference of one day— and yet what an enormous difference! For the bird it is easy enough to *be* rid of the next day—but to *get* rid of it! Oh, of all the enemies that with force or with slyness press in upon a person, perhaps none is as obtrusive as this next day, which is always *this* next day. To gain the mastery over one's mind is greater than to occupy a city,[76] but if a person is to gain mastery over his mind, he must begin by *getting* rid of the next day. The next day, yes, it is like a troll, which can assume all forms; it can look so enormously different, but for all that it is still—the next day.

The Christian does not have this care. The care about the next day is most often associated only with care about livelihood. This is a very superficial view. All earthly and worldly care is basically for the next day. The earthly and worldly care was made possible precisely by this, that the human being was compounded of the temporal and the eternal, became a self, but in his becoming a self, the next day came into existence for him. And basically this is where the battle is fought. Earthly and worldly care—when one mentions this phrase, what an enormous compendium of dissimilarities, what a motley multitude of passions, what a mixture of contrasts! And yet the whole thing is only one battle, the battle of the next day! The next day—such a little village it is, and yet it has become and remains renowned, because it was and is

X
76

there that the greatest and the most decisive battle is fought—
there temporality and eternity are decided. The next day—it is
the grappling iron with which the huge mass of cares seizes hold
of *the single individual's* small craft—if it succeeds, then he is in the
clutches of that power. The next day—it is the first link in the
chain that shackles a person, along with thousands, to the abundance of that care, which is of evil. The next day, yes, it is amaz-
ing—ordinarily when someone is sentenced for life, the sentence
says it is for life; but the person who sentences himself to care
about the next day sentences himself for life. Therefore, see
whether deliverance from the next day is not to be found in
heaven, since it is not found on earth; not even by dying on the
next day do you escape it—after all, it was until that day you
were alive. But if there is no next day for you, then all earthly
care is annihilated,[77] not only the care about livelihood, because
everything earthly and worldly is desirable only for the sake of
the next day—and insecure because of the next day. When the
next day comes, it loses its enchantment and its disquieting in-
security. If there is no next day for you, then either you are dying
or you are one who by dying to temporality grasped the eternal,
either one who is actually dying or one who is *really* living.

The Gospel says, "Each day has enough trouble of its own."
But is this a Gospel? It seems instead to be from a book of lamen-
tations; if each day has trouble enough of its own, this makes all
life, this admits that all life is, sheer trouble. One would think that
a Gospel would have to proclaim that every day is free from
trouble, or that there are only particular unlucky days. Yet it is a
Gospel, and it truly is not straining at a gnat and swallowing a
camel,[78] because it is aiming at the monster of self-torment—and
assumes that a person will manage the daily troubles all right.
Therefore it says in essence: Each day *will* have its troubles. Admittedly, these words are not in the Gospel, but it reads: "Tomorrow *will* worry about itself." But if it will worry about itself,
then you are to be without care for it and are to let it look after
itself. With regard to trouble, then, you *will* have enough in what
each day has, since you *must* let the next day look after itself. Is
this not the case? When the teacher says to a pupil, "You must

leave your seatmate alone; let him look after himself," he is also saying, "You have enough in attending to yourself, and you *will* have enough in that." Each day will have its trouble—that is, just make sure that you become free from the next day's trouble, be calmly and gladly satisfied with each day's trouble; you stand to gain thereby—by becoming free from the next day's trouble. Be content, therefore; have godliness with contentment,[79] since each day has *enough* trouble of its own. God takes care of us also in this regard; he measures out the trouble that is *enough* for each day; take no more than what is apportioned, which is just *enough*, whereas worry about the next day is covetousness.

To be properly positioned, to take the correct position, is important for everything in life. The Christian does this with regard to the next day because it does not exist for him. —It is well known that the actor, blinded as he is by the effect of the lighting, faces the deepest darkness, the blackest night. Now, one would think that this must disturb him, make him uneasy. But no, ask him and you will hear; he himself admits that precisely this supports him, calms him, keeps him in the enchantment of the illusion. It would, however, disturb him if he could see some particular, catch a glimpse of a particular spectator. So also with the next day. At times we lament and find it sad that the future lies so dark before us. Ah, the misfortune is precisely when it is not dark enough, when fear and presentiment and expectancy and earthly impatience catch a glimpse of the next day!

The one who rows a boat turns his back to the goal toward which he is working. So it is with the next day. When, with the help of the eternal, a person lives absorbed in today, he turns his back to the next day. The more he is eternally absorbed in today, the more decisively he turns his back to the next day; then he does not see it at all. When he turns around, the eternal becomes confused before his eyes and becomes the next day. But when, in order to work toward the goal (eternity) properly, he turns his back, he does not see the next day at all, whereas with the help of the eternal he sees today and its tasks with perfect clarity. But if the work today is to be done properly, a person must be turned in this way. It is always delaying and distracting impatiently to

X
78

want to inspect the goal every moment, to see whether one is coming a little closer, and then again a little closer. No, be forever and earnestly resolute; then you turn wholeheartedly to the work—and your back to the goal. This is the way one is turned when one rows a boat, but so also is one positioned when one believes. One might think that the believer would be most distanced from the eternal, he who has completely turned his back and is living today, whereas the glimpser stands and looks for it. And yet the believer is closest of all to the eternal, whereas the apocalypt is most distanced from the eternal. Faith turns its back to the eternal expressly in order to have it entirely present with it today. But if a person turns to the future, and especially with earthly passion, then he is most distanced from the eternal, then the next day becomes a monstrous confused figure, like that in a fairytale. Just like those daimons we read about in the book of Genesis who begot children with mortal women,[80] the future is the monstrous daimon that begets the next day with a person's womanly imagination.

But the Christian believes, and for that very reason he gets rid of the next day. Compared with the self-tormentor, the believer is in the exactly opposite position, because the self-tormentor completely forgets today in his concern for and preoccupation with the next day. The believer is one who is present [*Nærværende*] and also, as this word [*praesens*[81]] in that foreign language indicates, a person of power. The self-tormentor is an absentee, a powerless person. We frequently hear the wish to be contemporary with some great event or great man; the idea is that contemporaneity might develop one and make one into something great. Perhaps! But should being contemporary with oneself not be worth more than a wish! How rare is the person who actually is contemporary with himself; ordinarily most people are apocalyptically, in theatrical illusions, hundreds of thousands of miles ahead of themselves, or several generations ahead of themselves in feelings, in delusions, in intentions, in resolutions, in wishes, in longings. But the believer (the one present) is in the highest sense contemporary with himself. To be totally contemporary with oneself today with the help of the eternal is also the most formative and generative; it is the gaining of eternity. There certainly was never any contemporary event or any most honored contemporary as great—as eternity.

This contemporaneity today is the very task; when it is worked out, it is faith. This is why the Christian praises (as does one of the most rigorous church fathers[82]) a saying by Sirach, not as a sagacious rule but as devout fear of God (Sirach 30:23): "Love your soul and comfort your heart and drive care far from you"—who indeed would be as cruel as the self-tormentor is toward himself. But all his torments, all these cruelly devised and cruelly practiced torturing agonies are comprehended in this one phrase, "the next day." And now the remedy against it! It is told that in a library in Spain a book was found with the inscription on its spine, "The Best Remedy against Heretics." Upon opening the book or, rather, upon trying to open the book, one saw that it was not a book; it was a case in which lay a scourge. If one were to write a book called "The Best Remedy against Self-Torment," it would be very brief: "Let each day have trouble enough of its own." Therefore when the Christian works and when he prays, he speaks only of today: he prays for the daily bread *today*, for blessing upon his work *today*, to escape evil's snare *today*, to come closer to God's kingdom *today*. In other words, if a person, just because he has become acquainted with horror, were to pray thus with the passion of his soul, "Save me, O God, from myself and from the next day," he is not praying Christianly, and the next day already has too much power over him. The Christian prays, "Save me from evil today." This is the surest deliverance from the next day, but it is also intended to be prayed every day; if it is forgotten one day, the next day promptly makes its appearance. But the Christian does not forget to pray on any day; therefore he saves himself throughout life, and faith saves his courage, his joy, his hope. That fearful enemy, the next day, exists, but the Christian does not paint the devil on the wall, does not conjure up evil and temptation; he does not speak of the next day at all, but only of today—and he speaks about it with God.

To live in this way, to fill up the day today with the eternal and not with the next day, the Christian has learned or is learning (for the Christian is always a learner) from the prototype. How did he

X
79

conduct himself in living without care about the next day—he
who from the first moment he made his appearance as a teacher
knew how his life would end, that the next day would be his
crucifixion, knew it while the people were jubilantly hailing him
as king (what bitter knowledge at that very moment!), knew it
when they were shouting hosannas during his entry into Jerusalem,[83] knew that they would be shouting "Crucify him!"[84] and
that it was for this that he was entering Jerusalem—he who bore
the enormous weight of this superhuman knowledge every
day—how did he conduct himself in living without care about
the next day? Because he knew that the suffering was unavoidable, he who did not suffer as one who suffers the assault of adversity and hardships but who also at every moment has the possibility before him that it is still possible that everything could still
turn out all right; he who, with every additional sacrifice he
brought to the truth, knew that he was hastening his persecution
and downfall, and thus he had his own fate in his power and
could make sure of royal splendor and the adoring admiration of
his generation if he would relinquish the truth, but also with
even greater certainty would make sure of his downfall if he (oh,
what an eternally sure way to downfall!) betrayed the truth in
absolutely nothing—how did he conduct himself in living without care about the next day—he who was indeed not unacquainted with the suffering of this anxiety or with any other
human suffering, he who groaned in an outburst of pain,
"Would that the hour had already come"?

See, in the language of the military, one speaks of covering a
commander while he is attacking the enemy, of protecting him
lest someone attack him from the rear. While he was living the
day today, how did he manage to protect himself against the
enemy that would attack him from the rear, namely the next
day—just because he had the eternal with him in his today in a
sense totally different from the way any human being has, for that
very reason he turned his back on the next day. How did he
manage? Far be it from us presumptuously to try to gain popular-
ity by fathoming what should not be fathomed. We do not believe that he came to the world in order to give us subjects for

X
80

erudite research. He came to the world to set the task, in order to leave a footprint so that we would learn from him.[85] Therefore we have also already let the answer appear in the question, have recalled how he conducted himself and what we are to learn: he had the eternal with him in his today—therefore the next day had no power over him, it did not exist for him. It had no power over him before it came, and when it came and was the today, it had no other power over him than what was his Father's will, to which he, eternally free, had consented and to which he obediently submitted.

The pagan, however, does have this care, because paganism is precisely self-torment. Instead of casting all his cares upon God,[86] the pagan has every torment; he is without God and for that very reason is the tormented man, the self-tormentor. In other words, since he is without God, it cannot be God who lays any torment on him. The relation is not this: without God, without torment; with God, with torment—but this: with God, without torment; without God, with torment.

"Let us eat and drink, because tomorrow we shall die."[87] But then the pagan is indeed without care about the next day; after all, he himself says that there is no next day. No, he really does not deceive Christianity, and neither does he succeed in deceiving himself. This very remark echoes with the anxiety about the next day, the day of annihilation, the anxiety that insanely is supposed to signify joy although it is a shriek from the abyss. He is so anxious about the next day that he plunges himself into a frantic stupor in order, if possible, to forget it—and how anxious he is—is this what it means to be without care about the next day? If this is being without something, then it is being without understanding or being insane. Furthermore, tomorrow is also the refrain in the day's joy; indeed, the verse continually ends this way, "because tomorrow." We speak, to be sure, of a lust for life based on despair, which simply because it does not have the next day lives, as it is said, totally in the today. But this is an illusion, because one cannot exactly live that way in the today, least of all *totally*. A human being has the eternal within him, and therefore

X
81

he cannot possibly be *totally* in the purely momentary. The more he attempts to will to dispense with the eternal, the further away he is from living today. Whether the pagan will die tomorrow, we leave undecided; one thing is certain, he is not *living* today.

"But tomorrow!" Just as the Christian continually speaks only about today, so the pagan continually speaks only about tomorrow. It actually makes no difference to him what kind of day today is, glad or sad, lucky or unlucky—he is able neither to enjoy it nor to use it, because he cannot get away from the invisible writing on the wall[88] : tomorrow. Tomorrow I shall perhaps starve, even if I do not today; tomorrow the thieves will perhaps steal my wealth, or slanderers my honor, deterioration my beauty, life's envy my good fortune—tomorrow, tomorrow! Today I am standing on the pinnacle of good fortune—ah, tell me of some misfortune this very day, quickly, quickly—for otherwise tomorrow everything may be boundlessly lost. What is anxiety? It is the next day. And why was the pagan most anxious at the very moment when he was most fortunate? Because adversity and misfortune perhaps had served in part to quench the fire of his earthly care. Earthly care, breeding, gives birth to anxiety, which in turn, feeding, gives birth to care. In order to make the glowing ember burst into flame, there must be a draft. But craving, earthly craving, and uncertainty, earthly uncertainty, these two currents form the very draft that stirs up the fire of passion in which anxiety dwells.

With whom, then, does the pagan contend in anxiety? With himself, with a delusion, because the next day is a powerless nothing if you yourself do not give it your strength. If you totally give it all your strength, then you find out in a terrible way, as the pagan does, however strong you are—what a prodigious power the next day is! The next day, which the pagan approaches with horror, fighting against it like one who is being dragged to the place of execution, futilely resisting, like one who on a sinking ship desperately stretches his arms toward land, disconsolate like one who from land watches all his possessions sink into the sea!

In this way the pagan devours himself, or the next day devours him. Alas, *there* a human soul went out; he lost his self. No one knows how it happened; it was not need or misfortune or adversity. No one saw the dreadful power that devoured this person, but he was devoured. Like a baleful spirit that found no rest in the grave, he lives like a ghost—that is, he is not living. Just as we speak of the irregularity of turning night into day, so he desperately wants to turn today into the next day. Therefore he is not living today, and he will not live until the next day. "He will not live until tomorrow," we say of the patient whom the physician has given up; but the patient is still living today. But the self-tormentor will not, in the even stricter sense, live until tomorrow; he is given up because he gave up the eternal. He is not living even today, although he is living, still less until tomorrow, because in order to live until tomorrow one must be living today. Just like a bird that flies against a painted wall in order to perch in one of the trees and flies itself to the point of exhaustion, perhaps to death, by wanting to perch in one of those trees, so also the self-tormentor desouls his self by wanting to live the next day today. Just as the bird that became exhausted crossing the ocean sinks down with feeble wing strokes toward the sea and now can neither live nor die, so it is also with the self-tormentor who becomes exhausted on the way across the distance between today and the next day. To live is to exist today; when one is dead, there is no more today. But the self-tormentor lives, yet not today; he does not live until tomorrow, yet he goes on living day after day. Our Lord cannot throw light around him, because it remains just as dark around him and just as unblessed whether he lives or dies, he who neither lives nor dies and yet lives—yes, as in a hell.

Let us then in conclusion consider the bird, which was there in the Gospel and must be here in the discourse. The bird arrives at its far-off destination the same day; the Christian is in heaven, where his life is, the same day, "this very day";[89] the pagan never moves from the spot. The bird is a self-lover in a good sense, one who reasonably loves itself and therefore is no self-tormentor; the Christian loves God and therefore is no self-tormentor; the pagan hates himself (which God forbade and forbids)—he is a self-tormentor. The bird lives only one day; thus the next day does not exist for it. The Christian lives eternally; thus the next day does not exist for him. The pagan never lives; he is always prevented from living by the next day. The bird is free from all anxiety; the blessing upon the Christian delivers him from all anxiety; the pagan's care is the punishment upon him: self-torment—no sin punishes itself as self-torment does.

VII

The Care of Indecisiveness, Vacillation, and Disconsolateness

No one can serve two masters—the pagans seek all these things

This care the bird does not have. If the angels are God's messengers[90] who obey his every hint, if he uses the winds as his angels, the bird and the lily are just as obedient, even though God does not use them as messengers, even though it seems as if he has no use for them. The bird and the lily have no occasion to become self-important by the use that is made of them; they humbly feel like a superfluity. But this does not mean that they are less dear to God, nor is being a superfluity the worst fortune. Quite often in the busy life of people, it is precisely the unusually gifted person who is more or less a superfluity because he does not fit into anything of all that this busyness wants to assign to him, engage him in, use him for—and yet his very superfluity serves more to the honor of the Creator than all the pomposity of busyness. Just as Mary's sitting at Christ's feet honored him better than Martha's activity, in the same way the lily and the bird are a superfluity of beauty and joy that God has squandered on the creation. But just because they are a superfluity in this way, the most perfect obedience is required of them. Certainly everything that exists is by grace; but the one who owes everything to grace to the degree that he understands he is a superfluity, must be all the more obedient. Certainly everything that exists is nothing in the hands of the Omnipotent One, who created it from nothing, but that which in coming into existence advanced only to becoming a superfluity must understand most deeply that it is nothing. When parents give a party for their own children, they presumably require joyful obedience or the joy that is obedience; but when they give a party for poor children and also give everything just as if it were their own, then they require even more decisively the joy whose secret is unconditional obedience.

But the lily and the bird are just like that, serving only *the master*, without thought of any other master, and without one single thought that is not of him, more obedient in his hand than a supple plant in the gardener's, more obedient to his every hint than the seasoned dove to its master's. Everything that goes by the names "lily"and "bird" belongs to one master, but every bird and lily serves only this one master.

Therefore the bird is never indecisive. It is the very opposite, although it might seem to be out of *indecisiveness* that the bird flies to and fro—it is altogether certain that this is out of joy. This is not the erratic flight of indecisiveness; this is the easy soaring of perfect obedience. Admittedly the bird soon becomes tired of its habitat and flies far away, but this is not *vacillation*; it is the very opposite—it is the firm and definite decision of perfect obedience. Rarely perhaps was any human being's decision as definite and stood so firm. Admittedly we do at times see a bird perching and looking crestfallen; it can have distress, but this is not *disconsolateness*. The obedient bird is never without consolation, and its life is essentially freedom from care just because it serves only one master, and this in turn serves best both the bird and the human being, serves to free him from grieving disconsolately.

How, then, are the bird and the lily the teacher? Quite simply. The bird and the lily serve only one master and, what amounts to the same thing, serve him wholly. So be like the bird and the lily; you, too, serve only one master, serve him with all your heart, with all your mind, with all your strength[91]—then you also are without care. More eminent than the bird and the lily, you are in kinship with that master (the lily and the bird are like the poor children), yet in obedience you serve the same master if you, like the lily and the bird, serve him wholly.

^X
⁸⁶
The Christian does not have this care. [92]"No one can serve two masters," or there is only one master whom one can serve *wholly*. In the choice between the two masters, it is not true that if we choose only one of the two and then serve this one, no matter

which one, that we are then serving only one master. No, there is only one who is master in this way, is *the master*, so that if we serve him we serve only one master. It is also clear enough that when there "is only one master"one does not serve one master when one does not serve him. Therefore it is not true that the person who chose wholly to serve mammon serves only one master; against his will he is still in the service of the other master, in the service of *the master*. If a person chooses another master than God, he must hate God, "for he must either love the one and hate the other"[93]—that is, if he loves the one, he must hate the other; but however much he hates God, he nevertheless is not released from his service and still does not serve one master. With a person's servant-relationship to God it is not as with a servant in his relation to another human being. He can run away from his service and so far away that his first master cannot get hold of him, or he may even take refuge in a situation so different that his first master must give up his claim on him. No, regardless of how desperate his determined will was, the person who chose to serve any other master than *the master* still remains in the service of two masters. Precisely this self-contradiction is his punishment: to will the impossible, since it is impossible to serve two masters. But then it is also possible to serve one master only if one has chosen *wholly* to serve *the master*. It looks almost tempting, it is almost as if the Gospel wanted to let human arbitrariness loose by saying: You must choose one of two. Ah, but right here is eternity's terrible earnestness in exercising a restraining influence, because you can choose only the one in such a way that by choosing him you serve one master. Therefore it is not true that the person who entirely made up his mind to doubt serves only one master, doubt, because to doubt, as the word [*tvivle*] suggests, is to be at odds with oneself, to be split in two.[94] Neither is it true that the person who entirely made up his mind (however loathsome this may be) to be a villain serves only one master, the devil, because no more than there is agreement in a den of thieves is there agreement in the heart that is a den of thieves. But how would it be possible to serve *one master in disagreement*!

The Christian serves only one master, *the master*; and he not only serves him but he *loves* him; he loves the Lord his God with his whole mind and with his whole heart and with all his strength. For this very reason he serves him wholly, because only love unites wholly, unites the dissimilar in love, here unites the human being wholly in God, who is love. Love is the firmest of all bonds, since it makes the lover one with what he loves; no bond can bind more firmly, or no bond can bind so firmly. The love that loves God is perfection's bond that in perfect obedience makes a person one with the God he loves. Furthermore, the love that loves God is the most beneficial bond,[95] which by keeping a person solely in the service of God frees him from cares. This love unifies a person, makes him eternally at one with himself and with the master who is one; and it unifies a person in likeness to God. Oh, what blessed service, to serve God alone in this way! This is also why it sounds so ceremonial [*høitidelig*] when we express it in one phrase; this service is indeed *divine service* [*Guds-Tjeneste*], the Christian's life is unalloyed divine service. The bird never carried it so high [*høi*] that one could call its life divine service; the bird never became that *perfect* in obedience, even if it were just as obedient.

But then is the Christian even more obedient than the bird? Yes, indeed he is. The bird has no other will than God's will, but the Christian has another will, which in obedience he always sacrifices to God—so much more obedient is he. What a hard sacrifice but pleasing to God and thus so blessed! Oh, we speak of so many *different things* that an individual can love the most: a woman, one's child, one's father, one's country, one's art, one's scholarly studies; but what *every* human being basically loves most, more than his only child, the child of promise,[96] more than his only beloved in heaven and on earth—is nevertheless his own will. You must not therefore lay a hand on this your child—God is not cruel; you must not forsake your beloved—God is not hardhearted. There is something else, something even deeper within you, and it is for your own salvation that it is taken away from you, and yet to your own harm there is nothing you clutch so tightly and nothing that clutches you as tightly (the child would rather submit to being sacrificed and the girl to becoming the sacrifice): it is one's own will. See, the bird is promptly at hand to obey God's will; but from a long way off, in a certain sense, comes the Christian, who is yet even more obedient than

the bird! Indeed, which promptness is the greater, the promptness of one who is standing beside you and instantly turns to
obey, or the promptness of one who from a distance is instantly
on the spot! The bird comes as quickly as it can when God
calls—all honor to it, it is a joy to watch it; but the Christian
comes infinitely more quickly, because he comes just as quickly
from—giving up his own will.

This is also why the Christian, free from care, is never *indecisive*—he has faith; never *vacillating*—he is eternally resolved;
never *disconsolate*—he is always joyous, always giving thanks.[97]
That obedience is the way to this he has learned and is learning
from him who is the Way,[98] from him who himself learned obedience[99] and was obedient, obedient in everything, obedient in
giving up everything[100] (the glory that he had before the foundation of the world was laid[101]), obedient in doing without everything (even that on which he could lay his head), obedient in
taking everything upon himself (the sin of humankind), obedient
in suffering everything (the guilt of humankind), obedient in
subjecting himself to everything in life, obedient in death.

Thus the Christian in perfect obedience serves only one master. Just as the bird sings incessantly to the honor of the Creator,
so also is the Christian's life, or at least he understands and admits
that this is the way it ought to be, and this understanding, this
admission, is already a declaration of honor. Thus the Christian's
life is like a hymn of praise to *the master's* honor, because this life
obeys God even more willingly and in even more blessed harmony than the harmony of the spheres. This life is a hymn of
praise, since a human being can praise God only by obedience,
can praise him best by perfect obedience. But the tone of this
hymn of praise is pitched so high and is so deeply gripping because this humble, cheerful obedience does not praise what one
understands but what one does not understand. And this is why
the instrument used in this hymn of praise is not the human
understanding's toy tin trumpet but faith's celestial trombone. By
way of obedience the Christian praises only one thing: that God
does everything, and that everything God does is sheer grace and
wisdom. Thus it is actually a kind of impudence, an insubordination (which the Christian could never want to permit himself) to

thank God as a matter of course because something takes place in just the way one feels able to understand will be beneficial and gratifying to one. If such a thing happens to the Christian, he certainly gives thanks, he who always gives thanks, but precisely then he is doubtful and suspicious of himself; he prays to God for forgiveness if he should give thanks too vehemently, too vehemently because according to his childish notion what happened seemed to him to be beneficial and gratifying.

X
89

The proper praise, hymn, and canticle of praise is namely this: by joyous and unconditional obedience to praise God when one cannot understand him. To praise him on the day everything goes against you, when everything goes black before your eyes, when others might readily want to demonstrate to you that there is no God—then, instead of becoming self-important by *demonstrating* that there is a God, humbly to demonstrate that you *believe* that there is a God, to demonstrate it by joyous and unconditional obedience—this is the hymn of praise. The hymn of praise is not something higher than obedience, but obedience is the only true hymn of praise. The hymn of praise is in the obedience, and if the hymn of praise is truth, it is obedience. In relation to another person, you can actually do yourself harm by submitting to his will, even if the harm never becomes great, since it is still also a blessing for you yourself to sacrifice yourself for the sake of another. But would it also be possible for me to do myself harm in any way by obeying God's will—when his will is certainly my only true good! But if that is the case, should not obedience then always be joyous, should it hesitate for one single moment to be joyous—after all, it is simply and solely my own good that is advanced!

All creation praises God by obeying his hint. The Christian's life praises him by an even more perfect obedience, by joyous obedience even when he understands that he does not understand God. Why, then, should the door be left open or the back gate left unguarded through which indecisiveness or vacillation, to say nothing of disconsolateness, would be able to sneak into the Christian's soul! No, there is no fortress as secure as faith's! Every other fortress—even if the enemy found no gate open, no path cleared up the mountain or no possibility of clearing one,

he, by totally cutting it off from any connection with the surrounding world, from all supply, will finally starve it out and
force it to surrender. But the more you cut faith off from all
supplies from the surrounding world (the supplies of indecisiveness, vacillation, disconsolateness—indeed, there is nothing else
equivalent to what supplies a fortress's needs from the outside),
the more secure is the fortress. You err if you think that you are
attacking it—you are fortifying it. It is merely a pompous lie to
call a fortress a little world to itself. But the fortress of faith is a
world to itself, and it has life within its ramparts; and what it
needs least of all—indeed, alas, what harms it the most—are all
the supplies from the surrounding world. Cut faith off from all
connections with the surrounding world, starve it out—it becomes all the more impregnable, its life all the richer. And with
faith in this fortress lives obedience.

The pagan, however, does have this care. Paganism is precisely a dou-
bleness, the two wills, masterlessness, or what amounts to the
same thing, slavery. Paganism is a kingdom divided against itself,[102] a kingdom in continual rebellion, where one tyrant succeeds another, but where there still is never any master. Paganism
is a mind in rebellion; by the devil's help the devil of the moment
is driven out, and seven worse ones come in.[103] At rock bottom,
however variously it manifests itself, paganism is disobedience,
the powerless, self-contradictory attempt of wanting to serve two
masters. But this is also why the punishment on it is: "Woe to the
sinner who walks on two paths."[104] It is said that one can tell it
in a congregation when for many years there has been *no pastor*,
although there have been many pastors; in the same way one can
also tell it in the pagan that there are many masters, or that many
have been masters, but *no master* has ruled over this mind. There
is one thing in which all pagans resemble one another, disobedience to *the master*; and there is one thing that no pagan does, he
does not serve one master. He perhaps tries his hand at everything else, at wanting to serve one master who nevertheless is not
master, at wanting to have no master, at wanting to serve several
masters—and the more experienced he becomes in all such
things, the worse his last condition becomes than his first.

X
90

At first the pagan is *indecisive*. As long as he is indecisive, it looks as if there were still nothing blameworthy, as if the possibility of choosing the one master were still open for him, as if he were devoid of care and his indecisiveness were earnest deliberation. Perhaps one thinks that the longer a person deliberates the more earnest his decision becomes. Perhaps—if it does not entirely fail to come. Above all, do not forget that there certainly is something that does not require long deliberation. For example, with regard to a triviality—there a long deliberation would certainly be a very dubious sign. Now, there are many such trivialities in life, but there is still one thing about which a need for long deliberation is a very dubious sign: it is God, or choosing God. The triviality is out of all proportion to long deliberation; but God's majesty is also out of all proportion to long deliberation and reflection. Long deliberation here is so far from being earnestness that it demonstrates the very lack of earnestness and demonstrates it by showing itself to be indecisiveness. It is far from being the case that a person, the longer he deliberates and deliberates, comes closer to God; on the contrary, the longer the deliberation becomes, while the choice is being postponed, the more he distances himself from God.

To choose God is certainly the most decisive and highest choice; but woe to the person who needs long deliberation here, and woe to him the longer he needs it. It is precisely faith's impatient readiness, its infinite need, which refuses to hear about anything else, that is not only closest to the choice but is best prepared for the choice. The person guilty of the impiety of very calmly postponing the question whether he should choose God now or another master is obviously indecisive and probably to such a degree that he never gets out of it. Strangely enough, we ordinarily say that a family in poverty has a hard time getting out of it, but the one who in indecisiveness became rich in deliberation has a far more difficult time getting out of it. God is not like something one buys in a shop, or like a piece of property that one, after having sagaciously and circumspectly examined, measured, and calculated for a long time, decides is worth buying. With regard to God, it is the ungodly calmness with which the indecisive person wants to begin (indeed, he wants to begin with doubt), precisely this that is the insubordination, because in this way God is thrust down from the throne, from being *the master.* When one has done that, one actually has already chosen another master, self-will, and then becomes the slave of indecisiveness.

When indecisiveness has ruled long enough, *vacillation* (Luke 12:29[105]) comes into power. It perhaps seemed for a time as if indecisiveness concealed in itself the tension of choice, this possibility. If it was there at all, it is now dissipated and the pagan's soul is lax; what indecisiveness really conceals in itself is disclosed. In indecisiveness there is still a power to resist the thoughts; the indecisiveness still makes an attempt to be itself the master in the house and to join the thoughts together. But now the masterlessness of the thoughts, or the whim of the moment, comes to power. The whim rules, also with regard to the question of choosing God. In the whim of the moment it seems to the pagan that it would indeed be most appropriate to choose God, and then in turn to choose something else and a third thing. But these motions, which have no meaning, acquire no meaning either and leave no trace, except increased sluggishness and laxity. Just as in the sluggishness of stagnant water a bubble languidly rises and emptily bursts, so vacillation bubbles in the whim and then bubbles again.

When vacillation has ruled long enough and, of course, like all ungodly rulers has sucked the blood and wasted the marrow, *disconsolateness* comes to power. Then the pagan would prefer to get rid of the thought of God entirely; now he wants to sink into the emptiness of worldliness, there to seek forgetfulness, forgetfulness of the most dangerous (precisely because it is the most uplifting) of all thoughts, the thought of being remembered by God, of existing before God. Indeed, if one *wills* to sink, what is more dangerous than everything that will lift up! Yet he has, so he thinks, overcome his pain, expelled all delusions, learned to console himself. Well, in a way, yes, somewhat as when a person deeply downcast, in order to console himself (what dreadful disconsolateness!), says to someone the sight of whom reminds him of something higher: Let me be what I am. Then the light of the spirit goes out; a dull mist hangs before his eyes. He is listless, but still he does not want to die; he is living in his own way. What dreadful disintegration, worse than death's, to decay while living, without the energy even to despair over oneself and one's condition! But the light of the spirit has gone out, and the disconsolate person becomes insanely busy with all sorts of things, if only nothing will remind him of God. He slaves from morning to night, accumulates money, hoards, engages in business transactions—yes, if you speak with him you will incessantly hear him talk about the earnestness of life. What appalling earnestness! It would be almost better to lose one's mind!

What is disconsolateness? Not even the wildest scream of pain or the presumptuousness of despair, however terrible, is disconsolateness. But this understanding with oneself, arrived at in dead silence, that everything higher is lost, although one can still go on living if only nothing reminds one of it—this is disconsolateness. Not even to grieve disconsolately, but to have entirely ceased to grieve, to be able to lose God in such a way that one becomes utterly indifferent and does not even find life intolerable—that is disconsolateness and is also the most terrible kind of disobedience, more terrible than any defiance—to hate God, to curse him, is not so terrible as to lose him in this way or, what is the same thing, to lose oneself. To lose something trivial in such a way that one does not care to pick it up, well, that perhaps is all right, but to lose one's own self (to lose God) in such a way that one does not even care to bend down to pick it up, or in such a way that it entirely escapes one that one has lost it! Oh, what terrible perdition! Not only is there certainly an infinite difference between what one loses and what one loses, but also between *how* one loses. To lose God in such a way that repentance in brokenheartedness promptly rushes to recover what was lost; to lose God in such a way that one takes offense at him, is indignant with him or groans against him; to lose God in such a way that one despairs over it—but to lose God as if he were nothing, and as if it were nothing!

Let us then in conclusion consider the bird, which was there in the Gospel and must be here in the discourse. The bird obeys God in such a way that it is still doubtful whether this obedience is not identical with being self-willed; the Christian denies him-

X
93

self in such a way that this is identical with obeying God; the pagan is self-willed in such a way that it becomes forever obvious that he does not obey God. The bird has no self-will to give up; the Christian gives up his self-will; the pagan gives up God. The bird neither found nor lost God; the Christian found God, and as everything; the pagan lost God, and as nothing. The bird serves only one master, whom it does not know; the Christian serves only one master, whom he loves; the pagan serves the master who is the enemy of God. The bird obeys promptly when God calls; the Christian is even more obedient; to the pagan God cannot even call, because it is as if there were no one to call to. The bird's obedience serves to the glory of God; the Christian's more perfect obedience is even more to the glory of God; the pagan's disobedience does not honor God—he is good for nothing except to be thrown out as salt that has lost its strength.

Part Two

STATES OF MIND IN THE STRIFE OF SUFFERING[1]

CHRISTIAN DISCOURSES

"I will incline my ear to a proverb;
I will set my dark saying to the
music of the harp." Psalm 49:5.[2]

I

The Joy of It: That One Suffers Only Once But Is Victorious Eternally[3]

The one who wants an end must also want the means. But this implies the assumption or admission, does it not, that he knows what he wants. If this is assumed, we stop him at "the means" by saying, "*Then* you must also want the means." Sometimes, however, it may still be necessary to go back even further and say, "The one who wants something must first and foremost know what he wants, must be conscious of what it is that he wants." To the impatience that wants to attain its end at once, this already seems an appalling hindrance, this matter of the means to be used—oh, but what deadly slowness to begin as far back as "The one who wants something must also know what he wants, must be conscious of what it is that he wants."

So it is now with regard to what is indeed the task of the upbuilding discourse:[4] to build up, or rather with regard to being built up. Perhaps someone wants to be built up as something extra, wishes to be built up, and who, if he took the time to understand what he wants or took the time to have it explained to him, would have second thoughts about it and now there is nothing he wishes more to be excused from than from being built up. Such misunderstanding happens rather frequently in life. A person can vehemently, passionately, indeed, obstinately crave something of which he does not know the more precise nature at all—alas, the more precise nature of which is perhaps the very opposite of what the wisher thought it to be.[5] So also
with the upbuilding, which truly is a good thing in itself and for that very reason must require that the individual who wants to be built up has understood himself, lest he, wishing light-mindedly in a worldly way, thoughtlessly, take the upbuilding in vain and then decline with thanks when he finds out more precisely what it is.

What exactly is the upbuilding? The first answer to this is what the upbuilding is at first: it is the *terrifying*.[6] The upbuilding is not for the healthy but for the sick,[7] not for the strong but for the weak; thus for the presumably healthy and strong it is bound to appear at first as the terrifying. The sick person naturally agrees to be under a physician's treatment, but for a healthy person it would of course be terrifying to discover that he has fallen into the hands of a physician who summarily treated him as sick. So it is with the upbuilding, which at first is the terrifying; for the one without a broken and a contrite heart,[8] it is at first the crushing. Where there is nothing terrifying whatever and no terror whatever, there is nothing that builds up either, no upbuilding whatever. There is forgiveness of sin—that is upbuilding. The terrifying is that there is sin, and the magnitude of the terror in the inwardness of guilt-consciousness is proportionate to the dimension of the upbuilding. There is healing for all pain, victory in all strife, rescue in all danger—that is upbuilding. The terrifying is that there is pain, strife, danger; and the magnitude of the terrifying and the terror is proportionate to what builds up and to the upbuilding.

So deep lies the upbuilding. Finding the upbuilding resembles artesian-well drilling, in which one must dig many, many fathoms—then of course the jet spurts all the higher. One must first look closely to find the terrifying. The terrifying is to the upbuilding what the divining rod is to the spring: where the rod bends down, there in the ground is the spring; and where the terrifying is, there, close by at the bottom, is the upbuilding. Having looked closely to find the terrifying, if one then looks closely again, one finds the upbuilding.

So sure is the upbuilding of itself, so reliable in itself. One must not be afraid of the terrifying, as if it hindered the upbuilding, must not timorously keep it away in the hope of making the upbuilding more pleasant, because the upbuilding itself leaves with the terrifying. But, on the other hand, the upbuilding is precisely in the terrifying. So triumphant is the upbuilding that *whatever* at first glance could seem to be its enemy is made a presupposition, a servant, a friend. If the art of medicine successfully performs the difficult task of turning poison into a remedy, in the upbuilding the terrifying is far more gloriously transformed into the upbuilding.

So it is also with what is the subject of this discourse. One suffers only once. This is said so quickly that it almost sounds frivolous, like that frivolous saying so often heard in the world, "Enjoy life—you live only once."[9] But in order to find the upbuilding, one must first find the terrifying and thus take the time here to understand that in these words is contained the most somber view of life. One suffers only once—that is tantamount to saying of someone that he was sick only once in his life, was unhappy only once in his life—that is, throughout his whole life. See, now the upbuilding in the deepest sense begins. But earthly sagacity and impatience and worldly care that seek healing in a worldly way must not insist on the impossible, that one should be able to address them for upbuilding when one is to speak about the essentially Christian. Christianity really begins right there, or real Christianity begins right there where human impatience, whatever actual suffering it had to lament over, would find this to be infinitely increased—by the consolation—indeed, by consolation to the point of despair, because from the worldly point of view Christian consolation is much more to despair over than the hardest earthly suffering and the greatest temporal misfortune. *There* begins the upbuilding, the Christian upbuilding, which is named after him, our Lord and Savior, for he also suffered only once[10]—but his whole life was suffering.

So let us speak about

the joy of it: that one suffers only once but is victorious eternally.

[11]One suffers only once but is victorious eternally. If so, is one then victorious only once? Yes, indeed. But the difference is infinite—namely, *that the one time of suffering is a moment and the one time of victory is eternity; therefore the one time of suffering, when it is past, is no time; in another sense the one time of victory is no time, because it is never past; the one time of suffering is a transition or a passing through; the one time of victory is a victory lasting forever.*

The one time of suffering is a moment, or one suffers only once. If the suffering lasts seventy years, it is only once; if the one time is

seven times seventy times,[12] it is still only once. Temporality itself, the whole of it, is a moment; eternally understood, temporality is a moment, and a moment, eternally understood, is only
once. Temporality futilely wants to make itself important, counts
the moments, and counts and adds—when the eternal is allowed
to rule, temporality never gets further than, never becomes more
than, the one time. Eternity is the very opposite. It is not the
opposite of a single moment in temporality (this is meaningless);
it is the opposite of the whole of temporality, and with all the
powers of eternity it resists temporality's becoming more. Just as
God said to the water, "Up to here and no further,"[13] so eternity
says to temporality, "Up to here and no further; you are, no
matter how long you continue to be, a moment, neither more
nor less; this I, eternity, guarantee, or this I, eternity, compel you
to be." No more than the parasitic plant, no matter how long it
continues to grow or how widely it spreads along the ground,
ever grows in height, no more does temporality, no matter how
long it lasts, become more than a moment and the one time—
when eternity rules.

Therefore the youth who stands at the beginning of life says
with the same right as the old man who stands at the end of life
and gazes out over the past: One suffers only once. With the
same right—that is, by virtue of the eternal, but not with the
same truth, even if the statement is equally true. The youth *says
what is true*, but the old man has verified it, *has made true* that
which is indeed eternally true. This is the only difference, something that has been overlooked in these times, in which people
with all this demonstrating and demonstrating have completely
forgotten that the highest a person is capable of is to make [*gjøre*]
an eternal truth true, to make it true that it is true—by doing
[*gjøre*] it, by being oneself the demonstration, by a life that perhaps will also be able to convince others. Did Christ ever get
involved in demonstrating one or another truth, or in demonstrating the truth? No, but he made the truth true, or he made it
true that he is the truth.

One suffers only once. But just as that parasitic plant that
creeps along the ground shows at every moment, if you pay attention to it, a propensity to grow in height, and if along the way

it finds something on which it can entwine itself upward it sneaks upward in height or it counterfeits height—in the same way temporality, if in its insidious course it finds something on which it can hang, also wants to sneak upward to be something—with outside assistance. Yes, with outside assistance, and yet no, not with outside assistance, because if that happens, if temporality manages to become something in this way, then it happens with the assistance of the person to whom, to his misfortune, this happens.

When a person does not draw his power from the eternal and acquire by communion with the eternal the power to hold temporality down, temporality steals his power from him and through this stolen power it now becomes some enormous something; it becomes his impatience, his despair, perhaps his downfall. Pride strikes its own master, but temporality is just as ungrateful; it becomes something by stealing the power of eternity from a person and then in return remains with him and makes him its slave. Then, alas, the person comes to know a great deal about the moment; greater and greater become the numbers with which he calculates—ah, and this same calculation, when eternity is allowed to rule, is one times one. Now one day of suffering is long, one month terribly long, one year deadly long, not to be endured, to be despaired over; now one can remember this time and that time and that time and finally so many times that no one knows either the beginning or the end of the many times of suffering. But was not the master of the vineyard in the right when, according to the agreement, he had the workers paid an equal wage although they were called to work at different hours[14]—in the *eternal* sense, was he not in the right, because, in the eternal sense, they had worked only once? Therefore the workers who complained as if they had been wronged must have learned something from temporality that is not eternally true, and that, of course, was their mistake, and it was they who were in the wrong, not the master. The master is eternity, for whom the time distinction does not exist, for whom temporality is only one time; the equal pay is in turn the eternal. Therefore no one had reason for complaint, because with regard to the eternal only one agreement is possible, the one equal for everybody; and with regard to receiving eternity's wages, one person has not worked longer because he was called at the third hour, has not worked any longer than the person who was called at the eleventh hour.

O you suffering one, every evening you hear the cry, "Watch your candles and fires";[15] at times you perhaps also hear the cry, "Make use of your time." I would rather cry out to you and to me: Above all, take care to associate circumspectly with temporality, even more circumspectly than with fire and candles, lest it become more for you than the one time! Never begin the terrible calculating that wants to count the moments and the times, something that no one who started ever finished! Above all, take care promptly to reduce the fraction with the help of the eternal, in which all moments always cancel out and in such a way that they become only one time! Never let go of this upbuilding consolation, "One suffers only once"; protect yourself with this, that is, with the eternal, against ever coming in your life to suffer more than once! Once, ah, is it not true, a person can surely endure that; but if he only has to suffer twice— then impatience is up and doing. Is this not the way it is? Indeed, it was precisely impatience that taught him that it was a second time he suffered—with the help of eternity one suffers only once. Therefore, when evening comes, let the day's suffering be forgotten so that when the same suffering begins the next day you still are suffering only once! And when the year is over, let this year's suffering be forgotten so that when the same suffering begins the next year you still are suffering only once! And then when your last hour has come, let this life's suffering be forgotten—yes, is it not so, then it is forgotten, you suffered only once! Oh, whoever you are, even if you feel ever so grievously trapped in the lifelong confinement of suffering, alas, like a trapped animal in its cage—see, this prisoner paces around the cage every day, measures the length of the chain in order to have movement—so if you also measure the length of the chain by proceeding to the thought of death and eternity, you gain the movement enabling you to endure, and you gain zest for life! Suffer patiently, but everything, everything that can be said about suffering patiently is actually and essentially contained in this one sentence: Let eternity help you to suffer only once.

The one time of suffering is no time [*er ingen Gang.*] It is as the proverb says: Once does not make a habit [*er ingen Gang*]. Whether it holds true of what the proverb refers to, I do not decide. It is quite possible that the proverb is not true, and yet what the proverb says is true; a proverb, after all, is no eternal truth and speaks only of temporal things. It is eternally certain and never can it manifest itself as clearly and decisively that one time is no time as when the relation is—temporality/eternity. What indeed are seventy years compared with an eternity! In eternity it will be manifest that all this suffering, this one time, is no time. It will be altogether impossible to perceive on the sainted ones that they have suffered, perceive anything at all of what they have suffered. Every tear will be wiped away from the eyes[16] that now shine with joy; every need will be satisfied in the heart that now blessedly possesses everything and possesses it *there* (what blessed security of possession!), there where nothing can take the joy away from it, there where the sainted ones blessedly say: One time is no time.

[17]Only sin is a human being's corruption;[18] only sin has the power to mark a person in such a way that it is not immediately or totally, yes, in such a way that it perhaps is never overcome in eternity. All temporality's suffering—its one time is no time.

The one time [*Gang*] *of suffering is a transition* [*Overgang*], *a passing through* [*Gjennemgang*]. You must pass through it; and even if it lasts as long as life, and even if it is as heavy as a sword that passes through your heart,[19] it is still only a passing through. It is not so that it is the suffering that passes through you; you pass through it—in the eternal sense, totally unscathed. In temporality and in its understanding, it looks so terrible; by way of an optical illusion, it looks as if the suffering were piercing through you so you would perish in it, rather than that it is you who are passing through it. It is an optical illusion. It is as in the play when one actor kills the other; it looks exactly as if he pierced him, but we all know, of course, that it is not so, that he did not hurt a hair on his head.[20] But just as the murdered actor goes home unharmed, and Daniel went out of the lion's cage[21] unharmed, and the three walked into the red-hot furnace[22] unharmed—so a believer's soul goes into eternity unharmed by all temporality's suffering, unscathed by death. All temporality's suffering is a mirage, and death itself, in the eternal sense, is a buffoon! As little as moth and rust can consume the treasure of eternity (and what indeed is more impossible!), as little as thieves can steal it,[23] just as little can all the suffering of temporality, no matter how long it might last, injure the soul in the remotest way. Neither sickness, nor privation and need, nor cold and heat, however much they consume, is able to do it; neither slander nor insult nor personal attack nor persecution is able to do it, no matter what they steal and rob; death is not able to do it!

The one time of suffering is a passing through that leaves no mark at all upon the soul, or, even more glorious, it is a passing through that completely cleanses the soul, and as a result the purity becomes the mark the passing through leaves behind. Just as gold is purified in the fire, so the soul is purified in sufferings.[24] But what does the fire take away from the gold? Well, it is a curious way of talking to call it taking away; it takes away all the impure elements from the gold. What does gold lose in the fire? Well, it is a curious way of talking to call it losing; in the fire the gold loses all that is base—that is, the gold gains through the fire. So also with all temporal suffering, the hardest, the longest; powerless in itself, it is incapable of taking away anything, and if the suffering one lets eternity rule, it takes away the impure, that is, it gives purity.

Sin is man's corruption. Only the rust of sin can consume the soul—or eternally *corrupt* it. Indeed, this is the oddity whereby even that simple wise man of antiquity[25] demonstrates the immortality of the soul, that the sickness of the soul (sin) is not like the sickness of the body, which kills the body. Neither is sin a passage that one is to go through once, because one is to back away from it; sin is not a moment but is an eternal falling away from the eternal; therefore it is not one time, and thus its one time cannot possibly be no time. No, just as there was a chasmic abyss between that rich man in hell and Lazarus in Abraham's bosom,[26] so also there is a chasmic difference between suffering and sin. Let us not create confusion, so that the discourse about suffering perhaps became less frank because it also considered sin, and this less frank discourse became recklessly brazen inasmuch as it spoke this way about sin. Precisely this is the essentially Christian, that there is this infinite difference between evil and what is confusingly called evil; precisely this is Christianity, continually to speak about the suffering of temporality more and more frankly, more triumphantly, and more joyously because, from the Christian point of view, sin, only sin, is the corruption.

[27]*One suffers only once but is victorious eternally.* Let me illustrate this difference for you. In a church[28] somewhere here in our country, there is on the altar an artwork that presents an angel who holds out to Christ the cup of suffering.[29] As you look at the picture, it does indeed make the impression that the artist wanted to produce; you lose yourself in this impression, because this was indeed the way it was, it was held out to him, the cup of suffering! But if you remained a whole day sitting by the altar in order to look at this painting, or if you looked at it every Sunday year after year—oh, is it not true, however piously you are always reminded of his suffering, also praying to him to remind you of it continually, is it not true that there will come a moment when everything infinitely changes for you, when the picture blessedly turns around, as it were, when you will say to yourself, "No, surely it did not last that long; surely the angel did not keep on holding out the cup to him; he took it willingly from the angel's or obediently from God's hand. —He has indeed emptied it, the cup of suffering, because what he suffered he suffered only once, but he is victorious eternally!"

X
109

On the other hand, think of him in his victory. Yes, if any artist could portray this, I wonder, no matter how long you remained sitting, even if you piously contemplated this picture every Sunday, I wonder if the moment would ever come when you would say to yourself, "But this lasts too long; there is no end to it." Oh no, God be praised, precisely this is the eternal blessedness, that his victory never has an end! Yet his victory is only once, just as his suffering was only once; but the one time of victory is eternity, the one time of suffering a moment. It certainly can be impatience, which is unable to keep on looking at the picture where the cup is being held out to him, but it can also be faith, which accordingly does not impatiently turn away but in faith inserts the picture of victory under the picture of suffering.

O you suffering one, whoever you are, just as you begin every day with God, with praying to him to give you patience to suffer that day, so also pray to him every day to remind you that one suffers only once! In the Lord's Prayer a Christian prays for the daily bread today. We think that this petition is more particularly for the poor, whose task is to manage with the daily bread of poverty. But this petition is made also for you, who with regard to suffering may have been richly supplied with suffering in abundance from the beginning and for the whole of your life. For you the task is the reverse and yet the same: to manage with the daily of suffering so that sometime at the end of your life, just as the poor man says, "I pulled through all right and received the daily," so also you may be able to say, "I pulled through all right and received the daily." The poor man pulls through, defends himself against poverty, finds the daily. It is perhaps more difficult with the daily to pull through the abundance of suffering, but that is the task. Also take the following closely to heart. Consider that if a person had lived his whole life in undisturbed enjoyment of all the good things of this earth, consider that in the moment of death he has nothing whatever to recollect, nothing whatever with which to approach recollection's vast future. *Enjoyment* is pleasant at the moment but, just like the momentary in its emptiness, does not make a good showing for recollection and does not exist at all for eternal recollecting. On the other hand, there is no recollecting more blessed, and nothing more blessed to recollect, than sufferings over and done with in company with God; this is the secret of sufferings. So, then: either seventy years in all possible enjoyment, and nothing, nothing for eternity (of all the most dreadful lack, and also indeed the longest lasting!), or seventy years in suffering and then an eternity for blessed recollecting. Blessedly to recollect the sufferings over and done with in covenant with God! Most blessedly, of course, to recollect undeserved sufferings for a good cause, as the Lord indeed says, "When people insult you and say all sorts of evil

things about you and lie, then count yourselves blessed,"[30]—
indeed, to suffer blessedly in this way, a most blessed recollection! But this holds true of every suffering endured in covenant
with God; it is blessed to recollect it in eternity. One suffers only
once, but one is victorious eternally. How wonderful, the way it
turns around! Long duration, which seems to belong to temporality, the seventy years, is only one time if temporality is held
down, but then it comes again in eternity, where it is perma-
nently, enduringly blessed to recollect that one time!

II

³¹The Joy of It: That Hardship
Does Not Take Away
But Procures [*forhverve*³²] Hope

What a wonderful occupation, to acquire [*erhverve*] hope in that way! Is it not just as wonderful as if a merchant became rich by having no one enter his shop, or a traveler arrived at his destination by having been given wrong directions! Oh, the complaint is frequently made that life is so insignificant, so meaningless, so utterly lacking in diversion; it seems to me that in this thought alone there is diversion enough for an eternity! The complaint is frequently made that life is so empty, so monotonous, makes one so unstrung; it seems to me that in this one thought alone there is excitement enough for an eternity! Writers frequently portray in their stories a disguised character who in the decisive moment turns out to be entirely different from what he seemed; it seems to me that in this regard the creations of all the writers taken together are like child's play compared with this disguise devised by eternity, that it is hardship that undertakes to provide one with hope! Or does there appear in any fairy story, in any poem, someone who is supposed to be evil (and yet is basically good), who looks as terrifying as hardship—and then that it is hardship that procures hope! Can any thief be more sure of the effect of his thrust when he aims straight at the heart than hardship's aim seems to be at hope—and yet it is hardship that procures hope! How marvelous, it does not give hope, but it procures hope. Therefore it is not in a decisive moment that hardship throws off its disguise and says, "I just wanted to scare you; here you have hope"—no, it procures hope. So all the time it lasted, this is what it was working for; in deliberate slowness it was working simply and solely to obtain hope for the suffering one.

Yes, let us from the bottom of our hearts *wonder* at this! If there is anything we in these times have forgotten, it is to wonder, and therefore also to believe and to hope and to love. The highest is proclaimed, the most marvelous, but no one wonders. It is proclaimed that there is forgiveness of sins, but no one says, "It is impossible." Scarcely anyone turns away offended and says, "It is impossible"; even less does anyone say it in wonder or as the one says it who would like it to be true but does not dare to believe it, the one who still does not want to let go of it but unhappily loves this pronouncement that he does not dare to believe; even less is it said by one who just believes it, one whose repentance is mitigated into a quiet sorrow that in turn is transfigured into a blessed joy, the one who therefore, expressing his unspeakable gratitude to God, refreshes his soul by repeating, "It is impossible!" Oh, blessed refreshment, that the one who was brought close to despair because it was impossible now believes it, blessedly believes it, but in his soul's wonder continues to say, "It is impossible!" We all know, of course, what is told about a person who had heard a story that everyone laughed at when it was told but which no one laughed at when he told it, because he, as we know, had forgotten the most important point. But imagine an apostle living in these times, an apostle who certainly knew how to tell the marvelous story properly, imagine his sadness, or the sadness of the Holy Spirit within him, when he would have to say, "There is no one who wonders; they listen to it so indifferently, as if it were the most trivial of all, as if there were no one at all to whom it applies, no one at all for whom it is of importance, of enormous importance, whether it is possible or not possible, whether it is so or not so, whether it is true or a lie!"

Let us, then, as a beginning wonder over this, that hardship procures hope; let the soul be well disposed to wonder; let us call to it as the psalmist calls to his soul, "Wake up, zither and harp,"[33] and let us, then, speak about

the joy of it: that hardship does not take away but procures hope.

If one were to designate with one word what is characteristic of the life of childhood and of youth, one would certainly have to call it a dream-life. And we also say the same. How often, for example, an adult repeats these sad words, "They vanished, the dreams of my childhood and youth." They vanished—probably because the dreamer vanished, disappeared. How could there be dreams if there is no dreamer! But with what right do we call it a dream-life anyway and accordingly characterize the child and the youth as sleepers, as sleepwalkers? In another sense the child is certainly awake in a way no adult ever is, its senses open to every impression; the child is sheer life and motion, unalloyed attention all day long. And the youth is awake as an adult rarely is, his mind restless early and late, stirred in passion so he often can scarcely sleep. Yet the life of childhood and youth is a dream-life, because the innermost being, that which in the deepest sense is the person, is sleeping. The child is turned entirely outward; its inwardness is outwardness, and to that extent it is wide awake. But for a person to be awake is to be turned inward eternally in inwardness; therefore the child is dreaming, and it dreams itself sensately together with everything, indeed, almost as if it confuses itself with the sense-impression. Compared with the child, the youth is more inwardly turned, but in imagination; he is dreaming, or to him it is as if everything dreamed of him. On the other hand, the one who is turned inward in the sense of eternity perceives only what is of the spirit. With regard to sense perception, which is of flesh and blood, of temporality and of the imagination, he is, however, like one who is sleeping, is absentminded, has died—in him the spirit is awake and the lower nature sleeps; therefore he is awake. The term "dream-life" is connected with the more noble part; in the awakened person the spirit is awake, whereas there is indeed something that sleeps, namely, the lower nature. In the child and youth, it is the spirit that sleeps and the lower nature is awake; yet it is the destiny of spirit to awaken, and therefore that life is called a dream-life.

But the one who is dreaming must be awakened, and the deeper that is which is sleeping, or the more deeply it is sleeping, the more important it is that he be awakened, and the more vigorously he must be awakened. If there is nothing that awakens the youth, then this life continues into adulthood. To be sure, he thinks he is no longer dreaming, and in a certain sense he is not;

he perhaps makes light and is scornful of the dreams of youth, but precisely this shows that his life has miscarried. In a certain sense he is awakened; yet he is not awakened in the eternal or in the deepest sense. Thus his life is much poorer than the youth's; his own life is despicable, because he has become an unfruitful tree or like a tree that has died, whereas the youth's life is truly not to be despised. The dream-life of childhood and youth is the blossoming time. But in the case of a tree that is supposed to bear fruit, the blossoming time is also an immaturity. It does admittedly look like retrogression when the tree that once stood naked, then in blossom, throws off its blossoms, but it can also be progress. The blossoming time is beautiful, and the hope of blossomings in the child and the youth is beautiful, but it is an immaturity.

x
114

Then comes *hardship* to awaken the dreamer, hardship, which like a storm tears off the blossoms, hardship, *which nevertheless does not take away but procures hope.*

Where, then, is the hope? Is the hope in hardship's rushing gales? Ah, no, no more than God's voice was in the rushing gales but was in the gentle breeze.[34] Likewise hope, eternity's hope, is like a gentle breeze, like a whisper in a person's innermost being, only all too easy to ignore. But what, then, does hardship want? It wants to have this whisper brought forth in the innermost being. But then does not hardship work against itself, must not its storm simply drown out this voice? No, hardship can drown out every earthly voice; it is supposed to do just that, but it cannot drown out this voice of eternity deep within. Or the reverse. It is eternity's voice within that wants to be heard, and in order to gain a hearing it uses the clamor of hardship. When all irrelevant voices are silenced with the help of hardship, then it can be heard, this voice within.

O you suffering one, whoever you are, receive what is said to you! People continually think that it is the world, the environment, the circumstances, the situations that stand in one's way, in the way of one's fortune and peace and joy. Basically it is always the person himself who stands in his way, the person himself who is bound up too closely with the world and the environment and the circumstances and the situations so that he is unable to come to himself, to find rest, to hope. He is continually too much turned outward instead of being turned inward; therefore everything he says is true only in an illusion. The person himself maintains connection with the enemies, and the connection is: *the hope of youthfulness.*

X
115

But hardship *takes away* hope. You surely have experienced this yourself, have you not, even if you have not given up the connection with this ambiguous experience. You hoped that if you did not succeed this time, then at least another time, and if not that time, then yet another. In compensation for all your bad luck, you hoped to get a little restitution next time. You hoped that it would still be possible that some unforeseen help could come as it came even to the person who had been paralyzed for thirty-eight years;[35] his rescue was so close that it was always only one other who came first. After having given up all other friends, you finally placed your hope in this friend—but the hardship continued.[36]

Hardship procures hope. It does not *give* hope, but it *procures* [*forhverve*] it. It is the person himself who *acquires* [*erhverve*] it, eternity's hope, which is planted in him, hidden in his innermost being; but hardship procures it. Hardship ruthlessly (yes, ruthlessly from the point of view of childishness) prevents him from obtaining any other help or relief whatever; hardship ruthlessly (yes, ruthlessly from the point of view of youthfulness) forces him to let go of everything else; hardship ruthlessly (yes, ruthlessly from the point of view of immaturity) takes him to task, takes him to task very effectually so that he must learn to grasp the eternal and to cling to the eternal. Hardship does not help *directly*; it is not something that acquires or buys hope and presents it to the person; it helps *repellingly* and cannot do otherwise, simply because the hope is within the person himself. Hardship preaches for awakening.

Alas, unfortunately people are often all too insensitive, so that the terrors of powerful thoughts are of little help; hardship is better able to make itself understood. Unlike a witticism, its eloquence does not strike only once, but, as we say of a stick, it has striking capacity; that is a permanent quality it has. People would rather have the direct communication as assurance upon assurance; this is so comfortable, and most comfortable when nothing comes of it. Hardship, however, does not jest. When hardship begins its task of procuring hope, for a moment it seems as demented as if one wanted to attack a beggar, stick a pistol against his chest, and say, "Hand over your money!" Alas, the suffering one is just about to despair of hope (that is, the hope of youthfulness), which he would rather cling to, so he says—and then hardship attacks him and demands of him: hope (that is, eternity's hope). x 116

Hardship is no congratulating caller who comes with hope as a gift. Hardship is the bad one who cruelly (yes, from the point of view of childishness) says to the suffering one, "I'll procure hope for you, sure enough!" But just as it always happens in life that the person who is supposed to be the bad one never comes to be appreciated and no one takes the time to come to know him, how splendidly he is managing and doing his job, how splendidly, without being moved by any sighing and crying or by wheedling pleas—so also it goes with hardship: it is bound to be blamed. But this bothers hardship no more than it bothers the physician when the sick one scolds and yells in pain, yes, kicks at him. God be praised, it pays no attention to this—it procures hope. Just as Christianity demonstrates, precisely from all the disapprobation and persecution and wrong the truth must suffer, that justice must exist (what a marvelous way of drawing conclusions!), so also in the extremity of hardship, when it squeezes most terribly, there is this conclusion, this *ergo: ergo*, there is an eternity to hope for.

Imagine hidden in a very plain setting a secret chest in which the most precious treasure is placed—there is a spring that must be pressed, but the spring is concealed, and the pressure must be of a certain force so that an accidental pressure cannot be sufficient. The hope of eternity is concealed within a person's innermost being in the same way, and hardship is the pressure. When the pressure is put on the concealed spring, and forcefully enough, the content appears in all its glory!

Imagine a kernel of grain placed in the earth; if it is to grow, what does it need? First of all space; it must have space. Next, pressure; there must also be pressure—sprouting is making space for itself through an opposition. Eternity's hope is placed in a person's innermost being in the same way. But hardship makes space by setting everything else aside, everything provisional, which is brought to despair; thus hardship's pressure is what draws forth!

Imagine, as indeed is the case, an animal that has a defense weapon with which it defends itself but which it uses only in mortal danger. Eternity's hope is in a person's innermost being in the same way; hardship is the mortal danger!

Imagine a creeping animal that nevertheless has wings that it can use when it is brought to an extremity, but for everyday use it does not find it worth the trouble to use them. Eternity's hope is in a person's innermost being in the same way; he has wings, but he must be brought to an extremity in order to discover them, or in order to develop them, or in order to use them!

Imagine a really hardened criminal whom the court is unable to get to confess either by sagacity or by kind words but from whom a confession is extracted by means of the rack. Eternity's hope is in a person's innermost being in the same way. The natural man goes reluctantly, very reluctantly, to confession. He is quite willing to hope in the sense of the child and the youth. But to hope in eternity's sense is conditioned by an enormously painful effort, to which the natural man never submits willingly. A human being is born with pain, but he is born again to the eternal with perhaps even greater pain—yet in both cases the shriek signifies just as little, since it is supportive. There must be hardship, then, to extract the confession, hope's confession. Or imagine a stubborn witness who refuses to testify (and every human being must, after all, be a witness concerning the eternal and give testimony to it). Hardship does not let him go because he refuses to give evidence; day after day it imposes heavier and heavier fines for failure to comply, until he gives testimony. Or imagine, as we read in the poets, an evil woman who knows the remedy but maliciously continues to advise incorrectly—then when she is sentenced to burn at the stake, the words come out. Eternity's hope is in the natural man's innermost being in the same way. But he does not want his own good; therefore he does not want to come out with what is appropriate, hardly wishes to hear it spoken by someone else, still less by himself—until hardship rescues him by extracting it from him!

This is the way hardship procures hope. —But then will the hardship in turn cease, is the whole thing a painful operation? No, not necessarily. Once hardship has achieved what eternity wants with it, the relationship aligns itself properly; the pressure continues but continually makes itself known inversely as hope, converts itself into hope: the pressure is concealed underground; what is manifested is the hope. It is implicit in the thought itself: a pressure can press, but to press can also mean to lift. You see the jet of water, that it rises high in the air; you do not see the pressure or that there is a pressure and that it happens because of a pressure. There is a pressure that depresses, but there is also a pressure that elevates. The only person hardship can depress is the person who refuses to be helped eternally; hardship presses into the heights the person who wants it. The only person from whom hardship can take away hope is the person who does not want to have the hope of eternity; for the person who wants this hope, hardship procures it.

X
118

So it is with hardship. In life there is only one danger that decisively brings downfall along with it, and that is sin, because sin is a human being's corruption. Hardship, yes, even if it were more terrible than any person had ever experienced, hardship procures hope.

III

The Joy of It: That the Poorer You Become the Richer You Are Able to Make Others

There are many ways to riches. Whether a person succeeds in becoming rich by taking one of these many ways or he does not succeed, there is in the world always a lot of talk about and sufficient acquaintance with these many ways. But this way to riches—and it truly is the greatest wealth to be able to make others rich, this way to riches by becoming poor oneself, this way that is indeed *the way*—this is rarely mentioned, is rarely taken, is rarely recommended. Alas, in the world it is almost as if it did not exist at all—nor is there any idea in the world that precisely this is wealth: not to become or to be rich oneself, but to be able to make others rich.

Yet this marvelous way to riches does actually exist. But we understand it when we read in the poets' tales about how the one who has ventured into the robbers' hideout must be afraid, with every step he takes, lest there be a concealed secret trapdoor through which he can plunge into the abyss; we understand it when unbelief or fearfulness recites its doctrine of the uncertainty of life—because we are only all too inclined to believe in the possibility of downfall. But that life, that existence is blessedly secured with the help of eternity, that in the very danger there is a hidden trapdoor—to ascent—this we do not believe. Just when a person is closest to despairing, there is a place to step on (and in despair he is brought as close as possible to stepping on it), and everything changes infinitely. Then he walks along the same path, but in the opposite direction. Instead of sighing, worried, over walking the path of poverty, of lowliness, of being unappreciated, of persecution, he walks, joyful, along the same path, because he believes and in faith understands that the poorer he becomes the richer he can make others.

Since ordinarily this way to riches is not mentioned, we shall speak about it, about

the joy of it: that the poorer you become
the richer you are able to make others.

The difference is the internal one that infinitely changes everything, whether the suffering person, worried, will continue to stare at how poor he has become, how lowly, how unappreciated, or whether, as everything earthly is taken away from him, he will look away from that and now see his condition from its beautiful, indeed, its blessed side. If it is true even for the artist that he, when he is going to portray a person with one eye, sketches him from the side where he has the eye, should not the sorely suffering person be willing to look away from the distress in order to see the blessing! In the external sense there certainly is no change; the sufferer remains on the spot, in his condition, and yet there is the change, the wondrous change, the miracle of faith. Seen from the one side, it is a poor person who becomes poorer and poorer; seen from the other side, he is the poor person who, the poorer he becomes, makes others richer—yet in the external sense it is the same person.

[37]*Let us now proceed with the discourse in this way: let us first clarify for ourselves the difference between riches and riches (earthly/spiritual), and what follows from this difference for the possessor, in order to understand that one must indeed be poor in order to make others rich, and that therefore the poorer a person becomes the richer he can make others.*

Every earthly or worldly good is in itself selfish, begrudging [misundelig]*; its possession is begrudging or is envy* [Misundelse] *and in one way or another must make others poorer*—what I have someone else cannot have; the more I have, the less someone else must have. The unrighteous mammon[38] (with this term we perhaps may indeed designate every earthly good, also worldly honor, power, etc.) is in itself unjust and makes for injustice (quite apart here from the question of acquiring it or possessing it in an unlawful manner) and in itself cannot be acquired or possessed equally. If one person is to have much of it, there must be someone else who necessarily gets only a little, and what the one has the other cannot possibly have. Furthermore, all the time and energy, all the mental solicitude and concern that is applied to acquiring or possessing earthly goods is selfish, begrudging, or the person who is occupied in this way is selfish, at every such moment has no thought for others; at every such moment he is selfishly working for himself or selfishly for a few others, but not equally for himself and for everyone else. Even if a person is willing to share [*med-dele*[39]] his earthly goods, at every moment in which he is occupied with acquiring them or is engrossed in possessing them, he is selfish, just as that is which he possesses or acquires.

Not so with the goods of the spirit. In its concept, the good of the spirit is communication [*Meddelelse*]*, its possession merciful* [*miskundelig*]*, in itself communication.* If a person has *faith*, he truly has not thereby taken anything away from others; on the contrary—indeed, it is strange but true—by having faith, he has worked for all others (even apart from what he does directly to communicate to others); during the time he was working to acquire faith for himself, he was working for all others. The whole generation and every individual in the generation is a participant in one's having faith. By having faith, he expresses the purely human or that which is every human being's essential possibility. His having faith truly does not begrudge others anything; whereas the possession of money by the rich is a kind of envy that has taken it from the poor, who perhaps in turn envy the rich the money, because there is envy in both situations since earthly riches are in themselves envy. No, the believer has taken nothing from anyone, has in faith no begrudging; and no one should envy him it but instead every human being should be joyed by him. The believer has only what every human being can have, and to the degree that his faith is greater, to the same degree it is seen, but all the more clearly, that this glory and blessedness are possible as a common possession for all human beings.

If a person has *love* [*Kjerlighed*[40]]—shall I now say: Yes, even if he has it beyond all measure? No, this rhetorical intensification would certainly be wrong. It would seem that to the higher degree he has this good, love, the closer he must be to having taken something away from others. Yet it is just the opposite; to the higher degree he has love, the further he is from having taken anything from others. If, then, a person has love beyond all measure, he has not taken anything away from others; on the contrary, he has (even apart from what he actually does for others out of love) worked for all others. During all the time he was working to acquire love for himself, he was working for all others. If just for a moment we very scrupulously disregard the use he makes of his love, even in the possession he does not have it only for himself, because the whole generation and every individual in the generation is a participant in his having love.

If a person has *hope*, eternity's hope beyond all measure, he has not thereby in the slightest way taken anything away from anybody—on the contrary, he has thereby worked for all. That one person has hope, or that there is one person who has hope, is for all others a much more joyful news, just because it is much more reassuring, than the news that one ship has reached the goal is for all the other ships steering to the same goal. With regard to ships, accidental circumstances can determine the outcome for each one, and "the other" ships are not by an essential possibility participants in the one ship's good fortune. But that there is one person who has hope, or every time there is a person who has hope, is decisive for all, that they are able to have it. Here it holds true that one is all and all are one.

Thus the goods of the spirit are in themselves essentially communication; their acquirement, their possession, in itself a benefaction to all. The one who seeks or possesses these goods does not therefore do well only for himself but does a good deed for all; he is working for all, his striving to acquire these goods is in itself immediately enriching for others. The others see themselves in him just as spectators see themselves in the hero of a play. This is the humanity of spiritual goods in contrast to the inhumanity of earthly goods. What is humanity [*Menneskelighed*]? Human likeness [*menneskelige Lighed*] or equality [*Ligelighed*].[41] Even at the moment when he most seems to be working for himself in acquiring these goods, he is communicating; it lies in the very essence of the goods; their possession is communication. By acquiring hope you are not acquiring it only for yourself, but by your acquiring it (what blessed acquiring!) you are communicating, since even in immediate possession eternity's hope is communication. You do not only have hope, but even just by having it (what blessed possession!) you are one who is communicating, you are doing a good deed to others.

Oh, how all the blessing of heaven follows these goods of the spirit from first to last and at every moment—for "I do not weary of repeating the same thing,"[42] and to me it seems that the thought is so blessed that it could not be repeated often enough; indeed, it would not even be too often if a person's life were a repetition of this thought every day. Whereas earthly goods in themselves are begrudging and therefore (what immense latitude for accidental possibilities, what uncertainty!) it must, alas, depend on whether they happen to be possessed by someone who wants to do good with them; and whereas possession of them all too often only tempts the possessor to become begrudging just like the goods, the goods of the spirit are to such a degree a blessing that possession of them (quite apart from any mention of the use the possessor makes of them) is a blessing to others, is communication, sharing [*Meddelelse*]. It is just as impossible to possess the goods of the spirit for oneself in the selfish sense as it is impossible to prevent air from penetrating even the thickest walls. If we may speak this way, this is not due—and precisely this is what is so eternally reassuring—this is not even due to the possessor but is due to the goods themselves, which are communication, although it is self-evident that if the possessor does not correspond to the goods he does not possess the goods of the spirit either. Just as costly fragrant essence spreads fragrance not only when it is poured out but, to the extent that it contains fragrance in itself, is fragrance, so that it permeates the vial in which it is contained and even *in concealment spreads* fragrance— likewise to that degree the goods of the spirit are communication, so that possession is communication, and just to acquire them is to enrich others.

From this it follows, then, that all the time you spend on acquiring these goods, every moment you are rejoicing in their possession, you are so far removed from being selfishly occupied with yourself that you are immediately communicating.

So, in truth, it is with the true goods of the spirit, which also have the reassuring quality, that mark of truth, that they can be possessed only in truth. If someone wants to possess them self-

ishly, possess them for himself, have them for himself in the selfish sense, then he does not possess them either. But in contrast to
merely earthly and worldly goods, there are also spiritual goods,
less perfect spiritual goods. For example, insight, knowledge, capacities, gifts, etc. are spiritual goods. But here it still holds true
of the less perfect that the possessor decides the outcome, or that
what decides the outcome depends on the nature of the possessor, whether he is benevolent and communicating or he is selfish,
because these goods in themselves are still not communication.
If then the one who possesses such less perfect spiritual goods is
selfish, it also turns out that through him the goods themselves
become begrudging and make others poorer. The possessor simply incloses himself with these goods of his; during all the time
he is working to acquire them or to keep them, he is selfishly
inclosed, has neither the time nor the opportunity to concern
himself with others or with thought of others. The sagacious
person becomes more and more sagacious, but in the begrudging
sense, in such a way that he expressly wants to have the advantage
that others become simpler and simpler in comparison with his
increasing sagacity, wants to have these simple others more and
more—inhumanly in his power.[43] The learned person becomes
more and more learned, but in the begrudging sense, and finally
becomes so learned that no one can understand him, so learned
that he cannot communicate at all. In this way, by being possessed in untruth, these less perfect spiritual goods are transformed into worldly and earthly goods, whose characteristic is
that the possession of them makes others poorer in one way or
another. But of the true goods of the spirit it holds true that they
can be possessed only in truth, and the one who does not possess
them in truth does not possess them at all.

These, then, are the relations with regard to riches and riches,
and these relations must indeed underlie and define the thought:
to enrich others. On the one side are the earthly goods (or the less
perfect spiritual goods), the possession of which in itself is begrudging, the acquiring of which in itself is begrudging, and
therefore every hour, every thought that is occupied with possessing or acquiring them is begrudging; on the other side are
the true goods of the spirit, the possession of which in itself is

communication [*Meddelelse*], the acquisition of which in itself
is communication, and therefore every hour, every thought occupied with possessing or acquiring them is enriching for others.

How, then, can one person make another rich? Yes, someone
who has earthly goods can share [*meddele*] them. Very well, let us
assume that he does so and let us momentarily forget that earthly
goods nevertheless are not the true riches. So, then, he shares and
does good with what he has of earthly goods. It can be done very
briefly; he can do it once a month or one hour every day and still
give away very much. But note that in all the hours and days in
which he is occupied with acquiring, accumulating, preserving
the earthly goods he is selfish. Indeed, even if he accumulated in
order to share, as long as his thought is occupied with the earthly
goods it is selfish. In a certain sense it is not due to him; it lies in
the essential character of earthly goods. Therefore this proves to
be only a very imperfect way to make others rich, even if we
assume that the one who possesses the earthly goods is not cor-
rupted by them but is willing to give and to share, and even if we
momentarily forget that earthly goods are not the true riches.

No, the true way, the way of perfection, to make others truly
rich, must be: to communicate the goods of the spirit, in other
respects to be oneself solely occupied with acquiring and possessing these goods. When this is the case, a person truly makes
others rich, and it is the only thing he does, his sole task, and yet
the task of his whole life. The goods are the true riches. During
the time he himself is acquiring them, he is communicating and
immediately makes others rich. During the time he possesses
them, he is communicating and immediately makes others rich.
And since he is solely occupied with and concerned about these
riches, he will strive to increase them. But with regard to the true
riches, the nature of which is communication, increase is neither
more nor less than direct communication, and this is increased,
because here it is not as it is, paltry enough, in connection with
false riches, which certainly are not increased by being given
away. When he, instructing, admonishing, encouraging, comforting, communicates these goods, he does indeed very directly
make others rich.

X
125

Let us now consider our theme: The joy of it, that the poorer a person becomes, the richer he can make others. O you suffering one, whoever you are, if life has taken your riches away from you, if you have perhaps been reduced from prosperity to poverty—well, then, if you are willing to be helped and to understand it as being well-intentioned for you, then you will also be freed from wasting your time and your days and your thought on that with which one can occupy oneself only selfishly; and you will be all the more induced to occupy yourself solely with acquiring and possessing the goods of the spirit—oh, and at every moment spent in this way you make others rich! Or if life has taken your worldly reputation and influence away from you, well, then, if you are willing to be helped and to understand it as being well-intentioned for you, then you are also freed from using your time and your thought on keeping or enjoying that with which one can occupy oneself only selfishly; and you are all the more induced to occupy yourself solely with acquiring and possessing the goods of the spirit—and at every moment spent in this way you make others rich! Or if you are as if cast out from human society, if no one seeks your company, if no invitations disturb you, well, then, if you are willing to be helped and to understand it as well-intentioned for you, then you are also freed from wasting your time and your thought on chatter about futility and vanity, emptily engaged in killing time in order to escape boredom or in wasting it in meaningless pastimes; and you are all the more induced to occupy yourself solely with acquiring and possessing the goods of the spirit—and at every moment spent in this way you make others rich!

X
126

Do you perhaps find it hard to *become* poor in this way, poorer and poorer, because in the external sense it has now been settled once and for all? Does your soul perhaps still cling to things of this earth, selfishly preoccupied with the loss of them just as the one who possesses them is occupied with possession? But is it then also hard to make others rich? Do not be foolishly deceived. It looks so easy to give some money to the poor when one is oneself rich, to help someone else advance when one is oneself powerful—do not be deceived: the person who is occupied with acquiring faith, hope, and love—he, precisely he, makes others rich.

So, then, become even poorer, because you are perhaps maintaining a deceitful wish-connection with what has been lost, and you are perhaps nourishing a self-betraying hope of regaining it. Become even poorer; completely let go of what has been lost and then seek only the goods of the spirit so that you might make others rich. Blessed be every such hour, every such moment; you not only do good to yourself, but you make others rich, you do a good deed to others!

And when you have actually become poor, then you will also more and more have appropriated for yourself the goods of the spirit. Then you will also be able to make others rich in an even more abundant way by communicating the goods of the spirit, by communicating what in itself is communication. The poorer you become, the less frequent will be the moments in your life when you are selfishly occupied with yourself or with what in itself is selfish, the earthly, which draws a person's thought to himself in such a way that he no longer exists for others. But the less frequent such moments become, the more continually will the hours of your day be filled with acquiring and possessing the goods of the spirit (and do not forget, oh, do not forget that when you do that you also make others rich!) or with immediately communicating the goods of the spirit and thereby making others rich.

Think of our prototype, the Lord Jesus Christ! He was poor, but he certainly made others rich! And his life never expresses anything accidental, that he was poor in the accidental sense. No, his life is the essential truth and therefore showed that in order to make others rich one must oneself be poor. This is a divine thought, different from what arose in a human being's heart[44]: the rich man who makes others rich. Not only are earthly goods not the true riches, but the rich man, however generous he is in giving of his abundance, cannot escape having times when he is occupied with his riches, and for that length of time he is not occupied in making others rich. But he was poor as long as he lived here on earth; therefore it was his task as long as he lived, every day, every hour, every moment, to make others rich.

X
127

Himself poor, he gave himself solely to the work of making others rich, and he belonged to it totally only by being poor himself. He did not descend from heaven in order to become *poor*, but he descended in order to make *others rich*. But in order to make others rich, he had to be poor. He *became* poor,[45] not as if it happened at some time in his life after perhaps having been rich for a time. Yet he *became* poor, since it was his own free decision, his choice. He became poor, and *became* that in every sense, in every way. He lived as an outcast from human society, he associated only with sinners and publicans (what frivolousness to trifle with his reputation, what indefensible indifference to the opinion of others, to "what they say," what brazenness—which, thanks to himself, would have to bring him low, low in the eyes of all!). So he became poor in order to make others rich. His decision was not to become poor, but his decision was to make others rich, and *therefore* he became poor. —Think of the apostle Paul, who says these very words: Ourselves poor, we make others rich.[46] The apostle accepted being poor, cast out from human society, without even having a wife to whom he belonged or who belonged to him—he accepted it, and indeed why, if it was not simply because *in that* he found *the way* to make others rich.

This, then, is the joy of it, that the poorer you become the richer you can make others. Oh, then it actually means nothing that the world takes everything away from you, or that you lose the whole world; yes, it is even the best, if only you yourself think it is for the best! In the very moment of despair, when the need is greatest, the help is nearest, the change that infinitely changes everything: that you, the poor one, are the rich one—because the true riches, after all, are to make others rich. Thus here, too, the joy is hidden. Sin alone (and this is the way we want to end each of these discourses so that it becomes both really clear what we are talking about and clear how the eternally different must be talked about in a totally different way)—only sin is a human being's corruption.

X
128

IV

The Joy of It: That the Weaker You Become the Stronger God Becomes in You

Imagine a group of people gathered for sociable diversion. The conversation is in full swing, animated, almost vehement; the one can hardly wait until the other is finished so that he can have his say, and everyone present is more or less actively taking part in this verbal exchange—then a stranger enters, that is, comes right into the middle of this. He concludes from the faces and the loud voices that the subject of the conversation is one that occupies them very much and respectfully concludes that it therefore must be a rather important subject. Very calm, as he can easily be since he had not been involved in the heat, he asks what is really being talked about. Imagine, as certainly happens quite frequently, that it was a mere triviality! The stranger is completely innocent of the effect he produces; he has politely assumed that it was something significant. But what a surprising effect, suddenly to realize in this way that what has engaged a whole group for perhaps more than an hour, and almost passionately, is so insignificant that it can hardly be stated, that it is nothing—when a stranger calmly asks what the conversation is about!

But religious talk often produces an effect that is even more odd when it is heard amid the talk of the world. There is so much talk in the world about conflict and conflict and conflict. There is the talk about this man and that man who live in conflict with each other, about this man and his wife, who, although united in
the holy bonds of marriage, live in conflict with each other, about the scholarly conflict that has commenced between this one and that one, about someone who challenged someone else to a duel. There is talk about a riot that has broken out in the city, about the thousands of enemy troops who are advancing against the country, about an imminent European war, about the con-

flict of the elements that rages horribly. See, this is what is talked about in the world, day in and day out, by thousands and thousands. If you have something to tell about conflict in that sense, you will easily find an audience; and if you wish to hear something, you will easily find talkers.

But just suppose that someone took this talk about conflict as an occasion to speak about the conflict in which every human being must engage—with God—what an odd effect! Would it not very likely seem to most people that it was he who was talking about nothing, whereas all the others were talking about something, or even about something very important! How surprising! Travel around the world, make the acquaintance of the various nations, mix with people, become involved with them, visit them in their homes, go with them to their meetings—and listen closely to what it is that they are talking about. Take part in the many, many different conversations on the countless many, many different ways in which a person can come into conflict here in this world, engage in these conversations, but always in such a way that you yourself are not the one who introduces this subject into the discussion—and then tell me if you have ever heard mention of this conflict. And yet this conflict pertains to every human being; there is no other conflict of which it holds true to this degree that it unconditionally pertains to every human being. The conflict between people—well, there certainly are many who live peaceably throughout their lifetime without conflict with anyone. And conflict between married people—well, there certainly are many happy marriages that are untouched by this conflict. And it is indeed a rarity that a man is challenged to a duel; so this conflict pertains only to very few. Even during a European war, there are still many—yes, even if it is the worst of situations, there still are many, if not elsewhere at least in America, who go on living in peace. But this conflict with God pertains unconditionally to every human being.

But perhaps this conflict is regarded as too sacred and serious and for that reason is never discussed. Just as God is not directly perceivable in the world, where on the other hand the enormous mass of the multifarious draws attention to itself so that it seems

as if God did not exist at all, so this conflict is perhaps like a secret
everyone has but no one talks about, whereas everything else
talked about draws attention to itself as if that conflict did not
exist at all. Perhaps this is so, perhaps.

But surely every sufferer, in one way or another, has occasion
to become aware of this conflict. And to those who suffer these
discourses are indeed addressed. So, then, let us speak about this
conflict, about

the joy of it: that the weaker you become the stronger God becomes in you.

Is it not true, you suffering one, whoever you are, is this not
indeed joyful? Yet it holds true here, as in all these discourses,
that everything depends on how the relationship is viewed. If the
sufferer wants to go on staring despondently, dejectedly, perhaps
despairingly at how weak he has become—well, there is nothing
joyful in that. But if the sufferer will look away from that in order
to see what it means that he becomes weak, who it is who becomes strong, that it is God—then there surely *is* joy. At times
we hear someone who has suffered defeat say, "I was defeated,
became the weaker one (this is the pain of it), but what comforts
me, indeed, makes me rejoice, is that it was he who was victorious." Which *he*? Well, it must be someone whom the defeated
person likes very much, holds in very high esteem. Admittedly,
the joy is not perfect. He would rather have been the victor, but
he manages to see a more joyful side of the defeat; he grants the
victor the victory. But now when he who is victorious is God—
and in turn it is, of course, only an error of judgment on the part
of the sufferer if he stares *outwardly* at the fact that it is his enemies, his adversaries, who become stronger, for it is certainly
possible that they become stronger, that it is their very strength
that makes him weak, but the sufferer has nothing at all to do
with that. He becomes weak; *inwardly* understood, this simply
and solely means that God becomes strong. Consequently, when
he who is victorious is God! To grant God the victory, to comfort oneself because it is *he* who has been victorious—oh, that is
basically to grant oneself the victory! In relation to God a person
can truly be victorious only in this way, that God is victorious.[47]

But let us first try to make it really clear that a person's becoming weak means that God becomes strong in him **inwardly**. And this is what we first and foremost must ask of the sufferer, what we must require of him in order to be able to speak to him—that he look away from the external as quickly as possible, turn his gaze *inward*, lest his gaze, and he along with it, become stuck in an external view of the relation of his suffering to the surrounding world. When the former is done, when it is made clear that a person's becoming weak means that God becomes strong in him inwardly—*then it indeed follows of itself that it is joyful.*

A person who only rarely, and then fleetingly, is occupied with his relation to God scarcely thinks or dreams that he is so closely related to God, or that God is so close to him that between him and God there is an area of reciprocal relationship—indeed, the stronger a human being is, the weaker God is in him; the weaker he is, the stronger God is in him. Everyone who assumes that there is a God of course considers him the strongest, as he indeed eternally is—[48]he, the Omnipotent One,[49] who creates out of nothing, and to whom all creation is as nothing—but presumably he scarcely thinks of the possibility of a reciprocal relationship.

Yet for God, the infinitely strongest one, there is one obstacle. He himself has placed it—yes, he himself has lovingly, in incomprehensible love, placed it. He placed it and places it every time a human being comes into existence, whom he in his love makes into something in relation to himself. Oh, what wonderful omnipotence and love! A human being cannot bear to have his "creations" be something in relation to himself; they are supposed to be nothing, and therefore he calls them, and with disdain, "creations." But God, who creates from nothing, omnipotently takes from nothing and says, "Become"; he lovingly adds, "Become something even in relation to me." What wonderful love; even his omnipotence is in the power of love.

From this results the reciprocal relationship. If God were only the Omnipotent One, then there would be no reciprocal relationship, because for the Omnipotent One the creature is nothing. But for love it is something. What incomprehensible omnipotence of love! It seems as if one could, in comparison with this omnipotence, better comprehend what cannot be comprehended, the omnipotence that creates out of nothing. But this omnipotence that constrains itself (something more wonderful than the coming into existence of all creation!) and lovingly makes the created being something in relation to himself—what wonderful omnipotence of love! Just stretch your mind a little; it is not so difficult, and it is so very blessed. The omnipotence that creates out of nothing is not as incomprehensible as the omnipotent love that can make this wretched nothing for omnipotence into something for love.

But precisely for this reason love also requires something of human beings. Omnipotence does not require anything; it never occurs to omnipotence that a human being is anything other than nothing—for omnipotence he is nothing. It is said that it is the omnipotent God who requires something of human beings, and then, perhaps, it is the loving God who gives in a little. What a sad misunderstanding that forgets that God's infinite love must already exist in order for a person to exist in such a way for God that there can be any question of requiring anything of him. If the Omnipotent One required something of you, then at that very moment you are nothing. But the loving God, who in incomprehensible love made you something for him, lovingly requires something of you. In human relations it is the power of the mighty that requires something of you, his love that gives in. But this is not so in your relationship with God. There is no earthly power for whom you are nothing; therefore it is his power that requires. But for God you are nothing, and therefore it is his love, just as it made you to be something, that requires something of you. It is said that God's omnipotence crushes a human being. But this is not so; no human being is so much that God needs omnipotence to crush him, because for omnipotence he is nothing. It is God's love that even in the last moment manifests his love by making him to be something for it. Woe to him if omnipotence turned against him.

Thus love, which made the human being into something (omnipotence made him come into existence, but love made him come into existence *for* God), lovingly requires something of him. Now there is the reciprocal relationship. If a person selfishly wants to keep for himself this something into which love made him, selfishly wants to be this something, then he is, in the worldly sense, strong—but God is weak. It almost is as if the poor loving God has been tricked: in incomprehensible love he has made human beings into something—and then they deceive him, keep this something as if it were their own. The worldly person fortifies himself in the opinion that he is strong, is perhaps fortified in the same opinion by the worldly judgment of others, and with his presumed strength perhaps transforms the shape of the world—but God is weak.

If, however, a person himself gives up this something, the independence, the freedom to go his own way that love gave him, if he does not misuse this, his perfection, to exist for God by taking it in vain, if God perhaps helps him in this regard by hard sufferings, by taking away his dearest possession, by wounding him in the tenderest spot, by denying him his one and only wish, by taking his final hope away from him—then he is weak. Yes, everyone will tell him that and say that about him; that is how he will be regarded by all; no one will make common cause with him, because it seems as if he would only become a burden that their sympathy would have to bear. He is weak—but God is strong. He, the weak one, has totally given up this something into which love made him, has wholeheartedly consented to God's taking away from him all that could be taken. God is only waiting for him to give in love his humble, his glad consent and thereby to give it up completely, so he is utterly weak—and then God is strongest. There is only one who can hinder God, him who indeed is eternally strongest, in becoming the strongest— this one is the person himself. That God, then, is the strongest is recognized by one thing, that the person is utterly weak. There is only one obstacle for God, a person's selfishness, which comes between him and God like the earth's shadow when it causes the eclipse of the moon. If there is this selfishness, then he is strong, but his strength is God's weakness; if this selfishness is gone, then he is weak and God is strong; the weaker he becomes, the stronger God becomes in him.

But when this is the case, the relationship is in another sense, in the sense of truth, turned around, and now we stand at the joy of it.

X
134

The one who is strong without God is in fact weak. Compared with a child's strength, the strength with which he stands alone can be strength. But the strength with which he stands alone without God is weakness. God is the strong one to the degree to which he is all strength, *is strength.* Therefore, to be without God is to be without strength; to be strong without God is therefore to be strong—without strength. It is like being loving without loving God, that is, to be loving—without love, for God *is love.*[50]

But the one who became utterly weak—in him God became strong. The one who, worshiping and praising and loving, became weaker and weaker, himself less significant for God than a sparrow, like a nothing—in him God is stronger and stronger. *And this, that God is stronger and stronger in him, means that he is stronger and stronger.* —If you could become utterly weak in perfect obedience, so that, loving God, you would understand that you are capable of nothing at all, then all the mighty of the world, if they were to unite against you, would not be able to bend a hair on your head—what tremendous strength! But this is in fact not true, and above all let us not say anything untrue. They certainly would be able to do that; they are even able to kill you. And the great union of all the mighty of the world is not at all necessary for this; a much, much lesser power can do it, and easily enough. But if you were utterly weak in perfect obedience, then all the mighty of the earth in union would be unable to bend a hair on your head *in any way other* than God wills it. And if it is bent *in this way,* yes, and if you are insulted *in this way,* yes, and if you are put to death *in this way*—if you are utterly weak in perfect obedience, then you, loving, would understand that no harm is done to you, not in the least, that it is indeed your true welfare—what tremendous strength!

Even if it were not the case that the strongest is the one in whose weakness God is strong, it still is joy, blessedness, that God becomes stronger and stronger, that it is God who becomes stronger and stronger. Let us speak about a relationship between one person and another that corresponds somewhat, even though very imperfectly, to what in the relation between an individual and God is the truth of *worship;* let us speak about admiration. Admiration in itself is a duplexity, can be seen from two sides. Its first side is a feeling of weakness when the admiring one relates himself in admiration to superiority. But admiration is a happy relation to superiority, and therefore it is a blessed feeling; in true unanimity with oneself, it is perhaps more blessed to admire than to be the one admired. That admiration's first feeling is one of pain is seen in this, that if someone senses superiority but admits it reluctantly, not joyfully, then he is far from being happy: on the contrary he is exceedingly unhappy, in the most distressing pain. But as soon as he yields to the superiority that he still basically but unhappily admired, and yields in admiration, then the joy of this is victorious in him. The more surrendered he is, the more unanimous with himself in admiring, the closer he is to almost becoming superior to the superiority. In his admiration he is indescribably happily freed from every pressure of superiority; he does not succumb to the superiority, but he is victorious in admiration.

Let us then forget what imperfection there may be insofar as admiration in the relationship between one person and another could correspond to worship in the relationship between a person and God. God is infinitely the strongest; basically everyone believes that and to that extent, willing or not, feels God's infinite superiority and his own nothingness. But as long as he only believes that God is the stronger one—and, to mention something terrible, believes it even as the devil also does—and trembles[51]; as long as he only believes it in such a way that he shrinks from the admission, as long as he believes it only in such a way that he does not become joyful, the relationship is painful, unhappy, and his feeling of weakness is a tormenting sensation. *Defiance* is in relation to worship what envy is in relation to admiration. Defiance is weakness and feebleness, which makes itself unhappy by not willing to be weakness and feebleness, is the unhappy relation of weakness and feebleness to superiority, just as envy tortures itself because it does not will to be what it basically is, admiration. What is required of the human being, which is already suggested in the relationship of admiration (the admiring one loses himself in wonder over the far greater), is that he shall lose himself in wonder over God. If he does that with his whole heart, with all his strength, and with all his mind,[52] then he

x
136

is in a happy relationship with God as the strong one, then he worships. Never, never did any lover become as happy, never, never did the parched and drought-stricken earth sense the rain's refreshment as deliciously as the worshiper in his weakness blessedly senses God's strength. Now these two suit each other, God and the worshiper, happily and blissfully as lovers have never suited each other. Now the worshiper's only wish is to become weaker and weaker, because that would mean all the more worship; worship's only desire is that God will become stronger and stronger. The worshiper has lost himself, and in such a way that this is the only thing he wishes to be rid of, the only thing from which he flees; he has won God—so it is directly his concern that God will become stronger and stronger.

The worshiper is the weak one; this is how he must appear to others, and this is what is humbling. He is utterly weak; unlike others, he is not capable of coming to a decision for a whole lifetime, no, he is utterly weak; he is scarcely capable of making a decision for the next day without adding, "If God wills."[53] He is not capable of boasting of his strength, his talents, his gifts, his influence; he is not capable of speaking proud words about what he is able to do—because he is capable of nothing at all. This is what is humbling. But *inwardly*, what blessedness! This, his weakness, is love's secret with God, is worship. The weaker he himself becomes, the more fervently he can worship; and the more he worships, the weaker he becomes—and the more blessed.

Is it not joyful, then, that the weaker you become the stronger God becomes in you; or is it not joyful that you become weak? Is there basically anything to complain about because something grievous happened to you, something that you perhaps had dreaded most and that made you utterly feeble and weak—the weaker you become, the stronger God becomes in you. And that it is joyful—oh, you yourself will surely admit it! Think how impoverished a person would be if he could live through life, proud and self-satisfied, without ever having admired anything. But how horrible if a person could live through his life without ever having wondered over God, without ever, out of wonder over God, having lost himself in worship! But one can worship only by becoming weak oneself; your weakness is essentially worship. Woe to the presumptuous one who, supposedly strong, would, as strong, be brazen enough to worship God! The true God is worshiped only in spirit and truth[54]—but the truth is that you are utterly weak.

Therefore there is nothing to fear in the world, nothing that can take all your own power away from you and make you utterly weak, that can shatter all your self-confidence and make you utterly weak, that can completely subdue your earthly courage and make you utterly weak—because the weaker you become, the stronger God becomes in you.

No, understood in this way, there is nothing in the world to fear—because only sin is a human being's corruption.

V

The Joy of It: That What You Lose Temporally You Gain Eternally

That this is a gain, even so disproportionate that no merchant who made an advantageous transaction ever made one so advantageous, is easy to perceive. The difficulty lies elsewhere, or rather in the place where the transaction, if I may put it that way, must be concluded: that it is in temporality. If one were in eternity, one would easily be able to understand this. But in temporality and in the moment of the loss, where temporality accordingly asserts itself most strongly, it perhaps easily seems that eternity is infinitely far away, that this undoubtedly extraordinary gain will not come for such a long time—and what is the use of the great advantage if there are such difficulties! One bird in the hand is better than ten on the roof; a little less advantage seems preferable to the enormous—uncertain one. Yes, so it seems in temporality, which of course sees everything upside down. There is scarcely any more upside-down thought than this, that the eternal is the uncertain, and scarcely any more upside-down sagacity than that which lets go of the eternal—because it is the uncertain, and grasps the temporal—because it is the certain. If one does not immediately have the opportunity to discover that the eternal nevertheless is the certain, one will soon have the opportunity to experience that the temporal is the uncertain. Therefore scarcely any talk is more ridiculous than someone's saying when he holds the temporal in his hand, "I am holding on to what is certain." But, as stated, the difficulty lies in the place
where the transaction must be concluded. As soon as one has become clear about one's death, it is easy to exchange time and eternity; but in temporality to obtain eternity's understanding of replacing the temporal with the eternal, eternity's understanding that what is lost temporally is gained eternally—yes, that is difficult.

But the one who suffers has perceived life's difficulty in another way, how difficult it is to bear one's loss, the sorrow and pain of it; well, if the joy of the loss that is offered also has difficulty, this joy is still to be preferred. The difficulty is to bring eternity a little closer; when eternity is very close, the joy is complete. But this, to bring eternity a little closer, is decisive for every sufferer if he is to be comforted and if his comfort is to become joy. Whether the art of medicine has a miracle remedy, one for all sicknesses, I do not know; but spiritually there is one, only one—a very simple remedy: eternity. The difficulty is only to bring it very close. See, a child, for example, can perhaps also draw after a fashion, and someone who is not an artist can perhaps also draw after a fashion, but everything they draw they draw flat up and down on the paper. Ask the artist what the difficulty is, and you will hear him answer: the distance of perspective in the drawing. With regard to eternity, the difficulty is the reverse: eternity seems so far away; the task is to bring it as close as possible. In the sense of temporality, to the impatience of the unwise person (and the more temporality rules, the less wisdom and the more impatience) it looks as if, instead of recovering eternally what he lost, he instead would have to wait an eternity to recover it. But if eternity is very close to you, then you will still not recover what was lost, because that happens only in eternity, but nevertheless to you it is *eternally certain* that you will recover it eternally. When this is so, eternity is very close to you. How close it is to you can perhaps be illustrated in another situation. A wise man has said: Everyone who has deserved punishment fears punishment, but everyone who fears punishment suffers punishment.[55] In a certain sense the guilty person has not yet suffered his punishment; in another sense it hangs over him so close that he suffers it.

So let me try to constrain, if possible, the sufferer for his own good to become joyful, constrain him to bring eternity as close as possible as I speak about

the joy of it: that what you lose temporally you gain eternally.

Only the temporal can be lost temporally; temporality as such cannot possibly take away from you anything other than the temporal; when you know that it is temporality that has taken something away from you, you know at once that it must be something temporal it took. If the terrible thing happens that a person *temporally* loses *the eternal*, we are no longer talking about *loss* [*Tab*]— this is *perdition* [*Fortabelse*]. Loss is connected with the temporal. It is assumed, when there is a question about loss, about the pain and suffering of the loss—if anything is to be said for comfort, encouragement, and joy—it is assumed that the sufferer himself is not guilty of damaging his own soul,[56] something that is not due to any loss. If this happens and it is the eternal that he loses in time, then something entirely different must be said. Therefore the discourse presupposes that the sufferer to whom it is addressed, no matter how severe the pain of the loss may be, still has kept intact a relationship to the eternal, with the aid of which he is to be comforted. If the loss has gained power over him so that his "heart in sorrow has sinned,"[57] so that in despair he will be lost, then something altogether different must be said. Words unto repentance must first and foremost be spoken against sin before words of comfort are spoken; words unto comfort and joy against suffering can be spoken at once—even if the comforting discourse is "a hard saying,"[58] as indeed it is if it is Christian. Above all, let us not forget that not only stealing and murdering and drunkenness and the like are sin, but that sin essentially is: *temporally to lose the eternal.* We forget this all too often. Yes, even the authorized spiritual counselor is at times much too inclined (and therefore also fails) to want to comfort at once without, as is proper for a physician, first of all examining the sufferer's condition. Just as rigorousness in the wrong place can be harmful, so also can gentleness in the wrong place, gentleness when the sufferer himself basically feels that something rigorous should be said and therefore is disgusted both with the comfort and the comforter, who shows that he does not recognize the sickness.

Think of a woman, the most lovable of all; we can indeed imagine such a one. It would be odious to think of what we call the more flagrant sins together with her purity—ah, but also vanity and pride and envy and arrogance are alien to her lovable soul. She has lost her beloved—if her heart in sorrow has sinned, if in her despair she has said, "I don't care about either God or eternity," then certainly comfort, in a straightforward sense, would be the most harmful of all. And even if you yourself were ever so deeply gripped, shocked by the sight of her pain, yes, even if you were so sympathetic that you would willingly give everything, your very life, to comfort her if possible—how terrible, if you were the spiritual guide, if you did not have the courage to use rigorousness! Or what would you think of a physician who, because he himself had an impression of the horribleness of the feverish patient's thirst, did not dare to forbid him but prescribed—just say it and hear the contradiction—out of sympathy he prescribed cold water, that is, out of sympathy killed him!

So, then, if the suffering one, whatever he lost, is not personally guilty of disturbing the divine order of things, only the temporal can be lost temporally. Because a human being has something eternal within him, he can lose the eternal, but this is not to lose [*tabe*], it is to be lost [*fortabes*]; if there were nothing eternal in the human being, he could not be lost.

On the one side: only the temporal can be lost [*tabes*] temporally; on the other side: *only the eternal can be gained eternally.* If a person could be so presumptuous as to want to gain the eternal temporally, this again is perdition [*Fortabelse*]. If, for example, someone wanted to grasp the eternal in order to have *earthly* advantage from it, he is lost [*fortabt*]; if someone wanted to buy the Holy Spirit,[59] he is lost. Why is he lost? Because he *temporally lost the eternal*; he lost the eternal by wanting to reduce it to the temporal. The purpose or the objective is always higher than the means. If, then, someone wants to gain the eternal for the sake of earthly advantage, the earthly advantage is something higher for him than the eternal; but if that is the case, he has lost the eternal, and if a person has lost the eternal, he is lost. The eternal does not want to be mixed up with all this talk about this loss [*Tab*] and that loss; as soon as it is the eternal that is lost, everything, including the language, is changed—then it is perdition.[60]

Let us now draw the thoughts together in order to capture joy or the suffering one for joy. If only the temporal can be lost temporally and only the eternal can be lost eternally, the gain is indeed obvious: in losing temporality I gain eternity. O you suffering one, whatever you have lost, you have lost only something temporal; it is impossible to *lose* anything else; and whatever you have lost, there is something to gain, the eternal, which you gain eternally. If you do not want to be lost (and if that is to happen, you yourself must *will* it), if you shudder deep within your soul at this thought, if the rigorous earnestness of this thought and your shudder guarantee, if they jointly guarantee, that you do not personally avoid consolation by willing to be lost—then, however heavy your loss is, it will be manifest that the joy of it is really that what you lose temporally you gain eternally.

But perhaps you say: Will eternity give me back what I lost precisely as it was when my soul clung to it? Oh, certainly not, then the discourse certainly would not be about gain, which it is—you get it back eternally. But perhaps there is a bit of cunning concealed in this question of yours. In other words, insofar as you lost it, it has indeed been taken away from you; you have not done this yourself; but from this it still does not follow that you have really willed to let go of what was lost. Perhaps you are not far (oh, be on your guard!) from wanting to have eternity for assistance in order to recover in eternity the temporal just as it was in temporality, your eyes' delight and your heart's desire—this, too, is perdition. If that is the case, then what you want is not to gain the eternal eternally but to gain the eternal in order that in eternity it will give you the temporal that was lost—that is, you are willing to lose the eternal in order eternally to gain the temporal; and this is temporally to lose the eternal, which is perdition. If it was not earthly goods that you lost, if it was something that hurts more painfully, if it was, for example, your honor that you lost, which slander stole from you; if your soul clung to honor with insatiable passion so it was your only wish, your only desire, to enjoy vanity's and pride's satisfaction of being honored—well, eternity cannot give this back to you! If it was your beloved that you lost, whom death took from you, the beloved to whom you clung with all the vehemence of earthly passion, with the love of your one and only wish—your beloved, to whose transfiguration, if you had your way (just imagine, how cruel!), you would therefore be an obstacle—well, in that case

X
142

eternity cannot give him back to you! In eternity there is no
pomp and circumstance of worldly honor, and in eternity one
does not marry![61]

But why do you ask about some particular temporal thing you
want to have again if it is not because your soul is temporally
clinging to it? The discourse ventures to go much further, makes
the loss much greater, speaks about the whole of temporality,
about everything temporal—but then it also speaks about *letting
go of* the temporal that is lost. Why, then, do you talk about a
particular temporal thing—and so passionately? Oh, be on your
guard. It indeed seems as if you are about to will to lose something temporal in an eternal way, to fix a temporal loss eternally   X
fast in your soul, to recollect eternally a temporal loss—this, too,   143
is perdition. When something temporal is lost in this way, it cannot be due to the temporal, because the temporal can be lost only
temporally. Therefore it must be due to the loser, that he *wills* to
lose eternally something temporal—that is, temporally to lose
the eternal, that is, to be lost.

What you lose temporally you gain eternally. You do not receive it again in the sense of temporality; that is impossible, and
it would not be a gain either; but you receive it again in the sense
of eternity—if you lose it temporally, that is, if you do not yourself, alas, by *willing* to be lost, make the temporal into something
other than it is. If the loss of something temporal occupies you as
if it were not the temporal but the eternal, the fault surely does
not lie in the temporal, which according to its concept can be lost
only temporally, but in you. If the loss of the temporal occupies
you in such a way that you in despair do not even care about
gaining the eternal, this of course is surely not due to the temporal, which according to its concept can be lost only temporally,
but to you. That is, if you do not *will* to be lost (and in that case
talk about "loss" is meaningless), then it stands fast eternally that
what you lose temporally (be it whatever it may, be it regarded
by all others as the heaviest loss or regarded as such only by you
in your pain) you gain eternally.

It stands fast eternally; even if all the devils and all the sophists
would dispute with us, they would be unable to refute this.
Therefore if you lost an earthly friend, perhaps your only friend,

the best—if you do not lose him in any way other than that temporality took him away from you, that is, if you lose him temporally (*temporality* cannot possibly take him away from you in any other way unless you yourself *will* to be guilty of it, and temporality really cannot take the blame for this), you gain him eternally. So you lose an earthly friend—you gain one transfigured. Eternity does not give you back the lost temporality in the sense of temporality. No, precisely this is the gain of eternity: what was lost it gives back in the sense of eternity, and eternally—if you yourself, by being lost, do not prevent yourself from receiving it (oh, consider also the guilt toward the one lost!). If it was earthly riches that you lost—if you lost them temporally (and remember that *temporality* cannot possibly take them away from you in any other way), if you yourself did not incur the terrible guilt of losing them in a way totally different from the way temporality can take them away from you, namely, by losing yourself, if you were willing to let go of the lost temporal thing because you understood the truth that it was lost temporally—then you would gain the eternal. You lost the riches of temporality—you gained the riches of eternity. If you saw your fondest plan miscarry in the world, saw the cause for which you had sacrificed yourself collapse—yet if you lost only temporally (remember that *temporality* cannot destroy any plan or any cause in any other way), if you yourself did not incur the terrible guilt of suffering defeat in a way totally different from the way temporality is able to inflict it on you, namely, by losing yourself, if you were willing to let go of the lost temporal thing because you understood the truth that it was lost temporally—then you gained the eternal. You suffered defeat in temporality—you won eternity's victory. Then do you not gain eternally what you lose temporally? If a person in despair wants to be victorious here in time, well, then to him temporality's defeat is: all is lost. But this is not due to temporality, it is due to him. If, however, he is victorious over his mind, then for him the loss is absolutely nothing else than what it is, a temporal loss; he gains eternally.

X
144

But perhaps a suffering one says: Yes, but what I receive again is not the same as what I lost. Certainly not; after all, the discourse is about gain. Moreover, if what you received again was the same temporal thing, then of course you did not lose it temporally. Insofar as what you lost was a synthesis of the temporal and the eternal, and if temporality took away what belonged to it, you did lose that; but it did not take the eternal away from what you lost, and you receive that again in eternity. Therefore you do receive again what was lost. Or did your departed friend lose anything because death temporally took the temporal away from him if death was nevertheless compelled to let him keep the eternal; does an owner lose because his property gains? —But insofar as what you lost was something purely temporal, temporality did take it away from you and you did lose the temporal, but in the loss you gained the corresponding eternal, which you receive again in eternity. Thus you do indeed receive *eternally that*, precisely that, which you lost *temporally*.[62]

Is this not joyful, that in temporality, wherever there is loss and the pain of loss, eternity is right there to offer the sufferer more than compensation for the damage? After all, the sufferer himself is a synthesis of the temporal and the eternal. If now temporality inflicts upon him the greatest loss it is able to inflict, then the issue is whether he, traitorous to himself and to eternity, will give temporality's loss the power to become something totally different from what it is, whether he will lose the eternal, or whether he, true to himself and the eternal, does not allow temporality's loss to become anything else for him than what it is, a temporal loss. If he does this, then the eternal within him has won the victory. *To let go of the lost temporal thing in such a way that it is lost only temporally*, to lose the lost temporal thing only temporally, *is a qualification of the eternal within the loser*, is the sign that the eternal within him has been victorious.

For the sensate individual this triumphant joy does not exist at all; it totally escapes him that in all of a person's struggle here in life the actual struggle is about something entirely different from what it seems at first glance.[63] In other words, in the religious sense it makes absolutely no difference whether a person is struggling to get along in life or is at the head of hundreds of thousands under cannon fire; the struggle is continually about saving his soul—whether he *wills* to lose [*tabe*] the eternal temporally, which is to be lost [*fortabes*], or whether by losing the temporal temporally he gains the eternal. That this is what should be looked at escapes the worldly person entirely. Therefore, if in temporality he decisively loses the temporal, he despairs, that is, it becomes obvious that he was in despair.[64] But the one who in truth wants to save his soul looks at what ought to be looked at, and just by looking at that he simultaneously discovers the joy, that what one loses temporally one gains eternally. Alas, just as the teacher's strictness is necessary at times, not to punish [*straffe*] inattention but in order to get [*skaffe*] attention, in order to constrain the pupil to look at that which ought to be looked at instead of sitting distracted and being cheated by looking at all sorts of things—so also the fear of perdition must help the sufferer to look at that which ought to be looked at and thereby help him to discover the joy of it.

Only with the help of the eternal is a person able to let go of the lost temporal thing in such a way that he loses it only temporally. If the eternal does not help, then he loses much more than the temporal. But when the temporally losing of the lost temporal thing is a qualification of the eternal in the one who loses, then eternity is certainly very close to him. Indeed, the only thing there was to fear was that the compensation of eternity would not come for such a long time; that was the only hindrance to finding the joy of it, that what one loses temporally one gains eternally. In the eternal certitude that this is so, eternity is as close as possible to a person and as close as is necessary. But when eternity itself is helpful, if the loser only temporally loses the lost temporal thing, then eternity is indeed very close to him. And when that is so, then the joy of it is that what one loses temporally one gains eternally. You do not have to wait fifty years in uncertainty to recover what was lost. Oh no, it only seems like that in temporality if you are not willing temporally to let go of the lost temporal thing. If you are willing to do that, then the eternal in you has been victorious, or the eternal has been victorious in you, then the eternal has visited you, then you are eternally sure that you will receive it again, and then you can very easily wait. Therefore never shove the guilt onto the length of time, because an eternal certitude easily shortens it, even if it were a hundred years of expectancy, to one day. Do not shove [*skyde*] the blame [*Skyld*] onto temporality, because it took the temporal away from you only temporally. It can take nothing else and in no other way. Above all, do not impatiently hurry [*skynde*] to your own downfall, alas, "as the bird rushes to the snare."[65] Seek the fault in yourself; consider earnestly and rigorously how close perdition is; consider that, solely in the eternal sense, every temporal loss is a moment—if it takes you a long time to understand this, it is because the eternal within you does not have sufficient power. Let the eternal come very close to you in order to help you—oh, if only the eternal is very close to you, then this joy is for you.

There is, then, really no loss in the world but sheer gain. Every "loss" is temporal, but what you lose temporally you gain eternally; the loss of the temporal is the gain of the eternal. Only sin is a human being's corruption. But sin is precisely to lose the eternal temporally or to lose the lost temporal thing otherwise than temporally, which is perdition.

VI

The Joy of It: That When I "Gain Everything" I Lose Nothing at All[66]

"To gain everything," no one can ask for more, and if one gains everything, it is clearer than day that one loses nothing at all. And that this is joyful is certainly easy enough to perceive. Any child can *immediately* understand that; indeed, in the cravings of his desires, even the most confused and impatient young person can understand this *at once*. If only he does not misunderstand this and thereby the entire discourse. These discourses actually are not for a young person, at least not to be used at once; not until his life has first given him the text can he perhaps find use for them and better understand the theme.

But is it not surprising that the one burning most fiercely in the craving of youthful desires and the one who in renunciation gave up the most, that these two say the same thing, "to gain everything," whereas there is nevertheless a world of difference between them and they are as far as possible from talking about one and the same thing! God's Word does indeed promise the believer that he will "gain everything," and no young person, not the one utterly spoiled by having all his wishes satisfied, has craved more than to gain everything. How surprising! Just as in life there is a reversion, for example, when a person becomes like a child again, so also in the language of thought there is a reversion whereby the most dissimilar expressions turn out, so it seems, to say the same thing—and that is precisely when the dissimilarity is greatest. There is no one so different from a child, not the slightly older, not the somewhat older, not the much older, not the old man, not the very old man (all of this is direct comparison, in which the *likeness* is the point of departure for the dissimilarity)—there is no one so different from a child as the old person who became a child again, because this is the reverse comparison in which everything is turned around, in which the *dissimilarity* is the point of departure for the likeness. There is no one so different from a desirer, a craver, a coveter who wants to gain everything, not the one who gave up a little, not the one who gave up something, not the one who gave up much (all of this is direct comparison, so that the one who gave up little, something, much, can very well be a coveter who covets much, something, little)—no, no one is as different from a coveter who wants to gain everything as the person who gave up everything—yet he does not speak about this; strangely enough he speaks about gaining everything, and therefore no one is as different from a coveter who wants to gain everything as the very person who says the same thing.

But it remains just as certain that it is joyful to gain everything and that I, when I gain everything, lose nothing at all. So, then, let us speak about

the joy of it: that when I "gain everything" I lose nothing at all.

When the 'everything' I gain is in truth everything, then that which in another sense is called everything, the everything that I lose, must be the false everything; but when I lose the false everything, I indeed lose nothing. Therefore, when I lose the false everything, I lose nothing; and when I gain the true everything, I indeed lose the false everything—so I indeed lose nothing.[67]

You yourself perhaps know that for a moment it looks as if one could in two ways fight this joyful thought through to victory. One could strive to make it entirely clear to oneself that the everything one loses, that the false everything is nothing. Or one takes another way; one seeks the complete conviction of a positive spirit that the everything one gains is in truth everything. The latter method is the better of the two and thus is the only one. In order to have the power to understand that the false everything is nothing, one must have the true everything as an aid; otherwise the false everything takes all the power away from one. With the aid of nothing, it is really not possible to see that the false everything is nothing. There is a supposed wisdom

whose secret is nothing and that nevertheless considers itself able
to see that everything is nothing. But this is impossible; it is just
as impossible as it is to see in the dark by a candle that is not
lighted. There is much said in the world about there being two
ways to truth: the way of faith and the way of doubt. But this is
just as strange as to say that there are two ways to heaven, and one
of them leads to hell.

X
149

Therefore *the way* is to seek for a positive spirit's complete
conviction that you gain everything and that the everything you
gain is in truth everything. And what is it to seek in this way? It
is to have faith. Believe that you gain everything; then you lose
nothing at all. Wish to gain everything, crave to gain everything,
expect to gain everything—and you perhaps will lose everything. But believe that you gain everything—then you lose
nothing at all. The everything to which faith relates itself is the
true everything—therefore you lose nothing at all.

But believe! Ah, this matter of the essentially Christian is so
strange; in a certain sense it is so indescribably easy to understand,
and on the other hand it actually becomes difficult only when it
is that which must be believed. I know very well that a profound
upside-down worldly wisdom has managed to turn the relationship around: it is so easy to believe, so difficult to understand. But
test it, take what we are speaking about here. What is easier to
understand than: when I gain everything, I lose nothing at all?
Only when it must be believed does the difficulty actually arise.
What is easier to understand than that the whole world must
manifest itself to a person as Christianity says, must manifest itself
in this way—when he is one who is dead, dead in self-denial?
But *to become* the one who is dead, this: *when* he is one who is
dead!

Believe that you gain everything; you thereby die to the
world. And when you are one who is dead, you lose nothing by
losing that which in the understanding of the living is everything.
Lose gold and goods, lose power and might, lose honor and prestige, lose health and vigor, lose keen mental power, lose your
best friend, lose your beloved's love, lose much more than the
king who still spoke of losing everything when he said, "Everything is lost except honor"[68]—believe that you gain every-

thing—then you lose nothing at all! Nothing is more certain than this: if you gain everything, it is impossible to lose even the least little thing—if only you believe that you gain everything! It is, yes, I admit it, it is an unequal apportionment that the discourse has only the task of saying the same thing (that is, when one says that he who gains everything loses nothing at all, one is saying the same thing, because to gain everything and to lose nothing at all are one and the same), whereas you have the task to grasp the faith, in faith to hold it fast, that you gain everything—oh, but then the discourse does not have your joy either! Poor discourse, in a certain sense it never moves from the spot; it merely says one and the same thing. In another sense it hovers between heaven and earth, because if it does not stand fast that there is one who believes that he gains everything, then the discourse is empty. Therefore it is not the believer who needs the discourse; it is rather the believer who has compassion on the discourse. Every time one believes that he gains everything, the discourse becomes true; then this empty and meaningless, all-too-easy-to-understand discourse becomes very full, very rich, in the good sense of the word very difficult—but very true.

X
150

   Believe that you gain everything; then you become one who has died to the world. Just as ghosts flee before the dawn and apparitions collapse when they are called by name, and sorcery ceases when the Word is spoken, so also the world and what the world calls everything become nothing to you. Then lose the world, all its pleasures, its friendship, let it become your enemy who drives you out of every place of refuge, your enemy who hates you—believe that you gain everything, and you lose nothing at all! The world must hate someone who has died to the world; there is nothing that contemporaries tolerate less in a contemporary than living as one who has died to the world. It is disturbing to be in a room when a blind man walks around and cannot see what he is bumping into. But the believer is likewise a blind man; his eyes are blinded by the brightness of everything he gains; he can see nothing of the everything in which the world has its life and its pleasure; he can see nothing of this everything, because he has seen that it is nothing. Oh, what mad disregard on the part of faith, which out of regard for the true everything has become blind to all regard! It is disturbing in a social gathering to have a deaf person present who cannot hear what the others are saying and yet goes on conversing, inasmuch as he is heard transforming into meaninglessness what the others are saying. But the believer is likewise a deaf man; his ears ring with the gloriousness of the everything that he gains; he can hear nothing of the everything in which the world has its life and its pleasure. Oh, what mad disregard on the part of faith, which out of regard for the true everything has become deaf to all regard! But believe that you gain everything, and you lose nothing at all!

Yes, believe that you gain everything! See that expert, he had finished all his calculations, perhaps had spent many years to research and systematize all this, and now all was in order—he was waiting only for a point outside the world and he would be capable of lifting the whole world[69] by means of—calculations? Yes, or by means of the point. As long as he does not have the point, all his calculations, the fruit of many years of diligence, are a powerless nothing. And the discourse about one's losing nothing at all when one gains everything—indeed, if the speaker was a person who had pondered over only this thought all his life, or pondered over only this one thought, and if he was the most eloquent of all the eloquent and if he had completed the whole edifice of eloquence—the discourse is a powerless nothing if there is no one who believes that he gains everything. And if he is there, this believer who believes that he gains everything—he loses nothing, nothing at all, even if he received nothing at all from all this eloquence![70]

Oh, what victorious joy of faith! But then can the discourse do nothing at all because it cannot give you faith, because in regard to faith it is not higher (as is assumed by a wisdom that is higher—only in madness) but lower? Well, the discourse can tell you how blessed it is to believe. When one believes, then one gains everything; to gain everything is to believe, to believe that one gains everything; and when one gains everything, then of course one loses nothing at all. With regard to the various losses in life, there is perhaps an insurance company that pays one compensation for damages; but what security is there against all losses so that by them all one loses nothing—indeed, it is like being secured

X
151

against death by being one who is dead! If the desiring youth gained everything, what security does he have that he cannot lose it? But what security for gaining everything, so that one gained it by losing everything—and yet lost nothing at all!

Only the person who lost the true *everything*, only he in truth lost all. But this is perdition; only sin is a human being's corruption.

VII

The Joy of It: That Adversity Is Prosperity[71]

Adversity [*Modgang*] is prosperity [*Medgang*]. But do I hear someone say: This surely is only a jest and easy to understand, because if one just looks at everything turned around, it is quite correct: in a straightforward sense adversity is adversity, adversity turned around is prosperity. Such a statement is only a jest, just like guessing riddles, or when a jack-of-all-trades says, "Nothing is easier to do than this, provided one is in the habit of walking on one's head instead of on one's legs." Well, yes, but is it also so easy to do it? And just because it seems so very easy for thought, untried in the actuality of life and ignorant of any pressure, to swing up and down and down and up, to wheel around to the right and to the left, is it also so easy when adversity presses on the thought that should make the swing, is it then so easy when thought is to manage to turn around the one who in suffering and adversity continually wants to take the opposite position? That is, for thought, for aimless and ownerless thought, thought as such in general, thought that belongs nowhere and is not anybody's, thought that shadowboxes with unnamed names and definitions that define nothing: "here/there," "right/left," "straight ahead/turned around"—for thought as a vagrant it is easy enough to do the trick. But when it is thought with a name, when it is my thought, or when it is *your* thought and, when you are a sufferer, it consequently becomes an earnest matter that thought, which can turn easily enough, acquire in earnest this power over you to turn you around despite all the many things that manifoldly prevent you—is this, then, so easy?

Moreover, just because being able to walk on one's head instead of one's legs is a jest, is it also a jest to look at everything turned around? Far from it, or rather, just the opposite; it is precisely earnestness, the earnestness of eternity. That which is jest, a meaningless jest, as long as it is thought as such in general—when it becomes a matter of earnestness by being your thought that is supposed to turn you around: then it is the very earnestness of eternity. Eternity, which certainly is the source and stronghold of earnestness, says, "This is the task, because it is indeed my, eternity's, view of life to see everything turned around. You are to accustom yourself to looking at everything turned around. And you suffering one, if you want to be comforted in earnest, comforted so that even joy is victorious, then you must let me, eternity, help you—but then you, too, must look at everything turned around." This is the earnestness of eternity; this is eternity's comfort for the sufferer, the law that eternity dictates, the condition that eternity makes to which all promises are bound. Eternity knows only one procedure: look at everything turned around. Let us then look at the relation turned around and in this way find

the joy of it: that adversity is prosperity.

But let us proceed in such a way that we first try to orient the suffering one properly so that he might have an eye for the turned-aroundness, so that he might be willing to enter into this point of view and give it power over himself: then the joy will undoubtedly follow as a matter of course.

What is prosperity? Prosperity is what is helpful to me in reaching my goal, what leads me to my goal; and adversity is what will prevent me from reaching my goal.

But what, then, is the goal? As an assumption we have fixed firmly the one thought by defining what adversity and prosperity are; but since we need to define the other thought (of the goal), it is readily apparent that if the goal is different, is the opposite, then prosperity and adversity must also be changed accordingly.

We are standing at the beginning. But in another sense we are not standing at the beginning. The discourse addresses itself to one who is suffering. But one who is suffering is not first to begin his life now; on the contrary, he is in the midst of it and, alas, not just in the midst of life but in the midst of life's suffering. If so, then he knows very well what adversity is, he the sufficiently tested one. Perhaps. But we were agreed that the extent to which he knows what adversity is depends on whether he knows what the goal is. Only the one who has the true conception of what the goal is that is set before human beings, only he knows also what adversity is and what prosperity is. The one who has the false conception of the goal has also a false conception of prosperity and adversity; he calls prosperity that which leads him to—the false goal—and as a result prevents him from reaching *the goal* (the true goal). But that which prevents one from reaching the goal, that is indeed adversity.

Now, there are many different things for which people strive, but essentially there are only two goals: one goal that a person desires, craves to reach, and the other that he should reach. The one goal is temporality's; the other is eternity's. They are opposite to each other, but then prosperity and adversity must be turned around accordingly. If this discourse addressed itself to a young man, it would try to make this matter of the two goals very clear to him so that he might begin his life by choosing the right goal, begin by being properly positioned. Yet the discourse would perhaps not succeed, because the young man's soul probably will be in a dubious agreement with temporality's goal and accordingly with the false conception of prosperity and adversity. And now one who is suffering, who therefore does not stand at the beginning but on the contrary is far along in it, he knows all too well what adversity is; but the question, as stated, is whether he also really knows what the goal is. The more vehemently he speaks about his suffering and how everything is going against him, the more it only becomes obvious that he has the false conception of the goal. If he has the false conception of the goal, he cannot speak truthfully about prosperity and adversity.

It must, therefore, if he is to be helped, be required of him that he once again deliberate profoundly on what goal is set for human beings, lest he, deceived by the delusion of knowing very well what the goal is, proceed to complain. You certainly are suffering adversity; you cannot reach the goal you so eagerly desired very much to reach—but now what if the goal is the false goal!

What, then, is required? It is required of the suffering one that he halt his errant thinking, that he then make up his mind about what the goal is—that is, it is required that *he turn around*. With regard to sin, a turning around is required; with regard to eternity's comfort, the same is required but in a milder form—namely, that one turn around. To the sinner, the rigorousness of the Law says terrifyingly, "Turn around!" To the suffering one, eternity says gently, sympathetically, "Oh, just turn around." Accordingly, it is required that he turn around. Here eternity already manifests itself as the reverse of temporality. In other words, eternity presupposes that the natural man does not know at all what the goal is, that on the contrary he has the false conception. Temporality presupposes that everyone knows very well what the goal is, so that the only difference among people is whether they succeed in reaching it or not. Eternity, on the other hand, assumes that the difference among people is that the one knows what the goal is and steers by that, and the other does not know it—and steers by that, that is, steers wrong. You suffering one, whoever you are, you probably find it all too easy to make yourself understood by people in general when you complain about your suffering—even though they have no consolation for you, yet they understand you; but eternity will not understand you this way—and yet it is by this that you are to be helped.

So, then, turn around! Do let me say it—good Lord, it is so obvious that if a person is to reach the goal he must know what the goal is and be properly positioned; it is so obvious that if the person is to be delighted by the glorious prospect he must turn to the side where it can be seen and not to the opposite side. Do not be impatient, do not say, "Of course I know what adversity is." Do not try also to terrify us with a description of your suffering so that we, too, would turn the wrong way and lose sight of the goal. If your suffering is so terrible, why then do you want to stare at it; and if the terror is just that you cannot stop staring at it, it is still not impossible. Do not say, "When someone suffers as I am suffering, he knows what adversity is, and only the person who suffers as I am suffering knows what adversity is." No, do not say that, but please listen. In order not to wound you, we speak in another way; we do not deny that you know what adversity is; what we are speaking about is that you still do not know what the goal is.

And then when you have turned around and have caught sight of the goal (eternity's), let the goal become for you what it is and should be, become so important that there is no question about what the path is like but only about reaching the goal, so that you gain the courage to understand that whatever the path is like, the worst of all, the most painful of all—if it leads you to the goal, then it is prosperity. Is it not true that if there is a place that is so important for you to reach because you are indescribably eager to arrive there, then you say, "I will go backward or forward, I will ride or walk or creep—it makes no difference, if only I get there." It is this that eternity wants first and foremost, it wants to make the goal so important to you that it gains complete control over you and you gain control over yourself to take your thoughts, your mind, your eyes away from the hardship, the difficulty, away from *how* you arrive there, because the only important thing to you is to arrive *there*.

x
156

Accordingly, out of respect for the goal, it has now become a *matter of indifference* to you whether it is what is usually called prosperity or whether it is what is usually called adversity that will lead you to the goal: what leads you to the goal is prosperity. What a change! Do you believe that the sensate person could be indifferent to this? What comfort would it be to him that adversity led him to *the goal* if he is concerned only about the goal to which prosperity leads!

But perhaps you still cannot stop looking around for the distinction: what is ordinarily called adversity and prosperity. You have gained the right position but still no peace in it. Well, eternity will give you more help. Now, if what is ordinarily called adversity leads only to or even especially to *the goal*, is there then any reason to look around? If it is so, let us assume it, that you could come to the place you want so much to reach only by or indeed best by going backward, would it then be proper to say, "Whether I go forward or backward makes no difference"? Surely it would be better to say, "How fortunate that I had a chance to go backward." Likewise, if it is possible that what is ordinarily called prosperity could lead you more easily to *the goal*, there would then, of course, be room for a wish. But now nothing will tempt you—because adversity is leading you right to *the goal*. And is it not true, you do indeed want to stand by your word that whatever leads you to the goal is prosperity. Therefore adversity is prosperity.[72]

Let us now make this very clear to ourselves, that what we call prosperity and adversity do not both lead just as well to *the goal*, but only, or indeed especially, what is called adversity leads to *the goal*. What can prevent a person from reaching *the goal*? Surely it is the temporal, and how most of all? When what is ordinarily called prosperity leads a person to reach temporality's goal. In other words, when by means of prosperity he reaches temporality's goal, he is furthest away from reaching *the goal*. A person should strive toward eternity's goal, but by means of prosperity the temporal has delayed him. That temporality favors him does not lead him to the eternal, therefore not to *the goal*. If anything does that, it must be exactly the reverse, that temporality opposes him. But temporality's opposition to him is, of course, what is called adversity.

When it is said, "Seek *first* God's kingdom,"[73] eternity's goal is established for the human being as that which he should seek. If this is to be done, and exactly according to the words (oh, eternity does not allow itself to be mocked,[74] nor to be deceived!), then the point above all is that the human being not seek something else *first*. But what is the something else that he can seek? It is the temporal. If, then, he is to seek first the kingdom of God, he must renounce voluntarily all the goals of temporality. What a difficult task, when opportunity is offered perhaps in abundance, when everything beckons, when what is called prosperity is ready at once, if only he desires it, to lead him to the possession of all the delectable goods of temporality—then to renounce all this! The suffering one, however, has adversity; therefore he is called a sufferer. What is called adversity prevents the sufferer from reaching these goals of temporality; adversity makes it difficult for him, perhaps impossible. Oh, how hard to see difficulties pile up this way in front of the wish, how hard that fulfillment of the wish became impossible! Is it not true? Yes, I probably do not need to ask you about it, but is it not true (and would to God that it is) that it is rather you who now want to ask me whether I myself have now forgotten what the discourse is about? Say it, then; it was just this that I desired; just tell us what the discourse is about, while I listen with joy and hear you say: If what is called prosperity is the deterrent that prevents one from reaching *the goal*, then it is indeed good that what is called adversity makes it difficult or impossible for one—to be delayed, that is, then adversity leads one right to *the goal*.

O you suffering one, whoever you are, for just one moment tear yourself away from your suffering and the thoughts that want to force themselves upon you; try to think altogether impartially about life. Imagine, then, a person who possesses all the benefits of good fortune, favored on every side—but imagine that this person is also earnest enough to have directed his mind to the goal of eternity. He understands, therefore, that he is to renounce all this that has been given him. He is also willing to do this, but see, then a despondent concern awakens in his soul, an anxious self-concern, whether he still may be deceiving himself and this matter of renunciation is only a delusion, since, after all, he remains in possession of all the benefits. He does not dare to throw away everything that has been given to him, because he understands that this could be a presumptuous exaggeration that could easily become his corruption instead of a benefit. He has dolefully come to have a concerned mistrust of himself, whether he might not possibly be deceiving God and all his renunciation be pretense. Then he might very well wish that it would all have to be taken away from him, so that this matter of giving up the temporal in order to grasp the eternal might become something in earnest for him. If this does not happen, perhaps a sickness of mind develops in his innermost being, an incurable depression due to his having become in a profounder sense bewildered about himself.

Have you never thought of this? For you in particular it certainly would be a right point of view, since it places as much distance as possible between you and your possessions. Look at your situation from this point of view! You have indeed had and are having adversity enough; therefore you have only the task

X
158

of renouncing what has been denied you, whereas he has the task *of renouncing what has been given to him.* Second, you are freed from the concern about whether you actually, that is, in the external sense, have given it up, because inasmuch as you do not possess it, the matter is in this regard easy enough. How much more, then, you are assisted! You are denied what will prevent you from reaching *the goal;* you yourself have not cast it away and thereby taken upon yourself a responsibility that in a decisive moment would make your life so very difficult because you found yourself powerless before the task you voluntarily had assigned yourself. No, with regard to you, Governance has taken all the responsibility upon itself; it is Governance that has denied you this. All you have to do, then, is to lend assistance to Governance, the Governance that has helped you. Adversity is prosperity, and you do indeed have adversity.

So, then, adversity is prosperity. It is eternally certain; all the wiles of Satan are unable to make it doubtful. And you can very well understand it. You may, however, not really have faith that it is so. But (to offer you a little lighter fare[75] if the Scriptural text about first seeking God's kingdom should be too strong for you) then do you believe that the poet,[76] whose songs delight humankind, do you believe that he could have written these songs if adversity and hard sufferings had not been there to tune the soul! It is precisely in adversity, "when the heart sits in deepest gloom, then the harp of joy is tuned."[77] Or do you believe that the one who in truth knew how to comfort others, do you believe that he would have been able to do this if adversity had not been for him the requisite prosperity that had helped him to proficiency in this beautiful art! Perhaps he himself also found it hard enough in the beginning, almost cruel that his soul should be tortured in order to become resourceful in thinking of comfort for others. But finally he came to realize very well that without adversity he could not have become and could not be who he was; he learned to have faith that adversity is prosperity.

Therefore, may you also have faith that adversity is prosperity. To understand it is easy enough—but to believe it is difficult. Do not allow yourself to be deceived by the futile wisdom that wants to delude you into thinking that it is easy to have faith, difficult

x
159

to understand. But believe it. As long as you do not believe it, adversity is and remains adversity. It does not help you that it is eternally certain that adversity is prosperity; as long as you do not believe it, it is not true for you. See, the adult, unlike the child, knows what to do about nettles: just grasp them briskly, then they will not burn you. To the child this must seem most unreasonable of all, because, thinks the child, if nettles burn when one merely touches them, how much more so if one grasps tightly. The child is told this. But when the child is supposed to grasp, it does not really have the courage; it still does not grasp briskly enough and is burned. So it is also with this, that adversity is prosperity—if you have not made up your mind in faith, you will only have adversity out of it.

Therefore have faith that adversity is prosperity. It is certain; it only waits for you to believe it. Do not let yourself be disturbed in your faith by others; "have the faith by yourself before God" (Romans 14:22). If the seafarer is convinced that the wind now blowing is taking him to the goal—even if all the others call it a contrary wind, what does he care, he calls it a fair wind. The fair wind is the wind that takes one to the goal, and prosperity is everything that takes one to the goal; and adversity takes one to *the goal*—therefore adversity is prosperity.

That this is joyful need not be developed. The one who has faith that adversity is prosperity does not really need to have the discourse explain to him that this is joyful. And for the one who does not really believe it, it is more important not to waste a moment but to grasp the faith. There is no need, therefore, to speak of this, or only a word. Imagine, then, that everything ordinarily called grounds of comfort has been roused and gathered, as in a worldwide hunt, all those grounds of comfort that the fortunate have discovered to get rid of the unfortunate (I do think this to be so); and imagine, then, in comparison, eternity's comfort, this concise comfort that the concern has discovered, just as *it* has also discovered that it is a concerned person, one who is suffering, not a fortunate person, who will comfort others—this concise comfort: adversity is prosperity! You do find it entirely as it should be, do you not, and in a certain sense well advised, that the human grounds of comfort do not pretend to be able to make the sorrowing one happy but undertake only to comfort him somewhat, which they then do quite badly? On the other hand, when eternity comforts, it makes one joyful; its comfort truly is joy, is the true joy. It is with the human grounds of comfort as it is when the sick person, who has already had many physicians, has a new one who thinks of something new that temporarily produces a little change, but soon it is the same old story again. No, when eternity is brought in to the sick person, it not only cures him completely but makes him healthier than the healthy. It is with the human grounds of comfort as it is when the physician finds a new, perhaps more comfortable, kind of crutch for the person who uses crutches—give him healthy feet to walk on and strength in his knees, that the physician cannot do. But when eternity is brought in, the crutches are thrown away; then he can not only walk—oh no, in another sense we must say that he no longer walks—so lightly does he walk. Eternity provides feet to walk on. When in adversity it seems impossible to move from the spot, when in the powerlessness of suffering it seems as if one could not move a foot—then eternity makes adversity into prosperity.

In all adversity there is only one danger: if the suffering one refuses to have faith that adversity is prosperity. This is perdition; only sin is a human being's corruption.

Part Three

[1]THOUGHTS THAT WOUND FROM
BEHIND—FOR UPBUILDING

CHRISTIAN ADDRESSES

[2]The essentially Christian needs no *defense*, is not served by any *defense*—it is the *attacker*, to defend it is of all perversions the most indefensible, the most *inverted*, and the most dangerous—it is *unconsciously cunning treason*. Christianity is the attacker—in Christendom, of course, it attacks from behind.

I

Watch Your Step When You Go
to the House of the Lord[3]

How still, how secure everything is in God's house. To the one
who enters, it seems as if with a single step he had come to a
distant place, infinitely far away from all noise and clamor and
loud talk, from the terrors of existence, from the storms of life,
from scenes of dreadful events or the debilitating expectation
of them. Wherever you look in that place, everything will
make you secure and quiet. The lofty walls of the venerable
building stand so firm; they watch so trustworthily over this safe
refuge, under whose mighty dome you are free from every pressure. The beauty of the setting, its splendor, will make everything friendly for you, so inviting; it is as if the holy place wants
to ingratiate itself with you also by recollecting, something that
must indeed be assumed, the good and the quiet times that have
favored these works of peace. See, the man who carved these
pictures in stone took a long time to do it, and during all this long
time his life must have been protected and safeguarded so that
no one pushed [støde til] him and nothing happened [tilstøde] to
him that could in any way make his hand or his thought unsteady. As an artist he needed the most profound quietness of
peace—what he created therefore also reminds us of this quietness. See, the one who wove this velvet with which the pulpit is
adorned must have had the quietness to sit still at his work, at the
work that thrives in times of peace and is not necessary in times
of war. And the woman who embroidered it with gold must
have been allowed to sit undisturbed and busy at her work, occupied solely with it and with the thought of doing each stitch with
equal meticulousness.

   How quieting, how soothing—alas, and how much danger in
this security! This is why it is true that it really is only God in

heaven who in the actuality of life can preach very effectually to people, because he has the circumstances, has the destinies, has the situations at his disposal. The circumstances—and when *you* are in them, when they encompass *you* as the one concerned, well, their eloquence is penetrating and awakening. You surely have also experienced this. If you yourself were the sick one who lay sleepless on the sickbed in the midnight hour, or if you were only the person who sat by the sick one's bed of pain in the midnight hour and with disquieting clarity counted every stroke of the clock and every sigh of the sick one, but without finding the relief of uniformity or of counting—if you then were to hear that devout song, "It was in a midnight hour that our Savior was born,"[4] do you think that all the orators together would be able to produce this effect? Why not? Because the sickbed and the nighttime hour preach more powerfully than all the orators, know this secret of speaking to you in such a way that you come to perceive that it is you who is being addressed, *you* in particular, not the one who is sitting beside you, not those outside, but *you* in particular, you who are feeling alone, alone in the whole world, alone in the midnight hour by the sickbed. Or if a person is lying at the point of death and has been frankly and honestly told what people in these times do not wish to tell the dying person, the most important thing for him to know, that it is all over—do you not believe that the simple, comforting word from the most limited person will bring about an effect totally different from that of all the most famous orators on the person who, healthy and energetic, also in his own opinion mentally and spir-itually sound, sits secure in the magnificent temple and listens—and perhaps judges the address? Why will that simple word bring about a totally different effect? Because death knows how to make itself understood on the question, to whom does it apply, knows how to make you understand that it is *you*, that you are the one involved, that it is no one else, not your next-door neighbor, not the neighbor opposite or anyone else here in the city, but that *you* are the one who is going to die.

So it is in life's actuality when God is the one who with the help of circumstances preaches for awakening. But in God's house, in the magnificent house of God when the pastor

preaches—for tranquilization! Especially if he is trying to satisfy
the human demands or what are called the demands of the times.
While people in these times are becoming more and more timorous, more and more afraid of personally experiencing in actuality the terror implicit in the power of circumstances, they on
the other hand are becoming more and more fastidious in
craving the trumpery of eloquence. They do not want to hear
in earnest anything about the terror; they want to play at it,
much as soldiers in peacetime, or rather nonsoldiers, play war;
they demand everything artistic in the beauty of the surroundings, demand everything artistic of the speaker, but they themselves in a worldly and ungodly way want to sit in God's house
in absolute security because they know very well that no speaker
has the power, the power only Governance has, to grip a person,
to hurl him into the power of circumstances, and to let the ups
and downs and ordeals and spiritual trials preach to him in earnest
for awakening.

Ah, there is so much in the ordinary course of life that will lull
a person to sleep, teach him to say "peace and no danger."[5]
Therefore we go to God's house to be awakened from sleep and
to be pulled out of the spell. But when in turn there is at times so
much in God's house that will lull us to sleep! Even that which
in itself is awakening—thoughts, reflections, ideas—can completely lose meaning through the force of habit and monotony,
just as a spring can lose the tension by which alone it really is
what it is. Thus, to come closer to the theme of this discourse, it
is indeed right and defensible, it is a plain duty to invite people
again and again to come to the house of the Lord, to call to
them. But one can become so accustomed to hearing this invitation that it loses its meaning, so that finally one stays away and
the outcome is that the invitation preaches the church empty.
Or one may become so accustomed to hearing this invitation
that it generates false ideas in those who come, makes us self-
important because *we* are not like those who stay away, makes us
self-satisfied, secure, because it involves us in an illusion, as if it
were God who needed us since we have been so urgently invited, as if on the contrary it were not we who in fear and trembling[6] should think about what he may require of us, as if it were

not we who in honesty should thank God that he will have anything to do with us at all, that he will tolerate and allow that we
approach him, tolerate that we presume to believe that he cares
about us, that without being ashamed he wills to be known, to
be called our God and our Father.

On this subject, then, let us now speak in a different way as we
discuss this verse from Ecclesiastes:

Watch your step when you go to the house of the Lord.

Watch your step when you go to the house of the Lord. It is an extremely responsible matter to go up into[7] the house of the Lord.
Remember that he who is present is he who is in heaven—and
you are on earth. But do not imagine that he in his loftiness is far
away: this is exactly the earnestness and responsibility—that he,
the infinitely lofty one, is very close to you, closer than the people you have around you every day, closer than your most intimate friend before whom you feel that you can show yourself as
you are. Loftiness and distance seem to correspond to each other
so that the person who is lofty is also distant from you. Equality
and closeness also seem to correspond to each other so that the
person who is close to you is also your equal. But when loftiness
is very close to you and yet is loftiness, then you are in a difficult
position. Yet God himself, the infinitely lofty one, is in his loftiness very close to you in the house of the Lord, because with God
it is not as with a human being, who basically becomes less lofty
when he comes close to you, the lowly one, and gets involved
with you. No, God can come very close to the lowliest, and yet
he is in his infinite loftiness.

Oh, what earnestness of eternity, oh, what a difficult position!
Is it not true that ordinarily when only a stranger is present where
you are, you are somewhat changed, and when the most powerful and lofty person in the country is present you are very much
changed because he is so lofty and because you so rarely see him.
But God in heaven is lofty in a totally different way, and yet
when you go up into the house of the Lord, God in his infinite
loftiness is very close to you, closer than you are to yourself, since
he understands and discovers even your thoughts that you yourself do not understand. What an enormous weight of responsibil-

ity, that the infinitely lofty one, before whom you perhaps would prefer to show yourself in your best form, that he in his loftiness is still very close to you, sees you, and yet in his loftiness sees you very close at hand, sees you as not even the person who is with you every day sees you. Even if you, in view of your presenting yourself before the Most High, would try to appear different from what you are, you cannot do it—he is too infinitely lofty for that—yes, now it comes again, he is too close to you for that. If a person can lose his composure when he is placed before His Royal Majesty and can forget what he wanted to say, how terrible to be placed before God, because His Royal Majesty is neither as lofty as God nor can he come as close to you.

x
171

Therefore take care when you go to the house of the Lord. What do you want there? You want to invoke the Lord your God, to thank and praise him. But is that in all honesty actually your definite intention? As you know, language has no more solemn expression with regard to requiring honesty than to say to someone: Before God, is this your conviction, what you mean? In the house of the Lord you are indeed *before God*. Is then your invocation, which calls upon God, is it honestly meant before God? What is honesty before God? It is that your life expresses what you say. We human beings have to be satisfied with less, with one person's solemnly assuring the other that this and that is what he honestly means. But God in heaven, the infinitely lofty one or—yes, here it comes again—God, the knower of hearts,[8] who is very close to you: God understands only one kind of honesty, that a person's life expresses what he says. All other honesty, all other solemnity, all mere assurance that one means what one says is to God a deception, an untruth—such an invocation is presumptuousness toward him.

Take care, then, lest your invocation, instead of being able to please God, is presumptuousness toward God. Take care lest you, self-deceived because you do not understand yourself, presume to deceive God, as if you had in your heart the devout feelings that nevertheless do not have the power over you to change your life, to make your life be the expression of these feelings. Oh, we human beings frequently lament that we lack the words and expressions for our feelings, that language will not

come to our aid, that we, perhaps futilely, have to hunt for
words. Nothing like that will trouble you before God if only
your life expresses that you have these feelings; yes, then before
God you are honest, and that garrulous honesty is altogether
superfluous.

Or perhaps you go up into the house of the Lord in order to
pray to God for help and assistance. Take care what you do. Are
you rightly, are you before God, conscious of who it is you call
upon for help, what it means to invoke his help, what it commits
you to? If it is perhaps on account of worldly affairs, childish
concerns, and trivialities that you invoke his help—and not in
order that he might help you to forget them but in order to
occupy yourself with them—consequently, if it is on account of
trivialities, which you perhaps will have forgotten tomorrow and
with them also this by no means trivial thing, that you invoked
the assistance of the Most High—then you have indeed mocked
God, and he will not forget that you invoked his help. If a physician, and certainly with justification, becomes impatient when
childish parents send for him for every triviality that is all over
when he arrives and they have almost forgotten why they sent for
him—would God the Omnipotent One then be willing to be
treated this way! Or would you dare have the nerve to think that
it is God who should serve you, that he, the Most Exalted, should
promptly be ready to listen to your petitions and fulfill your
wishes—oh, if you become involved with him, then you are the
one who in so doing is unconditionally committed to obey and
serve. If you do not understand this, then it is presumptuousness
to become involved with him, presumptuousness to invoke his
help. Yes, he certainly is the Omnipotent One and can do everything he wills, and it does look almost tempting, as if you needed
only to wish. But take care. No thoughtless word is avenged as
is a thoughtless petition to God, and no word commits one as
does the petition that calls upon God for help, because it now
commits you unconditionally to let God help you as he wills.
You may ask a human being for help and have forgotten it when
he comes with the help; you may ask a human being for help,
and if he is unwilling to help you as you wish, you may say,
"That is not what I asked for." But if you have asked God for

help, then you are bound, bound to accept the help as he sees fit. How often we hear this cry for help and this cry that there is no help—truly, there is always sufficient help. But the human heart is so cunning and has so little fidelity to its word that, when the help proves to be what one most feared, one says, "But that certainly is no help!" But if this help is from God and if you have asked him for help, then you are committed to accepting the help and in faith and gratitude to call it help.

Or perhaps you go up to the house of the Lord in order with a vow to God to commit yourself to an intention, to a resolution for the future—take care what you do. Have you really been conscious of what it means to promise God something, that what you promise God is something a human being can and may promise God, that it is not something that we human beings can be tricked into promising one another, that it is something God will permit you to promise him—otherwise it is indeed presumptuousness—and have you rightly been conscious of how a promise to God commits you? "A promise is a snare,"[9] we say— and a promise to God, well, if it is what it should be and becomes what it should become, then it surely is as far as possible from being a snare, then it is a rescuing leading-string—but if it is not! If you are not conscious of what you are promising God, do not have the true conception of what you can and may promise God—then you lose God, then you pamper your soul into treating God and God's name light-mindedly and irresponsibly. And if you do not keep what you promise God, then you lose yourself. And yet there is always one whom a person cannot escape: oneself; and there is one more: God in heaven!

Take care, therefore, when you go to the house of the Lord; bear in mind the words of the Preacher: "Be not rash with your mouth and let not your heart be hasty in saying something before God's face, because God is in heaven and you upon earth. When you pledge a vow to God, do not put off paying it, because he has no pleasure in fools; pay what you pledge. It is better that you pledge nothing than that you pledge and do not pay it."[10]

Watch your step when you go to the house of the Lord. Perhaps you will come to know much more there than you really wish to know, and perhaps you will receive an impression that you

x
173

will later try in vain to get rid of—therefore take care with fire, it burns.

It is heard again and again; it is regarded in the world as definitely settled that people would like to know the truth if only they had the capacity and the time for it and if it could be made clear to them. What a superfluous concern, what an ingeniously fabricated evasion! Every human being truly has capacity enough to know the truth—would God in heaven be so inhuman as to have treated someone unfairly! And every human being, even the busiest, truly has time enough also to come to know the truth. Nothing is more certain, since he *shall* have time; that the busy person has just as little time for it as the idler is certainly by no means a refutation! And since everyone has capacity enough and time, neither can it be such a difficult matter to make it really clear—if a person himself *wants* to have it made clear. But precisely here lies the difficulty. It is so easy to shove the blame onto the lack of capacity, onto the lack of time, and onto the obscurity of the truth, and then on the other hand it looks so fine and is so easy to say that one would very much like to know the truth.

Truly, truly, this is not so. The one who has any knowledge of himself at all knows from his own experience that it is rather that one has in one's innermost being a secret anxiety about and wariness of the truth, a fear of getting to know too much. Or do you actually believe that it is everyone's honest desire to get to know very effectually what self-denial is, to get it made so clear that every excuse, every evasion, every extenuation, every refuge in the false but favorable opinion of others is cut off for him! Do you believe this? Well, I need not wait for your answer, because if it were the case, then everyone would in truth have self-denial, since precisely this is the first form of self-denial. Ah, but even the better person who has surmounted the first fear of the truth and does not flinch in an altogether worldly way from getting to know it—even he, he who therefore honestly admits that he knows very well from his own experience that one is not so very eager to get to know the truth—even he, or rather he especially, will certainly admit that with reason he too often mistrusts himself, that he still hides from the truth as Adam hid among the trees,[11] that he still sneaks away from something and still sneaks to something, that at times he would rather slip into darkness, where there is only twilight, than have the truth make it all too bright around him.

Take care, therefore, when you go up to the house of the Lord, because there you will get to hear the truth—for upbuilding. Yes, it is true, but take care with the upbuilding; there is nothing, nothing as gentle as the upbuilding, but neither is there anything as domineering. The upbuilding is least of all loose talk; there is nothing as binding. And in God's house you get to know the truth—not from the pastor, whose influence you can indeed easily and also in a certain sense should avoid, but from God or before God. The earnestness of truth, the truth, is just this—that you get to know it before God; what it depends on particularly is this: before God. In God's house there is someone present who together with you knows that you, precisely you, have learned the truth. Take care with this shared knowledge; you will never be able to slip back from this shared knowledge into ignorance. That is, you will not slip back [*slippe tilbage*] without guilt, nor will you escape [*undslippe*] the consciousness of this guilt.

Take care, therefore, lest you get to know too much, lest you get to know that the assurance—which, while underneath it your life went on merrily, made you look good in your own eyes, pleasing in the eyes of others—that the assurance that you very much desired to come to know the truth is a delusion, or even worse, an untruth. Take care lest there in God's house you get to know—but you do know it, of course; in all your great knowledge you perhaps even raise yourself above the simple speakers who want to speak about such outmoded things, which every child knows—but nevertheless take care lest there in God's house you get to know in such a way that you must understand it: that you can be required in self-denial to give up everything in which the natural man has his life, his pleasure, his diversion. Have you thought about what life-weariness[12] means? That life-weariness emerges just when everything finite is taken away from a person although he is still allowed to retain life, that then everything around him becomes desolate and empty and repugnant, time becomes so indescribably long, indeed, that to him it

x
175

is as if he were dead—yes, self-denial calls this dying to the
world—and the truth teaches that a person must die to finitude
(to its pleasures, its preoccupations, its projects, its diversions),
must go through this death to life, must taste (as it is said, to taste
death) and realize how empty is that with which busyness fills up
life, how trivial is that which is the lust of the eye and the craving
of the carnal heart. Alas, the natural man understands the matter
in exactly the opposite way. He thinks that the eternal is the
empty. Certainly there is no drive so strong in a human being as
that with which he clings to life—when death comes, we all pray
that we may be allowed to live, but self-denial's dying to the
world is just as bitter as death. And in the house of the Lord you
get to know the truth that you must die to the world, and if God
has found (which, of course, is unavoidable) that you have
learned this, then in all eternity no escape will help you. Therefore take care when you go to the house of the Lord.

Watch your step when you go to the house of the Lord. Even if you
fled into God's house from the horror on the outside, from the
most terrible thing in the world that can happen to a person, you
are coming to something still more terrible. Here in God's house
there is essentially discourse about a danger that the world does
not know, a danger in comparison with which everything the
world calls danger is child's play—the danger of sin. Here in
God's house there is essentially discourse about a horror that has
never occurred either before or after, in comparison with which
the most horrible thing that can happen to the most unfortunate
of all people is a triviality: the horror that the human race crucified God.

X
176 What, then, brings you to God's house? Is it poverty, or sickness, or other adversity, in short, any earthly need and misery
whatever—this is not spoken about in God's house, at least not
at first. What is spoken about first and must be spoken about first
is sin, that you are a sinner, that before God you are a sinner, that
in fear and trembling before this thought you are to forget your
earthly need. An odd way to comfort, is it not? Instead of solici-
tously asking how you feel, instead of giving you advice and
suggestions . . . . . if that is why you had recourse here, then you
have indeed made a mistake, because you are coming to some-

thing even more terrible. Instead of having sympathy for your earthly misery and busily remedying it, an even heavier weight is laid upon you—you are made a sinner. What is spoken of, therefore, and truly for upbuilding, is that there is a deliverance for sinners, comfort for the repentant. But perhaps all this does not pertain to you, you who, concerned only with your earthly suffering, fled to this place. Yet it does pertain to you; it is futile if you will say that it does not pertain to you, futile if you go away—it is said to you, and God and you both know that it was said to you and that you heard it!

What, then, brings you to God's house? Perhaps you have suffered wrong; possibly you are the innocent one, the lovable character, and yet perhaps people deceived you perfidiously; possibly you are the noble one, the good character, possibly some day you will even be counted among the benefactors of the human race, and yet, yet as a reward for that people perhaps ostracized you, mistreated, insulted, mocked you, indeed, tried to kill you—and you flee into God's house seeking comfort. Whoever you are, you are making a mistake—there you will come to something even more terrible! Here, in God's house, what is spoken is not, at least not at first, about you and me, about what we people in the world could suffer as a little wrong, which yet in another way we have honestly deserved. No, here, in God's house, what is spoken of is principally the horror, the like of which had never been seen and never will be seen later in the world's confusion, the wrong, the atrocious wrong that had never been committed before and never will be committed later, that rebellion, more terrible than the ocean's wildest, when the human race rebelled against God, and, not powerlessly as ordinarily, but triumphantly, as it were, seized him and crucified him. Therefore the one who flees in here from the horror outside is making a mistake—flees to something still more terrible! Yet the discourse must first and foremost be about that. The figure of him, our Lord Jesus Christ, must be called forth, not in such a way as the artist finds time and takes his time to portray it, not in such a way that it is taken out of the environment of horror and set forth as an object for tranquil contemplation. No, he must be brought to mind at the moment of danger and horror, when the

X
177

tranquil spectator no doubt would rather stay at home, since it would have aroused suspicion if anyone had looked worshipfully or merely lovingly at him, when there was nothing to see except this "See what a man,"[13] when there was not even time to look at him because the horror averted one's eyes and fastened them fixedly on oneself. Moreover, Christ's suffering is not to be brought to mind as a past event[14]—oh, save your sympathy! No, when this horror is portrayed, it is something present, and you are present, and I, at something present, and as—accomplices in guilt!

But in that case you made a mistake when you went to the house of the Lord. Instead of getting to hear words of consolation that could comfort you in whatever wrong you are suffering, instead of being shown to be in the right against the people who are treating you unjustly, instead of that you are shown to be in the wrong, you, precisely you, the innocently persecuted, insulted, and wronged one! You get a guilt, a glaring guilt, laid upon your conscience—namely, that you, too, are an accomplice in his innocent suffering and death. Oh, what harsh consoling words! Who can listen to them![15] What a rigorous way to disperse your dark and mournful thoughts—to give you something even more terrible to weep over!

Watch your step when you go to the house of the Lord—and why? Precisely because in the house of the Lord the one and only deliverance, the most blessed comfort is offered to you; the highest of all, God's friendship, his grace in Christ Jesus is offered to you. Therefore we should not cease to invite people to come to God's house; we should always be willing to pray, on behalf of others as for ourselves, that our visit to God's house may be blessed. But therefore, for that very reason, we should not hesitate to cry out to people: For God's sake, take care, above all be on guard, so that you worthily use what is offered to you— precisely because there is everything to win, there is also everything to lose *there.* Use it in faith! There is no conviction as fervent, as strong, and as blessed as faith's conviction. But faith's conviction is not something one is born with, the confidence of a youthful, cheerful mind; even less is faith something one snatches out of the air. Faith is the conviction, the blessed conviction, which is in fear and trembling. When faith is seen from its one side, the heavenly, only the reflection of eternal salvation is seen in it; but seen from its other side, the merely human side, one sees sheer fear and trembling. But then the discourse is indeed false that continually, and never in any other way than invitingly, enticingly, attractively, wants to speak about the visit to God's house, because, seen from the other side, it is terrifying. But that discourse is also false that finally ends by frightening people away from coming to the house of the Lord, because from the other side it is blessed; one day in God's house is better than a thousand[16] anywhere else. This is why it is a difficult matter to steer rightly, and this is why a person very seldom succeeds in doing it, and always in frailty. It is easy to win people by enticing; it is also easy to frighten them away by repelling. But, if possible, with a fervent inwardness that no one could resist, to invite them to come, and in addition with a terror that could teach even the bravest to shudder, to cry out, "Take care!"—indeed, that is difficult. In other words, what the speaker maintains applies also to him. To the speaker it says: Use all the ability granted to you, ready for every sacrifice and compliance in self-denial; use it to win people—but woe to you if you win them in such a way that you leave out the terror. Therefore use all the ability given you, ready for every sacrifice in self-denial; use it to terrify people—but woe to you if you do not use it essentially to win them for the truth.

II

"See, We Have Left Everything and Followed You; What Shall We Have?" (Matthew 19:27)—and What Shall We Have?

The words quoted are the Apostle Peter's, spoken on the occasion of Christ's declaration about how difficult it is to enter into the kingdom of God. The ending of the question pertains to all of us: What shall we have, what does Christianity promise us? But now the beginning of the question, "We have left everything and followed you," does that pertain also to us? Certainly. Does it fit us? Perhaps. It is of course possible that it can fit different people in different ways. Blessed is the one whom these words fit perfectly; blessed is the one also who dares to say: I have left everything in order to follow Christ. Yet in also another way the words can fit perfectly—as a mockery of those who say and think they are Christians, that is, follow Christ, and yet cling wholeheartedly to the things of this world. In a more detailed account, one could try to show that the Christianity of such people is a delusion, a deception; but one can also deal with the whole thing more briefly, yet in a way that is less likely to fail in its effect, by merely quoting Peter's words: "See, we have left everything and followed you"—they fit perfectly!

Frequently there is talk about how glorious it is to be a Christian, about the great good in being a Christian, about what the one who is a Christian possesses and someday will receive more fully, about what good is offered a person in Christ, and this good is recommended in the highest and strongest terms. This, of course, is entirely in order, proper and defensible; it is a plain duty that it be done in this way. But one can say the same thing, exactly the same thing, in another, perhaps more awakening way. Which of these two actually speaks more truthfully about the gloriousness of this good, the one who describes it in the most glorious terms or the one who says, "See, I have left everything for the sake of this good"? Thus he says nothing direct about how glorious the good is; he uses, he wastes not a single word on that. He thinks it is better to say: See, I have left everything; examine, test my life, its external conditions, the innermost state of my soul, its wishes and longings and cravings, and you will see that I have left everything. Or is it not also a very suspicious kind of self-contradiction that a person is altogether convinced of the gloriousness of the good, which nevertheless did not have such power over him that for its sake he would give up the slightest of what is in conflict with and cannot be possessed together with this good? Is this not an excellent way to test how glorious a good is for one, this: how much one has given up for its sake? If there was one lover who in the most beautiful and glowing terms praised the beloved's perfections and merits, and if there was a second lover who did not say a single word about this but merely said, "For her sake I have left everything"—which of these two would speak more gloriously in her praise! Nothing runs as easily as the tongue, and nothing is so easy as to let the tongue run. Only this is just as easy: by means of the tongue to run away from oneself in what one says and to be many, many thousands of miles ahead of oneself.

Therefore, if you want to praise Christianity—oh, do not wish for the tongues of angels, the art of all poets, the eloquence of all orators—to the same degree that your life shows how much you have given up for its sake, to the same degree you praise Christianity. If we want to test our Christian conviction, whether we actually are assured and convinced about the gloriousness of the good that Christianity promises, then let us not seek in some speaker a felicitous presentation we sanction completely and make our own, nor ourselves attempt, if we are speakers, in written or spoken word to praise the gloriousness of this good. But let us turn our gaze inward upon ourselves, and as we honestly test our lives listen to these words by Peter, words said about us,

"See, we have left everything"—and then ourselves say the last words: What are we going to have?

"See, we have left everything and followed you." The apostle, then, is not portraying himself here as a man who has had great loss in the world, a man from whom God has perhaps taken everything—he is not a Job who says, "The Lord took."[17] No, the apostle uses another expression; he says, we have *left* everything. Job did not do that, Job did not leave the slightest thing; on the contrary, the Lord took everything away from him down to the slightest thing. Job's piety is that, when the Lord had taken away everything, he said, "May the Lord's name be praised," that he humbly and faithfully, indeed, praising and thanking God, consented to reconciling himself to the loss or to regarding the loss as being for his own good. Not so with the apostle; he has left everything, that is, has given it up voluntarily; no force was used against him in order to take away even the slightest thing—no, but he voluntarily gave up everything. This is the essentially Christian. Reconciling oneself to unavoidable loss is also seen in paganism. Reconciling oneself to unavoidable loss in such a way that one not only does not lose faith in God but in faith worships and praises his love—that is Jewish piety. But to give up everything *voluntarily*—that is Christianity.

Oh, false talk is frequently heard that wants to delude people into thinking that voluntarily to give up the goods of this earth would be tempting God, that voluntarily venturing into the danger one could avoid would be tempting God. It is thought that this is tempting God and, in criticism of the person who gets into danger this way, it is said, "It is his own fault." Yes, it certainly is—it is his own fault, and precisely this is the eulogy on him. If he had sagaciously held back and out of fear of tempting God had allowed himself to make a fool of God, he presumably would have remained out of danger and in secure possession of everything he owned. But the apostle says, "See, we have left everything," and on this occasion he is so far from any thought of self-reproach that he clearly considers it to be in their favor as something that must be pleasing to God. But of course he adds, "and followed you (Christ)," because it is self-evident that if one gives up and leaves everything in order to follow one's own way, one is then tempting God.

It is, however, actually true that Christ requires of the Christian that he shall voluntarily give up and leave everything. This was not required in the Old Testament days; God did not require of Job that he himself should give up anything and, testing, explicitly required of Abraham only Isaac. But Christianity is indeed the religion of freedom, and precisely the voluntary is essentially Christian. Voluntarily to give up everything to follow Christ means to be convinced of the gloriousness of the good that Christianity promises. Cowardly and timorously not to dare venture it out of the fear of tempting God is a slavish spirit; cunningly to pretend that it was out of the fear of tempting God is making a fool of God. There is something that God cannot take away from a human being, namely, the voluntary, and it is precisely this that Christianity requires. God can take everything away from a human being, but he has left it up to the individual to give up everything voluntarily, and this is exactly what Christianity requires. Humanly speaking, it holds true of those glorious ones who voluntarily gave up everything to follow Christ that it was their own fault that they had all those troubles and hardships, exposed themselves to all those insults and persecutions; it was their own fault that they suffered death. At one time it was in their power (yes, this must be said, in the eyes of the world to their disparagement, in the eyes of God to their honor) to hold back, to avoid all these dangers, but they voluntarily left everything. This is the essentially Christian—and for that very reason gives offense. The world can well comprehend that little consolation is found for those who suffer unavoidable loss. But that one should voluntarily expose oneself to loss and danger, this is madness in the eyes of the world—and it is altogether properly the essentially Christian.

Voluntarily to leave everything in order to follow Christ, which the world neither wants nor is able to hear without being offended, is also that which so-called Christendom prefers to have suppressed or, if it is said, would very much like to ignore, or in any case hears in such a way that something different comes out of it. Thus it would not be impossible that even a discourse

x
182

intended to terrify could have a lulling effect. For example, one could portray it as very terrible, as indeed it is, when in Christendom's long-vanished ages, the ages of persecution, one perhaps ventured out and wanted to be a martyr, and then, possibly after already having suffered in many ways and for a long time, at the last moment, the moment of mortal danger, of painful death, became discouraged and renounced—disavowed Christianity. This would be something terrifying, as indeed it is.

But where, then, is the possibility of the lulling? The lulling is or would be the wrong application, if the addition was made, or if the hearer was allowed tacitly to add: We have not denied Christianity in this way—we, we who in our cowardly sagacity perhaps know how to avoid any danger in which our Christianity could be tested. Alas, which kind of denial is worse? Certainly the latter, the cowardly, ingeniously calculated, daily denial of Christ, continued year after year, dragging on through a whole lifetime incessantly, daily (how terrible to obey Christ's command about daily denial in this way!). Of course, this denial does not become as obvious (at least not in the dramatic sense—but for the Knower of Hearts and the Omnipresent One it certainly is obvious enough) as it is when such an unfortunate one at the decisive moment of painful death denies Christ. But which is worse—about that there can be no doubt. There still are and always are deliverance and hope for everyone whose sin became really notorious; salvation is closer to him the more terrible the form in which his sin must appear to him. But there is no salvation for this cunning game of sagacity; the secret consists simply in maintaining the appearance that one has not, after all, denied Christ.

That there is a difference between sin and sin, everyone knows, but there is a difference of which we do not always seem to be adequately aware, the difference between the sin of the moment, or the sin at the moment, and the incessant daily sin, or a life that consciously and with clarity about the circumstances has adapted itself to sin, moreover, has provided itself with the requisite hypocrisy to maintain the appearance of the good. The proverb says, "To sin is human, but to continue in sin is diabolical." Yet what we are talking about is even more terrible, this

ingenious and conscious adapting of life to sin, or if not with full
consciousness of it, at least with the consciousness that one is
maintaining an unclarity in one's soul about something that one
for good reasons does not wish to clarify.

That there is a difference between sin and sin, everyone
knows, but there is a difference of which we are perhaps not
always adequately aware: between the sin that the world regards as loathsome and the sin that the world regards as the good,
or for which it has mitigating and euphemistic names. The latter
sin is obviously the worse, since it is impossible that the sin the
world regards as sin can be the worse—then the world itself
would of course have to be good. All sin is of evil, but the sin for
which the world has the mitigating name in readiness is sin in an
even stricter sense, is doubly of evil; indeed, it has its stronghold and its approval in the wickedness that is the world's sin. In
God's eyes, therefore, there is no sin as loathsome as the sin of
sagacity, simply because this has the world's approval. Or to
continue with the example given, what is it, if the world were to
be honest, what is it really that it condemns in such an unfortunate one who in the decisive moment denies the faith? What else
is it really but just this, that he was unsagacious enough to venture so far out that his denial could become notorious in such a
decisive way. Therefore it is his starting point, the beginning,
that is condemned, but precisely the beginning was indeed
good. The one who does not begin in this way never attains the
glory of remaining faithful to his conviction in painful death.
The sin of sagacity is to sin in such a way that one ingeniously
knows how to avoid punishment, yes, ingeniously knows how
to give the appearance of the good. The sin of sagacity is ingeniously to avoid every decision and in that way to win the
distinction of never having denied—this the world regards as
something extraordinary. The world does not truly hate evil but
loathes and hates what is unsagacious, that is, it loves evil. ——
"See, we have left everything and followed you"—and *we*, what
shall we have?

"See, we have left everything and followed you." The Apostle Peter
is no youth who at the beginning of life enthusiastically talks that

X
184

way about leaving everything. He knew very well what he meant by it, and we know how true it was when he said it, how true it became in his later life, how true it is that the apostle had left everything.

He left his customary occupation, a quiet and simple life that, content with a modest income, was spent in security. He left the reassuring trust in the probable, within which a person usually has his life, untried in anything other than what usually happens—*he left the certain and chose the uncertain.* Christ, in imitation [*Efterfølgelse*] of whom he left everything, was no man of independent means who could give his disciples a fixed income annually or guarantee them a permanent job and a livelihood—he, the poorest of all, he who as far as his own life was concerned was sure of only one thing: that he would be sacrificed. But as soon as Christ called him, he left all this, as is written in Matthew 4:20. This was a noble decision, and we must not imagine Peter, a human being like ourselves, as perhaps being without moments when his lower nature was ready with misgivings and cares, because true greatness is not like that, is not free from cares and misgivings but is what it is by overcoming these. He came, however, to the noble decision to leave all this. But for nobility the difficulty is always twofold: first, to conquer the low and earthly in oneself. Then, when this is done, the second difficulty comes—namely, that in every generation the contemporaries find nobility fatuous and foolish. That someone chooses a life by which he wins many advantages (which is not at all noble), this the world admires; but that someone gives up all advantages, even that of being honored by the world (which is precisely the noble), this the world finds ludicrous. —So Peter left the certain and chose the uncertain, chose to be Christ's disciple, the disciple of him who did not even have a place to lay his head.[18] Peter chose the uncertain, and yet, no, he did not choose the uncertain. The one to whom he attached himself was no adventurer who kept possibility uniformly open: the possibility of becoming something great in the world and the possibility of losing everything. Christ did not leave his disciples uncertain about what was in store for them and for him—certain downfall. Therefore Peter chose certain downfall.

X
185

He left family and friends and peers, the concepts and ideas in which his associates had had their lives; he became more foreign to them than the one who speaks a foreign language. An even greater difference, more immense than a difference in language, is the difference between two people, one of whom thinks and speaks only about heavenly things, about God's kingdom and his righteousness, and the other only about a job and livelihood and wife and children, about what is new in the city, and about becoming something in the world. He left all this, even though in the beginning his family and friends in their language certainly found it queer and extreme of him and therefore changed into his unfriends who mocked him and later, when they saw how full of danger his life became, went about saying: It is his own fault.

He left the faith of his fathers and therefore had to hate his father and mother. This is indeed the meaning of Christ's words: that the one who for his sake does not hate his father and mother is unworthy of him[19]—and Peter was worthy of him. If there is a difference of religion, that is, an eternal, decisive difference of eternity between father and son, and the son ardently believes with all his heart, with all his strength, and with all his soul[20] that only in this religion is there salvation—then he indeed hates the father, that is, his love for something else is so great that his love for the father is like hate. If someone has a legitimate claim, has a sacred claim, has first claim on your love, then to love someone else, even if this means only becoming indifferent to that first one, is indeed like hating him, simply because he has a claim on your love. But to love something so greatly that one believes that in it alone are deliverance and salvation to be found and outside it perdition, and if the father to whom you are joined by the most fervent bond of love does not believe the same, if, then, the believer, the more fervently he himself holds fast in love to the one and only in which there is salvation, is compelled (what horror, almost like laying violent hands upon his father!), is compelled to assume (what horror, just like being able to deny his father the necessities of life!), must find it in his heart to assume that the father accordingly is lost—this is indeed hating the father. Is this not hating another person, to believe him lost—is this any less, however indescribably hard it is for one! Therefore it is hating the father,

x
186

or, rather, it is hating him and yet loving him! Oh, what unparalleled abomination, to hate the beloved, so one's love turns to hate. Oh, of all the sufferings of the soul, this is the hardest, the most agonizing, to hate the beloved and yet to love him. To be willing to do everything for him, to be willing to sacrifice one's life for him—but to be bound, bound, yes, or crucified, or nailed to the condition that is not in one's power, the condition that attaches salvation to one provision so that without this there is no salvation, so that the choice must be either to give up one's own salvation in order to become lost with the beloved or oneself to believe unto salvation—alas, and in this way, hating, to let go of[21] the beloved!

He left the faith of his fathers and thereby *the people to whom he belonged, the fatherland, the love of which binds with the strongest bonds.* He no longer belonged to any people; he belonged only to the Lord Jesus. In faith he had to understand that God's chosen people, to whom he belonged by birth, was disowned, that there no longer existed a chosen people; in faith he had to understand that what once had certainly been his proudest thought, to belong to God's chosen people, from now on was hardness of heart and perdition in everyone who continued to hold fast to this thought.

In this way the apostle left everything, broke with everything that binds a person to the earth, and with everything that confines to the earth. In love for Christ or in hatred for the world he left everything, his position in life, livelihood, family, friends, human language, love for father and mother, love of fatherland, the faith of the fathers; he left the God he had worshiped until this time. He left it in a way *different* from that of one who is separated by the ocean from his fatherland; he left it *more inwardly* than does the man who leaves father and mother in order to cling to his wife,[22] *more passionately* than the woman who leaves her parental home—he did not even turn around to look back, to say nothing of requesting time to bury the dead.[23] He left everything—yes, and in the most decisive way, because he stayed in that place, surrounded by everything he left. The daily hardships of his life were the attested expression of his having left it. He remained among those he left—that he left them was expressed in their hatred and persecution of him. He did not go away from

X
187

it all—no, he remained in order to bear witness that he had left it, exposing himself to all the consequences, which in turn were testimony to his having left everything.

"See, we have left everything and followed you; what shall we have?" The apostle had left everything—and, as has been shown, it was in the strictest sense in earnest that he left everything; with him it was not as with us who, without the slightest change in externals, affirm that we are willing to forsake everything if it is required of us. Now the apostle asks, "What shall we have?"—and I ask, or better, you ask yourself, my listener (for this is both the best and most useful way), you ask: What shall we have?

Oh, there is nothing as deceitful and as cunning as a human heart, resourceful in seeking escapes and finding excuses; and there surely is nothing as difficult and as rare as genuine honesty before God. Truly, we should guard against delivering a censorious sermon here, should in relation to others especially guard ourselves against wanting to be the ones who would have to collect, so to speak, God's accounts payable. It certainly is true that God can require honesty of every human being—consequently of *me*; but that does not at all mean that I am called upon to require it of others on God's behalf. If I pretended to have such an assignment, I would be guilty of dishonesty toward God. No, we shall not terrify in that way. But what is terrible about being dishonest toward God has another side. For every human being, no matter whether any other help is available to him or all other help is at an end, there is still only one help in heaven and on earth, this, that God helps him. But how would God be able to help a person if he is not honest toward God? Perhaps one often thinks that God is slow to help, or that the complexity of the infinitely many circumstances in governing the world makes the help so slow in being to one's benefit. Oh, far from it, God is swift to help, swifter than thought, and for God there is no complexity. But the human being is dishonest toward God in craving help and in any case is very slow about becoming honest.

If a person asserts that he would be willing to leave everything for Christ's sake if it is required of him—well, how would I dare

x
188

to say that this is untrue. But see, in those ages when having to leave everything was actually in earnest, were there at that time very many who were willing, and the few who were found, were they not found just among the poor and the lowly? But now, now when it is not so easy to be actually in earnest about literally leaving everything in earnest, now we are all willing—if it is required. Let us not deceive ourselves, and not deceive God. It will not do to think that highly of oneself: to remain in possession of everything and then, in addition, to consider oneself to be such a person.

If God does not require of us that we leave everything, he still does require honesty of us. Far from impatiently and vehemently urging someone impatiently and vehemently to try his hand at leaving everything, which God perhaps does not require, does not require of him, we shall instead recommend honesty, which God does require of all. It is, however, very wrong to make this into a platitude or in a platitudinous way to say about all of us something that, if it is actually in earnest, is carried out only by one in thousands and thousands.

Perhaps God does not require it of him; that is, it is required of everyone, but it is not *unconditionally* required of everyone; that is, it is entrusted to freedom. The one who, believing, therefore humbly does this is acting Christianly; the one who is humbly conscious that he is not doing it, humbly thinks lowly of himself, is also acting Christianly. Perhaps God does not require this; that is, perhaps God does not require it in this way of us who are living in Christendom. Moreover, the voluntary, voluntarily to leave everything, is in every case the essentially Christian only when, as has been shown, it is done in order to follow Christ, thus in accord with God's requirement; and in Christendom this voluntary act is to be recommended only when before God it then is a consciousness of the essential difference, that the apostles and earliest Christians did what they did surrounded by Jews and pagans, that is, by non-Christians. For the one who lives in Christendom—there is in any case one thing he should not leave that the apostle did leave: the faith of the fathers; and there is and remains a distinctive difficulty in relation to being persecuted: to be put to death, not by Jews, not by pagans, but by Christians—for the sake of Christianity.

There was a time in Christendom when people thought they could do penance only by actually leaving everything and fleeing out into the solitude of the desert, or by striving to be persecuted in the throngs of the cities. There is another way to do penance, that of being genuinely honest toward God. I do not know—and if I did know otherwise, I hope to God that I would dare to speak otherwise—I do not know that it is anywhere unconditionally required of a person in Christendom that in order to be a Christian and in order to be blessed he must in the literal sense leave everything, or indeed that he must even sacrifice his life, be put to death for the sake of Christianity. But this I do know, that God cannot be involved with a dishonest person. According to my conception, therefore, the words by Peter we have chosen are a theme for a call to repentance: "See, we have left everything and followed you; what shall we have?" It is the theme if you are prompted by them to ask yourself: What shall we have? No person is saved except by grace; the apostle, too, was accepted only by grace. But there is one sin that makes grace impossible, that is dishonesty; and there is one thing God unconditionally must require, that is honesty. If, however, a person keeps God away through dishonesty, such a person can come *neither* to understand that he, if God should require it, in the more rigorous sense would leave everything, *nor* to understand himself in humbly admitting that he certainly did not in the literal sense leave everything but still entrusts himself to God's grace.

Ah, however different it is, humanly understood, when the apostle says, "See, we have left everything and followed you; what shall we have?" and when a person, who humbly confesses that he is not tested in this way and honestly admits before God that he certainly did not dare to believe himself capable of this, says: What shall we have—by God's grace they both receive exactly the same.

III

All Things Must Serve Us for Good— *When* We Love God[24]

If a person in the most solemn and strongest terms asserted that he loved God, that God, God alone, was his love, his only, his first love, and this person, when asked why, answered, "Because God is the highest, the holiest, the most perfect being"; and if this person, when asked whether he had ever loved God for any other reason, whether he did not sometimes love God for another reason, answered no—we might well be suspicious of him, that he was a fanatic, might very well earnestly warn him to watch out lest this fanatic mood end in presumptuousness. The simple and humble way is to love God because one needs him. Admittedly it seems very natural that in order to love God one must soar high up into heaven where God dwells, but in loving God humbly it is most fitting and sure to remain on earth. Admittedly it seems very elevated to love God because he is so perfect; it seems very selfish to love God because one needs him—yet the latter is the only way in which a person can truly love God. Woe to the presumptuous who would dare to love God without needing him! In relationships among people there can perhaps be a fanatic kind of love that loves someone solely for the beloved's perfection, but the fundamental and primary basis for a person's love of God is completely to understand that one needs God, loves him simply because one needs him. The person who most profoundly recognizes his need of God loves him most truly. You are not to presume to love God for God's sake. You are humbly to understand that your own welfare eternally depends on this need, and therefore you are to love him.

For the sake of one's own welfare, then, let each one ask himself whether he loves God. In the profoundest sense, the question "Do I love God?" is a question of welfare. If the answer is yes, then your welfare is indeed eternally assured, because "all things must serve for good those who love God." Oh, how often these words are said and repeated again and again, explained and expounded for upbuilding, for comfort, for reassurance. It has been shown how experience has confirmed its truth, how everything *actually* has served for good those who loved God. Doubts have been dispelled; it has been made obvious that it is so: that however different everything appears at the time or times of suffering, ordeal, and spiritual trial, yet finally everything must serve for good those who love God, that there is no rest for thought, that no doubt can stand up against this assurance but finally must give up and submit.

But what then? Because it is eternally certain that all things serve for good those who love God, does it follow from this that *I* love God? And this indeed is precisely the decisive question. The more one impersonally struggles against all the objections of doubt and then, after having refuted all these objections, pretends that everything is now decided, the more one's attention is diverted from what is really decisive. Yes, people have often been busy in a strange way in the wrong place. They struggle and struggle, ponder and ponder, in order to demonstrate the truth of Christianity, and when it is demonstrated they reassure themselves and think that now everything is as it should be. This is settling down to rest at the beginning, which one really ought not do before the end, and which is especially strange in these times when one is usually very busy with going further.[25] The person who has just a little understanding of the matter easily sees that everything else is only preliminary, an introduction to the main issue: Is this the way it is **for me**? But the matter has been all turned around, and therefore a work has been opened up that Christianity had least dreamed of. Christianity was proclaimed with divine authority; its intention was that not a single moment should be wasted on demonstrating that it is true, but that each one individually should turn to himself and say: How do you relate yourself to Christianity? This self-concern, this fear and trembling with regard to whether one is oneself a believer, is the best means against all doubt about the truth of the doctrine, because the self-concerned person works with all the power of his

X
192

soul in a totally different place. But because this self-concern has been altogether abolished, a kind of doubt has been opened up that Satan himself cannot combat but does indeed invent, a kind of doubt that is impossible to combat because to combat it actually requires one to go over to its side—that is, to conquer it one must oneself betray Christianity. In the Christian sense, the only weapon against doubt is, "Be still," or, Luther-like, "Shut your mouth!" Doubt, however, says, "Get involved with me, fight me—with my own weapons." What irrationality, and what an impossibility! If a liar were to say, "Get involved with me, fight me with my own weapons," could truth be served with this proposal or with winning such a victory!

Now, because this is the way it is, and very commonly, it is surely of benefit to turn the matter around and replace the coil spring of personality that has been removed from the essentially Christian. So also in this discourse; instead of demonstrating that it is true that all things serve for good those who love God, we shall quite simply, as is proper, assume this to be eternally decided, to be the most certain of all certainties, and instead discuss that

all things must serve us for good—"when" we love God.

The discourse, then, will actually revolve around the word "when." It is a little word, but it has enormous meaning. It is a little word around which, however, a world, the world of personality, revolves. You probably know about that nation that was famous for expressing itself briefly, and you presumably also know that short reply: *When.* The superior force had haughtily announced what its countless troops would do when they had conquered everything; the terse reply was "*When.*"[26] So it is also in a similar sense with this demonstrating again and again and the refuting that in proud words talks about its capability—although it is still incapable of doing the least thing *when* it does not itself believe, although it still does not have the slightest benefit from all this demonstrating *when* it does not itself believe, although it still cannot benefit you in the least *when* you do not believe, cannot in the slightest way assist you to faith *when* you do not believe, and on the other hand is of no importance whatever to you *when* you do believe. Yes, it is a little word, this "when"! If God is love, then it is self-evident that all things must serve for good those who love God, but from God's being love it does not at all follow that you believe that God is love, or that you love him. But if *you* believe, then it is self-evident that you must believe that all things serve *you* for good, because this is indeed implicit in what you believe about God. In the one case, it is the individual who presumes to want to become thoroughly familiar with God, so to speak, and to demonstrate something about him, demonstrate that he is love and what follows from that. In the other case, the individual humbly understands that the issue is whether *he* believes that God is love, because if he believes this, then everything else follows without any demonstration—from the demonstration nothing follows *for me*; from faith everything follows *for me*.

So, then, the discourse is about this "when" and thus about faith, which of all the goods is the highest and the only true good. Of all other goods it holds true that there is still a "but"—that they have a side from which it becomes doubtful whether this good is indeed a good, whether it would not have been better for one not to have received this good. But faith is the good that is of such a nature that if you believe, provided that you do believe, when you believe, insofar as you do believe—even if what you most feared did happen to you, you will in faith understand that it must be the best for you, that is, a good. Although doubt has power over everything that is ordinarily called goods, power to make them dubious, faith has power over all the good and over all the evil that can befall you, power to make it undoubted that it is a good.

All things must serve us for good—**when** *we love God*. Imagine someone who possesses all the goods of good fortune, is untroubled by all pain and adversity, unacquainted with any suffering or danger, indulged in his every wish, envied by the petty-minded, considered fortunate by the young—does he dare to consider himself fortunate? Yes—*when* he believes that God is love, because then all these things serve him for good. "When"—it is a bad little word, this "when"! Yes, woe to the

x
194

person who ventures to cast doubt about God into another person's heart, because all this doubt is sinful, and to awaken this doubt in another is to seduce. But honor be to the person, praise be to him, thanks be to him, to him the earnest one who has no fear of awakening in another person the doubt that teaches him to have doubts about himself, the doubt that is the origin of self-concern. Therefore, *when!* This "when," it is the preacher of repentance. Perhaps you think that a preacher of repentance is like a rushing violent wind that terrifies physically. No, the true preacher of repentance, like God's voice, also comes in a gentle breeze[27]—yet it is not soft but rigorous, as rigorous as the earnestness of eternity. The true preacher of repentance has only one aim, to press hard on you or me, on the single individual, to wound him in such a way that he himself now becomes essentially his own preacher of repentance. Take care with this "when"—in another sense, see to it that you love this "when," because if you do not, you will be your own downfall. But take care with this "when"—if it has struck you, it can perhaps take you ages before you are finished with it, or rather, if in truth it has struck you, you will never be completely finished with this "when"—nor should you be either. This "when" becomes like an arrow in your heart; it will remain there until the end. Therefore do not be afraid of the preacher of repentance who perhaps has terror in his countenance and wrath in his voice, who scolds and castigates and thunders. All that is just a game and becomes merely a kind of shuddering entertainment. No, deep within every person's heart, there dwells his preacher of repentance. If he speaks, he does not preach to others, he does not make you into a preacher of repentance—he preaches only to you. He does not preach in any church to an assembled crowd; he preaches in the secret recesses of the soul—and to you, whether you want to listen to him or not. He has nothing whatever to attend to than to attend to you, and he sees to it that he is heard at the moment when everything around you is still, when the stillness makes you completely solitary.

You fortunate one, you whom so many envy and so many consider fortunate—if you are wounded by this "when" or if you have wounded yourself on it, you will seek in vain to find rest in anyone else's assurance that you are fortunate—yes, even if all people joined together in order to assure you of that, it will not give you the slightest certainty. You are dealing now with your-self, with the preacher of repentance in your own inner being. He does not use many words; he is too well informed for that. He says only "when." And whether you want to deliver a long speech to him or ask him a brief question, he says only "when." If, in view of your riches, with the thought of how it is in your hands to make your life as cozy and pleasurable as possible, and what is even more glorious, that it is in your hands to do good to so many, if in view of all this you consider yourself fortunate, then the preacher of repentance says, "Yes—*when* you believe that God is love, *when* you love God, because then all this serves you for good." It is a bit unsettling, this answer. In a certain sense it is so cold, so calm in its ambiguity; it is neither yes nor no! If you ask him, "Do I then not love God?" he answers, "I do not know anything about that; I am saying it only as it is: *When* you love God, then . . . . . ." If you were to beseech and implore him finally to answer yes, if you were to threaten him with death to say yes, you will move him just as little. You cannot win him over by flattery or by pleas; you cannot put him to death, except in a very metaphorical sense, and in any case he does not fear death. But as long as he lives, as long as you still hear his voice, he repeats this "when." If you were to say to him, "I will give half of my riches to the poor[28] if only I may have certainty that the rest of it will truly serve me for good," and he gave you no answer because he cannot reply to this talk, or he answered, "Yes, when"—if you, then, brought to the limit by perceiving what power lies in this "when" said by *him* to *you*, if you were to say, "I will give all my riches to the poor if only I may have the certainty that poverty truly serves me for good," then he will answer, "Yes—when you love God."

When you love God—or when you believe that God is love, because if you believe that God is love, then you also love him, and then all things serve you for good. But do not make a mis-take, do not go ahead and love God in the overflowing feeling of your good fortune, as if you did not really need him because you are fortunate enough. No, you must learn to need God, to love

X
195

him because you need him, you the most fortunate of all. Your welfare is by no means, oh, by no means decided by all your good fortune; it is first decided when—but then it is also eternally decided—when you believe that God is love, when you love God. O you fortunate one [Lykkelige]—when you believe it— congratulations [til Lykke]! Then all this serves you for good— your riches, your good health, your glorious mental gifts, your joy at the side of your beloved, your honor and prestige among people, the blissful cheer of your children: it all serves you for good—when you love God, and then you are actually blessed. In other words, however fortunate a person is, we still say that he lacks one thing if he is not conscious of his good fortune. But the true consciousness of his good fortune is to have this con- sciousness (without which, as stated, good fortune is not good fortune) contained in, set in the consciousness that God is love. A knowledge that God is love is still not a consciousness of it. Consciousness, personal consciousness, requires that in my knowledge I also have knowledge of myself and my relation to my knowledge. This is to believe, here to believe that God is love, and to believe that God is love is to love him.

You surely have often heard people speak of the power of the word, of what the one is able to do who has the word really in his power, and yet this little "when" has infinitely more power when in a person's inner being it is the preacher of repentance who says the word to *this person*. The power of the word has overturned thrones, changed the shape of the world. But this little "when" has an even greater power; it is an even greater change when a person is eternally changed by this "when." When a person comes to love God, it is an eternal change more remarkable than the most remarkable event in the world. Whether it happens, when it happens, no one can tell him. The preacher of repentance in his inner being can help him to be- come aware, can help him in self-concern to seek the certitude of the spirit as God's Spirit witnesses with this person's spirit that *he* loves God.[29] But only God can give him this certitude. Keep him awake in incertitude in order to seek after certitude, this the preacher of repentance can do; he says: All things serve you for good *when* you love God. With this word he calls to the youth in the morning of life; with this word he calls to the adult many times and in many ways in the busy days of life; with this word he prevents the old person from becoming lethargic and apathetic. He does not add one syllable, he does not take one syllable away, he does not change his voice, does not accentuate the word differently; as unchanged as a dead person, as calm as eternity, he repeats "when."[30]

All things must serve us for good—**when** *we love God*. Imagine a person, the most wretched of all—already a long time ago, human sympathy gave him up and abandoned him, does not dare, alas, for its own sake, to come close to him, desires only, alas, for its own sake, to remain unaware of all his misery and thereby unaware that it can actually happen that a human being can become so wretched—would he now dare to say, "Only evil happens to me, and from that comes only more evil"? Not at all—well, if he does not love God, then he may be right in that, but then the discourse is really about something entirely different from what he is talking about. In the divine sense, not to love God is a human being's crucial wretchedness, whether he otherwise is fortunate or unfortunate. But what human language calls need, adversity, suffering, sheer wretchedness: that can still serve a person for good—when he loves God.

x
197

But it is a strange double entity, this "when." Yet this is quite as it should be. Is it not true that the preacher of repentance, if he is genuine, is always the comforter as well, who knows how to comfort and endure long after human help is futile and has given up the sufferer? That is why he is loved just as much as he is feared. In the dark night of despair, when every light has gone out for the sufferer, there is still one place where the light is kept burning—it is along this way the despairing one must go, which is the way out: *when* you love God. In the fearful moment of disconsolateness, when there is no more talk or thought of any concluding clause, but humanly speaking the meaning is ended—there is still one clause left, a courageous clause of comfort that intrepidly penetrates into the greatest terror and creates new meaning: *when* you love God. In the dreadful moment of decisiveness, when humanly speaking no turn is any longer possible, when there is everywhere only wretchedness wherever you turn and however you turn—there is still one more turn possible; it will miraculously turn everything into the good for you: *when* you love God.

But who is it, then, who says this to a person? Oh, deep within every person there dwells a comfort; it is also in there that the preacher of repentance dwells. It is of only little help to you if another person wanted to preach repentance to you. He cannot do it; it becomes an empty game. The most he can do is to help you become your own preacher of repentance. Likewise it is of only little help to you if another person wants to comfort you. If you are being tested in hard decisions, another person's comfort will not understand you and therefore cannot help you either; and if you really became wretched, then in fairness you cannot demand that another person's sympathy shall venture in to you. But deep within yourself, there where the preacher of repentance dwells, there dwells the comfort, this "when." And just as this word does not allow itself to be bribed by the flattery and pleas of the fortunate one and defies his threats, so also, God be praised, it is undaunted on the day of need. You are mistaken if you think that the most morbid and troubled imagination could invent a horror that could silence this word. Tell this comforter anything you wish, confide to him what is about to gain power over you, that however much you shudder at it you are close to concluding, yet with conflicting emotions, that "God is not love"—he is not shocked; he only repeats: *When* you love God, then this will also serve you for good.

X
198

O final comfort, O blessed comfort, O comfort beyond all measure! As stated, when human sympathy ceases, when the one person does not dare to go in to the other, deep within a person there is a comfort. Just as Scripture says, "Have salt in yourselves,"[31] so also it holds true that there is the comfort deep within every person. But still this comforter has in no way denied his character as a preacher of repentance. If you, by all your misery, by any cry of pain in your suffering, or by any cry of anxiety over the suffering you fear, were to attempt to move him to give you an assurance that you love God, he would answer, "*When* you love God." Do not imagine either that it is actually out of sympathy for all your wretchedness that he says and repeats this word of comfort. No, it is because he fears that in your despair you would plunge yourself into what, in the divine sense, is a person's wretchedness, into the wretchedness of not loving God. He is not engaged in wanting your suffering removed, nor does he give you what he cannot give, the certitude that you love God. But while the wretchedness preaches repentance to you, he preaches comfort, not human but divine comfort; and in the divine comfort, repentance is always contained and required.

O you suffering one, *when* you believe that God is love, or what is the same, *when* you love God (for if you believe that God is love, then you also love him), then all this serves you for good. Do not say that you cannot understand how all this wretchedness would serve you for good, and do not surrender to the error of doubt either, so that you begin to question whether God is love. Fear for yourself, but also find comfort within yourself; pay attention to these words that sound in your innermost being, *when* you love God. If the words cannot give you the certitude that you love God—if the words cannot do this, then only God can give you this when his Spirit witnesses with your spirit that you love him, when you know with him that you believe that he is love. But the words can help you to aspire to this certitude. When despair wants to close in over you, the words still create a prospect of deliverance; when you want to collapse in exhaustion and give up, these words still hold open the possibility of help, *when* you love God.

x
199

*All things must serve us for good—***when** *we love God.* Imagine a person endowed, if possible, with more than extraordinary mental gifts, with a depth in pondering, a sharpness in comprehending, a clarity in expounding, a thinker the likes of whom has never been seen and never will be. He has pondered the nature of God, that God is love; he has pondered what follows from that—namely, that the world must be the best and that all things serve for good. He has recorded his ponderings in a book that is regarded as the property of the whole human race, its pride; it is translated into every language, is referred to on every scholarly occasion, is made the basis of lectures, and from this book the pastors derive their demonstrations. This thinker, protected by favorable conditions, which are indeed a necessity for scholarly research, has until now lived unacquainted with the world. Then it so happens to him that he is forced out into a decision; he must act in a difficult matter and at a decisive moment. This act is followed by a consequence such as he had least expected, a consequence that plunged him and many others into wretchedness. It is the consequence of his action—and yet he is convinced that he could not have acted in any other way than he, after the most honest deliberation, did act. Therefore the point here is not just the misfortune but that he is responsible for it, however innocent he knows he is. Now he is wounded; a doubt awakens in his soul whether this, too, can serve him for good. The direction of thought this doubt immediately takes in him, the thinker, is whether God is indeed love—in the believer doubt takes another direction, that of self-concern. Meanwhile the concern acquires more and more power over him, until finally he is at his wit's end. In this condition he goes to a pastor who does not know him personally. He opens himself to him and seeks comfort. The clergyman, who has gone along with the times and is a thinker of sorts, now wants to demonstrate to him that this, too, must be for the best and must serve him for good, since God is love, but he is soon convinced that he is not the man to enter into an intellectual bout with this stranger. After several futile attempts, the clergyman says, "Well, I know just one resource; there is a book about God's love by so and so. Read it, study it; if it cannot help you, then no one can help you." The stranger replies, "I myself am the author of that book."

See, now, what the thinker had put down in that book was excellent; indeed, how would I dare question it? What the thinker had understood about God was surely also true and profound. But the thinker had not understood himself; until now he had lived under the delusion that when it had been demonstrated that God is love it followed as a matter of course that you and I believe it. As a thinker, he perhaps has taken a very dim view of faith, until—as a human being he learned to take a somewhat dimmer view of thought, especially of pure thought. The train of his thought turned around; his train of thought became different.

He did not say: God is love; ergo all things serve for one's good. But he said: *When* I believe that God is love, then all things serve *me* for good. What was it that turned everything around for him—it was this "when." Now the thinker was matured for life as a human being, because until now there had been something inhuman about him. What it means as a baby to acquire the name one is to be called throughout one's whole life is akin, at some time in one's life, to being wounded decisively, eternally on this "when" and thereby coming to love God, while subsequently this "when" is still always ready to keep eternally young the love with which one loves God—eternally young, as God is eternal, in the first tension of passion, but more and more inwardly.

All things must serve us for good—**when** *we love God*. Is this so, is it actually so, can I demonstrate it? Ah, when *you* believe it, if *you* believe it, you will be blessedly sure that, as usual, what you are seeking is not only here, so that you need not go out to seek it, but that you have found it, that you have it. If you believe that, you will easily understand that every demonstration only leads you away from what you have, although this demonstration deceptively pretends to lead you to it.

Let us understand each other. You are most likely familiar (and who is not!) with that very felicitous and fervent line by the noble poet who has the unhappy girl say something like this, "I ask for nothing more, I have lived and I have loved,"³² or what in her thinking would be the very same, "I have loved—and lived." Why? Because she humanly regards erotic love [*Elskov*] as the highest good, and therefore she makes these two concepts entirely synonymous: to live and to love. To love is to live, to live is to love; if her beloved is taken away from her, then life is over—but she has loved. We do not wish to quarrel with this loving girl—and, moreover, she is of course the stronger. She is stronger than all our understanding—because she *believes* in erotic love. She is stronger than all worldly power; in a certain sense she has vanquished death, does not fear it, because life has already been taken away from her; after all, life to her was indeed her love—alas, and she *has* loved.

But now, to love God! Surely it is the highest good; what the girl, piously deceived by her heart, held true of love surely holds true, with eternity's truth, of loving God: to love God is to live. *To live!* When the words are used this way with special emphasis, one indicates the full, rich life that is in possession of the conditions for living, indicates a life that is truly worth living, a life that, so to speak, overflows with a blissful sense of life. One lives this way only when one possesses the highest good, but the highest good is to love God. But in that case, no matter what happens to him, the one who loves God indeed possesses the highest good, because to love God is the highest good. Oh, is this not true! If you will permit me for the sake of a pious jest to make fun just once of this demonstrating conceit, I shall add: *quod erat demonstrandum* [which was to be demonstrated]!

The same thing holds true when we speak of loss. In speaking about loss, about what a person can lose in the world, one usually forgets that the highest good is to love God! Then if a person loses everything in the world—if he does not lose faith in God's love [*Kjerlighed*]—he does not lose the highest good. Imagine two people, both of whom lost everything, but the one also lost faith in God's love—what is the difference between these two? Shall we in a wretched way say that the difference is that the one is still somewhat better off than the other? No, let us speak the truth, the difference is: the one really did lose everything; the other really lost nothing at all, since he indeed retained the highest good.

"—**When** *we love God!*" O my listener, you who are perhaps accustomed to demanding everything from the speaker, here you see how everything lies with the listener. Will you deny that the speaker is speaking the truth who says, "All things serve you for good—*when* you love God"? You certainly will not do that. All right, but then you would certainly be asking the impossible of him if you demanded that he bring about one specific effect: to reassure or to terrify. The effect this truthful discourse will bring about depends solely on who the listener is. Perhaps there is someone whom this discourse could make more anxious than he has ever been before, but this is not the fault of the discourse—it lies with the listener. Perhaps there is someone who in complete agreement said yes and amen to it, heard it as the most blessed reassurance; but this is not the merit of the discourse, it lies with the listener. It is not the discourse that has terrified the one, and it is not the discourse that has reassured the other; it is the one and the other who in the discourse have understood themselves.

IV

There Will Be the Resurrection of the Dead, of the Righteous— and of the Unrighteous[33]

My listener, you yourself may have been in this situation, or you know, do you not, that such is the case with very many: at various times in his life a person has wished that someone could demonstrate to him the immortality of the soul. He has not required that these demonstrations should make all effort on his part superfluous; he was willing to participate in the task with his own thinking. He has obtained one or another book on the subject, has sat calmly and read it, or he has attended a lecture that undertook to demonstrate the immortality of the soul. What is this person's state of mind amid all this, how should I describe it? In civic life we say that there is security in the city: public security is maintained; we calmly walk home even late at night without fearing any danger; we seldom hear of theft, and then only a little insignificant "appropriation for use"; assault never occurs. Therefore we are secure, live in security. So it is also with being secure in the intellectual sense: the thoughts come and go, even the most decisive ones pass by the soul; one deals with even the most appalling things, thinks about them more or less, but deep inside the security is maintained, and one is secure or, as it perhaps could be called even more correctly, one's mind is at ease.

But this discourse about immortality—yes, it aims to violate public or, more correctly here, private security; it intends to disturb peace of mind. It is like an assault, bold as an assault in broad daylight, as terrifying as an assault at night. Before it demonstrates anything—but, no, let us not divert the mind in a delusion—it does not want to *demonstrate* anything at all. It divides people into the righteous and the unrighteous and in so doing asks you whether you count yourself among the righteous or among the unrighteous. It places this question in the closest connection with immortality—indeed, it does not speak about immortality but about this distinction. Is this not like an assault! It certainly never occurred to any of the demonstrators to make this division or to raise this question—that would be pressing too closely to the listener or reader; one is afraid of pressing too closely to the listener or reader—that would be unscholarly and uncultured. Strangely enough, one is afraid of pressing too closely to the listener or reader—although one is engaged in demonstrating to him that which of all things most closely pertains to a person; indeed, there is nothing that pertains to a person more closely than his immortality. Yet one wants to demonstrate it to him without pressing too closely to him. Presumably, by virtue of the demonstration, he will also after a fashion assume his immortality without pressing too closely to *himself* or to *his* immortality. In a way, demonstrating immortality becomes a kind of game. And when this game is continued for a long time and becomes very popular, it is like an assault when a discourse, assuming immortality as the most certain of all, presses as closely as possible to a person by unceremoniously bringing up what follows from that instead of wanting to demonstrate immortality (since that places it at a distance and keeps it at a distance from one). Instead of begging you to give it your attention and to listen calmly while it demonstrates immortality, it assaults you somewhat like this: "Nothing is more certain than immortality; you are not to worry about, not to waste your time on, not to seek an escape by— wanting to demonstrate it or wishing to have it demonstrated. Fear it, it is only all too certain; do not doubt whether you are immortal—tremble, because you are immortal."

The words are by Paul,[34] and very likely both the Pharisees and the Sadducees became equally enraged at him. Scripture tells specifically that the Sadducees, who did not assume immortality, became indignant when Paul spoke about immortality; but would not this be due especially to the way in which he spoke, so that the Pharisees became essentially just as incensed? For Paul it had indeed been the most favorable opportunity; yes, in the circumstances there seemed to be a summons to him; it was

almost as if the age demanded of him that he produce some evidence of the immortality of the soul. If he had done that, if he
had invited people to a meeting where he proposed to deliver
some lectures on the evidence of the immortality of the soul—
well, even the Sadducees would probably have had no objection
to that. As scholarly, cultured people, they presumably would
have been broad-minded enough to think something like this:
"Although we deny the immortality of the soul, there may still
be something to be said for the other side, and of course one can
listen to him." But to hurl or throw oneself upon someone in this
way with the question about the righteous and the unrighteous,
to upset the point of view completely in this way, to abandon the
scholarly in order to go over to the personal—well, no wonder
that people become indignant over such behavior! They gather
as men of culture, a circle of serious people who want to hear
something about immortality, whether there is an immortality,
whether there actually is an immortality, a personal immortality, whether they actually will recognize one another again,
about how they will pass the time in eternity, whether in those
lofty vaulted chambers in the hereafter one will actually find
oneself again in one's own person, the happiest moments of one's
life (when one was a bride, when one charmed everyone in the
social club[35]), embroidered in the tapestry of recollection—and
then instead of all this, instead of spending a pleasant hour and
later, as an earnest person, being able to say afterward: "There is
still a question about immortality"—instead of this, to have the
matter decided in such a way that one becomes anxious and
afraid!

Well, yes—truly, the one who never had his immortality decided in such a way that he became anxious and afraid has never
really believed in his immortality. This has been quite forgotten
in these times that, in complete conformity with this, are so busy
demonstrating immortality, in these times when one is almost
ready brazenly to let it stand open as left up to everyone's discre-
tion whether he will or he will not, whether he for the most part,
nearly, almost, to a certain degree, or after a fashion wants to
believe a little bit in immortality. Immortality is on the way to
becoming a kind of luxury to people, left up to whatever one

likes. For that reason, for that very reason, so many books are written that after a fashion *demonstrate* the immortality of the soul—and for that very reason it is certainly made necessary to give the matter another turn. So we shall speak about these words:

There will be the resurrection of the dead, of the righteous—and of the unrighteous, or about the demonstration of the immortality of the soul formulated in this way: it is only all too certain, fear it!

Immortality is judgment. Immortality is not a continued life, a continued life as such in perpetuity, but immortality is the eternal separation between the righteous and the unrighteous; immortality is no continuation that results as a matter of course but a separation that results from the past.

What is it that has given rise to this whole error about immortality? It is that the placement of the issue has been shifted, that immortality has been turned into a question, that what is a task has been turned into a question, what is a task for action has been turned into a question for thought. Of all errors and evasions, this is by far the most corruptive. Indeed, would not the most corrupt of all ages be one that managed to have "duty" completely changed into a problem for thought? What is duty? Duty is what one *ought to do.* There ought not to be a question about duty, but there ought to be only the question about whether I am doing my duty. There ought not to be a question about immortality, whether there is an immortality, but the question ought to be whether I am living in such a way as my immortality requires of me. There ought not to be discussion about immortality, whether there is an immortality, but about what my immortality requires of me, about my enormous responsibility in my being immortal.

This means: immortality and judgment are one and the same. Immortality can be discussed properly only when there is discussion about judgment, and of course when there is discussion about judgment there is discussion about immortality. This was why Felix became afraid of Paul's discussion about immortality; Paul refused to speak in any other way than to speak about

judgment, about the separation between the righteous and the
unrighteous.[36] If Paul had been willing to speak in a different
way, had separated, according to modern taste, judgment and
immortality, had spoken, or babbled, about immortality without
saying a word about judgment, spoken about immortality and
pretended that there is no judgment—well, then I am sure that
Felix would not have become afraid, then Felix surely would
have listened with the attentiveness of a cultured man and afterward would have said, "It is really entertaining to listen to the
man, although it is a kind of fanaticism that nevertheless can be
diverting as long as one listens to it; it has something in common
with a fireworks display."

Immortality is judgment. There is not one more word to say
about immortality; the one who says one more word or a word
in another direction had better beware of judgment. But immortality has been turned into something entirely different and has
therefore been subverted. It has been sapped of its strength, has
been tricked out of its authority—because people have wanted
to *demonstrate* it, and then it has been left standing open, whether
one will accept it; but instead it is just the opposite: either you
will or you will not; the question is not raised at all about
whether you are immortal—just beware! If a public official who
has authority orders something, if then a few people, who presumably want to be helpful to him by demonstrating that he is a
very sagacious man etc., wanted to persuade the subordinates to
obey this public official—what then? Then these eloquent people would have cheated him out of his authority, because he
should not be obeyed because he is sagacious, should not be
obeyed for this reason or that etc., but because he has authority.
When duty, instead of being the imperative, is set aside as a problem, even if people did *what* duty commands, they would still not
be doing *their duty*; duty is to be done because it *ought* to be done.
Likewise, if someone by means of all sorts of demonstrations
managed after a fashion to carry it to the point of assuming his
immortality, he still does not *believe* in his immortality. With several reasons you will not carry it any further than the probability
that you are immortal. No, God has totally excused you from
that trouble; you are immortal, and you are to make an account-

X
207

ing to God of how you have lived, you immortal one! Precisely
because you are immortal, you will not be able to escape God,
will not be able to mislay yourself in a grave and behave as if
nothing has happened; and the criterion by which you will be
judged by God is that you are immortal.

Immortality is judgment, or the separation between the righteous and the unrighteous. This is how Paul also joins the two. He
does not waste a word talking about immortality, whether there
is an immortality; he speaks about what immortality is, that it is
the separation between the righteous and the unrighteous. The
imperfection of this earthly life, its earthliness, is precisely that it
cannot show this difference between the righteous and the unrighteous. Here in this earthly life there is the confusion that the
unrighteous one can have the appearance of being the righteous,
that the righteous one may suffer as if he were the unrighteous,
that an impenetrable darkness covers who is the righteous one
and who is the unrighteous, that righteousness seems to be humankind's own invention, so that the righteous is what the majority regard as righteous. Thus righteousness seems to have the
same character as everything else earthly, to be only to a certain
degree, so that just as beauty requires being neither too large nor
too small, likewise righteousness is a kind of middle way [*Mid-
delvej*], so that it must not be sought after immoderately, and
therefore it is justified when (as a consequence of the world's
mediocrity [*Middelmaadighed*]) suffering and the opposition of
people become the lot of the one who wants only righteousness,
who loves righteousness more than his life. But the truth and
perfection of eternal life are eternally to show the difference between right and wrong with the rigorousness of eternity, scrupulous as only eternity is, with a majesty that to the earthly-minded
must seem pettiness and eccentricity. In eternity, therefore, it
will be easy enough to distinguish between right and wrong, but
the point is that you are not to do this first in eternity; you will
be judged in eternity as to whether you in your earthly life have
done this as eternity wants to have it done.

What, then, is the eternal? It is the difference between right
and wrong. All else is transitory: heaven and earth will collapse;
all other differences are evanescent; all differences between one

human being and another are a part of the interlude of human life
on earth and therefore something terminating. But the difference
between right and wrong remains eternally, just as he remains,
the Eternal One, who established this difference *from eternity* (unlike the difference he established *in the beginning* between heaven
and earth[37]) and remains *for eternity* just as he, the Eternal One,
remains, he who rolls up the heavens like a garment,[38] changes
everything, but never himself—and therefore never changes this
either, eternity's difference. The eternal is the difference between right and wrong; therefore immortality is the separation
between the righteous and the unrighteous. Immortality is not a
continuation, is not related to present life in such a way that this
is continued, but it is the separation in such a way that life indeed
continues, but in separation. It is a futile, an indolent, a flabby
thought to desire a life after death in the sense of a long life; it is
eternity's thought that people part in this earthly life—the separation *is* in eternity.

But how can the eternal be a difference? To be a difference—
is it not a much too imperfect being to be able to be the eternal?
Well, now, the eternal is not the difference either; the eternal is
righteousness. But the being of righteousness has this perfection,
that it contains a redoubling [*Fordoblelse*]; this redoubling that it
has within itself is the difference between right and wrong. A
being that has no difference whatever in itself is a very imperfect
being, in part an imaginary being, such as the being of a mathe-
matical point. A being that has the difference outside itself is a
vanishing being; this is the case with the dissimilarities of this
earthly life, which therefore vanish. The eternal, righteousness,
has the difference in itself, the difference between right and
wrong. But if someone, instead of becoming accustomed to believing that there is an eternal difference between right and
wrong, instead of practicing this so that he might have his life in
it (which costs much time and effort, for which this whole
earthly life therefore is intended)—if someone instead turns away
from it, becomes accustomed to thinking that there is a difference of sorts between right and wrong but that he ought not to
become pedantic about it either, that it probably is good to make
the distinction once in a while, but it would spoil everything to

make it a daily practice—then it appears difficult to grasp what otherwise is implicit in the matter itself, that in eternity there would be an eternal difference between right and wrong. If there is an eternal difference between right and wrong (something that should be seen already in this life, but, alas, it is not), how, then, would it not be so in eternity! Take any earthly difference whatever to illustrate that a difference is naturally seen best where it has its abode. Take the difference: noble and common. If the nobleman lives in a city where he is the only nobleman and all others are commoners, he cannot maintain his difference—the commoners overpower it by superior numbers; but when he comes together with his own class, strengthened by being together with them, then you see the difference. So also with the eternal difference between right and wrong. Here in earthly life it is overwhelmed, so to speak, cannot properly assert itself, is debased, but when it comes home in eternity, it is in its full power. Whether people believe that this difference exists in eternity or not, it does exist in eternity. And with eternity it is not as it so often is with the powerful, the insightful, a thinker, a teacher, that he, overwhelmed by the great numbers, *in the end* must give in! Just the opposite! Indeed, in temporality it does rather look as if eternity had already given in; therefore it does not yield *in the end*—no, *in the end* it comes in a terrible way. It tests people here in earthly life; at times it lets itself be mocked here in earthly life, but in the end, in the end it judges, because immortality is judgment.

Immortality is judgment, and this pertains to **me***; in* **my** *view it pertains to* **me** *most of all, just as in* **your** *view it pertains to* **you** *most of all.* I have been able to understand this matter in no other way. But that may be due to my own limitations. In my view it is incomprehensible that there are people who put the matter altogether differently. They are sure enough about what will happen to them in that separation of eternity, are sure enough about the matter of their own salvation, that they are the righteous, or sure enough that they are believers—and now they raise the question whether others can be saved. For me the matter has never appeared that way; nothing has ever crossed my mind but that every other person would easily be saved; in *my* view it was

X
210

doubtful only in regard to *me*. Yes, if I had caught myself doubting the salvation of anyone else at all, it would have been enough to make me despair of my own.

But the matter must be put in one of two ways; one cannot be in two places at one time or work with one's thoughts in two places at one time! *Either* one works unceasingly with all the effort of one's soul, in fear and trembling, on self-concern's thought, "whether one will oneself be saved," and then one truly has no time or thought to doubt the salvation of others, nor does one care to. *Or* one has become completely sure about one's own part—and then one has time to think about the salvation of others, time to step forward concerned and to shudder on their behalf, time to take positions and make gestures of concern, time to practice the art of looking horrified while one shudders on behalf of someone else.

But the one who has become so completely sure, so sure of his hand as he handles this eternally decisive question (more worthy of admiration than a surgeon's sureness in using his scalpel, because with regard to this question of an eternal salvation it is impossible to cut someone else without cutting oneself), he has most likely not always been so sure. So he has changed in the course of time. Obviously a person does change in the course of time. See, when a person grows older, a physical change takes place: the fine velvety skin becomes wrinkled, the smooth joints stiffen, the tendons tighten, the bones calcify—is this change, this sureness, is it for the better? The young girl who once upon a time blushed to hear "his" name mentioned, blushed when she said it aloud to herself in solitude, the young girl whose heart beat violently every time the clock struck the hour when "he" was to come, the young girl who at one time shuddered at the thought of having displeased him in the slightest way and could not sleep for having done it, the young girl who at one time became cold as death out of anxiety because "he" for one moment was not as affectionate toward her as usual—this young girl has now been married to him for many years. Now she has become sure, sure that she is indeed good enough for him; she is aware of none of those maidenly feelings. As far as she is concerned, she is completely sure. She is pleased with herself; if it should happen that she was not pleased—I almost said "with the beloved," but that is out of the question; she has no beloved even though she has him as a husband. She is occupied only with judging other wives; she is completely satisfied with herself even in her changed state. She is not even like that old man who walked around stooped over and whose beard reached his knees, and when he was asked why he was so downcast, he replied as he threw up his hands, "I have lost my youth on earth, and now I am trying to find it everywhere." She is not trying to find anything; she who once tried with all the ardor of love to please is now pleased with herself; she is completely sure. Is this sureness a change for the better!

No, away, pernicious sureness. Save me, O God, from ever becoming completely sure; keep me unsure until the end so that then, if I receive eternal blessedness, I might be completely sure that I have it by grace! It is empty shadowboxing to give assurances that one believes that it is by grace—and then to be completely sure. The true, the essential expression of its being by grace is the very fear and trembling of unsureness. *There* lies faith—as far, just as far, from despair and from sureness. The one who fritters away his life without thinking of immortality perhaps cannot be said to scorn the highest good; but the one who became completely sure, that one scorns it. The one who trifled away his life can certainly be said to be throwing away his immortality; but the one who became completely sure threw it away even more appallingly. Eternal God, therefore keep my deepest concern silent in my innermost being, understood only by you, so that I may never speak directly of it to anyone. Otherwise I probably would soon carry it to the point of being just as sure as some others, more sure than several others—and completely sure—would become practiced in assurances and assurances until I became completely sure. Save me from people, and save me from deceiving any other person, because this deception lies all too close when one treats one's relationship with God as if it were a direct relationship with other human beings, so that one gets into comparisons and human sureness. If someone, regarded by many as extraordinarily noble and upright, were to continue in fear and trembling to work out his salvation,[39] the others would become furious with him. In other words, they would want to have his sureness as an excuse for their peace of mind, and they would want their own peace of mind to be his sureness. But, my God and Father, the question of my salvation indeed pertains to no other person, but only to me—and to you. Is there not bound to be unsureness in fear and trembling until the end if I am who I am and you are who you are, I here on earth, you in heaven, and, alas, the infinitely greater difference, I a sinner, you the Holy One! Should there not be, ought there not be, and must there not be fear and trembling until the end? Was this not the fault of the foolish bridesmaids, that they became sure and went to sleep—the sensible ones, however, stayed awake.[40] But what is it to stay awake? It is unsureness in fear and trembling. And what is faith but an empty delusion if it is not awake? And if faith is not awake, what else is it but that pernicious sureness? The person who never concerned himself about his salvation did not become sure either; but the faith that fell asleep, that is sureness.

So this pertains to *me*, in *my* view most of all to *me*, and I can understand that likewise in *your* view it pertains to *you* most of all. I cannot understand you in any other way, I do not wish to understand you in any other way, and I do not wish to be understood by you in any other way. I know nothing concerning *my* salvation, because what I know I know only with God in fear and trembling, and therefore I cannot speak about it. When there has been a discussion about something in a meeting of the ministers of state but it has not yet been decided, is it then not a crime to report it in the city—and *my* salvation is not yet decided. And I know nothing about *your* salvation; only you can know about that with God. But this I do believe, that there will be the resurrection of the dead, of the righteous—and of the unrighteous.

My listener, this discourse is nevertheless reassuring, is it not? Indeed, one cannot speak more reassuringly than when one says to a person who so eagerly *would like* to believe in immortality, who so eagerly *would like* to see it *demonstrated*, "In this regard, be entirely at ease; you are immortal whether you want to be or not"—one cannot speak more reassuringly, unless this turns out to be exactly what is disquieting. But if it is disquieting, then it must have been deceit in the mouth and in the heart of the person who so eagerly would like etc. And if he was deceitful, then his disquiet is not my fault, since I must have spoken to his disquiet if what he said was true in him. If there was deceit in him, then he was really the very opposite of what he claimed to be, he was afraid of immortality—therefore he so eagerly would like to have it *demonstrated*, because he dimly understood that by becoming an object of demonstrations immortality is hurled from the throne, deposed, a powerless wretch one can make sport of as the Philistines did of the captive Samson.[41]

There is a shrewdness in humankind, in the human race, that is more cunning than the shrewdest statesman. It is this very shrewdness of the human race that has managed to get the position of immortality turned wrong. The individuals are always far from understanding how sly this whole thing is and therefore with a kind of gullibility say what is almost in the air because it lies in human nature. It is the human race that has wanted to rebel against God; it is the human race that has wanted to abolish immortality and has managed to have it made into a problem. With immortality (and what it implies, the immortality of every *individual*), God is the lord and ruler, and *the single individual* relates himself to him. But when immortality becomes a problem, then God is abolished and the human race is God. The individuals perhaps do not perceive how they are in the power of the human race and that it is the human race that is speaking through them; therefore they think that the person who calls to them and calls them *individuals* is a rebel—and so he is indeed; in the name of God he rebels against making the human race into God and immortality into a problem. In the name of God he rebels, and he appeals to God's word: that there will be the resurrection of the dead, of the righteous—and of the unrighteous!

V

We Are Closer to Salvation Now—Than When We Became Believers[42]

"My God, where are we?" shouts the ship captain in the dead of
night when the ship refuses to obey the rudder and no stars are
visible, when everything is pitch dark, while the storm is raging,
when every determination of location is impossible—"My God,
where are we!" But the one who in these times is to proclaim
Christianity, must not he also say: Where are we! We are in
Christendom, yes, it is true; there—so and so many Christians are
born every year, there so many are baptized, there so many are
confirmed; we are so and so many Christians, just about as many
as there are inhabitants in the land, but what does that mean? Is
it a determination of location? Or should the one who proclaims
Christianity keep the whole matter at a distance from actuality in
order not to come too close, speak about Christianity but leave
undecided to whom it is that he speaks? Is he to speak about our
being closer to salvation now than when we became believers
but to leave altogether unspecified who these "we" are, whether
it is those who are living now or those who lived centuries or
eighteen hundred years ago—is he to speak this way and in so
doing shadowbox, so that to proclaim Christianity is boxing in
the air?[43] Where are we! The one who is to speak about Christianity in Christendom, is he a missionary who is to propagate
Christianity—so that all this about Christendom is a delusion? Or
is he to assume that we all are Christians, or is he to make a
distinction, and if so, how is he to make a distinction—where
are we?

People in these times seem to be quite unaware of this difficulty. Christianity is regarded as a sum of doctrines; lectures are
given on it in the same way as on ancient philosophy, Hebrew,
or any branch of knowledge whatever, with the listener's or the

learner's relation to it left as a matter of indifference. Basically this is paganism. The essentially Christian is precisely this: the relation to Christianity is what is decisive. Someone can know all about Christianity, can know how to explain, discuss, expound—but if in addition he thinks that his own personal relation to Christianity is a matter of indifference, then he is a pagan. But, just as all regimes have been overthrown, so also has Christianity been overthrown. Rather than that it should rule over people, transform their lives, not only on Sunday but every day, intervene decisively in all relationships of life, it is kept at a scholarly distance as mere doctrine, the agreement between its various doctrines is shown—but your life and my life, the agreement or nonagreement of the lives of people with this doctrine—that is a matter of indifference.

This is why we have chosen these words to speak about. Lest this discourse be altogether meaningless, we must in one way or another come closer to people, or rather prompt them to come closer to themselves. This is what we want to do. It is not at all our intention to judge Christendom or any single person in Christendom; we are doing our best to come as close as possible to ourselves, the best way to keep us from coming judgingly too close to others. But it is indeed our intention to give the listener occasion to become aware of where *he* is, to test himself, his life, his Christianity. And to discuss these words "we are closer now" etc. without determining who *we* are would be just as futile as to journey from Copenhagen to Jerusalem on a map. To discuss these words without determining this *now* and this *when* is just as meaningless as to travel in imagination from one planet to another.

We are closer to salvation now— than when we became believers.

Every determination of location always requires two points. To say that a city lies *there*, that a road goes *there*, that a man lives *there* is to make a fool of the person with whom one is speaking and to make a fool of oneself if one did not intend to banter with the other but meant to speak earnestly. If there is to be any sense or earnestness in the discourse, and if the person spoken to is to have any benefit from it, there must be one given point, the location of which he knows, a point in relation to which one then determines the *there*. The reason a stranger gets lost in the desert and a person experiences giddiness at sea is that he has no *there* in relation to which he can determine where he is, or that he has no point in relation to which he can determine the *there*.[44]

The same applies to the determination of time. If I am to determine where I am *now*, I must have another definite point of time in relation to which I determine this *now*. Therefore the verse chosen as the subject of this discourse quite properly has another determinant with the aid of which those speaking determine this *now*: We are closer to salvation *now* than *when* we became believers. This makes excellent sense. If a man says, "I am now further along in this and that work than when I began," it makes sense and there is a determination of time; he has one point of time with the aid of which it is firmly established that he has begun, and he measures the distance from the beginning to see where he is now. But if this man had never begun this work, well, then his talk makes no sense; it is meaningless to say that one is closer *now* than *when* one began if one did not begin at all. If someone who had never become a believer were to repeat unthinkingly these words, "We are closer to salvation now than when we became believers," it would be meaningless.

Apply these words to yourself, then, in order to test your own life with their aid and to find out where you are *now*. If you are to learn this, you must first of all make sure that you know definitely when that time was *when* you became a believer, or that the decision has taken place in your life so that you became a believer. Are you really aware of this difficulty that comes, as it were, from behind? The question is not whether you have gone backward since the time you became a believer, whether you have abandoned the faith. One could indeed draw a conclusion in this way: it is self-evident that I am closer to salvation *now* than *when* I became a believer, because *now* is a later moment than *when*; therefore it is self-evident, unless, as said, you have since that time abandoned the faith. Nothing, however, is self-evident if it is not certain that at some time you became a believer, that you have experienced the moment when you became a believer.

When, then, did you become a believer? It is of enormous importance that you get this determined if you are going to be able to
determine where you are *now*. And if the circumstances of life are
of such a nature that they may contribute to leaving it in a haze
of uncertainty as to whether you actually did become a believer,
then you certainly realize how close to meaninglessness you are,
how it seems to inclose you, and realize how easily you could
spend your whole life in meaninglessness—and therefore how
important it is that you tear yourself out of all the illusions that
will prevent you from finding out whether you ever did become
a believer, all the illusions that will help you even to be able to
listen to a sermon on this text, "We are closer to salvation now
than when we became believers," without discovering that these
words sound like a mockery of you, who still remain entirely
calm, convinced in your meaninglessness that *now* you are closer
to salvation than *when* you became a believer—you who never
did become a believer. But perhaps you had been made aware of
this, so that you tested yourself as to whether you had not later
denied the faith. In this regard you were meanwhile conscious of
nothing; you ransacked your life but found that you boldly dared
to say that you had never denied or consciously abandoned the
faith. Thus you must indeed also be closer to salvation *now* than
at the time *when* you became a believer. Alas, it remained hidden
for you that the tragedy was that you never did become a believer; so only to that extent was it correct that you certainly had
not—later abandoned it.

When did you become a believer or, it amounts to the same
thing, are you essentially conscious that you have experienced
this decision to become a believer? It is not important whether it
was at twelve o'clock noon and the like. No, it is all a spiritual
matter and therefore has true earnestness, which certainly does
not ask the hour or the minute. But on the other hand it is also
obvious that it would become a game like "Go to the Next
House"[45] if a person, if asked as an old man when he became a
believer, would answer, "Well, it was a long time ago." "As an
adult, perhaps?" "No, it was longer ago than that." "Was it as a
youth, then?" "No, it was longer ago than that. In short, it was
so long ago that I cannot remember when." It is obvious that this

would become a game and that then it is meaningless for this man to say where he is *now* with regard to his salvation if the decision by which he became a believer recedes into the dimness of fable and fairy tale.

When did you become a believer; have you become a believer? It is, of course, not the same today as in those difficult times when a Jew or a pagan became a Christian at a more mature age, because he readily knew definitely when and that he had become a believer. Now we live in a—more favorable situation, in Christendom; now it is much easier to become a Christian—at least it is much easier to be fooled into passing one's whole life under a delusion. You are baptized as an infant, brought up in the Christian religion, are confirmed; everyone regards you as a Christian, and you call yourself a Christian when there is some occasion to state your name, your occupation, and your religion. Whether you are going to be a merchant or scholar or artist or soldier etc., whether you are going to marry this one or that one, where you are going to live, in the city or out in the country, etc.—you no doubt at some time in your life have had occasion to put all such questions to yourself and to reply; you will also be able to say *when* and therefore in all these matters will be able to decide where you are *now*. But the question whether you have become a believer has perhaps never come up for you at all; as long as you can remember, it has been assumed that you were a believer; so you certainly must also have become that at some time—God knows when.

And where are you **now**; are you closer to your salvation **now**? You surely have heard about that simple wise man of old who was so artful in asking questions.[46] This question may very well sound like the kind intended to put one in an awkward position, to expose the muddleheadedness of the person being questioned. I now neither wish nor am able to ask you, but imagine that it was he, that simple wise man, who asked you. Even in Christendom, you know, the catechetical art is patterned on him, but no catechist has ever been able to ask questions as he did. Imagine this simple wise man, this determined hater of all evasions and excuses and muddleheadedness and dubiousness, and in addition the equally shrewd, cunning, deft, and undaunted ferreter of the same; he who had no doctrine that he expounded at a distance to people but as a teacher so probed people to the core that to the person conversing with him it seemed as if he were conversing with himself, as if his innermost being became disclosed to him; he who not only fetched wisdom down from heaven but knew how to make it penetrate into "the single individual."[47] Imagine that it is this simple wise man who is questioning you; imagine how he could go on teasing a person with the question whether he is closer to his salvation *now*; imagine how he could turn and twist this question in countless ways, but always teasingly, always with that smile on his face that was so characteristic of him when he surmised that the person with whom he was talking did not himself know definitely what was what, whether he did or did not understand something, whether he had become a believer or had not become a believer. Imagine his persistence, until he, the simple man, trapped the one being questioned and managed to make it clear that he had been under an illusion. "Are you closer to it (salvation) *now*?" "Yes." "But closer than when?" Well, here perhaps it stops, and if it stops here, this pause acquires the power to throw the whole conversation into confusion. You are *closer* now; this "closer" is a comparison, but with what are you comparing? Can one say that one person is larger than another who simply does not exist? There is something tempting, something persuasive in this "more" of comparison; it coaxes one, as if it were quite easy, as if one should not be disheartened, because at least it is going forward. But if it is not firmly fixed that there was a beginning, then all this coaxing ends only in meaninglessness. Just as someone on board a ship never leaves the ship no matter how many hours he walks the deck and how many miles he covers, so also the person who never began the course that takes one closer and closer does not come closer to something. But the way to deliverance is faith, and only when it is definitely fixed that one has become a believer can there be any mention of being closer *now*.

Where are you now; are you closer to your **salvation** *now?* Your salvation! It is your salvation that is being discussed, coming closer to one's own salvation. And if that is what the discussion is about, then something else is indeed being discussed at the

same time—namely, perdition. Your perdition! The discussion is
about your perdition, about sinking deeper and deeper into perdition! See, if you made a mistake in life and became a grocer
when you actually should have been an artist—well, good Lord,
that can be hard enough but the bad luck can still be surmounted.
If you made a mistake in life, if you married the girl, but her sister
would have suited you much better—well, good Lord, one can
resign oneself to missing out on one's luck in this way. But what
if a person missed out on his salvation! See, if at the peak of your
youthful energy you conceived a plan for a gigantic work you
wanted to carry out and that would be your life work, but you
were delayed along the way, you were hindered in many ways,
nor were your capacities up to it; in short, at the end of your life
you had not come much closer to accomplishing the task than
you were at the beginning—well, good Lord, there is consolation for this sorrow also. But what if at the end of your life you
had not come closer to your salvation! Is there anything more
terrible than to be at a distance from one's salvation? To be at a
distance from one's salvation, to be in this condition, this, after
all, means to distance oneself more and more. Salvation corresponds to being in danger; the one who is not in danger cannot
be saved either. Therefore if you are in danger and you do not
come closer to your salvation—then you are of course sinking
deeper and deeper into danger. Just as the shipwrecked person
who saved himself by means of a plank and now, tossed by the
waves and hovering over the abyss between life and death, strains
his eyes for land, so indeed should a person be concerned about
his salvation. But can a person be further away from his salvation
than when he does not even know definitely whether he has
begun to want to be saved?

Test yourself, then, with the help of these words. It is a blessed
comfort to dare to know "that one is closer to one's salvation
now than when one became a believer"—but is it not true that
then one must be sure that one has become a believer? These
words, therefore, can serve as comfort, but they can also, so to
speak, take one by surprise. If it so happens that a person becomes aware of this, it certainly is terrifying—oh, but even in this
terror, in this salutary terror, there is some comfort. There is

some comfort, because when a person has become aware that he has not even begun, he is always somewhat *closer* to his salvation than he was as long as he went on living secure in an illusion and a delusion.

Just one more thing—let us not forget that the words in the apostle's mouth sound somewhat different from the words as we have used them. He says, "Our salvation is closer now than when we became believers." The words as we have used them concentrate all thought on self-activity and therefore are used to make people aware. The apostolic words also stress that salvation is from God. He does not say *that we come closer to salvation* but *that salvation comes closer to us*. It could be necessary to discuss this also, so that *the believer* would be reminded not to be in a hurry, not to think that he himself will acquire what essentially is given. It could very well be necessary to speak about this—if only it is always clear where we are. But in order to become aware of that, we must first know whether we have become believers.

VI

But It Is Blessed—to Suffer Mockery for a Good Cause[48]

"Blessedness [*Salighed*[49]]" is certainly the highest good; what holds true of the lesser goods must also hold true of this good. In other words, if a speaker or a poet really wanted to describe the gloriousness of one or another earthly good, would he not make people desire it so they would scarcely be able to keep calm during the discourse but would impatiently want to be off to lay hold of it? And how very justified would not their rage be at this speaker because he had only dangled the desirable good before their eyes and then ended the speech by saying that it was chance that distributed these goods! If this had not been the case, they might well have thought that they could never adequately thank the speaker who knew how to describe so invitingly and so enchantingly the goods that everyone could possess. But *blessedness* is the highest good, and every person can come into possession of this good. Therefore it may be assumed that people would scarcely be able to listen to the discourse to the end in their impatience to acquire this good, the highest good, which every person can acquire. It may be assumed that the concern will awaken in them whether the moment spent listening to the discourse was not indeed almost a wasted moment, since in the strictest sense it was not used for acquiring this good.

We have such a discourse on blessedness[50] from a time long vanished. It was delivered on a mountain, afterward called Mount of the Beatitudes—because blessedness, compared with all earthly goods, is solid and unshaken like a mountain, and similarly blessedness, compared with all earthly goods, is elevated like a mountain over the low-lying regions. This discourse was delivered by *him*, the only one who from the very first could talk about blessedness, since this is linked to his name, the only name[51] in which there is blessedness. In this discourse it says: "Blessed are those who suffer persecution for the sake of righteousness, for theirs is the kingdom of heaven. Blessed are you when people insult and persecute you and speak every kind of evil against you for my sake and lie. Rejoice and be glad, for your reward will be great in heaven; so have they persecuted the prophets who were before you."[52]

These words will be the basis for the following discourse:

But it is blessed—to suffer mockery for a good cause,

in order that really for upbuilding we might become aware of the comfort, or rather, the joy, that Christianity proclaims, because these discourses are for upbuilding even if they, as is said, wound from behind.

But lest, alas, this joy be taken in vain in any way, let us therefore first repeat for verification the only conditions under which this can be said to be blessed. It must be for a good cause that one suffers mockery, or as Christ says, "for the sake of righteousness." And what the mockery says about one must be untrue, as Christ says, "when people speak every kind of evil against you and lie." But if this is the case, if everything in this regard is as it should be, then it is blessed—to suffer mockery.

Be comforted, then, you who are mocked, or rather, rejoice, you who are mocked! —What is the only thing that can deprive a person of the joy of having done a good deed? It is to receive a reward for it. But what if you are rewarded with mockery! All other repayment diminishes the good one has done; the repayment of mockery increases it: how blessed to suffer mockery for a good cause! —What is the only instance in which a person can have genuine merit? When he suffers because he does right. If he does right and is rewarded, he is an unworthy servant and has no merit;[53] how blessed, therefore, to suffer mockery for a good cause!

What is necessary for mutual understanding? Likeness; only like understands like. What is required for a covenant? Dedication; only the dedicated one is in covenant with the dedicated. Those glorious ones whom humankind disowned, mocked, insulted, persecuted, put to death—they certainly do exist for all people; many perhaps are able to give an account of their lives and describe them. But this understanding is that of the undedicated person, for whom those glorious ones do not exist in a deeper sense since they are not understood by him, just as they do not understand him. Only that person understood them and was understood, only that person was dedicated in covenant with them, only that person who himself suffered in like manner— how blessed to suffer mockery for a good cause!

What does the one inquire about who must change his residence for a time, must move from the city to the country or from the country to the city? He asks about the society. But the one who is mocked, when he some day must move away and wander, when he leaves the society in which he has lived and been mocked—then he, by having suffered mockery, has for an eternity secured for himself the society of those glorious ones, intimate, daily association with them, the innermost understanding of loving conversation with them—how blessed, therefore, to suffer mockery for a good cause!

What is the only distinction God makes? The one between right and wrong. And what distinction does he make? That he is wrath and malediction upon the one who does wrong.[54] In making this distinction, he makes still another: the distinction between the one who does right and is rewarded for it and the one who does right and suffers for it. But the greater the distinction he makes, the closer to him is the person who relates himself to him in this distinction: how blessed, therefore, to suffer mockery for a good cause!

Why does God never leave himself without witness?[55] Because in being good he is *unchanged*, the same, the same unchanged one.[56] When today, as thousands of years ago, all creation looks to him and asks for food and clothing, he opens his generous hand and satisfies with blessing everything that lives.[57] But when the one who suffers innocently for a good cause looks pleadingly to God, this look *moves* him, this look that is capable of doing nothing on earth, nothing at all, *moves* God; it constrains him to an even stronger witness: how blessed, therefore, to suffer mockery for a good cause!

What communion between human beings is the most deeply felt? The communion of suffering. Which of a person's communions is the most blessed? The communion with God. But when this is a communion of suffering, how blessed: how blessed to suffer mockery for a good cause!

Who has more: the one who has God and also something else, or the one who, deprived of everything else, has God alone? Surely the latter, since "all else is loss."[58] But who was deprived of more? The one who received not what was his right but mockery as his reward; the only thing a person has essentially is the right he has—he has everything else only accidentally; therefore it is not really his possession. The one who is mocked is deprived of everything; isolated from human society, he has only God—he the richest of all. He has only God—how blessed to be alone in having God. Praised be all the persecution, the scorn, the mockery that taught him, that compelled him, to be alone with God, to have only God—how blessed to suffer mockery for a good cause!

X
225

Where is Christ present? Wherever his name is called upon; even if only two or three are gathered in his name, he is present there.[59] Yes, and where someone suffers innocently for the sake of righteousness and calls upon his name, *there*, in addition to the voice that calls upon him, is something that calls upon him even more powerfully, and therefore the communion of his sufferings[60] and the power of his resurrection are *there*: how blessed to suffer mockery for a good cause!

What does a person desire as the highest reward? To have his name inscribed immortally in the annals of history. But that the person who is mocked, just by suffering mockery, receives the highest reward—has his name inscribed in the Book of Life![61] All of us are indeed immortal, also those who do wrong, also the most ungodly of all the ungodly. But to have one's name inscribed in the Book of Life: how blessed to suffer mockery for a good cause! What blessed, blessed comfort, what blessed, blessed joy!

But to whom is the discourse addressed—where is he, has he not completely forgotten himself! Perhaps there is no one at all in this most honorable gathering who has been mocked; perhaps, but no, that is an impossibility; how would a victim of mockery dare to venture into this most honorable gathering! After all, one cannot simultaneously be mocked and then be together where the honored and esteemed are assembled. The one who is mocked is indeed like a leper; his place is assigned among the graves, shunned by everyone.[62] "Yes, but he is being mocked for a good cause." But by whom, then, is he mocked? Certainly not by those who are themselves despised, since that is to be among the esteemed. Nor can the victim of mockery simultaneously be mocked and, by the same people who mock him, also be honored because he is mocked for a good cause; [63]not even in comedy could the same people be used simultaneously in two places: to mock him and to honor him because he is being mocked. What a strange difficulty!

Strangely enough, this difficulty does not appear when one looks at history. See, that truth-witness, it is now several centuries since he lived, but when he was living he was mocked and persecuted. In serving the truth, he had gained such a lead that limping justice could not overtake him as long as he lived, especially since, without hanging back one moment for limping justice, he made giant steps forward every day. Then he died and became still in the grave—then limping justice caught up to him: his name is honored and praised in history. We are now so accustomed to honoring and praising it that eventually someone will no doubt make the mistake of believing that he was honored and esteemed while he was living. Time exercises its foreshortening power. His name lives now, honored and praised for three centuries—and he, well, he indeed lived the customary human span of only sixty to seventy years—thus we can almost say that he has continually lived honored and esteemed. Well, yes, in a way, if one wishes to talk at random—otherwise, not. He has never lived honored and esteemed—he lived despised, persecuted, and derided as long as he lived. And at the time he was living, it certainly must have been the honored and esteemed who despised him—just as it is now the honored and esteemed who praise his name. But the truth-witness triumphed, and just as in other ways he changed the shape of the world, so also did he change the conception of honor: after his death he became the honored one, and his contemporaries, the honored and the esteemed at the time, now stand in another light. As long as he was living, this was not the case. Then he had to comfort himself with Christianity's doctrine: it is blessed to suffer for the sake of righteousness; he has both verified and understood these words. Whereas by looking at history backward many get only confusion out of it, Christianity, on the other hand, turns unchanged to the one who is living and proclaims to him that it is blessed—to suffer mockery for a good cause.

This means that on the whole Christianity is suspicious of being honored and esteemed in one's lifetime. Far be it from Christianity to be so foolish as to say that everyone who was mocked while he lived was on the right road. It only says: The true Christian must normally be found among those who were mocked while they lived. This is Christianity's view: what is eternal, what is true, cannot possibly win the approval of the moment, must inevitably win its disapproval. Thus Christianity does not understand being among the honored and esteemed simply as being in high positions and offices—something it is especially important to emphasize and indefensible to suppress in regard to the claim of this age, rebellious against all rule, that this rebellion is even supposed to be Christianity. It is also certain that such a life in power and eminence is often led in genuine sacrifice of being really honored and esteemed. No, from the Christian point of view, to be honored and esteemed is this: forgetting the eternal, idolatrously only to be in the service of and solely to belong to and never belong to anything else than what has power at the moment, to live only for the moment, to covet the moment first[64] and foremost and in so doing to harvest the applause of the moment, that is, to use a foreign word, it is to be in *Velten*[65] (and Christianity is not fond of the world); it is to be on top; it is, as is said of a certain kind of culture, to be a man of the world—in short, it is worldliness. Christianity, on the other hand, requires self-denial with regard to honor and prestige, even more definitely than with regard to money. Money is something purely external, but honor is a concept. The Christian is all the more committed to reject all this honor and prestige. To be a Christian is a matter of honor, and therefore every Christian is bound by his own and Christianity's honor to safeguard the true concept of honor lest by accepting the honor and respect of worldliness and the applause of the moment he become an accomplice in the dissemination of the false concept.

But to whom is this discourse addressed? Does it not, instead of utilizing the time and place, disappoint every reasonable expectation that might expect that *here* would be discussed what a great good honor and prestige are, how glorious it is to be honored and esteemed, as well as by what means one gains this very important good, since indeed, as the proverb says, "He who loses his honor cuts off his right hand," and therefore he is incapable of accomplishing anything—which is seen in the example of the apostles and all the truth-witnesses, since they have been incapable of accomplishing anything. To be sure, the discourse disappoints this expectation, but nevertheless certainly not the expectation of the one who expected that it would proclaim Christianity.

"But is it still not a great good to be honored and esteemed?" The discourse knows nothing at all about that; it knows only that it is blessed to suffer mockery for a good cause, and that this is Christianity. "But did that not hold true only in the first years of Christianity when it was contending with Jews and pagans; should the same be the case in Christendom, in the Church triumphant?" Well, yes, it surely is obvious that if one imagined a place where none but true Christians lived, it obviously would have to be evidence that one was a true Christian if one had the approval of and was honored and esteemed by those who themselves wanted what is true and had the true conception, were eager for knowledge of the truth. But is this place the so-called Christendom? If so, then it would of course be the consummation—and then, then we would have to assume that Christ had become lost in thought, had forgotten himself, had forgotten to come again, inasmuch as his coming again indeed corresponds to the consummation. But Christ has not yet come again—and if he came again, came to his own people[66] in an even stricter sense of the word than before—what would his reception be in Christendom?

See, there is much that has made me wonder, much that I find strange and inexplicable. When I hear someone say the right thing—but it does not occur to him at all to do any of it—I am amazed and cannot understand him. But, for example, it has become a very common witticism—I have read it and heard it said so frequently, said by the most diverse people, but always palmed off as current coin that no one examines carefully, something one does only with rare, unknown foreign coins, since it is sufficiently well known as conventional coin, as a good idea, a felicitous comment a witty person once made and clever people vie with each other to repeat—If Christ came again to the world now, he would be crucified again, unless the death penalty had been abolished by this time. People drop this remark as casually as they say "Good day," only with greater pretentiousness; and people find it said so aptly and strikingly, and it does not occur at all, not in the remotest way, to the person who says it to question whether he himself is a Christian; it does not occur to the person who says it to become aware of this whole mirage of Christendom. Truly this is inexplicable to me. It has become almost a saying in Christendom that if Christ came again he would meet the same fate as before, when he came to non-Christians—and yet Christendom is supposed to be the Church triumphant, which presumably, when all is said and done, would add to its triumphs the new one of crucifying Christ. Well, it goes without saying that the "Church triumphant" has triumphed over the world in an external sense, that is, it has in a worldly way triumphed over the world (since triumphing over it in the religious sense can be done only internally)—so, just as for all victors, there is only one victory left—to triumph over oneself, to become a Christian. As long as one is not aware of this, the concept "Christendom" is the most dangerous of all illusions. In Christendom, therefore, Christianity is continually still militant. No more than the person who has bought and had beautifully bound the books he needs to use for his studies and final examination for a university degree can be truthfully said to have taken his examination, no more is Christendom in the Christian sense the Church triumphant. There may be quite a number of true Christians in Christendom, but every such one is also militant.

"But is it actually Christianity's intention to recommend the suffering of mockery even if it is for a good cause? It is something else, after all, to have comfort in readiness for the one who was so unfortunate as to come to grief in this manner." Indeed, that is something else, but this something else is simply not the essentially Christian. There must remain no dubiousness as to how this is to be understood. The words in Matthew read as follows: "Blessed are you when people insult and persecute you and speak every kind of evil against you for my sake and lie. Rejoice and be glad, your reward will be great in heaven; so have they persecuted the prophets who were before you." The corresponding passage in Luke (6:26) reads as follows: "Woe to you when all people speak well of you; their fathers did the very same with the false prophets." Woe to you when all speak well of you! "And lie" is not added here. Presumably it is not necessary; it is assumed that if all speak well of someone it is a lie, and that one's life is a lie. Woe to you when all people speak well of you! That is, it is Christianity's meaning (and if this were not its meaning, there would be no meaning in Christianity) that a person is to have his life in such decisiveness, is to confess so definitely and publicly what he wants, what he believes and hopes, that it is impossible for all to speak well of him. To reach this can perhaps be quite difficult, this perniciousness, that all speak well of one, but should it succeed, it can succeed only for a sagacious, cowardly flabbiness that Christianity abhors and condemns. If it is to succeed, a person must be like a reed in the wind,[67] since even the smallest bush still puts up a little resistance; he must be devoid of a more profound conviction, empty in his innermost being, so that, if you were to compare the age to the weather, he can easily be blown away by any breeze, and, if you compare the age to a stream, he can just as readily float easily upon it. He must never be courageous except when the many are cowardly. He must be silent when he should speak, speak when he should be silent; he must say yes when he should say no, and no when he should say yes; he must answer evasively when he should answer decisively, decisively even if it means death. He must sleep when he should stay awake—indeed, do his best to keep others awake. He must flee every danger in which the abandoned truth may be and join up with every popular folly; he must completely forget God and the responsibility of eternity and everything that is high and holy—then perhaps he can succeed—woe to him! As seen from Christ's words, this is not only the most wretched posthumous reputation a person can leave behind, that all spoke well of him, but it is the judgment: woe to him that he succeeded! Either he must have been a dastardly inhuman wretch who out of fear of people went so far as to despise himself or he must have been a false prophet.

Yet it is blessed—to suffer mockery for a good cause! Woe to you when all speak well of you. There remains no dubiousness as to how these words are to be understood. It is blessed to suffer mockery for a good cause, and this is Christianity.

Is this difficult to understand? Not at all. Is it difficult to say? Not at all, at least not if the one to whom it is spoken is left completely unspecified. But is it possible for the discourse to bring about one specific effect? No, the effect the discourse will bring about depends on who the listener is. The difficulty with the essentially Christian emerges every time it is to be *made present*, every time it is to be said as it is and said now, at this moment, at this specific moment of actuality, and said to those, precisely to those [68]who are living now.[69] This is why people like very much to keep the essentially Christian at a little distance. Either they do not want to say it exactly as it is (so it is, of course, at a distance) *or they want to let it remain unspecified whether it is really to those who are living now that it is addressed.* [70]Therefore the speaker shadow-boxes and says, "That is how wrong it was eighteen hundred years ago, and seventeen hundred years ago, and a thousand years ago, and three hundred years ago, and fifty years ago, and thirty-three years ago; but now it is not that way." How strange! And if one stares fixedly at the reassuring speaker to see whether he is absolutely certain about what he is saying, he becomes a bit uneasy at this glance that falls upon him unexpectedly and, wavering somewhat, momentarily abandons his manuscript and adds extemporaneously, "Yes, well—I will not say that the world has become perfect, but it is not quite like that now, at least not in most recent times." How strange! This much is certain—if one goes through the calculation in reverse, at that time it was just the same as it is now. Seventeen hundred years ago, people said, "It was that way a hundred years ago, but it is not that way now—well, perhaps it is not quite like that now, at least not in most recent times." And three hundred years ago, people said, "It was that way fifteen hundred years ago and a thousand years ago and three hundred years ago, but it is not that way now—well, perhaps it is not quite like that now, at least not in most recent times." There must be something underneath this "most recent times." Indeed there is! One goes as close to it as possible if only one can avoid speaking to the living—and the living, of course, are the most recent times. If an audience of young people was being addressed, one certainly would say, "the very most recent times," because, since the very old and the elderly would not be present, one can readily chastise them—but particularly the dead; one chastises them severely, despite the beautiful rule about speaking only good of the dead.

So this is how it is with Christianity's doctrine that it is blessed to suffer mockery. If this is to be spoken in a moment of actuality, the discourse must find a group of the moment's honored and esteemed. If, then, the discourse addresses itself to such an assembly, then Christianity's blessed comfort, its joy, will sound like the most profound sarcasm. This is not due to the discourse. But it certainly would be difficult for a poet to invent a more profound sarcasm than this: Christianity's doctrine about blessedness delivered before an assembly of—Christians who have their lives in altogether different categories and who therefore, although they call themselves Christians, would prefer to decline with thanks that kind of comfort and who very likely would find it enough to drive one mad that the object of their greatest dread is supposed to be comfort.[71] Imagine a gathering of worldly-minded, timorous people whose highest law in everything is a slavish regard for what others, what "they" will say and judge, whose sole concern is that unchristian concern that "everywhere *they* speak well" of them, whose admired goal is to be just like the others, whose sole inspiring and whose sole terrifying idea is the majority, the crowd, its approval— its disapproval. Imagine such an assembly or crowd of worshipers and devotees of the fear of people, that is, an assembly of the honored and esteemed (why should such people not honor and esteem one another—to honor the other is, after all, to flatter oneself!)—and imagine that this assembly is supposed (yes, as it is in a comedy), is supposed to be Christians. Before this Christian assembly a sermon is delivered on these words: It is blessed to suffer mockery for a good cause!

But it *is* blessed to suffer mockery for a good cause!

VII

He Was Believed in the World

I Timothy 3:16. And great beyond all question is the
mystery of godliness: God was revealed in the flesh,
was justified in the Spirit, seen by angels, preached
among the pagans, believed in the world, taken up in
glory.

My listener, you indeed readily recognize this Bible passage, recognize it from your earliest childhood; you know it by heart; you
have heard it quoted often, again and again, perhaps have quoted
it yourself. If someone refers to the first part of this passage, you
can add the rest from memory; if someone quotes a single part,
you promptly remember the rest. For memory, then, this passage
has acquired a roundness so that it almost involuntarily joins together what for it irrevocably belongs together. You can begin at
the end and at the beginning and in the middle, but wherever
you begin your memory is immediately able to put it all together
and you no doubt prefer to quote it complete.

Yet there is—but perhaps this has escaped your *attention*, because it does not pertain to *memory*—there is a very remarkable
difference between the separate statements. Or rather there is
one among them—if you catch sight of it or it, as it were, catches
sight of you, then everything is changed. In a strange way it takes
possession of you so that it does not occur at all to your memory
to want to add the rest, because this part gained a power over you
so that to you it is rather as if you had forgotten the rest, at least
for a moment. See, "God was manifested in the flesh" does not
pertain to you; it pertains to him. Neither does "he is justified in
the Spirit" pertain to you. It was he who was justified in the
Spirit. Nor was it you who "was seen by angels"; it was he. And

it was he who "was proclaimed among the pagans" and he who "was taken up in glory." But this "He was believed in the world"! This does pertain to you, does it not; it pertains to you. Take special care; if you are properly aware of this, it pertains to you alone, or it is for you as if it pertained only to you, you alone in the whole world!

It is of this we wish to speak:

He was believed in the world.

It seems, then, as if the apostle is saying only something historical about Christ, and so indeed he is. But in the middle of the historical he has used a few words that are directed to you. "He was believed in the world"; that is, have you, then, believed him? There perhaps is no way to question in such a penetrating, such a gripping way as just this. If one wishes to pose a question of conscience to a person, but precisely in such a way that it really becomes a question of conscience, that is, in such a way that it does not become something to which his reply to the questioner is yes or no (because then the relationship of conscience is already somewhat interfered with), but poses it in such a way that it becomes a question the person must answer for himself, so that this question establishes itself firmly in his inner being and gives him no rest until he answers it for himself before God—then one may do as follows.

One tells him a story. This now puts him completely at ease, because he understands well enough that since it is a story the discourse is not about him. A few words are introduced into this story that perhaps do not immediately have their effect but sometime later are suddenly transformed into a question of conscience. In this way the matter becomes all the more inward. Paul does not come to you and ask you if you have believed, with a demand to hear your yes or your no, but he says, "He was believed in the world"—now it is left up to you yourself, to your conscience, to answer for yourself. This may be called placing a question on someone's conscience, and the one on whom it has this effect may be said to understand that he is being asked a question. Strangely enough, over the centuries countless interpretations of this passage have been written, difficulties have been created and difficulties have been removed; every part has been gone through in prolix and detailed exposition. The only part, as far as I know, that has not been made the object of interpretation (naturally because it was found so easy to understand that every child can understand it) is precisely this, "He was believed in the world." It is indeed easy to understand, but nevertheless watch out—this part is the question to *you*.

You surely are living in the world, are you not? Then when it is said, "He was believed in the world," the occasion has been placed as close as possible for you to ask yourself: Have I, then, believed in him? But who is it indeed who is asking the question? No one, no one! Yet you know very well that the most terrible, the most earnest question is the one of which it must be said: There is no one who is asking the question, and yet there is a question—and a question to *you personally*. If that is the case, then it is the conscience that is asking the question.

You no doubt have also heard about that shrewd person[72] who thought it impossible for *anyone* to outwit him with a question that he would not be able to answer in such a way that the questioner would become the victim; you have no doubt heard that the only thing he feared, sure of getting the worst of it, was the situation in which there was *no one* who asked him the question. You no doubt have personally sensed the solemnity there can be in the solitude of the forest, out there in the open, when one is utterly alone in the stillness of the night, when everything is sleeping—that is, how solemn it is when there is *no one*; as soon as there is *someone*, the solemnity is diminished. There, where there is *no one* who asks and where there nevertheless is a personal question, an invisible one is there, the questioner; there in the deepest sense *you* are involved with yourself, and this is the relationship of conscience. Therefore this question has such fearful power, because when someone asks you a question, you can manage to deceive him if it does not please you to answer him, or you can become angry with him and indignantly ask him who he is that he dares to ask you this question, what right does he have to do that; but here—here it is no one!

He was believed in the world. Yes, it is altogether certain; you know how many thousands have believed in him, have lived in this faith, and have died in this faith. And yet, no, this is not so. If you yourself do not believe, then you cannot know whether there is one who has believed in him; and if you yourself believe, then you know that he was believed in the world, that there is one who has believed in him. One person cannot peer into another person's heart, where faith lives, or rather, where it is seen whether faith is present or not—that is, only the single individual knows in himself before God whether or not he believes. Everyone else must be satisfied with the *assurance.* Therefore you cannot know that so and so many thousands have believed; you know only (for you surely will not claim or pretend to know what *cannot be known*) that so and so many have affirmed that they have believed, that so and so many have died for this faith—but what am I saying, you of course do not know that; you know only that they have been put to death for this faith (by those who still could not know whether they had this faith); you know only that they have affirmed that they died for this faith. More you do not know. This is not because your knowledge is limited but because of the limitation placed on all human knowledge—namely, that it is not the omniscience of the Knower of Hearts. This is not because you know only a few people; on the contrary, the more people you are thinking about, the less, of course, can there be any question of penetrating into their innermost being, the more necessary it is to be content with the assurance. But even if you selected one single person whom you made the object of all your attention—you cannot know whether he is a believer; you can know only that he affirms it. If you yourself have never been in love, you do not know whether anyone has ever been loved in this world, although you do know how many have affirmed that they have loved, have affirmed that they have sacrificed their lives for erotic love [*Elskov*]. But whether they actually have loved, you cannot know; and if you yourself have loved, then you know that you have loved. The blind person cannot know color differences; he must be content that others have assured him that they do exist and that they are thus and so.

Do not say that this stretches [*spaende*] thought too much, that this is an extravagance [*Overspaendthed*]. Far from it, this is precisely earnestness. Indeed, what is more earnest than the question

whether *you* have believed or not? See, therefore it is in the nature of faith to ward off all curiosity in order to concentrate the
entire mind on earnestness; therefore it is the nature of faith to
want above all to prevent the error that one can acquire or have
faith at second hand. And therefore it is of service to you properly
to understand that you cannot actually know whether another
person has believed. In order that all the power and the attention
of mind, which otherwise diverted could be wasted on being
busy with the question and curiosity about other people's faith,
can be concentrated in the service of earnestness, it is of service
to you (instead of light-mindedly running with the others—in
missing out on faith) that you come to feel the full weight of the
truth that it is you who alone are assigned to yourself, have nothing, nothing at all, to do with others, but have all the more, or
rather, everything to do with yourself, that concerning faith you
actually can know nothing about others. *Historically* the question
is how many have believed—that is the question history poses.
But faith is certainly not history. Faith's question, on the other
hand, is to *you*: Have *you* believed? This question pertains to
faith, the other to history. Faith is related to the personality. But
if *I* have believed, then in the personal sense how many and how
many also have believed is unimportant; and if *I* have not believed, then it is unimportant how many and how many have
believed or have not believed.

The question about how many have believed is a historical
question. "Now, since there are so and so many, so countless
many who have believed, then whether or not I have faith is
nothing to make a fuss about; then I do of course have it since so
many have it. No, if faith were something with which a person
is alone, well, that would be another matter." But you are indeed
alone with faith—if you have it; if you are not alone with it, then
you do not have it either. Is this mad vanity, is it an arrogant
derangement that can lead only to losing one's mind? No, it is
earnestness, the only thing, if you do not have faith, that can lead
you to having it, the only thing, if you have faith, that can keep
you in it. Is it perhaps also mad vanity, is it also an arrogant
derangement that you, if death took away your beloved, do not
want to understand, do not want to hear anything about but are

only disgusted by this talk as something loathsome: that, if one assumes that the earth is populated by many thousand millions of people, people die by the thousands every day and presumably every day also many loved ones? I would think that it was madness if the soul of a person was so volatilized, so weakened, so abominably historically dissipated that it could completely escape him that the one who died was *his* beloved; I would think that this was the surest evidence that he had never loved. On the other hand, I would think that it was lovely, truly human, that it was earnestness, insofar as earnestness can be related to erotic love, when the lover in his sorrow over the loss of his beloved understood only one thing; that it was *his* beloved, that it was *he* who had lost *his* beloved. And I would also regard it as madness, evidence of such an inner weakening that earnestness was out of the question, if year after year someone could recite by rote this Bible verse, "He was believed in the world; He was believed in the world," without having the question ever occur to him, have *I* then believed in him?

He was believed in the world. Therefore the one who understood Paul understands that there is a question here. But if the one who understood it were to answer, "Yes, he certainly was believed in the world; with every century that passes one can say this with more and more justification; continually more and more people are becoming believers; Christianity has been propagated everywhere, and especially since the discovery of America"—I wonder if Paul would not feel as one feels, alas, when speaking with a deranged person. It unquestionably is derangement when that garrulous man talks continually about himself and his little journey,[73] but it is also derangement when one is asked about faith to talk about the whole world but not about oneself.

X
238

But the one who understood the question and answered, "*I* have believed in him," he understood himself. And if he answered, "*I* have not believed in him," he still understood himself. Instead of the historical "He was believed in the world," the personal is "I have believed in him," when the single individual says, "I have believed in him."

"I have believed very much about things in the world, what trustworthy men have told me about things I myself have not heard or seen, and I have believed the testimony of history; in daily life I have believed others in a great variety of ways. Among the things I have believed this way, there is much that is trivial that is forgotten the next day, much that has occupied me for a time, much that I converted into my soul's possession and reluctantly relinquished—but yet, suppose all of this to be untrue: I could still recover from this loss. But I have believed in him—if I am deceived here also, then I am not only the most wretched of all[74] but my life at its deepest root is annihilated, then everything else can neither benefit nor harm. I have not procrastinated year after year, waiting for ever new certainty in order to dare to believe—no, with a decision of eternity I have secured my life by believing in him—if he is a mirage, then my life is lost. But this is not the case, this I *believe*. I have also suffered through the spiritual trial of venturing everything upon uncertainty, which is to believe. But faith has conquered; I believe in him. If someone were to say to me, 'But what if!' I would no longer understand that. I understood it at one time, in the moment of decision; now I no longer understand it. If someone were to become anxious and afraid on my behalf, afraid that I have ventured out too far on an 'if' or despite an 'if'—then let him not feel sorry for me but rather for himself. I am not living on any 'if.' Dead set against an 'if' and troubled by this 'if,' I have ventured out (it is called taking a risk), and now I believe. But that which has to be understood first before one grasps faith, the word 'if,' is in turn the word and that which faith understands least of all."

This is how the single individual would have to speak. And let him go on speaking so that he can interpret this part of that Scripture passage, the part that ordinarily is never interpreted. Of course, no particular individual is speaking here; neither you nor I, and therefore it is a *poetical* attempt; this is the only thing the discourse wants: it wants to make it plain how one speaks as an individual.

"I have admired the noble, great, and glorious things that have been produced among people. I do not think I know it all, but I know that with regard to what I do know of it my soul is not unacquainted with the delight of admiration, its blissful joy, its simultaneously depressing and uplifting joy—so I do know what it is to admire. Perhaps I have known only very little of what is great, but that makes no difference here. Indeed, if it were the case, in this connection (where the discussion is not about how *much* one has admired but of how *much* one has admired what one has admired), if it were the case that I admired joyously, enthusiastically, and with total devotion the little I knew, it would add rather than subtract. To take an example that, humanly speaking, is unique in the world and that we usually place closest to Christianity, I have admired that noble, simple wise man of antiquity.[75] Reading about him has made my heart beat as violently as did the young man's heart when he[76] conversed with him; the thought of him has been the inspiration of my youth and has filled my soul; my longing for conversation with him has been entirely different from the longing for conversation with anyone with whom I have ever spoken. Many a time, after being together with those who have comprehended everything and know how to talk about everything possible, I have longed for his ignorance and to listen to him, who always said the same thing—'and about the same thing.'[77] I have admired his wisdom, that in his wisdom he became simple! That in his wisdom he became simple so that he could trap the sagacious![78] That in his wisdom he became simple so that, without having many thoughts and without using many words, he could devote his life in the service of truth—oh, what moving simplicity! That face-to-face with death he spoke about himself, the condemned one, just as simply as he ever did in the marketplace with a passerby on the most everyday subjects;[79] that with the cup of poison in his hand he maintained the beautiful festive mood and spoke just as simply as he ever did at a banquet[80]—oh, what sublime simplicity!

"But I have never believed in him; that has never occurred to me. I do not find it to be either wisdom or profundity to make a comparison between him, the simple wise man, and him in whom I believe—I find that to be blasphemy. As soon as I think about the matter of my eternal salvation, then he, the simple wise man, is a very unimportant person, a sheer nonentity, a nobody. Nor could I ever find it in my head or in my heart or on my lips to answer the blasphemous question: to whom of these two do

I owe more—the simple wise man or him in whom I believe? But, on the other hand, I truly can answer the question, to whom do I owe most—should I not know to whom I owe most, most of all, most beyond all comparison? To him, namely, in whom I have believed, to him who has given his life also for me, given his life, not as one person may do for another in order to *preserve* the other one's life—no, in order to *give* me life. Without him it is a matter of indifference whether I live or die; it is an empty phrase to say that someone has saved my life when this life he saved for me still amounts to being dead. But he is life; in the eternal sense I owe him life, him in whom I believe.

"In the feeling in which I am myself, I am deeply attached in filial devotion to the person to whom I owe life, but I beg to be excused from answering the question: to whom do I owe more, to him, my father, or to him in whom I have believed? If it were required of me, that is, if he required it of me, I would not hesitate to wound myself as deeply and inwardly as no human being could wound me, to relinquish a son's love—out of love for him in whom I believe. I love my wife as my own self. If it were possible that she could be unfaithful to me, I would sorrow as someone who in this regard had lost everything in the most grievous way, because I could love only one. If death takes her away from me, I will confess, and on my deathbed I will again confess, what I have always said—that she was my only love. But if he in whom I believe, if it were possible that he required it of me, I will relinquish this erotic love [*Elskov*]—out of love [*Kjerlighed*] for him in whom I believe. I patiently bear my own loss, and I bear all her anger and misunderstanding because she cannot understand me until she in eternity will understand me—he will see to that, he in whom I believe. I love my children. I will do everything for them that lies in a person's power; I would not know how I could sufficiently thank the one who in word and deed truly helped me to benefit them; I would give my life for them. But if he in whom I believe, if it were possible that he could request it of me, I would relinquish this love—out of love for him in whom I believe. I take upon myself the pain of faithful suffering and the burden of responsibility; I patiently bear every judgment of condemnation upon me, even that of my

X
241

loved ones, until they sometime in eternity will understand me—he will see to that, he in whom I believe. —So, then, I love very much, in various ways, to various degrees; but if he in whom I believe requires it of me, I will relinquish all this love— out of love for him in whom I believe.

"If someone were to say to me, 'That would really be a dreadful "if"; how is it possible to endure life with such an "if" that indeed must kill all zest for life, with such an "if" hanging over your head in the spiderweb of possibility? Moreover, is it not a kind of faithlessness to live in all these life relationships, in the most deeply intimate relationships to other persons, and then at any time to have thought an "if" like that'—then I would reply: Yes, it certainly is dreadful, terrifying, this "if"; I perceived this in the moment of decision when I became a believer. In this terror lies the daring act of faith. But, truly, one can live under this 'if' and not feel it as a weight of anxiety but as a blessing upon oneself. That this 'if' has existed for me is part of my covenant with him, and through this 'if' he blesses every relationship I have to what is beneficial for me to love. Without this 'if' it is impossible to believe, because the obedience of faith must go that far, but from that it does not follow that he requires this of me. And I do believe that it is his will that the son shall love his father, the husband his wife, the father his children, and so on—I do believe this to be his will, if there is not a difference of faith between them. Therefore it still is not faithlessness that I know such an 'if'—indeed it is faithlessness only to them who do not know and do not want to know him, who do not have and do not want to have faith. Therefore it is also impossible that I, on the basis of this 'if' (my soul's fear and trembling, but also my love, my only love, because in it I love him in whom I believe) would feel alienated in the circle of my loved ones with whom I have the faith in common. But I certainly do feel alienated in Christendom insofar as all Christendom is supposed to be only Christians, more alienated than if I lived among pagans. A person cannot be as alienated by the indifference to his faith on the part of those who have another faith, another God, as he must feel alienated by the indifference of those who say they have the same faith—to the same faith. It is one thing, after all, to be indifferent to what

x
242

occupies me when someone has something else that occupies him; it is another matter that two people are occupied with the same thing, and then the one is so indifferent to it and the other so occupied with it—and it is the same thing that occupies both! I feel alienated in Christendom, alienated because people in Christendom think that what occupies me early and late can at most occupy only those whose livelihood it is, but otherwise it would be eccentric and exaggerated if anyone would be occupied with this. From this I draw no conclusions regarding the extent to which all those who live in Christendom actually are believers. I know absolutely nothing about others with regard to faith. But this I do know, 'He was believed in the world,' and I know it quite simply from this, that I have believed in and do believe in him."

My listener, this is indeed also a creed, or at least a confession of faith. For a person to be a Christian, it certainly is required that what he believes is a *definite* something, but then with equal certainty it is also required that it be *entirely definite* that *he* believes. To the same degree that you draw attention exclusively to the definite something he is to believe, to the same degree *he* moves away from faith. To the same degree that one gives the appearance that it will be very difficult to make definite what it is that a person is to believe, to the same degree one leads people away from faith. God does not allow a species of fish to come into existence in a particular lake unless the plant that is its nourishment is also growing there. Therefore one can draw a conclusion in two ways: this plant grows here, ergo this fish is also here; but even more surely, this fish is found here, ergo this plant grows here. Truly, no more than God allows a species of fish to come into existence in a particular lake unless the plant that is its nourishment is also growing there, no more will God allow the truly concerned person to be ignorant of what he is to believe. That is, the need brings its nourishment along with it; what is sought is in the seeking that seeks it; faith is in the concern over not having faith; love is in the self-concern over not loving. The need brings the *nourishment* [*Næring*] along with it—oh, so near [*nær*] (the word indeed says it) it is, so near it is, if only the need is there. The need brings the nourishment along with it, not *by itself*, as if the need produced the nourishment, but by virtue of a divine determination that joins the two, the need and the nourishment. Consequently, if one says this is the case, one must add "as sure as there is a God"; if God did not exist, then neither would this be as it is.

Do not be deceived by appearances. There is much deception in the language of people's daily conversation. When, for example, someone says, "I had fully resolved to venture this and that for this and that cause, but then this one and that one talked me out of my resolution," this sounds quite acceptable. But the one who knows the human heart sees very well the connection: the man has not been resolved in the deepest sense, because then he would not have turned to this one and that one but would have acted. The one whom falling in love does not make silent is not in love, and so also with the true resolution. So is it also when someone living in Christendom says he would very much like to believe if only he could get settled definitely what he is to believe. This sounds quite acceptable, and yet there is deceit in it. He is unwilling to venture out into the dangers and decisions where faith comes into existence; he is unwilling to become alone, alone in the life-perils of the spirit, and therefore he speaks about this difficulty; in the anxiety of his soul he is not willing to risk everything, and therefore he talks in this other way. He who is the object of faith, he is surely a good deal nearer to a person than at the distance of eighteen hundred years through the submerged connection of tradition or, if there is the slightest doubt here, through the delays and possible misunderstandings of eighteen hundred years. The nearest way is the way of life-perils; the most comfortable way, which, however, does not lead to faith, is to begin to get busy about not being able to make historically definite what it is one is to believe. The most reliable information is received in life-peril, where one hears (what one basically knows) with a clarity that only life-peril provides, because in life-peril one becomes infinitely ready to hear and is infinitely close to what one is to hear.[81] Everyone who lives in Christendom ordinarily has received more than enough information about Christianity (even the government sees to that); many perhaps have received all too much. What is lacking is certainly something entirely different, is the inner transformation of the whole mind, by which a person in life-peril of the spirit comes in earnest, in true inwardness, to believe at least something—of the considerable Christianity that he knows. Ordinarily everyone who lives in Christendom has unconditionally enough knowledge about Christianity to be able to invoke and supplicate, to be able to turn in prayer to Christ. If he does that with the need of inwardness and in honesty of heart, he surely will become a believer. If only it is altogether definite before God that this person feels the need to believe, he will very definitely find out what he is to believe. The opposite is: without a need to believe, to go on researching, ruminating, and pondering, more and more wanting nigglingly to waste year after year of one's life, and finally one's eternal salvation, on getting absolutely and precisely definite, down to a dot over a letter, what one is to believe. This opposite is empty shadowboxing that merely becomes more and more self-important, or it is a scholarly, learned practice in the wrong place, therefore a scholarly, learned malpractice, or it is cowardly, inhuman, and to that extent also ungodly pusillanimity.

Part Four

DISCOURSES AT THE COMMUNION
ON FRIDAYS[1]

CHRISTIAN DISCOURSES

Two (II and III) of these discourses, which still lack something essential to be, and therefore are not called, sermons, were delivered in Frue Church.[3] Even if he is not told, the knowledgeable reader will no doubt himself readily recognize in the form and treatment that these two are "delivered discourses," written to be delivered, or written as they were delivered.

February 1848

S.K.

I

Luke 22:15[4]

PRAYER

Father in heaven! We know very well that you are the one who gives both to will and to accomplish, and that the longing,[5] when it draws us to renew fellowship with our Savior and Redeemer, is also from you. But when longing grasps hold of us, oh, that we may also grasp hold of the longing; when it wants to carry us away, that we may also surrender ourselves; when you are close to us in the call, that we might also keep close to you in our calling to you; when in the longing you offer us the highest, that we may purchase its opportune moment, hold it fast, sanctify it in the quiet hours by earnest thoughts, by devout resolves, so that it might become the strong but also the well-tested, heartfelt longing that is required of those who worthily want to partake of the holy meal of Communion! Father in heaven, longing is your gift; no one can give it to himself; if it is not given, no one can purchase it, even if he were to sell everything—but when you give it, he can still sell everything in order to purchase it. We pray that those who are gathered here today may come to the Lord's table with heartfelt longing, and that when they leave it they may go with intensified longing for him, our Savior and Redeemer.[6]

Luke 22:15. **I have longed with all my heart to eat this Passover with you before I suffer.**

The sacred words just read, Christ's own words, do not belong to the institution of the Lord's Supper, it is true; yet they have the closest connection to it in the words of narrative; the words of institution follow immediately after these words. [7]It was in the night when he was betrayed, or rather, he was already betrayed;

Judas had already been bought to sell him and had already sold him; now the betrayer was only seeking "the opportune time so he could betray him to the high priests without any disturbance" (Luke 22:6). For that he chose the quiet of the night in which Christ was now together with his apostles for the last time. "And when the hour came, he sat down at supper and the twelve apostles with him. And he said to them: I have longed with all my heart to eat this Passover with you before I suffer." [8]—That this would be the last time, he did not find out afterward; he knew beforehand that it is the last time. Yet he did not have the heart to initiate the apostles entirely into how close the danger was, that it was this very night, and what the danger was, that it was the danger of the most ignominious death, and how unavoidable it was. He who bore alone the sin of the world[9] also here bears alone his terrible knowledge of what will happen. He who struggled alone in Gethsemane, alone because his disciples slept,[10] is alone here also, even though he is sitting at supper with his only intimate friends. Therefore, what will happen that night, how it will happen, by whom it will happen, only one person in that little circle knew, he who was betrayed—yes, and then one more, the betrayer, who was also present. So Christ sits down to supper with the apostles, and as he sits down to supper he says: I have longed with all my heart for this meal.

Does it not seem to you, my listener, that this belongs to the Lord's Supper in a more profound sense, both inwardly and in an exemplary way and not merely in the way it belongs historically to the sacred account? Is it not true that heartfelt longing belongs essentially to Holy Communion? Would it not also be the most terrible contrast to the sacred account of how the instituter longed with all his heart for this meal, would it not be the most terrible contrast if it were possible for someone, by force of habit or because it was the custom, or perhaps motivated by quite incidental circumstances, in short, if someone went to the holy meal of the Lord's Supper without heartfelt longing! The sacred words just read are, then, if I may say so, the introductory words to the institution of the Lord's Supper, and this in turn is for every single individual the true devout introduction or entrance: to come with heartfelt longing.

Let us then use the prescribed moments before the Communion to speak about

the heartfelt longing for the holy meal of
the Lord's Supper.

It is not anything new we want to teach you; even less do we want to lead you into more difficult investigations by leading you outside faith. We want only to try to express what was stirring within you when you felt the longing to receive Communion, the heartfelt longing with which you came here today.

X
257

The wind blows where it will; you are aware of its soughing, but no one knows whence it comes or whither it goes.[11] So also with longing, the longing for God and the eternal, the longing for our Savior and Redeemer. Comprehend it you cannot, nor should you; indeed, you dare not even want to attempt it—but you are to use the longing. Would the merchant be responsible if he does not use the opportune moment; would the sailor be responsible if he does not use the favorable wind—how much more, then, is the one who does not use the occasion of longing when it is offered. Oh, it is piously said that one must not waste God's gifts, but in a deeper sense what would better be called God's gifts than every prompting of the Spirit, every pull of the soul, every fervent stirring of the heart, every holy state of mind, every devout longing, which are indeed God's gifts in a far deeper sense than food and clothing, not only because it is God who gives them but because God gives himself in these gifts! And yet how often does a person waste these gifts of God! Alas, if you could look deeply into people's innermost beings and very deeply into your own, you would surely discover with terror how God, who never leaves himself without witness,[12] lavishes these his best gifts on every human being, and how, on the other hand, every human being more or less wastes [*spilde*] these gifts, perhaps forfeits [*forspilde*] them entirely. What a terrible responsibility when at some time, if not sooner, then in eternity, a person's recollections rise up accusingly against him, recollections of the many times and the many ways God spoke to him, but futilely, in his inner being. Recollections, yes, because even if he himself has long since forgotten what was wasted, so that he

therefore does not recollect it, God and eternity have not forgotten it; he is reminded of it, and in eternity it becomes his
recollection.

So also with longing. A person can ignore its call; he can
change it into an impulse of the moment, into a whim that van-
ishes without a trace the next moment. He can resist it; he can
prevent its deeper generation within him; he can let it die unused
as a barren mood. But if you accept it with gratitude as a gift of
God, it will indeed become a blessing to you. Oh, therefore
never let the holy longing return empty-handed when it wants
to visit you; even if it sometimes seems to you that by following
it you would return empty-handed—do not believe it, it is not
so, it cannot possibly be so; it still may become a blessing to you.

So, then, longing awakened in your soul. Even if it was inexplicable, inasmuch as it is indeed from God, who in it is drawing
you; even if it was inexplicable, inasmuch as it is through him
"who lifted up from the earth will draw all to himself" (John
12:32);[13] even if it was inexplicable, inasmuch as it is the working
of the Spirit in you—you still understood what was required of
you. Truly, even though God gives everything, he also requires
everything, that the person himself shall do everything to use
rightly what God gives. Oh, in the customary pursuits of daily
life, how easy it is, in the spiritual sense, to doze off; in the habitual routine of sameness, how difficult to find a break! In connection with this, God came to your aid with the longing that he
awakened in your soul. Then you did promise yourself and God,
did you not, that now you would also gratefully use it. You said
to yourself: Just as longing has torn me away from what so easily
entangles one in a spell, so by earnest thoughts will I also cooper-
ate so that I may tear myself completely away from what still
might hold me back. By holy resolutions I will strive to hold
myself fast in what the earnest thoughts make me understand,
because the resolution is beneficial for this, for securing oneself in
what one has understood.

"What sheer vanity the earthly and temporal is! Even if until
now my life was so fortunate, so free from care, so entirely unacquainted with terrifying or even merely sad experiences, I will
now summon the earnest thoughts; in covenant with the longing

for the eternal and with the Holy Supper before my eyes, to which no one dares to come unless well prepared, I will not be afraid to become earnest. Christianity certainly is not heavy-mindedness; on the contrary, it is so joyful that it is the joyful news to all the heavy-minded; it can make gloomy only the light-minded and defiant. —Everything, all that I see, is vanity and vicissitude as long as it exists, and finally it is the prey of corruption. Therefore, when the moon rises in its radiance, I will together with that devout man[14] say to the star, 'I do not care for you; after all, you are now eclipsed'; and then when the sun rises in all its splendor and darkens the moon, I will say to the moon, 'I do not care for you; after all, you are now eclipsed'; and when the sun goes down, I will say, 'I thought as much, because all is vanity.' When I see the brook running along so briskly, I will say: Just keep on running; you will never fill the sea. To the wind I will say, yes, even if it tears trees up by the roots, I will say to it: Just keep on blowing; there is no meaning or thought in you, you symbol of inconstancy. Even if the loveliness of the field, which charmingly captivates the eye, and even if the melodious-ness of the birds' singing, which deliciously falls upon the ear, and even if the peacefulness of the forest, which invitingly re-freshes the heart—even if they were to use all their persuasive-ness, I will still not allow myself to be persuaded, will not allow myself to be beguiled; I will still call to mind that all of it is deception. Even though through thousands of years the stars re-main so fixed and without changing their positions in the sky, I will still not allow myself to be deceived by this reliability; I will call to mind that they at some time will fall down.

"So I will call to mind how uncertain everything is, that a person is thrown out at birth into the world and from that mo-ment lies out upon the depths of thousands of fathoms,[15] and at every moment the future before him, yes, at every moment, is like the darkest night. I will remind myself that never has anyone been so fortunate that he could not become unfortunate,[16] and never anyone so unfortunate that he could not become more unfortunate! I will remind myself that even if I should succeed in having all my wishes fulfilled, in having them erected in one building—that still no one, no one, will be able to guarantee to me that the whole building will not at the very same moment collapse upon me. And if I succeeded (if it can be called success at all) in rescuing a wretched scrap of my former good fortune out of this downfall, and if I adapted my soul to be patiently satisfied with this—that still no one, no one, will be able to guarantee to me that this remnant, too, will not at the next moment be taken away from me! And if there was some misfortune, some horror, a brief or slowly torturing one, that I especially dreaded, and if I had already become an old man—that still no one, no one, will be able to guarantee to me that it cannot come upon me even at the last moment!

"Then I will remind myself that just as every uncertainty of the next moment is like the dark night, so in turn the explanation of every event or occurrence is like a riddle that no one has solved; that no one who, in the eternal sense, wants to speak the truth can with certainty tell me which is which, whether it actually would be more to my benefit that I had all my wishes fulfilled or that they all be denied to me. Even if I, like a shipwrecked person, saved myself on a plank from certain death, and even if my dear ones joyously greeted me on the shore and marveled at my rescue—even so, the wise man will be able to stand by and say, 'Perhaps it would have been better for you if you had perished in the waves,'[17] and perhaps, perhaps he is simply telling the truth! I will call to mind that the wisest person who ever lived and the most limited person who ever lived get equally far when it is a matter of guaranteeing the next moment, and when it is a matter of explaining the least little event get equally far, arrive at a 'perhaps' and that the greater the passion with which someone dashes toward this 'perhaps' the closer he is only to losing his mind. No mortal has broken or forced his way through; indeed, the prisoner who is sitting within walls fourteen feet thick, chained hand and foot, bolted to the wall, is not bound in the way every mortal is in this fetter made from nothing, in this 'perhaps.' I will call to mind that even if I had my soul concentrated in one single wish and even if I had it concentrated therein so desperately that I could willingly throw away my eternal salvation for the fulfillment of this wish—that still no one can with certainty tell me in advance whether my wish, if it is fulfilled, would still not seem empty and meaningless to me. And what is more miserable, that the wish would not be fulfilled and I would retain the sad and painful idea of the—missed good fortune—or that the wish would be fulfilled and I would retain it, embittered by the certainty of how empty it was!

"So I will bear in mind that death is the only certainty, that it, mocking, mocking me and all the uncertainty of earthly life, which at every moment is equally uncertain, is equally certain at every moment; that death is no more certain for the old than for the infant born yesterday; that whether I am overflowing with health or lying on a sickbed, death is equally certain at every moment, something of which only earthly lethargy can remain ignorant. I will remember that no covenant between individuals is entered into, not the most loving, not the most fervent, without being entered into also with death, which is present ex officio in everything.

"And I will remind myself that, after all, every human being is alone, alone in the infinite world. Yes, in good days, in fair weather when good fortune smiles, then it does indeed seem as if we lived in association with one another, but I will call to mind that no one can know when the news will come to me, the news of tragedy, of misery, of horror,[18] news that along with the terror will also make me alone or make it evident how alone I am, as is every human being, will make me alone, abandoned by my nearest and dearest, misunderstood by my best friend, an object of anxiety that everyone shuns. I will remind myself of the horrors that no scream of alarm, no tears, no pleas warded off, the horrors that have separated a lover from the beloved, friend from friend, parents from children; and I will remind myself of how a little misunderstanding, if it came so fatally ill-starred, was sometimes enough to separate them dreadfully. I will remind myself that, *humanly* speaking, there is no one, no, no one at all, to depend on, not even God in heaven. If I really hold to him, I would become his friend—ah, who has suffered more, who has been more tested in every suffering than the devout person who was God's friend."

This is how you talked with yourself, and the more you surrendered to these thoughts, the more the longing for the eternal

x
261

conquered in you, the longing for fellowship with God through your Redeemer, and you said: I long with all my heart for this supper. Oh, there is indeed only one friend, one trustworthy friend in heaven and on earth, our Lord Jesus Christ. Alas, how many words a person uses and how many times he goes to find another person to do him a favor, and if this other one with only some sacrifice does him the favor, he who has learned to know human beings and knows how rarely favors are done when the favor cannot be returned, how he will cling tightly to his bene-factor! But he, who also for me, yes, for me (that he did the same for all others certainly ought not to diminish my gratitude, which is for what he has done for me), he who went to his death for me—should I not long for fellowship with him! No friend has ever been able to be more than faithful *unto* death,[19] but he re-mained faithful *in* death—his death was indeed my salvation. And no friend can at most do more by his death than *save* an-other's life, but he *gave* me life by his death; it was I who was dead, and his death gave me life.

"But *sin* is the corruption of the nations[20] and of every human being; how then could I think earnestly about life without prop-erly considering what Christianity teaches me, that the world lies in evil![21] And even if my life up until now has gone on so quietly and peacefully, undisturbed by the evil world's attacks and perse-cutions, and even if it seems to me that the few people I have known are indeed all good and loving and kind, I will bear in mind that this may well be due to the fact that neither they nor I are led out into the kind of life-perilous spiritual decisions in which the magnitude of the events makes it really clear on an enormous scale what good or what evil dwells in a human being. It may be so, and therefore it is necessary that the revelation teach what the human being cannot know by himself—how deep hu-mankind has sunk.

"Then I will remind myself what I have heard about all the atrocities people have committed against people, enemy against enemy, alas, and friend against friend, about the violence and murder and bloodthirstiness and bestial cruelty, about all the in-nocently and yet so cruelly shed blood that cries to high heaven,[22] about slyness and cunning and deceit and faithlessness,

X
262

about all those who, innocent, were nevertheless horribly stran-
gled, as it were, whose blood was not in fact shed, although they
were destroyed. Above all, I will recall the experience of the
Holy One when he walked here upon earth, what opposition he
suffered from sinners,[23] how his whole life was sheer suffering of
mind and spirit through belonging to the fallen human race,
which he wanted to save and which did not want to be saved,
that a living person cruelly chained to a corpse cannot suffer
more torturously than he suffered in mind and spirit by being
embodied as man in the human race! I will bear in mind how he
was mocked, and how everyone was received with great applause when he could think up a new insult, how there was no
longer any mention, to say nothing of thought, of his innocence,
of his holiness, how the only mitigating words that were spoken
were the commiserating words: See what a man![24]

"Suppose that I had lived at the time of that dreadful episode,
suppose I had been present in 'the crowd' that insulted him and
spat upon him! Suppose that I had been present in the crowd—I
dare not believe that I among a whole generation would have
been one of the twelve—suppose that I had been present! Well,
but neither can I think it of myself that I would have been present
in order to take part in the mockery. But just suppose that the
bystanders became aware of me, that I was not taking part—ah,
already I see those savage glances, see the attack turned for a
moment against me; already I hear the cry, 'He, too, is a Galilean,
a follower; kill him, or make him take part in the mockery, in the
people's cause!' Good heavens! Alas, how many are there in each
generation who have the courage to stick to a conviction when
it involves the danger of insults, when it involves life and death,
and when in addition the decisiveness of the unforeseen danger
stands appallingly over one! And I, who was indeed not a believer, a follower, from where would I receive the strength to
risk, or how would it be possible for me to become a believer at
that moment so that the decisiveness of the danger would help
me just as wonderfully, even though in another way, as it helped
the robber on the cross;[25] and if I am not changed in this way,
from where would I receive the courage to risk this for someone who, after all, was a stranger to me! Good heavens, then I

x
263

certainly would have taken part in the mockery—in order to save my life I would have screamed with the others, 'His blood be on me'[26]—in order to save my life; yes, it is true, it would be in order to save my life! I know well enough that the pastor speaks in another way. When he speaks, he describes the dreadful blindness of those contemporaries—but we, we who are present at his sermon are not that kind of people. Perhaps the pastor does not have the heart to speak severely to us—yes, if I were the pastor, I would not talk any other way either. I would not dare to tell any other person that he would have behaved in this way; there are things one person does not dare to say to another. Ah, but to myself I do dare to say it, and regrettably I must say it: I would have acted no better than the crowd of people!"

This is how you talked with yourself. And the more you surrendered to these thoughts, the more the longing for fellowship with him, the Holy One, conquered in you, and you said to yourself: I long with all my heart for this supper; I long for fellowship with him, away from this evil world where sin prevails! Away from it, but that is not so easy. I can wish myself away from the world's vanity and corruption, and even if a wish cannot do it, the heartfelt longing for the eternal is still able to lead me away, because in the longing itself the eternal *is*, just as God *is* in the longing that is *for* him.[27] But sin has a peculiar power to hold back; it has an outstanding account to settle, a debt it wants paid by the sinner before it lets him go. Moreover, sin knows how to stand up for its rights, certainly does not let itself be deceived by loose words, not even if people completely abolished the word *sin* and put *weakness* in its place, not even if, strictly speaking, a person became guilty only in weakness. But this is why I long in an all the more heartfelt way to renew my fellowship with him, who has atoned for my sin also, has atoned for my every slightest actual sin, but also for the one that may lurk most deeply in my soul without my being aware of it and that possibly would yet burst out if I am led into the most terrible decision. Were those Jews worse criminals than other people? Oh no, but that they were contemporary with the Holy One made their crime infinitely more terrible.

X
264

I long with all my heart for this supper, for this supper that is in his remembrance.[28] But when someone has participated with heartfelt longing in the Lord's Supper, is the longing then stilled, does the longing diminish as he departs from it? See, if someone dear to you has died, it will certainly happen that again and again the longing to remember him will awaken in you. Then you perhaps go to his grave; and just as he now lies sunk in the bosom of the earth, so you sink your soul into the recollection of him. The longing is thereby somewhat satisfied. Life once again exercises its power over you; and even if you faithfully continue to recall the departed one and often long for him, it still cannot mean that you should live more and more apart from life in order to live in the grave with the departed one, so that the longing for him would intensify each time you visited his grave. Surely you yourself will admit that if this happened to a person, there still would be, however much we honor his loyalty to the dead, something morbid in his grief. No, you understand that your paths are essentially separated, that you belong to life and to the claims life has upon you; you understand that longing should not increase with the years so that you more and more become a co-tenant of the grave. Oh, but the longing for fellowship with your Savior and Redeemer should increase every time you remember him. He is not one who is dead and departed but one who is living. Indeed, you are really to live in and together with him; he is to be and become your life, so that you do not live to yourself, no longer live yourself, but Christ lives in you.[29] Therefore, just as heartfelt longing belongs to worthy remembrance, so in turn it belongs to heartfelt longing that the longing is increased through remembrance, so only that one went worthily to the Lord's table who went there with heartfelt longing and went from there with increased heartfelt longing.

II

Matthew 11:28

PRAYER

Father in heaven, just as the congregation's intercessory prayer usually asks that you yourself will comfort all who are sick and sorrowful, so in this hour it asks that you give rest for their souls to those who labor and are burdened. And yet this is no intercession; who would dare to think himself so healthy that he would pray only for others. Alas, no, everyone is praying for himself, praying that you will give him rest for his soul. Give, O God, rest for the soul to each one individually whom you see laboring and burdened in the consciousness of sins.

Matthew 11:28 **Come here to me, all who labor and are burdened, and I will give you rest.**

"Come here, all you who labor and are burdened." What a surprising invitation! Ordinarily when people are gathered together for celebration or for work together, they say to the strong and to the cheerful: Come here, join with us, join your strengths with ours. But about someone troubled, they say: No, we do not want him along; he will only spoil the fun and hold up the work. Yes, the troubled person understands it very well without being told, and so many a troubled one perhaps stands apart and alone, will not participate with the others lest he spoil their fun or hold up the work. But this invitation to *all* those who labor and are burdened must surely apply to him since it applies to all who are troubled; how would anyone troubled dare to say here: No, the invitation does not apply to me!

"All those who labor and are burdened," all of them, no one is excluded, not a single one. Alas, what manifold dissimilarity these words signify. Those who *labor*. Not only that person labors

who in the sweat of his brow works for the daily bread;[30] not only that person labors who endures the toil and the heat of the day[31] in a lowly job. Oh, also that one labors who is struggling with weighty thoughts; also that one labors who in concern has the care of one or of many; also that one labors who is immersed in doubt, indeed, just as the swimmer is said to be laboring. Those who are *burdened*! Not only is that one burdened who visibly carries a heavy burden, who visibly is in difficult circumstances, but also that one is indeed burdened whose burden no one sees, who may even work to conceal it. And not only is that one burdened who perhaps faces a long life of privation and hardships, of troubled recollection, but also the one for whom, alas, there seems to be no future.

But how would this discourse ever end if it were to mention all these dissimilarities, and even if it were to attempt to do so, it would perhaps misguide [*vildlede*] instead of guide [*veilede*], would draw [*henlede*] attention distractingly to the dissimilarities instead of concentrating the mind on the one thing needful.[32] Even if there are ever so many dissimilarities, is it really the meaning of the Gospel that there is to remain a little remnant or a greater number of people who might be called the fortunate ones, exempt from labor and troubles? When it invites all who labor and are burdened, is it the meaning of the Gospel that there are still some to whom this invitation does not apply because they actually are healthy and do not need healing?[33] This is indeed how we talk ordinarily. If you see a happy group of children and there is one child who is sick, to whom a kind person says: Come to me, my child; we will play together—he is saying, of course, that this child is sick, but also that the other children actually are healthy. Now, is the Gospel speaking in the same manner, or should we speak foolishly this way about the Gospel? If this were the case, then the Gospel would not pertain to all; then it would not proclaim equality for all human beings but on the contrary would establish a distinction, would exclude the happy people, just as human invitations tend to exclude the troubled. See, this is why the invitation is to be understood differently. It invites everyone; the Gospel does not want to be an escape, a comfort and solace for a few troubled people. No, it addresses itself to all those who labor and are burdened; that is, it addresses itself to all and *requires* of every human being that he shall know what it means to labor and to be burdened. If you, for example, are the most fortunate of all, alas, so that you are even envied by many—the Gospel nevertheless addresses itself just as much to you and requires of you that you labor and be burdened. Or if, for example, you are not the most fortunate, the uniquely privileged person, and yet you are living in happy contentment, with your most cherished wishes fulfilled, lacking nothing, the Gospel, with the requirement of the invitation, nevertheless addresses itself just as much to you. And if you are in earthly need and indigence, you nevertheless are not the only one about whom the Gospel speaks. Yes, if you are so wretched that you have become a kind of proverb, you nevertheless are not the only one about whom the Gospel speaks.

The invitation, then, does not wish to be taken in vain in a worldly way. Therefore it contains a *requirement*; it requires that the invited person labor and be burdened in the more profound sense. There is a longing for God;[34] it pertains to nothing earthly and temporal, not to your external conditions, not to your future; it is a longing for God. The person who is carrying this longing silently, humbly in his heart—that person is laboring. And there is a heavy burden; no worldly power can lay it on your shoulders, but neither can any human being take it away any more than you can—it is guilt and the consciousness of guilt, or even heavier, sin and the consciousness of sin. The one who bears this burden—alas, yes, he is burdened, extremely burdened, but yet he is also burdened in the very way the Gospel's invitation requires it. Moreover, there is a concern, a deep, an eternal concern; it pertains not to externals, not to your fortunes, past or future; it pertains to your actions and, alas, it pertains to those very ones that a person would prefer to have forgotten, because it pertains to the actions, secret or open, by which you offended against God or against other persons. This concern is repentance; the one who sighs repenting—yes, he labors burdened. No one, no one else labors burdened in this way, and yet this is exactly what the Gospel's invitation requires.

But just as the Gospel through its invitation requires, *so also does it declare the promise*: "*I will give you rest for your soul.*" Rest! That is what the exhausted laborer, the fatigued traveler, desires; and the sailor who is tossed about on the sea seeks rest; and the weary old man longs for rest; and the sick one who lies restless on his bed and does not find an alleviating position craves rest; and the doubter who does not find a foothold in the ocean of thoughts craves rest. Ah, but only the penitent properly understands what it is to pray for rest for the soul, rest in the one and only thought in which there is rest for a penitent, that there is forgiveness; rest in the one and only declaration that can reassure a penitent, that he is forgiven; rest on the one and only ground that can support a penitent, that atonement has been made.

X
270

But the Gospel does indeed promise this, that he will find rest for his soul. And it is indeed in response to this invitation that you have come here in this hour, attentive listener. And even if it cannot be given in such a way that with this one time it would be settled forever and you would never again need to come to this holy place in order to seek rest—yet rest is promised for your soul. You are on the way, and God's house is a biding place [*Bedested*[35]] where you seek rest for your soul; but even if you come again to seek this rest, it is still certain that it is the same rest in which you someday, when your last moment has come, will seek rest for your soul for the last time. Whether you have come here today seeking rest in the time of youth or at an advanced age—oh, when your final hour comes and in the hour of death you are abandoned and alone, then you will crave as the last thing in the world to which you will no longer belong, you will crave what you crave today.

This was the promise in the invitation. But who, then, is the *inviter*! It certainly would be terribly confusing speech if the invitation "Come here" was heard in the world but it was not stated where one should go. Therefore, if there was no inviter, or if forgetfulness and doubt had taken the inviter away, what benefit would it be that the words of the invitation were repeated; then it would be impossible to accept the invitation, since there would be no possibility of finding the place. But you, my listener, of course know who the inviter is, and you have accepted the invitation in order to cling more closely to him. See, he stretches out his arms[36] and says: Come here, come here to **me**, all you who labor and are burdened. See, he opens his arms, in which all of us can rest equally secure and equally blessed, for it was only in our Savior's earthly life that John lay closest to him upon his breast.[37] How you come here now, how you can be said to be laboring burdened now, whether your offense was major or minor, whether the guilt is old and, yet no, it is not forgotten, no, but old and often repented, or it is new and no mitigating recollection has eased it—oh, with him you will find rest for your soul. I do not know what in particular troubles you, my listener; perhaps I would not understand your sorrow either or know how to speak about it with insight. But you are not going to any human being; from having confessed in secret before God you are going to him, the merciful inviter, to him who knows all human sorrows, to him who himself was tested in everything, yet without sin.[38] He also knew earthly needs, he who hungered in the desert,[39] he who thirsted upon the cross.[40] He also knew poverty, he who had nowhere to lay his head.[41] His soul has been sorrowful unto death.[42] Indeed, he has experienced all human sorrow more grievously than any human being, he who at the very end was abandoned by God[43]—when he bore all the sin of the world. Moreover, he is not only your spiritual guide; he is also your Savior. He not only understands all your sorrow better than you understand it yourself, but he wants to take the burden from you and to give you rest for the soul. It is hard, yes, it is true, it is hard not to be understood, but of what help would it be to you if there was someone who could completely understand all your sorrow but could not take it away from you, could completely understand all your struggles but not give you rest!

So it was an invitation: Come here, all you who labor and are burdened; and the invitation included a requirement: that the invited one labor, burdened in the consciousness of sins. And there is the trustworthy inviter, he who still stands there by his words and invites all. God grant that the one who is seeking may also find, that the one who is seeking the right thing may also find the one thing needful, that the one who is seeking the right place may also find rest for the soul. It is certainly a restful position when you kneel at the foot of the altar, but God grant that this truly be only a dim intimation of your soul's finding rest in God through the consciousness of the forgiveness of sins.

III[44]

John 10:27

PRAYER

Father in heaven! Your grace and mercy do not vary[45] with the changing of the times, do not age with the years, as if, like a human being, you were more gracious one day than on another, more gracious on the first day than on the last. Your grace remains unchanged, just as you are unchanged, the same, eternally young, new every new day—because you say "this very day"[46] every day. Oh, but if a person pays attention to this phrase, is gripped by it, and in holy resolution earnestly says to himself, "this very day"—then for him this means that he desires to be changed on this very day, desires that this very day might become more significant for him than other days, significant through renewed strengthening in the good he once chose, or perhaps significant precisely by choosing the good. It is your grace and mercy, unchanged, to say "this very day" every day, but it is throwing away your mercy and time of grace if a human being, thus unchanged, would say "this very day" from one day to the next. You are indeed the one who "this very day" gives the time of grace, but the human being is the one who "this very day" should seize the time of grace. We speak this way with you, O God; there is a language difference between us, and yet we strive to understand you and to make ourselves intelligible to you, and you are not ashamed to be called our God. That phrase, which when you say it, O God, is the eternal expression of your unchanged grace and mercy, that same phrase, when a human being repeats it in the right sense, is the most powerful expression of the most profound change and decision—yes, as if everything would be lost if this change and decision did not take place this very day. Grant, then, to those assembled here today, those who without any external summons, therefore all the more inwardly,

have resolved this very day to seek reconciliation with you in the
confession of sins, grant that this day may be a true blessing for
them, that they may have heard the voice of him whom you sent
to the world, the voice of the Good Shepherd, that he may know
them, and that they may follow him.

**John 10:27 "My sheep hear my voice, and I know them,
and they follow me."**

When the congregation assembles in the Lord's house on the
holy days, God himself has indeed so commanded and prescribed
it. Today, however, is not a holy day, and yet a little group has
gathered here in the sanctuary, not because it is prescribed for all
(since it is prescribed for none), but because each individual of
those present must have especially felt, even though in different
ways, the need to resort to this place precisely today. Today is not
a holy day; today everyone goes routinely to his fields, to his
business, to his work;[47] only these few individuals came to the
Lord's house today.

So, then, the single individual left his home to come here.
When on a holy day the one who is himself going to church
meets a passerby, he spontaneously assumes that probably this
passerby is also going to church, because on a holy day, even if
this is far from always being the case, the passerby is: someone
who is going to church. But the one who, moved by some inner
need, came here today—I wonder if it would occur to anyone
who met him in passing that he was on his way to God's house?
Should this visit to God's house therefore be less solemn? It seems
to me that this mysteriousness might, if possible, make it even
more inward. Openly before everyone's eyes and yet secretly,
the single individual came to church today, secretly or along the
secret way. No one except God knew his way; it did not occur
to any passerby that you were going to God's house, something
you yourself do not say, since you say that you are going to Holy
Communion, as if this were even more inward and solemn than
going to church. You did not expect, as on a holy day, that the
passerby would be going the same way and with the same
thoughts; and therefore you went secretly, as a stranger, in the

midst of all those many people. You did not expect to see the
same purpose on the faces of those passing by; therefore you kept
your eyes to yourself, did not formally greet people as on a festival day. No, the person passing by simply did not exist for you;
with downcast eyes, you secretly fled, so to speak, to this place.
Nor was it your intention only to worship, to praise, and to thank
God, as on the festival days, when you therefore could not wish
to be alone. Your intention is to seek the forgiveness of sins—so
you must want to be alone. How still and how solemn it is now!
On a holy day everything is quiet outside also; the customary
work is suspended; even the one who is not visiting God's house
still notices that it is a holy day. Today, however, is not a holy
day. The noise of the daily activity of life out there sounds almost
audibly within this vaulted space, where this sacred stillness is
therefore even all the greater. The stillness that public authority
can command civilly is nevertheless not godly stillness, but this
stillness, while the world makes noise, is the godly stillness.

So it was not your duty to come here today; it was a need
within you. It was no external summons that determined you;
you yourself must have inwardly made the decision; no one
could reproach you if you had not come. It is your own free
choice to come; you did not do it because the others were doing
it, because the others, after all, on this very day went each to his
fields, to his business, to his work—but you came to God's
house, to the Lord's table.

In so doing, you have very specifically expressed that you
count yourself among those who want to belong to Christ, those
described in the sacred text just read, which was taken from the
Gospel in which Christ compares himself to the good shepherd
and the true believers to the sheep. Three statements are made
about them: They hear his (Christ's) voice; he (Christ) knows
them; they follow him (Christ).

They hear his voice. Today it is very particularly, is simply and
solely, *his* voice that is to be heard. Everything otherwise done
here is only for the purpose of concentrating the attention of the
mind on this, that it is *his* voice that is to be heard. Today no
sermon is preached. A confessional address is not a sermon; it
does not want to instruct you or impress upon you the old famil-

X
277

iar doctrines; it only wants to have you pause on the way to the Communion table so that through the speaker's voice you yourself confess privately and secretly before God. From a confessional address you are not to learn what it means to confess; it would also be too late; but through it you make your confession before God. Today no sermon is preached. What we say here in the prescribed brief moment is, again, no sermon, and when we have said Amen, the divine service is not as usual essentially over, but then the essential begins. Our address therefore only wants to have you pause for a moment on the way to the Communion table, because today the divine service does not as usual center on the pulpit but on the Communion table. And at the Communion table the point above all is to hear *his* voice. Certainly a sermon should also bear witness to him, proclaim his word and his teaching, but a sermon is still not *his* voice. At the Communion table, however, it is *his* voice you are to hear. If another human being said to you what is said at the Communion table, if all people would join together in saying it to you—if you do not hear *his* voice, then you would receive Holy Communion in vain. When there at the Communion table every word by the Lord's servant is said accurately as handed down from the fathers, when you listen accurately to every word so that not the least escapes you, not one jot or tittle—if you do not hear *his* voice, hear that it is he who is saying it, then you would receive Holy Communion in vain. If you, believing, appropriate every word that is said, if you earnestly decide to take it to heart and to order your life in accord with it—if you do not hear *his* voice, then you would receive Holy Communion in vain. It must be *his* voice you hear when he says: Come here, all you who labor and are burdened—therefore his voice that invites you. And it must be his voice you hear when he says: This is my body. At the Communion table there is no speaking about him; there he himself is present in person; there it is he who is speaking—if not, then you are not at the Communion table. In the physical sense, one can point to the Communion table and say, "There it is"; but, in the spiritual sense, it is actually *there* only if you hear *his* voice *there*.

He knows them. In other words, he does not know those who do not hear his voice, and neither are those his own whom he does not know. It is not with him as with a human being, who may very well have a friend and an adherent without knowing it, without knowing him; but the one Christ does not know is not his own, because Christ is all-knowing. —He knows them, and he knows each one individually. The sacrifice he offered he did not offer for people in general, nor did he want to save people in general—and it cannot be done in that way either. No, he sacrificed himself in order to save each one individually—would he then not know each one individually; would a person not know the one for whom he has sacrificed his life! —When the congregation gathers in great numbers on the festival days, he knows them also, and those he does not know are not his own. Yet on such an occasion someone may easily deceive himself, as if the single individual were concealed in the crowd. Not so at the Communion table; however many assembled there, indeed, even if all were assembled at the Communion table, there is no crowd at the Communion table. He is himself personally present, and he knows those who are his own. He knows you, whoever you are, known by many or unknown by all; if you are his own, he knows you. Oh, what earnestness of eternity to be known by him. Oh, what blessed comfort to be known by him. Yes, even if you fled to the uttermost parts of the world, he knows you; even if you hid in the bottomless pit, he knows you[48]—but there is no reason to flee, no reason to seek a hiding place, because the blessedness is precisely this, that he knows you. Yet no third party can know whether he knows you; this you must know with him and with yourself—but if he does not know you, then neither are you his own.

Behold, every morning the sun rises over the earth at day's dawning. Its rays penetrate everywhere at every point; there is no place so remote that the sun's rays do not illuminatingly penetrate there. But it makes no distinction in its acquaintance with earth; it shines equally everywhere and knows every place. But he, humankind's eternal sun—his acquaintance with humankind also penetrates to everyone everywhere like rays of light, but he makes a distinction. There are also those he does not know, those to whom he will say: "I do not know you, I never knew you,"[49]

X
279

those to whom he will say this even though they insist that they know him!

If you went up to the Lord's table and took part in the sacred act, if you could definitely certify that you had been to Communion, if the Lord's servant corroborates that he has handed the bread and wine to you in particular, just as to each of the others—if *he* did not know you, then you would receive Holy Communion in vain. One can point physically to the Communion table and say, "See, there it is," but in the spiritual sense the Communion table is *there* only if you are *known there* by him.

They follow him. You do not remain and are not to remain at the Communion table. You return again to your task, to your work, to the joy that perhaps awaits you, or, alas, to the sorrow— all such things you have put aside for today, but if you are *his own*, then you follow him. And when you follow him, you do indeed leave the Communion table when you go away from it, but then it is as if the Communion table followed you, for where he is, there is the Communion table—and when you follow him, he accompanies you. What earnestness of eternity, that wherever you go, whatever you do, he still accompanies you. What blessed comfort, that he accompanies you; what marvelous congruity, that the earnestness of eternity is also the most blessed comfort! The Communion table, to be sure, remains standing there, and you go to the Communion table, but yet it is the Communion table only if *he* is present *there*—therefore where he is, there is the Communion table.

He himself declares, "If you are offering your gift at the altar and you there remember that someone has something against you, then first go and become reconciled with your enemy and then come and offer your gift."[50] Which offering do you think is more precious to him, the offering you bring by becoming reconciled with your enemy, that is, by offering God your anger— or the gift you could offer on the altar! But if the offering of reconciliation is more precious to God, to Christ, then certainly the altar is indeed *there* where the most pleasing offering is brought! Abel offered a sacrifice on the altar, but Cain did not; God had regard for Abel's offering—that was why it was an

X
280

altar—but he had no regard for Cain's offering.[51] Oh, do not forget that where he is, there is the altar,[52] that his altar is neither on Moriah nor on Gerizim,[53] nor any visible *there*, but that it is there where he is. If this were not so, then you of course would have to remain at the Communion table, take up residence there, never budge from the spot, but such superstition is not Christianity.

[54]Today is not a holy day; today there is divine service on a weekday—oh, but a Christian's life is a divine service every day! [55]It is not as if everything were settled by someone's going to Communion on rare occasions; no, the task is to remain at the Communion table when you leave the Communion table. Today everything else we said was only for the purpose of concentrating your attention on the Communion table. But when you leave here, remember that the event is not finished—oh no, it is just begun, the good event, or, as Scripture says, the good work in you that God who began it will complete on the day of our Lord Jesus Christ.[56] No doubt you perhaps could devoutly call this day today, if what God will give you really has meaning for you, a day of Jesus Christ, but still there is only one day that really is called the day of Jesus Christ. The day today, however, will soon be over. God grant that when it is long since gone and forgotten—the blessing of this day, recollected again and again, may still be a vivid recollection for you, so that the remembrance of the blessing may be a blessing.

Pass on, O day, that never more
My eyes in time will see.
Fall into sleep by night surrounded!
I pass ahead to heaven bright,
My God to see, eternal light.
On that my faith is founded![57]

IV

I Corinthians 11:23

Remind, O Jesus, oft my heart
Of your pangs, torment, and need,
Remind me of your soul's pain.[58]

Yes, you our Lord and Savior, not even in this do we dare to trust
our own strength, as if by ourselves we were able to summon
deeply enough or constantly to hold fast your memory, we who
much prefer to dwell on the joyful than on the sorrowful, we
who all crave good days, the peace and security of happy times,
we who so very much wish to remain in the deeper sense ignorant of the horrors lest they, as we foolishly think, would make
our happy life dark and earnest, or our unhappy, so it seems to us,
life even darker and more earnest. Therefore we pray to you, you
who are the one we want to remember, we pray to you that you
yourself will remind us of it. What a strange language a human
being speaks when he is to speak with you. It indeed seems to
become unfit for use when it is to describe our relationship with
you or yours with us. Is this also a remembrance when the one
who is to be recollected must himself remind the one recollecting! Humanly, only the high and mighty person who has so
many and such important things to think about speaks this way.
He says to his subordinate: You must yourself remind me so that
I remember you. Alas, we say the same to you, you the Savior
and Redeemer of the world. Alas, and these same words, when
we say them to you, are the very expression of our lowliness, our
nothingness in comparison with you, you who with God are
exalted above all the heavens. We pray that you yourself will
remind us of your suffering and death, remind us often at our
work, in our joy and in our sorrow, of the night when you were

betrayed. We pray to you for this, and we thank you when you remind us; so we also thank you now as do those gathered here today in going up to your Communion table to renew their fellowship with you.

I Corinthians 11:23 **. . . the Lord Jesus, on the night when he was betrayed.**

[59]*On the night when he was betrayed*. Let it now become only night around you; indeed, this belongs to the holy act. You who are gathered here to share, in remembrance of our Lord Jesus Christ, in the supper that was instituted that night, you yourselves surely have prayed to him that he will bring his suffering and death very vividly before your eyes. Oh, there are those who perhaps pray that it might be granted them to see what kings and princes futilely desired to see,[60] one of his days of glory. Do not regret your choice, for truly that person chose the better part[61] who first and foremost prays that the terror might stand vividly before him. —On the night when he was betrayed. It was in this way, humanly speaking, that he has now come down in the world. He whom the people at one time would have proclaimed king,[62] he on whom the high priests later did not dare lay hands because all the people clung to him,[63] he who by his mighty works had collected a large crowd around him, he before whose authority as a teacher all had bowed, the Pharisees defiantly but constrained, the people happily and expectantly—he is now as if cast out of the world; he is sitting apart in a room with the twelve.[64] But the die has been cast; his fate has been decided by the decree of the Father and the high priests. When he rises from the table to go out into the night, he is also going to meet his death. Then begins the drama of horror for which everything is in readiness; then he will again experience the past in the repetition of the horror, in a certain sense terribly end with the beginning. He will be hailed as king, but in mockery; he will actually wear the purple robe, but as an insult; he will collect an even greater number of people around him, but the high priests will no longer be afraid to lay their hands on him but instead be forced to restrain the people's hands so that it can have the appearance that he—is

condemned to death. It was, after all, a legal proceeding; he was arrested "as one arrests a robber" and "crucified as a criminal"![65]

Thus his life was retrogression instead of progression, the opposite of what the human mentality naturally thinks and covets. In a worldly way, a person ascends rung by rung in honor and prestige and power; steadily more and more people accept his cause, until he who was continually in the majority, finally admired by everyone, stands on the highest rung. But he, in reverse, descended rung by rung, and yet he ascended; and this is how truth must suffer—or be singled out for distinction in the world—so truly was he the truth. At first it seemed to please all the people, but the more manifest it gradually became, the more definite and clear, the more decisive, the more the trappings of the illusions fell away, the greater was also the number of those who continually fell away—at last he stands alone. But he does not stop even there; now he ascends rung by rung through all the marks of abasement, until finally he is crucified.

Finally, yet the last did not take very long, because from the moment the drama of horror had its beginning on the night when he was betrayed the decision has been present with the speed of the sudden, just as when the storm darkens earth and sky in the twinkling of an eye. This night is the boundary line, and then what a change! And yet in a certain sense everything is the same. The place is the same, the high priests are the same, the same governor, the people are the same—yes, and he also is the same. When at one time they wanted to proclaim him king, he *fled*, and when they come armed to arrest him, he *goes to meet* the sentry and says, "Whom do you seek?"[66] He no doubt once greeted Judas as apostle with a kiss, nor does he deny Judas the kiss that he knows will betray him[67]—is he then not the same?

O my listener, just as a person perhaps at times has a day or a night that he must want to have out of his life, so also the human race must want to have this night out of its history! If the midnight hour in which he was born was dark, this night on which he was betrayed was even darker! The human race must want to have this night out of its history—indeed, and every individual must want to have it out of the history of the race. This event is not an event finished and long since past; we should not and dare not recall Christ's suffering as we recall the suffering of the glorious ones who met an innocent death, about which we say: That is now long since past. His innocent sacrifice is not past even though the cup of suffering is empty, is not a bygone event although it is past, is not an event finished and done with although it was eighteen hundred years ago, would not become that even if it were eighteen thousand years ago.

He did not die a natural death on a sickbed; nor did he meet his end by accident; nor was it a few individuals who attacked and killed him; nor was it that generation that crucified him—it was the *human race*, and we certainly do belong to that if we are human beings at all, and in this way we are indeed present if we are human beings at all. Consequently we dare not wash our hands—at least we cannot do it except as Pilate could do it;[68] consequently we are not spectators and observers at a past event—we are indeed accomplices in a present event. Therefore we do not presumptuously delude ourselves into thinking that it is sympathy in the fashion of the poets that is required of us—it is indeed his blood that is required also of us, who belong to the human race. Even the imitator [*Efterfølger*] of Christ who resembled him most,[69] who did not, as superstition so coveted, bear his wounds on his body but whose life was also retrogression instead of progression, who also, according to the Christian order of precedence, ascended from rung to rung, ridiculed, insulted, persecuted, crucified—even he when he is reminded of that night and it is very vividly present to his thoughts, even he is present as an accomplice! And when the congregation, every time these words are said, "Our Lord Jesus Christ on the night when he was betrayed," surround him anxiously but fervently, as if to ward off the treason, as if to pledge him their loyalty even though everyone else deserted him[70]—let no one dare to forget that on that night he was along as an accomplice, let no one dare to forget this pitiful prototype whom in other ways he scarcely resembles—the Apostle Peter. Alas, we human beings, even if we are of the truth,[71] are still alongside *the truth*; when we walk side by side with the man who is *the Truth*, when *the Truth* is the criterion, we are still like children alongside a giant; in the moment of decision we still remain—accomplices.

On the night when he was betrayed. What crime has greater like-ness to that night than an act of treason; and what crime is more unlike love than an act of treason—and most of all when it occurs by means of a kiss! Judas is certainly the traitor, but basically they are all traitors, except that Judas is the only one who does it for the sake of money. Judas betrays him to the high priests, and the high priests betray him to the people, and the people to Pilate; and Pilate betrays him to death out of fear of the emperor, and the disciples who flee in the night and Peter who denies him in the courtyard do the same out of fear of people.[72] This was the last—oh, just as when the last spark goes out, then everything is dark. In the whole human race there is not one person, not one single person, who will have anything to do with *him*—and he is *the truth*! If you think that you would never have done this, you would never have laid hands upon him or taken part in insulting him—but betray him, that you would have done: you would have fled or you would have prudently stayed at home, would have stayed out of it, would have let your servant report what happened there. Alas, but to betray is the most painful blow you can inflict upon love; there is no suffering, not even the most excruciating physical suffering, in which love agonizes as it ago-nizes soulfully in being betrayed, because for love [*Kjerlighed*] there is nothing as blessed as faithfulness!

Oh, that this happened is to me enough to make it impossible ever to be happy in the thoughtless and worldly way the natural man is, as the youth in his inexperience is, as the child in its innocence is. I do not need to see more, if indeed anything more terrible has happened in the world, something that can terrify the heart more, since there probably is something that can terrify the senses more. Nor is there need for anything terrible to hap-pen to me—this is enough for me: I have seen *love* betrayed, and I have understood something about myself, that I also am a human being, and to be a human being is to be a sinful human being. I have not become misanthropic because of that, least of all so that I would hate other people, but I will never forget this sight nor what I have understood about myself. The one whom the human race crucified was the Redeemer; as someone be-longing to the human race, I, for this very reason feel the need for a redeemer—never has the need for a redeemer been clearer than when the human race crucified the Redeemer. From this moment I will no longer believe in myself; I will not let myself be deceived, as if I were better because I was not tried as were those contemporaries. No, apprehensive about myself as I have become, I will seek my refuge with him, the Crucified One. I will beseech him to save me from evil and to save me from myself. Only when saved by him and with him, only when he holds me fast, do I know that I will not betray him. The anxiety that wants to frighten me away from him, so that I, too, could betray him, is precisely what will attach me to him; then I dare to hope that I will hold fast to him—how would I not dare to hope this when that which wants to frighten me away is what binds me to him! I will not and I cannot do it, because he moves me irresistibly; I will not inclose myself in myself with this anxiety for myself without having confidence in him; I will not inclose myself in myself with this anxiety or with this guilt consciousness that I, too, have betrayed him—I would rather, as a guilty one, belong to him redeemed. Oh, when he walked about in Judea, he moved many by his beneficial miracles; but nailed to the cross he performs an even greater miracle, he performs love's miracle, so that, without doing anything—by suffering he moves every person who has a heart!

He was betrayed—but he was Love: *on the night when he was betrayed*, he instituted the meal of love! Always same! Those who crucified him, for them he prayed;[73] and on the night when he was betrayed, he uses the occasion (how infinitely deep the love that finds this very moment convenient!), he uses the occasion to institute the meal of reconciliation. Truly, he did not come into the world to be served[74] without making repayment! A woman anoints his head[75]—in repayment she is recollected through all the centuries! Yes, he makes repayment for what they do against him! They crucify him—in repayment his death on the cross is the sacrifice of Atonement for the sin of the world, also for this, that they crucified him! They betray him—in repayment he institutes the meal of reconciliation for all! If Peter had not denied him, then there would have been at least one person who would not, just like every other individual in the human race, have needed reconciliation. But now they all betrayed him, and thus all need to take part in the meal of reconciliation!

[76]Behold, everything is now prepared;[77] blessed is the one who for his part is also prepared! Behold, he is waiting there at his holy table—do this, then, in remembrance of him and for blessing to yourself!

V

II Timothy 2:12–13

PRAYER

Lord Jesus Christ, you who loved us first, you who until the last loved those whom you had loved from the beginning, you who until the end of time continue to love everyone who wants to belong to you—your faithfulness cannot deny itself. Alas, only when a person denies you can he force you, so to speak, you the loving one, also to deny him. May this be our comfort when we must indict ourselves for the offense we have committed, for what we have left undone, for our weakness in temptations, for our slow progress in the good, that is, for our unfaithfulness to you, to whom we once in our early youth and repeatedly thereafter promised faithfulness—may it be our comfort that even if we are unfaithful you still remain faithful; you cannot deny yourself.[78]

II Timothy 2:12–13 **If we deny, he also will deny us; if we are faithless, he still remains faithful; he cannot deny himself.**

The Holy Word just read might seem to contain a contradiction, and if this were so, it could not merely seem but would be strange to call attention to such a verse. This, however, is not at all the case. The contradiction presumably would be that in the first clause it is said that if we deny, he will also deny us, and that in the next clause it is said that he cannot deny himself. But should there be no difference, then, between denying him and being unfaithful to him? After all, it is certainly clear enough that the person who denies him is also unfaithful to him, because no one can deny him without having belonged to him; but from this

it does not follow that everyone who is unfaithful to him also denies him. If this is so, there is no contradiction. The one clause is rigorous, the other lenient—in fact, here there is Law and Gospel, but both clauses are the truth. There is no duplexity in the verse, but it is one and the same word of truth, which separates people, just as the eternal truth, both in time and eternity, separates them, in good and in evil. It is just as is told in the sacred narratives, that not until the Pharisees had departed did Christ begin to speak intimately with the disciples;[79] in the same way the first words remove, send away—alas, as if to the left side— those who deny him, whom he also will deny; the latter words, the gentle words of comfort, are spoken as to those on the right side.[80] He bade his disciples not to cast their pearls before swine,[81] and his love, even if it wants to save all, is not a weakness that plaintively stands in need of those who should be saved, but it is the mercy to everyone who needs to be saved.

But you who are gathered here to take part in this holy supper, you certainly have not denied him, or in any case you are indeed gathered here today to confess him, or by being gathered here today and with the purpose of being gathered you do indeed confess him. Therefore, even though it can be beneficial that the rigorous words are brought to recollection, are heard simultaneously, just as they inseparably belong together so that we at no time separate what God has joined together[82] in Christ, neither add anything nor subtract anything, do not subtract the rigorousness from the leniency that is in them, do not subtract from the Gospel the Law that is in it, do not subtract from the salvation the perdition that is in it —yet the latter words are more suitable for meditating upon today. We let the terrifying thought pass by, not as something that does not pertain to us—oh, no, in that way no one is saved; as long as one lives it is still possible that one could be lost. As long as there is life there is hope—but as long as there is life there certainly is also the possibility of danger, consequently of fear, and consequently there will also be fear and trembling just as long. We let the terrifying thought pass by, but then we trust to God that we dare to let it pass by and to cross over as we take comfort in the Gospel's gentle word.

He still remains faithful. In your relation to him, then, you have one concern fewer, or rather one blessing more than any human

x
297

being can ever possibly have in relation to another person. Humanly speaking, in the relation between two people, each of them always has a dual concern; he has the one for himself, that he will remain faithful, but in addition he has the one about whether the other will also remain faithful. But he, Jesus Christ, he remains faithful. In this relationship, therefore, the peace and blessedness of eternity is complete; you have only one concern, the self-concern that you remain faithful to Christ—for he remains eternally faithful. Oh, there certainly is no perfectly happy love except that with which a person loves God, and no perfectly blessed faithfulness except that with which a person clings to Christ. Everything, unconditionally everything that God does is of service to you; you need not fear that anything that could be of benefit to you will escape him, because he alone knows what is to your benefit. You need not fear that you would not be able to make yourself understood by him, because he understands you perfectly, far better than you understand yourself; you have only to rejoice (what infinite joy of love!) in his love—to be silent and to give thanks! To be silent and to give thanks, yes, because when you are silent you understand him, and best when you are completely silent; and when you give thanks, then he understands you, and best when you give thanks always. So happy is a person's love with which he loves God.

But it is also the same with the faithfulness that joins one to Christ. Deep within every person's soul there is a secret anxiety that even the one in whom he had the most faith could also become unfaithful to him. No merely human love can completely drive out this anxiety, which can very well remain hidden and undetected in the friendly security of a happy life-relationship, but which at times can inexplicably stir deep within and which, when the storms of life begin, is immediately at hand. There is only one whose faithfulness can drive out this anxiety, and that is Jesus Christ. He remains faithful; yes, even if every other loyalty failed, he still remains faithful, every day of your life, whatever happens to you; he remains faithful to you in death; he meets you again in the hereafter as a trustworthy friend. In your relation to him, you have no concern whatever about his unfaithfulness; this anxiety, that he could become unfaithful to you after you had given yourself completely to him, had your whole life in him, will never, indeed, it cannot ever, visit you. No, strengthened by eternity's certainty of his faithfulness, you have increased strength, and this also is his gift, to devote everything so that you might be faithful to him. You are not to be engaged in two places, as is usually the case with troubled thoughts; by his own faithfulness, which he himself eternally guarantees, he wants to make you unconcerned, to set your mind at rest, to undergird you, but of course by that kind of faithfulness he also wants to call you to remain faithful to him.

If we are faithless, he still remains faithful. In your relation to him, then, you have one concern fewer, or rather one blessing more than any human being can ever possibly have in relation to another person. If in the relationship between two people one became unfaithful but repented of his unfaithfulness and re-turned—alas, perhaps his unfaithfulness would have had the power to change the other person so that he could not bring himself to forgive him. But he, our Lord Jesus Christ, remains faithful to himself. It would be presumptuous and blasphemous if someone would think that by his unfaithfulness he has the power to change him, the power to make him less loving than he was—that is, than he is. But it is also ungodly if someone could take his faithfulness in vain. [83]You shall not take the Lord your God's name in vain[84]—oh, but also be mindful lest you take Christ's faithfulness in vain, so that you make it into a punishment upon yourself, for is not his unchanged faithfulness, just as it is forgiveness for the penitent, is it not similarly a curse on the person who impotently rebels and hardens himself!

Even if we are faithless, he still remains faithful. When he walked here on earth, no sufferer came to him without finding help, no troubled person ever went away from him uncomforted, no sick person ever touched the hem of his cloak without being healed (Mark 6:56)—but if someone had come to him the seventieth time and asked forgiveness for his faithlessness, do you think he would have become weary, or if it had been seven times seventy times![85] No, heaven will become weary of carrying the stars and will cast them away before he becomes weary of forgiving and thrusts the penitent away from himself. Oh, what a blessed thought that there still exists a faithful, a trustworthy friend, that he is that; what a blessed thought, if a person dares to entertain this thought at all, how all the more blessed, therefore, that he is the trustworthy friend of the penitent, of the faithless!

Alas, complete faithfulness was never found in the world—if anyone was at all justified in seeking it in others. But complete faithfulness in return for faithlessness, that is found only with our heavenly teacher and friend—and surely we all need to seek that. Yes, if it were possible for you, our teacher and Savior, ever to become weary of our perpetual assurances of faithfulness, these assurances that certainly are not hypocritical or fictive, but yet to you must often or always sound so feeble, so childish; if at some time you could find it in your heart to test our faithfulness in earnest; if you were to thrust us out in the stream, as the teacher usually does with a pupil, and say, "Now, I am not going to help you at all but only test your faithfulness"—then we would indeed be lost at once!

When it comes to describing our relation to the Deity, this human language is certainly second-rate and half-true. Even when we speak in the strongest expressions about God's testing us, our speech is still meaningless unless the meaning is implicitly understood: that basically God is holding on to us. When we see a mother play with her child the game that the child is walking alone although the mother is holding on behind—and we then see the child's indescribable, radiant face, its self-satisfied look and its manly bearing—we smile at the child because we see the whole pattern. But when we ourselves speak of our relationship with God, then it must be in dead earnest about our walking alone, then we speak in the strongest expressions about God's laying his hand heavily on us, as if he actually did not use his hand for anything else at all, or as if he did not have two hands, so that even in such a moment he was holding onto us with one hand. Thus we truly do not presume to ask that you, our Teacher and Savior, should apply a test to our faithfulness to you, because we very well know that in the moment of the ordeal you yourself must hold on to us, we know very well that *fundamentally* we are faithless and that at every moment and *fundamentally* it is you who are holding on to us.

X
299

Devout listeners, you are gathered here today to renew your pledge of faithfulness, but what path are you taking to your decision? It is through confession. Is this not a detour? Why do you not go directly to the Communion table? Oh, even if it were not prescribed by sacred tradition, would not you yourself feel the need to go along this path to the Communion table! The confession does not want to burden you with the guilt of faithlessness; on the contrary, it wants to help you, through confession, to lay aside the burden. The confession does not want to make you confess; on the contrary it wants to unburden you through a confession; in the confessional there is no one who accuses you if you do not accuse yourself.

My listeners, all of you heard what the pastor said in the confessional, but no one except you, who said it, and God, who heard it, knows what you alone by yourself said to yourself. Yet it is not the pastor who is to receive Communion, but it is you. Nor was it the pastor who confessed; he did not even hear your confession, but it was you who confessed before God in secret. God has heard this, but what God has heard he also has heard, he whom you seek at the Communion table. If you have forgotten something, alas, or if you have deceptively forgotten something, God knows it, and he also knows it, he whom you seek at the Communion table. Far be it from us even to try with the discourse to get us to examine ourselves with regard to what faithlessness a person can reproach himself for, which can indeed be extremely varied. No, according to the sacred tradition of the Church, this is entrusted to your honesty toward God.

But nevertheless bear in mind, even if the interval since you last renewed your fellowship with your Savior was in what one, humanly speaking, would have to call a better time—alas, how much faithlessness there still may be in your relation to him to whom you promised faithfulness, not in something particular, not in this or in that, but unqualifiedly in everything. Alas, who does know himself! Is it not exactly this to which the earnest and honest self-examination finally leads as its last and truest, this humble confession: "Who knows his errors? From my hidden faults cleanse thou me" (Psalm 19:12). And when a person examines his relation to Christ, who then is the human being who

x
300

completely knows his faithlessness, who the human being who would dare to think that in his very self-examination there could not be faithlessness! Therefore you do not find rest this way. So, then, rest; then seek rest for your soul in the blessed comfort that, even if we are faithless, he still is faithful.

He cannot deny himself. No, he cannot inclose himself with his love within himself, he who out of love sacrificed himself for the world. But the one who incloses himself within himself and refuses to have anything to do with others, he indeed denies himself. He pretends to be out when you come in search of him, and if you did get to see him, you would seek in vain to grasp his hand, because he pulls it back and denies himself. You would seek in vain to catch his eye, because he averts it and denies himself; you would seek in vain an expression of sympathy in his countenance, because he withdraws and denies himself. But he, our Lord Jesus Christ, he does not deny himself, he cannot deny himself. This is why up there at the altar he stretches out his arms,[86] he opens his arms to all; you see it on him—he does not deny himself. He does not deny himself, and neither does he deny you what you ask of him when you now renew your pledge of faithfulness to him. He is the same; he was and he remains faithful to you.

VI

I John 3:20

PRAYER

Great are you, O God; although we know you only as in an obscure saying and as in a mirror, yet in wonder we worship your greatness—how much more we shall praise it at some time when we come to know it more fully! When under the arch of heaven I stand surrounded by the wonders of creation, I rapturously and adoringly praise your greatness, you who lightly hold the stars in the infinite and concern yourself fatherly with the sparrow. But when we are gathered here in your holy house we are also surrounded on all sides by what calls to mind your greatness in a deeper sense. You are indeed great, Creator and Sustainer of the world; but when you, O God, forgave the sin of the world and reconciled yourself with the fallen human race, then you were even greater in your incomprehensible compassion! How would we not, then, in faith praise and thank and worship you here in your holy house, where everything reminds us of this, especially those who are gathered here today to receive the forgiveness of sins and to appropriate anew reconciliation with you in Christ![87]

[88]I John 3:20 . . . **even if our hearts condemn us, God is greater than our hearts.**

Even if our hearts condemn us. When the Pharisees and the Scribes had brought to Christ in the temple a woman seized in open sin in order to accuse her and when later, shamed by his answer, they had all gone away, Christ said to her, "Has no one condemned you?" but she said, "No one, Lord."[89] Thus there was no one who condemned her. So is it also here in this sanctuary, there is no one who condemns you; if your heart condemns you, you yourself alone must know. No one else can know it, because this other one also is occupied today with his own heart, whether it condemns him. Whether your heart condemns you is no one else's concern, because this other person also has only his own heart to deal with, its accusing or its acquitting thoughts. How you feel when you hear these words read aloud, "even though our hearts condemn us," is no one else's concern, because this other one also applies everything devoutly to himself, thinks only of how he felt, whether the words surprised him like a sudden thought, or he heard, alas, what he had said to himself, or he heard what he thought did not apply to himself. A heart may indeed accuse itself, but from this it still does not follow that it must condemn itself; and we of course do not teach heavy-minded exaggeration any more than we teach light-minded indulgence. But when it is a matter of speaking about the words just read, how would one find better hearers than on a day such as this and better than such as these who have come here today, not from the distractions of the world, but from the concentration of the confessional, where each one separately has made an accounting to God, where each one separately has let his heart be the accuser, which it can indeed do best since it is the confidant, and which it also had better do betimes lest at some time it must in a terrible way become that against a person's own will. Yet there certainly is a difference between guilt and guilt; there is a difference between owing five hundred shillings and only fifty.[90] One person can have much, much more to reproach himself for than another; there can also be the one who must say to himself that his heart condemns him. Perhaps there is such a person present here, or perhaps there is no such person present, but nevertheless we all are in need of comfort. Moreover, it certainly cannot be discomforting to anyone that the words of comfort are so rich in compassion that they include everyone; this certainly cannot be discomforting to anyone, even if his heart does not condemn him. Yet we all, we whose hearts do not acquit us, essentially need the same comfort: [91]God's greatness, that he is greater than our hearts.

God's greatness is in forgiving, in showing mercy, and in this, his greatness, he is greater than the heart that condemns itself. See, this is the greatness of God about which we should speak particularly in the holy places, because here we do indeed know God in a different way, more intimately, if one may say so, than out there, where he surely is manifest, is known in his works, whereas here he is known as he has revealed himself as he wants to be known by the Christian. Everyone, *marveling*, can see the signs by which God's greatness in nature is known,[92] or rather there actually is no sign, because the works themselves are the signs. For example, everyone can of course see the rainbow and must marvel when he sees it. But the sign of God's greatness in showing mercy is only *for faith*; this sign is indeed the sacrament. God's greatness in nature is *manifest*, but God's greatness in showing mercy is a *mystery*, which must be believed. Precisely because it is not directly manifest to everyone, precisely for that reason it is, and is called, the *revealed*. God's greatness in nature promptly awakens *astonishment* and then *adoration*; God's greatness in showing mercy is first an occasion *for offense* and then is *for faith*. When God had created everything, he looked at it and behold, "it was all very good,"[93] and every one of his works seems to bear the appendage: *Praise, thank, worship the Creator.* But appended to his greatness in showing mercy is: *Blessed is he who is not offended.*[94]

All our language about God is, naturally, human language. However much we try to preclude misunderstanding by in turn revoking what we say—if we do not wish to be completely silent, we are obliged to use human criteria when we, as human beings, speak about God. What, then, is true human greatness? Surely it is greatness of heart. We do not by rights say that someone is great who has much power and dominion, yes, even if there lived or had lived a king whose sovereignty was over the whole world—however hasty our amazement is in promptly calling him great—the more profound person does not allow himself to be disturbed by externality. On the other hand, if it were the lowliest person who has ever lived—when you are witness to his action in the moment of decision, when you see him truly act nobly, and with his whole heart magnanimously forgive his enemy, in self-denial bring the ultimate sacrifice, or when you are witness to the inner forbearance with which he lovingly endures evil year after year—then you say, "He certainly is great; he is truly great." Therefore greatness of heart is the true human greatness, but greatness of heart is to master one-self in love [*Kjerlighed*].

When we, then, human beings as we are, want to form a conception of God's greatness, we must think about true human greatness, that is, about love and about the love that forgives and shows mercy. But what does this mean, would the meaning be that we want to compare God to a human being, even if this human being were the noblest, the purest, the most reconciling, the most loving person who has ever lived? Far from it. The apostle does not speak that way either. He does not say that God is greater than the most loving human being, but that he is greater than the heart that condemns itself. God and the human being resemble each other only inversely. You do not reach the possibility of comparison by the ladder of direct likeness: great, greater, greatest; it is possible only inversely. Neither does a human being come closer and closer to God by lifting up his head higher and higher, but inversely by casting himself down ever more deeply in worship. The broken heart[95] that condemns itself cannot have, seeks in vain to find, an expression that is strong enough to describe its guilt, its wretchedness, its defilement—God is even greater in showing mercy!

What a strange comparison! All human purity, all human mercy is not good enough for comparison; but a repenting heart that condemns itself—with this is compared God's greatness in showing mercy, except that God's greatness is even greater: as deep as this heart can lower itself, and yet never itself deep enough, so infinitely elevated, or infinitely more elevated, is God's greatness in showing mercy! See, language seems to burst and break in order to describe God's greatness in showing mercy. Thought tried in vain to find a comparison, then finally found it, something that, humanly speaking, is no comparison, the brokenness of a repentant heart—God's mercy is even greater. A repentant heart when in brokenness and contrition it condemns itself, yes, this heart would give itself no rest, not for one single moment; it would find no hiding place where it could flee from itself. It would find no excuse possible, would find it a new, the most terrible, guilt to seek an excuse. It would find no relief, none; even the most compassionate word that the most compassionate inwardness is able to think up would sound to this heart, which would not dare and would not allow itself to be comforted, like a new condemnation upon it—so infinite is God's greatness in showing mercy, or it is even greater.

It limps, this comparison—a human being always does after wrestling with God.[96] It is far-fetched, this comparison—indeed it is, because it was found by God-fearingly rejecting all human likeness. If a human being does not dare to make for himself any image of God,[97] then surely he does not dare to imagine that the human could be a direct comparison. Let no one be in a hurry in seeking, let no one be too hasty in wanting to have found a comparison for God's greatness in showing mercy. Every mouth is to be stopped;[98] everyone is to beat his breast—because there is only one comparison that is any at all, a troubled heart that condemns itself.

But God is greater than this heart! Be comforted, then. Perhaps you learned earlier from experience how hard it is for such a heart to be brought before the judgment of Pharisees and Scribes, or to encounter the misunderstanding that knows only how to tear it to pieces even more, or the pettiness that disquiets the heart even more—you, who so greatly needed someone who was great. God in heaven is greater. He is not greater than the Pharisees and Scribes, nor is he greater than misunderstanding and pettiness; nor is he greater than the person who nevertheless knew how to say a soothing word to you, with whom you found some solace because he was not pettyminded, did not want to put you down even more but wanted to raise you up—God is not greater than he (what a disconsolate comparison!)—no, God is greater than your own heart! Ah, whether it was a sickness of soul that so darkened your mind every night that finally in deadly anxiety, brought almost to the point of madness by the conception of God's holiness, you thought you had to condemn yourself; whether it was something terrible that so weighed upon your conscience that your heart condemned itself—God is greater! If you will not believe, if you dare not believe without seeing a sign, it is now offered to you. He who came to the world and died, he died also for you, also for you. He did not die for people as such in general—oh, just the opposite, if he died for

anyone in particular, then it was indeed for the one, not for the
ninety and nine[99]—alas, and you are too wretched to be included
at random in the round number; the weight of wretchedness and
guilt fell so terribly upon your heart that you are counted out.
And he who died for you when you were a stranger to him,[100]
would he abandon his own! If God so loved the world that he
gave his only begotten Son in order that no one would be lost,[101]
why would he not keep those who were so dearly bought! Oh,
do not torture yourself; if it is the anxieties of depression that
ensnare you, then God knows everything—and he is great! And
if it is a ton of guilt that rests upon you, he who on his own
initiative (something that did not arise in any human heart[102])
showed mercy upon the world, he is great! Do not torture yourself, remember that woman, that there was no one who condemned her, and bear in mind that this same thing can be expressed also in another way: Christ was present. Precisely because
he was present, there was no one who condemned her. He res-
cued her from the condemnation of the Pharisees and Scribes;
they went away ashamed; because Christ was present, there was
no one who condemned her. Then Christ alone remained with
her—but there was no one who condemned her. Just this, that he
alone remained with her, signifies in a far deeper sense that there
was no one who condemned her. It would have been of only
little help to her that the Pharisees and Scribes went away; after
all, they could come again with their condemnation. But the
Savior alone remained with her: therefore there was no one who
condemned her. Alas, there is only one guilt that God cannot
forgive—it is to refuse to believe in his greatness!

He is greater than the heart that condemns itself. But, on the
other hand, there is nothing about his being greater than the
worldly, frivolous, foolish heart that fatuously counts on God's
imagined greatness in forgiving. No, God is and can be just as
scrupulous as he is great and can be great in showing mercy. For
example, God's nature always joins opposites, just as in the miracle of the five small loaves.[103] The people had nothing to eat—
through a miracle a superabundance was created, but see, then
Christ commands that everything left over be carefully collected.
How divine! One person can be wasteful, another thrifty; but if

there were a human being who through a miracle could at any moment divinely create a superabundance, do you not think that he humanly would have disdained the fragments, do you think that he—divinely would have collected the fragments! So also with God's greatness in showing mercy; a human being scarcely has the slightest idea of how scrupulous God can be. Let us not deceive ourselves, let us not lie to ourselves, and let us not, which amounts to the same thing, depreciate God's greatness by wanting to make ourselves out to be better than we are, less guilty, or by naming our guilt with more frivolous names; in so doing we depreciate the greatness of God, which is in forgiving. But neither let us insanely want to sin even more in order to make the forgiveness even greater,[104] because God is just as great in his being scrupulous.

    X
    309

    Let us then here in your holy house praise your greatness, O God, you who incomprehensibly showed mercy and reconciled the world to yourself. Out there the stars proclaim your majesty, and the perfection of everything proclaims your greatness, but in here it is the imperfect, it is sinners who praise your even greater greatness! —The supper of remembrance is once again prepared; may you then beforehand be brought to mind and thanked for your greatness in showing mercy.

VII

Luke 24:51

PRAYER

You who came down from heaven to bring blessing to the fallen human race, you who walked here upon earth in poverty and lowliness, despised, betrayed, insulted, condemned—but blessing; you who while blessing were parted from your own, you who ascended again into heaven: our Savior and Redeemer, bless also those who are assembled here today, bless their taking part in this holy meal in your remembrance. Oh, there is always something lacking in every meal, but if the blessing is lacking, what would this Lord's Supper be without your blessing; it would not exist at all, since it is indeed the meal of the blessing!

Luke 24:51 **And it happened, as he blessed them, he was parted from them.**[105]

"As he blessed them, he was parted from them." These words contain the report of his ascension. He was parted from them "and was carried up into heaven"(Luke 24:51); "a cloud took him out of their sight" (Acts 1:9), but the blessing remained behind; they never saw him again, but they were keenly aware of the blessing. "They gazed up toward heaven" (Acts 1:10), because he, blessing them, was parted from them. But this, of course, is always how he is parted from his own—blessing them; and this is always how he comes to his own—blessing them; and this is always how he is with his own—blessing them. He is not parted from anyone in any other way, unless that one bears the terrible responsibility for it himself. Just as that progenitor of the Hebrew people who wrestled with God said, "I will not let you go unless you bless me,"[106] so it is as though he says, "I will not leave you without blessing you, and every time you meet with me I will not part from you without blessing you." When those who are gathered here today to meet with him return home from this meeting, may there be for them a blessing, because one is convinced that when they were parted from him, or when he was parted from them, he blessed them.

Devout listeners, whatever a person is going to undertake, whether the work is great and significant or lowly and insignificant, he is able to do nothing if God does not give his blessing. The master builder builds in vain if God does not give his blessing;[107] the wise man ponders in vain if God does not give his blessing; the rich man accumulates abundance in vain if God does not give his blessing. It is the same either way; it is the blessing that satisfies when you have abundance, and it is the blessing that makes poverty into abundance. But is it indeed true that no work succeeds and progresses unless God blesses it? Ah, we often see the human undertaking that succeeds, even extraordinarily, although God certainly did not bless it. Yes, this is so, and therefore we must say that the one who only wants—to have God's blessing for assistance just so that his undertaking will succeed, humanly speaking—does not pray worthily; he himself is not conscious of what he is asking, or he even presumes to want God to serve him rather than that he is to serve God. No, the blessing is the good in itself; it is the one thing needful, is infinitely more glorious and blessed than all success. What, then, is the blessing? The blessing is God's consent to the undertaking that a person prays God to bless. And what does it mean that he prays for the blessing? It means that he dedicates himself and his undertaking to serving God—regardless of whether or not it, humanly speaking, succeeds or progresses. Therefore we must say that every godly undertaking is futile if God does not bless it, because it is a godly undertaking only through God's giving it his blessing.

Every undertaking certainly can be and ought to be a godly undertaking, but the more decisively it is a godly undertaking and the more clearly a person is aware that what he has in mind is a godly undertaking, the more clearly and deeply he also feels that he needs the blessing and that it is futile if God does not bless it. For example, to pray is a godly undertaking, but is this not also

the thought that lies closest to the one who prays, that God will
bless his prayer—not primarily that God will grant his request,
but that God will bless his praying so that it might be or become
the right praying! What does a person pray for? For the blessing—but therefore first and foremost for the blessing upon the
praying or for the praying. It is a godly undertaking to go to
the house of the Lord, but is not the thought lying closest indeed
the thought that it might become a blessing! What does a person
seek in God's house? The blessing—but first and foremost that
God will, as it is devoutly phrased, bless his coming in. The
clearer it becomes that it is a godly act you have in mind, to the
same degree the need of the blessing will also become more profoundly clear to you, because the more you become involved
with God, the clearer it will be how much less you yourself are
capable of doing. If you become involved with him with all your
mind and with all your strength, then it will be entirely clear that
you yourself are capable of nothing, and it will be all the more
clear that you are entirely in need of the blessing.

But receiving Holy Communion is indeed in the strictest
sense a holy act, a godly undertaking. You are to receive Holy
Communion—it is for this holy act that you are gathered here
today. You receive Holy Communion in order to meet him, for
whom you long more every time you are parted from him. But
if as a human being you are nothing before God, therefore entirely in need—at the Communion table as a sinner you are in
relation to the Redeemer less than nothing—you feel all the
more deeply the need of the blessing. At the Communion table
you are capable of doing nothing at all. And yet it is there at the
Communion table that declaration is made of satisfaction for
guilt and sin, for your guilt and your sin. The greater the requirement is that you be capable of something and the more necessary
this is when you nevertheless are capable of nothing, all the more
clear it therefore becomes, and all the more deeply do you realize, that you are capable of less than nothing—but then all the
more clear is the need for the blessing, or that it is everything. At
the Communion table you are capable of nothing at all. Satisfaction is made there—but by someone else; the sacrifice is offered—but by someone else; the Atonement is accomplished—

by the Redeemer. All the more clear it therefore becomes that the blessing is everything and does everything. At the Communion table you are capable of less than nothing. At the Communion table it is you who are in the debt of sin, you who are separated from God by sin, you who are so infinitely far away, you who forfeited everything, you who dared not step forward; it is someone else who paid the debt, someone else who accomplished the reconciliation, someone else who brought you close to God, someone else who suffered and died in order to restore everything, someone else who steps forward for you. If at the Communion table you want to be capable of the least little thing yourself, even merely to step forward yourself, you confuse everything, you prevent the reconciliation, make the satisfaction impossible. [108]It holds true at the Communion table as it was said to that impious man who in a storm implored heaven for deliverance, "By all means do not let God notice that you are present."[109] Everything depends on someone else's being present at whom God looks instead of looking at you, someone else you count on because you yourself only subtract. At the Communion table, therefore, he is present, blessing, he who, blessing, was parted from his own, he to whom you are related as the infant was related to him when he blessed it,[110] he your Savior and Redeemer. You cannot meet him before the Communion table as a co-worker as you indeed can meet God in your work as a co-worker.[111] You cannot be Christ's co-worker in connection with the reconciliation, not in the remotest way. You are totally in debt; he is totally the satisfaction. [112]It is indeed all the more clear that the blessing is everything. What is the blessing? The blessing is what God does; everything that God does is the blessing; the part of the work in which you call yourself God's co-worker, the part God does, is the blessing. But at the Communion table Christ is the blessing. The divine work of reconciliation is Christ's work, and in it a human being can do only less than nothing—therefore the blessing is everything, but if the work is Christ's, then Christ is indeed the blessing.

At the Communion table you are able to do nothing at all, not even this, that you hold fast the thought of your unworthiness and in this make yourself receptive to the blessing. Or would you

X
316

dare, and even if it were only at the last moment as you come up to the Communion table, would you dare even with regard to the thought that recognizes your own unworthiness, would you dare to guarantee yourself, trust in yourself, that you would be able to keep away everything disturbing, every anxious thought of recollection that, alas, wounds from behind, every suddenly aroused mistrust that turns against you as if you were still not adequately prepared, every most transient delusion of security in yourself! Alas, no, you are capable of nothing, not even of holding your soul by yourself at the peak of consciousness that you stand totally in need of grace and the blessing. Just as someone else supported Moses when he prayed,[113] so also at the Communion table you must be supported by the blessing; when you are to receive the blessing, it must encompassingly support you as it is communicated to you.

The pastor who is present at the Communion table is not able to communicate the blessing to you, nor is he able to support you. Only he who is personally present is able to do that, he who not only communicates but is the blessing at the Communion table. He himself is present; he blesses the bread when it is broken; it is his blessing in the cup that is handed to you. But it is not only the gifts that are blessed—no, the supper itself is the blessing. You partake not only of the bread and wine as blessed, but when you partake of the bread and the wine you partake of the blessing, and this is really the supper. Only he who instituted this supper, only he can prepare it—because at the Communion table he is the blessing.

See, therefore he stretches out his arms at the Communion table; he bows his head toward you—blessing! In this way he is present at the Communion table. Then you are parted from him again, or then he is parted from you again—but blessing. God grant that it might also become a blessing to you!

THE CRISIS AND A CRISIS IN THE LIFE OF AN ACTRESS

by Inter et Inter

The thought of being an actress, that is, one of eminence, no doubt promptly evokes in most people the idea of a situation in life so enchanting and splendid that in the thought of it they often entirely forget the thorns: the incredibly many banalities, all the unfairness, or at least the misunderstanding with which an actress may have to contend especially in the decisive moments. X 323

Let us imagine a situation as propitious as possible; let us imagine an actress who is in the possession of all that is required for being unconditionally eminent. Let us imagine that she receives the recognition of admiration and that she is fortunate enough not to become the target (which is indubitably a tremendous good fortune) of some spiteful person's persecution—so then she goes on living year after year, the envied fortunate object of incessantly continuing appreciative admiration. It seems so glorious, it seems as if it were something; but if one looks more closely and sees the kind of coin in which this appreciative admiration is paid, sees the meager sum of shabby banalities that in the world of theater critics constitutes the fund *ad usus publicos* [for public use][1] (and it is indeed from this fund that the incessant appreciative admiration is normally paid), it may very well be possible that even this most fortunate situation for an actress is quite shoddy and cheap. —If it is true, as is said, that the wardrobe of the Royal Theater is thought to be very expensive and valuable, it is certain that the wardrobe of the newspaper critics is dreadfully shabby. X 324

Further. The admired artist goes on living year after year. Just as in middle-class households one knows exactly in advance what will be served for dinner each day, so also does she know exactly the season's perquisites in advance. Two or three times a week she will be praised and admired, cited for excellence; already in the course of the first three months, she will more than once have looked through the sum of stock phrases in the newspaper reviews—and turns of speech [*Vendinger*], as they with special emphasis may be called, since they return [*vende tilbage*] again and again. Once or twice, in good years thrice, she will be celebrated by some unsuccessful seedy fellow or would-be poet; her portrait will be painted for every art exhibition; she will be lithographed and, if fortune favors her very much, her portrait will even be printed on handkerchiefs and hat crowns. And she, who as a woman is jealous of her name—as a woman, she knows that her name is on everyone's lips even when they wipe their mouths with the handkerchief; she knows that she is the object of everyone's admiring discussion, also of those who are dying to have something to chatter about. She goes on living like this year after year. It seems so glorious, it seems as if this were something, but insofar as she is to live in the more positive sense on the costly nourishment of this admiration, find encouragement in it, be strengthened and stirred by it to ever new effort, even the most superbly talented person, and especially a woman, in a weaker moment may still look around despondently for an expression of genuine appreciation. Then at such a time she will really feel, something she of course has often sensed herself, how empty all this is and how unfair to envy her this burdensome glory.[2]

Meanwhile, the years go by, yet not many in these times of curiosity and impatience; so there is already gossip going around that she is getting older, and so—well, yes, we do indeed live in Christian countries, but just as one often enough sees examples of esthetic bestiality, so, too, the cannibalistic taste for human sacrifices has far from become obsolete in Christendom. The same fervid insipidity that without ceasing beat the big drum of banality in her praise and celebrated her eloquently on the cymbals,[3] the same insipidity now becomes bored with its idolized artist; it wants to get rid of her, does not want to see her anymore—she may thank God if it does not wish to have her exterminated. The same insipidity acquires a new sixteen-year-old idol, and in her honor the former idol has to experience the total disfavor of banality—because the great difficulty bound up with being an idol is that it is almost inconceivable that one can receive honorable discharge from this appointment. Or if this is not the case or is not as crude as presented here, then at times something else happens that seems much better but basically is just as bad. Coming on the run from the past, banality has such a good momentum with admiration that the idolized one is still allowed to go on with terminal velocity for a time after she, as they say, has become older. To all appearances no change in banality's expressions about the idolized artist has occurred; yet one seems to sense a certain uncertainty that betrays that the eulogizing Rosiflengius[4] begins to fancy just a little that he is doing the artist a favor by *chivalrously* continuing to say the same thing. But to be chivalrous to an artist is the very height of effrontery, a sticky impertinence, and the most loathsome obtrusiveness. Anyone who is somebody and is essentially somebody *eo ipso* [precisely thereby] has a claim to being recognized for this very qualification, no more and no less. —If it is so, as is said, that the theater is a sanctuary, [5]profanation is at least not far off. How burdensome and painful at the age of sixteen to have to endure in the form of art criticism the hypocritical bowing and scraping and declarations of love from old bald-headed or half-witted reviewers; how bitter sometime later to have to put up with the brashness of chivalry!

But why, now, this inhumanity that causes so much unfairness, yes, cruelty, to women dedicated to the service of art, why, if it is not that esthetic culture is so rare among people? When it comes to the feminine, most people's art criticism has categories and thought-patterns essentially in common with every butcher's assistant, national guardsman, and store clerk, who talk enthusiastically about a damned pretty and devilishly pert wench of eighteen years. These eighteen years, this damned prettiness and this devilish pertness—this is art criticism—and also its bestiality. On the other hand, at the point where, from the esthetic point of view, the interest really begins, there where the inner being beautifully and with intense meaning becomes manifest in the metamorphosis—there the crowd of people falls away. If one continues to admire, then they think one is chivalrous or is lenient, because when she is only thirty years old she is basically *perdue* [undone]!

It would really be desirable, especially for the sake of the people themselves, lest they be excluded or exclude themselves from the most meaningful pleasures, if this prejudice could be effectually eradicated. And a prejudice it actually is, yes, a bestial

x
326

prejudice, because it is not true that a woman becomes an actress in her eighteenth year; if she becomes that at all, she becomes that rather in her thirtieth year or later, inasmuch as this acting in comedies in the eighteenth year is esthetically a dubious sort of thing. To begin one's admiration with the second stage of development is so far from being chivalry that the opposite, to admire a little miss of sixteen years, is easily flattery. I do not really think that an essentially cultured esthetician could persuade himself to make an actress of sixteen years the subject of a review, especially if she is very beautiful etc. He would undoubtedly *perhorrescere* [shudder greatly at] this dubiousness. True, it will often happen that the girl who at eighteen has created a sensation does not carry through. Be that as it may, but in that case she has not essentially been an actress either; so she has created a sensation on stage in quite the same sense as when a young girl creates a sensation in the social club[6] for a winter or two. On the other hand, it is also true that if the metamorphosis is successful, chivalry is out of the question, because then and only then is the admiration, in the esthetic sense, seriously appropriate.

See, much is done in the theater to secure the future of the actresses. I think that it would also be very beneficial to get this altogether unesthetic superstition about the eighteen years completely eradicated and to get it made completely clear that the important decision comes much later—this would also serve to safeguard the actresses' future. The issue itself has not only esthetic interest but to a high degree psychological interest also; therefore I am amazed that it is not more frequently made a subject of consideration. What is of interest is, with the help of the psychological, to be able purely esthetically to figure out the metamorphosis, or at least to be able to explain it when it has occurred.

A little article in a newspaper, however, is not the place that lends itself to a more detailed investigation that examines several instances. Therefore I shall here attempt to describe purely psychologically and esthetically only one metamorphosis, certainly a difficult one, but for that very reason a beautiful and significant one. In other words, the more that has been given and therefore the more that is invested in the first extension,[7] the more difficult

X
327

it is to get a new extension; and the more a basically unesthetic public, idolizing and noisy, has been aware of the first extension, the more easily this same public is transformed into an alarmed, suspicious, or even sullen opposition to the metamorphosis. An actress who has never had the good fortune to be in decisive possession of what captivates and enchants the unesthetic spectators to such a high degree perhaps can have, in compensation for that, the good fortune to make her metamorphosis in all quietness. This, too, is beautiful, and precisely because it takes place so quietly; but it is also easier, just because the quiet transformation preliminary to the metamorphosis is not sought after by curiosity and is not disturbed by misunderstanding but is cut off from the public's whims and caprices. The public is strange; when time in the course of ten years, for example, has taken the liberty of making its declared favorite ten years older, the public becomes angry—with the favorite.

II

I have in mind, therefore, an actress at the very beginning of her career, in the first success of her early youth, at the moment when she first made her appearance and the first time she scored a brilliant success.[8] It is esthetically appropriate for me to speak of this here and to have the joy of speaking of it, because this investigation is ideal and does not concern itself with an actual actress of sixteen years who is contemporary.[9] It is esthetically proper, also for another reason, for me to describe such a first youth; since the real subject of the investigation is the metamorphosis, not even in the thought of the essay am I contemporary with that youthfulness. The description of the first period is to prepare the ground, is a poetical and philosophical recollection entirely devoid of sadness. The first period is not dwelt upon but instead is hastily superseded just as one always hastens on to what is higher, and the author is indeed esthetically convinced that the metamorphosis is the highest.

She makes her debut, then, in her seventeenth year. She possesses—well, what she possesses is very difficult to define, simply because it is an indefinable something that nevertheless omnipotently asserts itself and is unconditionally obeyed. The grumpiest, the most boring person—it is useless for him to harden himself, he must obey. A mathematician—it is useless for him to rear up pugnaciously and ask, "What, then, does it demonstrate?"—he must obey, he is basically convinced. Ergo, she possesses—well, what she possesses is very difficult to define simply because it is an indefinable something. How strange! Ordinarily one is able to say exactly what a person possesses, and when one can do that, one can in turn see exactly how far along he comes—with what he possesses. A young actress, on the other hand, who possesses this indefinable possession instantly impoverishes, so to speak, all property holders.

This indefinable possession is, in order to come yet a little closer to defining it, *good fortune*; she has good fortune. Here good fortune does not mean that she is lucky enough to have good friends and important connections, or lucky enough to be engaged by the theater on advantageous terms, or so lucky that the director and the critics are interested in her—no, here good fortune means what Caesar told the ship captain about when he said to him: You are carrying Caesar—and his good fortune.[10] Yes, if it would not challenge her good fortune, she could rashly dare to have printed on the poster every night she is playing: Miss Jane Doe and her good fortune—to that degree does she possess good fortune. She does not bring good fortune with her, and it is a great thing that this omnipotent force is pleased to escort a young girl—no, good fortune itself is at her beck and call. And insofar as she cannot be said to be in possession of good fortune, then it must be because she is as if possessed by good fortune—to such a degree that it accompanies her where she walks and stands, in everything she undertakes, in the slightest motion of her hand, in every intimation of her eyes, in every toss of her head, in every turn of her body, in her walk, in her voice, in her gestures. In short, good fortune accompanies her in such a way that it does not allow the expert critic to see for one second what she would be able to do without good fortune, even if he were already esthetically aware of whether the best of all this still does not, in an altogether different sense, belong to her.

Her indefinable possession, in order to come yet a little closer to defining it, further signifies *youthfulness*. This does not mean statistics, that exactly one week ago Monday she turned sixteen, nor that she is a young girl who by reason of her beauty and the like is properly put on *show* [*Skue*] and to that extent is improperly called an *actress* [*Skuespillerinde*]; no, her youthfulness is again an indefinable wealth. First and foremost it is animation's play of powers, what could also be called the robust, copious restlessness of youth, which one always and involuntarily speaks of with partiality, as when one says that the fortunately gifted child is the fidgeter in the family. Restlessness, in the sense of the hubbub of finitude, soon palls; but restlessness in the pregnant sense, the restlessness of infinity,[11] the joyous, robust originality that, rejuvenating, invigorating, healing, stirs the water[12] is a great rarity, and it is in this sense that she is restlessness. Yet in turn this restlessness signifies something, and something very great; it signifies the first fieriness of an essential genius. And this restlessness does not signify anything accidental; it does not mean that she cannot stand still; on the contrary, it signifies that even when she is standing still one has an intimation of this inner restlessness, but, note well, in repose. It does not mean that she comes running onto the stage; on the contrary, it means that when she is merely moving one has an intimation of the impetus of infinity. It does not mean that she talks so fast that one cannot follow her; on the contrary, it means that when she speaks very slowly one senses the animation and inspiration. This restlessness does not mean that she must very soon become tired; just the opposite, it discloses an elementary indefatigableness, like that of the wind, of the sounds of nature;[13] it discloses that her roguishness is inexhaustibly rich, so that it continually only betrays that she possesses ever so much more; it discloses that her coquetry (and a character such as this utterly without coquetry is unthinkable) is nothing else than a happy, innocent mind's joyful, triumphant awareness of its indescribable good fortune. Therefore this is not actually coquetry but is an added stimulus for the spectator; that is, it safeguards the trustworthiness of the whole and protects the exuberance with complete security.

One would think that trustworthiness on the one hand and on the other roguishness, animation, good fortune, and youthfulness are utterly heterogeneous qualifications that do not belong together at all. Yet this is by no means the case—they do absolutely belong together. If roguishness and animation are not unconditionally safeguarded by a complete trustworthiness that here is enough, enough for her, enough for a half dozen others, then the performance is *eo ipso* ill-starred and enjoyment is essentially absent. Their inseparability is also recognizable in the altogether consistent matching of roguishness and trustworthiness, as when an elderly but still lively man with total partiality for a roguish young girl says, "By Jove, that's a trustworthy little miss." He is not saying that she is roguish, but that she is trustworthy, and yet in so saying he is explicitly declaring that she is roguish, and this is not his invention, but she extorts, as it were, this statement from him by her roguishness.

X
330

One would think that exuberance on the one hand and a completely secure safeguard on the other would be heterogeneous qualifications that do not belong together at all or that only muddleheadedness could think of putting together, and yet they are precisely inseparable, and the dialectic is the deviser of this compounding. It holds true of everything that is a natural qualification, and as such something single, something uncompounded, that it must be completely secured. In what is compounded, something can very well be missing, but something that is single, is immediacy, must be complete or, which amounts to the same thing, when it is, it is complete. A little exuberance is *eo ipso* to be rejected as something ungraceful. Just because of its completely secure safeguard, genuine exuberance has first and foremost a calming effect on the spectator, something that may escape the attention of most people, who are of the opinion that exuberance has a stimulating effect, which is true only of a false exuberance or of a little exuberance.

Let us take an example from the immediate comic, from caprice.[14] When on an evening we see Rosenkilde[15] come onstage as if directly from infinity and with its momentum, possessed by all the spirits of caprice, when promptly at first sight we involuntarily say to ourselves: "Well, tonight he's going to be a riot," we feel *eo ipso* indescribably calmed. We take a deep breath in order really to relax; we settle down comfortably as if we intend to remain sitting in the same position for a long time; we almost lament not having brought some food along, because the trustworthiness and the safeguard that induce tranquillity are so great that we forget that it is only a matter of one hour in the theater. While we laugh and laugh and privately revel in the exuberance of the caprice, we continually feel calmed, indescribably persuaded, and lulled, as it were, by the complete safeguard, because his caprice gives the impression that this can go on for any length of time. On the other hand, if a spontaneous comedian does not calm first and foremost, if there remains just a little bit of anxiety in the spectator as to how far his caprice will extend, the enjoyment is virtually lost. Ordinarily it is said that a comedian must be able to make the spectators laugh; perhaps it would be more correct to say he must first and foremost be able to calm completely, and then the laughter will come by itself, because genuine laughter, this laughter right from the bottom of the heart, does not break forth because of a stimulation but because of a calming. x
331

So also with exuberance. It must first and foremost calm by a complete safeguard; that is, if it is truly present in an actress, its first effect is completely calming. It is in this calm, induced by the complete safeguard and trustworthiness, that the spectator in turn surrenders—in exuberance. See, here it is again: exuberance and trustworthiness seem to be a strange compound. To say that exuberance is reliable is a strange way of talking, and yet it is the correct and only a new expression for roguishness, because trustworthy exuberance is precisely roguishness.

Her indefinable possession, in order to come yet a little closer to defining it, further signifies: *expressiveness of soul*—that in the mood of immediate passion she is attuned to idea and thought, that her as yet unreflective inwardness is essentially in harmony with ideality, that every touch of a thought or idea strikes a note and gives a sonorous echo, and that she has an original and unique sensitiveness. Thus she relates herself soulfully to the author's words, but she relates herself to herself in the something more that very properly may be called resonance in relation to the lines and consonance in relation to the whole character. She does not merely take the author's words correctly from his mouth, but she gives them back to him in such a way that in the co-sounding of roguishness, in the co-knowledge of ingeniousness, it is as if she were also saying: Can you do the same thing that I do?

Her indefinable possession finally signifies: *that she is in proper rapport with the onstage tension.* Every tension can affect in a twofold way; this is the dialectic's own dialectic. It can make the exertion manifest, but it can also do the opposite; it can conceal the exertion, and not only conceal it but continually convert, transform, and transfigure it into lightness. The lightness, then, is invisibly based on the exertion of the tension, but this is not seen, is not even intimated—only the lightness is made manifest. A weight can press something down, but it can also inversely conceal that it is pressing down and express the pressure by the opposite, by lifting something up. We speak colloquially of making ourselves light by casting off burdens, and this view is the basis of all banal life-views. In a higher, in a poetical and philosophical sense, the opposite holds true: one becomes light by means of—weight; one soars high and free by means of—a pressure. The celestial bodies, for example, hover in space by means of a great weight; the bird flies by means of a great weight; the light hovering of faith is precisely by means of an enormous weight; the highest soaring flight of hope is precisely by means of hardship and the pressure of adversity. But the onstage illusion and the weight of all those eyes are an enormous weight that is laid upon a person. Therefore, where this fortunate rapport is lacking, not even proficiency to an ever so high degree can entirely conceal the weight of the burden, but where this fortunate rapport is present, the weight of the burden continually transforms itself into lightness.

So it is with the young actress. She is in her element in the tension of the stage; precisely there she is light as a bird. The very weight gives her lightness, and the pressure gives her the soaring flight. There is not a trace of anxiety. In the wings she perhaps is anxious, but onstage she is happy and light as a bird that has gained its freedom, because it is only now, under pressure, that she is free and has gained freedom. What at home in her study, what in the wings manifests itself as anxiety is not lack of power but, exactly the opposite, is elasticity, which makes her anxious simply because she has no weight upon her. In the theatrical tension, this anxiety very happily transforms itself into intensification. After all, it is a very narrow view that a performer must not be anxious and above all a mediocre sign of the great performer that he is not anxious. Indeed, the more powers he has, the greater is his anxiety as long as he is outside the tension that is exactly proportionate to his powers. If in a personification the force of nature that supports the celestial bodies is pictured as removed from its task and waiting for that which it is to undertake, then it would be sitting in deadly anxiety and not until it shouldered the burden would it be carefree and light. Therefore one of the worst agonies for a person is to have too much elasticity in relation to the tension of the little world in which he lives. Such an unfortunate never comes to feel entirely free, just because he cannot obtain sufficient weight upon himself. The important thing is only that the anxiety strike altogether properly, so that with regard to the dramatic artist it is always offstage, never onstage, which is usually the case with someone who is not anxious offstage.

Her *definable possession* is, of course, easy to indicate. She has not only natural charm but has training also. As an auxiliary element, she has the most of what a dancer does her utmost to have. Her diction is correct and precise. Her voice is not misused but is cultivated; without stridency, without interruptions, it completely and distinctly embraces the words, which she does not keep to herself or for herself, but neither does she project them awkwardly. She articulates superbly, even when she whispers. She knows how to use her voice and, above all, something that very fortunately befits her qualifications, knows how to use it in the slight, easily tossed off digressions of the conversational lines. X
333

She makes her debut, then, in her seventeenth year. Her first public appearance is naturally a triumph, and at the same time her life turns into a national affair. Just as the daughter of the regiment is regarded as a daughter by the whole regiment,[16] so she becomes the nation's daughter. Merely the first sight of her is sufficient to convince everyone that it would be difficult to find more than one specimen of such a uniquely fortunate feminine talent in each generation. Therefore it becomes a national duty to admire and a common concern to protect this rare plant. Alas, and even if it cannot be called exactly a duty, still it becomes, as an inevitable result of human weakness, an interest of curiosity to see how long she now is able to last. Yes, human joy over the rarity is strange; almost at the first and highest moment of joy, curiosity's assassination begins. This is not envy, far from it; it is a kind of discomfiture on the part of the admiration, which in its jubilation is at its wit's end, so to speak, until, sure enough, in the very first year it hits upon the creating of this deleterious tension, which out of sheer admiration admires almost suspiciously.

To bring to mind once again something that has been frequently stated: if there lived an essential esthetician at the time and he was asked to appraise this actress or one of her performances, he would no doubt say: No, her time has not really come yet.

III

Fourteen years have passed and she is now in her thirty-first year. During these not so few years, she has been the object of that incessantly admiring recognition. Allow me to suggest this passage of time by using this interval for a few comments.[17] Let us not, on the basis of appearances, be deceived by a rough estimate of the sum of her perquisites and be led by that to envy her unfairly the admiration. Let us instead bear in mind how much bungling is mixed up in the incessant overflowing of this banal recognition, and above all let us not forget what it means and signifies that during these fourteen years it has actually become a habit for her contemporaries to admire her. If we want to reckon correctly, let us not forget, unfairly to her, to subtract this from the presumed glory of the admiration. Oh, how rarely is there a person, to say nothing of a generation, that does not indulge in the fraud of habit, so that even if the expression is not changed, yet this unchanged expression becomes something else through habit, so that now this verbatim sameness nevertheless sounds very weak, very mechanical, very flat, although the same thing is said. Oh, there is a lot of talk in the world about seducers and seductions, but how many indeed are those who are self-deceived through habit, so that they seem unchanged but yet are as if emaciated in their inner beings, so that they do, to be sure, love the same people, love them, but very dully and very meagerly, so that they do, to be sure, use the same tender expressions but very weakly, very powerlessly, very devoid of soul.

If a king were to visit a humble family—yes, the family would feel honored, proud, almost overwhelmed by their good fortune. But if his majesty were to keep on visiting the same family every day, how long would it be before the king would almost have to make an effort to find a little meaning in his visiting the family, who out of habit went on saying without change: We thank you for the great honor. Of all sophists, time is the most dangerous, and of all dangerous sophists, habit is the most cunning. It is already difficult enough to realize that one changes little by little over the years, but the fraud of habit is that one is the same, unchanged, that one says the same thing, unchanged, and yet is very changed and yet says it, very changed.

Just for that reason, all truly unworthy [*unyttig*], that is, unselfish [*uegennyttig*] servants of the truth, whose life is sheer struggle with the sophisms of existence, whose concern is not how one can best come out of it oneself but how one can most truly serve the truth and in truth benefit people—they have known how to use [*benytte*] illusions: in order to test people. When, for example, a distinguished man lives very secluded,[18] when he only seldom makes an appearance, [19]people are not spoiled by seeing him. There develops, however, a splendid, an expedient, *si placet* [if you please], illusion that this distinguished man must be somebody altogether extraordinary. Why? Is it because people know how to evaluate his splendid qualities? Alas, no—it is because they see him so seldom that the rare sight produces a fantastic effect. Past experience shows that this can be done. The method, masterfully described by Shakespeare in Henry IV's charge to Prince Henry,[20] has been used successfully by a great number of kings and emperors and ecclesiastics and

Jesuits and diplomats and schemers etc., among whom there no doubt were many excellent people, some of whom also wanted to serve the truth, but all of whom were nevertheless united in wanting to influence with the aid of an illusion, whether it was merely to profit from it themselves by making sure of the *stupor* [astonishment] of the crowd, or whether they devoutly, perhaps also sagaciously, thought they were securing for the truth a more universal propagation with the aid of—an illusion. The unconditionally unselfish servants of the truth, however, have always had the practice of associating considerably with the people; they have never played hide-and-seek with the crowd in order to play in turn the wonder game[21] when, on the rare occasion, they appear in public as the surprising object of wonder.[22] On the contrary, they have always appeared regularly in everyday clothes, have lived with the common man, have talked on the highways and byways, thus relinquishing all esteem—for when the crowd sees a man every day, then the crowd thinks something like this: Is that all? Alas, yes, "*mundus vult decipi* [the world wants to be deceived],"[23] but the unselfish witnesses to the truth have never wanted to enter into this illusion, they have never wanted to go halves with the crowd on the next part: "*decipiatur ergo* [therefore let it be deceived]." They have, on the contrary, deceived by doing the opposite, that is, they have judged the world by appearing unimportant.[24]

If an author who neither has a considerable fund of ideas nor is very industrious were to publish at long intervals an elegant copybook that is especially ornate and is resplendently provided with many blank pages—the crowd gazes at this elegant phenomenon with amazement and admiration and thinks that if he has been such a long time in writing it and if there is so little on the page it really must be something extraordinary. If, on the other hand, an idea-rich author who has something else to think about than elegance and making a profit from an illusion, exerting himself with ever greater diligence, finds himself able to work at an unusual speed, the crowd soon becomes accustomed to it and thinks: It must be slovenly stuff. The crowd, of course, cannot judge whether something is well worked out or not; it sticks to—the illusion. If a pastor, for example the otherwise so highly gifted late Court Chaplain in Berlin, Theremin,[25] preaches only every eighth Sunday or even only every twelfth, but then, of course, in the most exalted and royal presence of their majesties and the entire royal house[26]—there immediately develops an illusion with regard to such a Chief Court Chaplain.[27] He becomes—well, in truth he remains what he truly is, a highly gifted man, but in the eyes of the crowd he becomes, in addition to being Chief Court Chaplain, also City Chaplain [*Stadsprædikant*] or a magnificent [*stadselig*] Chief Court Chaplain, a magnificent specimen, something like the king's golden carriage that one sees with amazement a few times a year.[28] [29]The crowd will be astonished; in its wisdom it will think something like this: If such a speaker takes three months solely for working out one sermon and learning it by heart, it must indeed be something extraordinary. See, the crush of people would be so great on that inquisitively and long awaited eighth or twelfth Sunday that the Chief Court Chaplain would hardly be able to get up into the pulpit—if he had preached only once a year, the crush of people certainly would be so great that he would not have been able to get down again, or armed sextons and policemen would be required to procure the coming in and the going out of[30] the Venerable Chief Court Chaplain. [31]So great would be the crush of people, and if it so happened that someone was trampled to death in the crush, then the crush of people would be even greater next time, because it holds not only of the truth but also of curiosity that "*sanguis martyrum est semen ecclesiae* [the blood of the martyrs is the seed of the Church]."[32]

And now an actress who for fourteen years has constantly been an object of admiration. By this time, of course, people have seen her very often and have become lethargic in their admiration. They know, of course, that she will stay in this country; if she were one of those who travel in Europe, she could still have her hope for the assistance of the illusion. They know, of course, that she must remain here in the city, because Denmark has only one city and one theater. They know, of course, that she must act, since she is under contract; many people, despite their admiration, are perhaps shameless enough to realize that she *must* act because it is her livelihood. They know, of course, that they can

x
337

get to see her as often as twice a week. It goes without saying that they still continue to admire, but in a generation how many are there likely to be who know how to preserve the vigilance of fervency and appreciation so that in the fourteenth year of admiration they can see her with the same originality—with the same originality that she preserves! No, in this regard humankind resembles children in the marketplace;[33] when they perceive that they have something and are permitted to keep it, they become ungrateful, and if not plainly ungrateful, then at least lazy in the habit of admiration. To no one, therefore, are people so ungrateful as to God—simply because they have a lazy idea that they can always have him—alas, he cannot by dying ever make them feel what they lost. O human admiration, what sheer vanity you are, and not least when you think you are being constant!

No change, then, has taken place in the expression of admiration and recognition, only in the intonation; the *spiritus asper* [aspirated sound][34] of that first impression has diminished into the softer breathing of a perishable, habitual admiration. The actress's stock stands unchanged at the quoted price, yet not at all so firmly; a sneaky, uneasy, basically well-meaning but yet in its curiosity treasonable reflection is beginning to whisper that she is getting older. No one will admit it, and yet it is said, and yet no one will admit to having said it. The tension of the awkward situation is all the more painful simply because her existence has been a national affair. People do wish her well (we shall not dwell on the part the envy of individuals may have in the genesis of such an opinion); they are really angry with time, that it will make her older now when they have cozily settled down into the admiration's habit of thinking that she should always remain eighteen years old. But yet, yet they cannot be at ease with this idea that she is getting older. No one considers how they ungratefully make her metamorphosis more and more difficult, how ungratefully they repay her by changing recollection into opposition at the decisive moment—and no one considers that this whole thing may be balderdash that is totally out of place, at least in esthetics, since her era will really begin with the metamorphosis.

IV
(Final Article)

So now to the metamorphosis. The essential constituent of this actress was not what is ordinarily called feminine youthfulness. In that sense, this youthfulness is the prey of the years; however lovingly, however carefully time takes away, it nevertheless takes away this temporary quality. But there was in this actress an essential genius that related itself to the idea: feminine youthfulness. This is an idea, and an idea is something totally different from the externality of being seventeen years old, which is also the case with the most idea-less girl who becomes seventeen years old. If there had not been this relation of genius to the idea, a metamorphosis would be out of the question; but just because this is the case and the idea is what it is, the metamorphosis can become the rare occurrence. Just as nature preserves continuity by its foresight and its recollecting hindsight, which natural scientists have beautifully called the Promethean and the Epimethean,[35] so also in the realm of spirit, that which is actually to constitute the metamorphosis must be present from the beginning, although it is not decisively used or does not decisively make its appearance before some time has passed—precisely this is the metamorphosis.

The one who has feminine youthfulness only in the simple sense can have no metamorphosis, because feminine youthfulness in this sense is not intrinsically dialectical, is only one life, which upon the supervention of the dialectical cannot be divided and separated but only consumed. Time is the dialectical element that comes from without, and therefore it consumes, swiftly or slowly, the undialectical youthfulness. But where there is one additional life, there time, as it is taking something away from the simple youthfulness, will make the genius more and more manifest, and manifest in ideality's purely esthetic relation to the idea. Of course she will not be young again in the ridiculous sense in which butcher assistants and the public speak of a devilishly pert wench, but only in the sense of ideality will she be young and younger. Now she is very properly a subject for an essential critique, now when for the second time and raised to the second power she relates herself to the same idea or, expressed more exactly, just because it is the second time she relates herself purely ideally to the idea.

The matter is quite simple. The question can be posed this way: what setting corresponds essentially to a genius whose idea is feminine youthfulness? Most people, unfortunately, will very likely answer: It is feminine youthfulness or being seventeen years old. But certainly this is a misunderstanding that conflicts with the distinctive thought process of the dialectical. Purely ideally and dialectically, the requirement is that the setting, or that in which the idea is, relate itself to the idea at a distance from the idea. With regard to all natural qualifications, it holds true that the first time is the highest, is the culmination. In the sense of ideality, it holds true that the second time is the highest, since what is ideality other than precisely—the second time. The idea of youthfulness as a task and being very young oneself certainly do not correspond correctly to each other in the understanding of ideality. Insofar as unesthetic spectators are of the opposite opinion, it is because they are deceived by an illusion that confuses the joy over Miss Jane Doe's external youthfulness with the actress's essential ideality.

Let us take another example. There is a lyricism that might be called the lyricism of youthfulness; every young person *erectioris ingenii* [of more gifted nature] has a little of it. But then there is a young man who *qua* youth has this lyricism of youthfulness and also has genius, the idea of which is the lyricism of youthfulness. Now the question is, when will he produce his best lyrical poetry—in his twentieth year? By no means. His best lyrics will come at a somewhat older age, when time has taken away the fortunate accidentals of his youthfulness so that he now relates himself to his idea purely ideally and thereby, *serving*, also relates himself in a profounder sense to his idea. Those who have a sense only for the fortunate accidentals of that first youthfulness lack esthetic culture and therefore do not discover that this good fortune is the accidental and the perishable, whereas the genius and the relation to the idea are the eternal and the essential.

The most significant assignment given to an actress who relates herself to the idea of feminine youthfulness raised to its most
lyrical power is surely the role of Juliet in *Romeo and Juliet*. I
wonder if it would ever actually occur to an esthetician that an
actress of seventeen years could play Juliet? There is a great hue
and cry, it is true, about the full play of powers, this flame, this
fire, and many other things of that sort, but talk about them is
actually only in gallery categories, and categories of that sort are
inadequate for judging a conception of Juliet. What the gallery
wants to see is, of course, not an ideal performance, a representa-
tion of the ideality—the gallery wants to see Miss Juliet, a devilishly lovely and damnably pert wench of eighteen years who
plays Juliet or passes herself off as Juliet, while the gallery is enter-
tained by the thought that it is Miss Jane Doe. Therefore the
gallery can, of course, never get it into its head that in order to
represent Juliet an actress must essentially have a distance in age
from Juliet. Yet this is how it is, and that much admired excess of
powers in the eighteenth year is actually, from the esthetic point
of view, a misunderstanding, because in ideality it holds true that
the best power is the consciousness and transparency that know
how to make use of the essential powers, but note well, in the
service of an idea. No doubt there are assignments for an actress
in which the eighteen years are *quod desideratur* [what was
wanted], but those assignments are definitely not the eminent
ones. There are assignments in which the excess of powers of the
first youthfulness should be used as a charming game. Such an
actress can undertake these assignments, and this can be regarded
as a beautiful and also as a meaningful pastime until she becomes
so mature that with the essential powers she can assume the eminent assignments. To portray a little miss of sixteen years in a
French play will be the appropriate assignment. But to bear with
this superficial, frolicking fragility is also to be reckoned as nothing compared with having to carry the weight of Juliet's intense
complexity. It is self-evident that it would be a misunderstanding to suppose that everyone who at one time could portray such
an almost merely sketchy character could therefore in time also
be able to undertake the eminent assignments. No, far from it.

But for that very reason it is a rarity when the one who, continually animated and rejuvenated, has altogether successfully fashioned herself in the light characters of the fleeting sea nymphs[36]—when in the fullness of time she transforms herself in an eminent hypostasis.

The metamorphosis, then, will in an eminent sense become a return to her first state. This will be elucidated in some detail by indicating the dialectical determinants in the metamorphosis. Time, as stated, is the dialectical element that comes from outside, but she was in herself originally dialectical and for that very reason she can resist time; therefore its dialectic only makes manifest the dialectical in her—in the metamorphosis.

Time has asserted its rights; it has taken away something from the immediate, the first, the simple, the accidental youthfulness. But in so doing time will in turn specifically make her genius more essentially manifest. In the eyes of the gallery, she has lost; in the sense of ideality, she has gained. The time of the gallery's confusion of identities is over. If she is to play Juliet, it can no longer be a matter of creating a *furore* [sensation] as Miss Juliet. If she is to play that part, it must become an eminent performance or, even more correctly, a performance in the eminent sense. And precisely this is the metamorphosis. Force against force, as they say, and so also here: dialectics against dialectics. Then time has no power actually to take away; it is only a serving power that serves to make manifest.

Time has asserted its rights; it has taken away something from the fortunate accidentals or the accidental good fortune of that first youthfulness, but, forming and refining, it has also developed her so that now, in full and conscious, in acquired and dedicated command of her essential power, she is truly able to be a servant of her idea, which is the essential esthetic relation and essentially different from the immediate relation of the seventeen-year-old to distinctive youthfulness. It is this serving relation to the idea that is actually the culmination; precisely this conscious self-submission under the idea is the expression of the eminent elevation of the performance. The youthfulness of the seventeen-year-old is much too coy, much too self-confident, much too happy to serve in the deepest sense or, which is the same, in the highest sense. But wholly to serve is inwardness; the inwardness of the seventeen-year-old is essentially a hankering outward that with all its happiness can never be secure in the face of one or another accidental. Or if the emergence of the accidental is avoided, one still must say each time: That was lucky, since it is always possible. Only in the completely serving relation to the idea is the accidental made completely impossible.

Time has asserted its rights; there is something that has become a thing of the past. But then in turn an ideality of recollection will vividly illuminate the whole performance, an incarnation that was not present even in those days of the first youthfulness. Only in recollection is there complete tranquillity,[37] and therefore the calm fire of the eternal, its imperishable glow. She has been calmed in the eternity of her essential genius; she will not childishly or plaintively long for the blazing of what has vanished, because in the metamorphosis itself she has become too warm and too rich for that. This pure, calmed, and rejuvenating recollecting, like an idealizing light, will transilluminate the whole performance, which in this illumination will be completely transparent.

These are the elements of the metamorphosis. In order to illuminate its distinctiveness from yet another side, let us now in conclusion place another metamorphosis alongside for comparison. We choose one that is qualitatively different; this itself will give the comparison essential interest and at the same time prevent all curious quantifying as to which is more excellent etc. This other metamorphosis is the metamorphosis of continuity, which in turn, more closely defined, is a process, a succession, a steady transformation over the years, so that the actress as she grows older gradually changes her sphere, takes older roles, again with the same perfection with which she at a younger age filled younger roles. This metamorphosis could be called straightforward perfectibility. It has especially ethical interest and therefore will exceedingly please, indeed convince, as it were, an ethicist who, fighting for his life-view, proudly points to such a phenomenon as his victory and, in quiet inner gratitude, calls such an actress his omnipotent ally, because she, better than he and precisely at one of the most dangerous points, demonstrates his theory.[38] The metamorphosis, however, of which we have been speaking is the metamorphosis of potentiation, or it is a more and more intensive return to the beginning. This metamorphosis will completely engage an esthetician, because the dialectic of potentiation is the esthetic-metaphysical dialectic. Happier than even Archimedes, he will dithyrambically cry "Eureka!"[39] as he points at the phenomenon. Intoxicated in admiration and yet sober in dialectical levelheadedness, he will have eyes for this alone and will understand it as his call to create room so that this marvel can be seen and admired precisely as such.

Over the years the metamorphosis of continuity will spread evenly over the essential range of assignments within the idea of femininity. Over the years the metamorphosis of potentiation will stand in an ever more intensive relation to the same idea, which, note well, esthetically understood, is the idea of femininity *sensu eminentissimo* [in the most eminent sense]. If it is said of the actress who measures up to the metamorphosis of continuity that in the sense of ideality she will indeed become older but not older in the sense of temporality, then of the other one it must be said that she becomes younger. But it may be said of both of them that time has no power over them. There is, namely, one resistance to the power of the years—it is perfectibility, and it is precisely over the years that it develops. And there is another resistance to the power of the years; it is potentiation, and it is precisely over the years that it becomes manifest. Both phenomena are essential rarities, and both have this in common, that they become more rare with each year. Just because they are dialectically compounded, their existence year after year will also remain dialectical. Each year will make the attempt to demonstrate its thesis about the power of the years, but perfectibility and potentiation will triumphantly refute the thesis of the years. This again makes the spectator completely calm, because the youthfulness of the seventeenth year is still fragile, but perfectibility and potentiation are complete trustworthiness.

If with this little article I may have succeeded in contributing something to making it clear how safeguarded, despite the years, the future of the essential actress is, it would be a cherished satisfaction to me, all the more so because I am convinced that in

many ways there is enough misunderstanding of the proper conception of an actress's future, while the same misunderstanding
that mistakenly and unesthetically overrates the beginning mistakenly and unesthetically takes a wrong view of what comes
later or, more correctly, of the highest.

Summer 1847

Inter et Inter[40]

Addendum

PHISTER AS CAPTAIN SCIPIO

BY PROCUL[41]

Phister as Captain Scipio
(in the Comic Opera *Ludovic*[42])

It may seem accidental and strange to take just a single performance by such a wide-ranging actor as Phister, and if one does
take a single performance, then it may in turn again seem accidental and strange to select Captain Scipio in particular. Well, as
a matter of fact the latter is accidental, or there is something
accidental in it, but so it is and so it must be—least of all is there
any intimation of the silly notion that this role is the best, the
most splendid, etc. No, there is something accidental in it—
namely, "Captain Scipio" is an outstanding performance in what
is Phister's greatest strength: reflection—accordingly it is essentially appropriate to make it the subject of a review. The characteristic of the critical review commensurate with reflection is that
it concentrates on details, goes into detail; accordingly, with regard to Phister, it is essentially appropriate to make a single performance the subject of a review and of a detailed review—
rather than of a general discussion that here says very little. The
accidental aspect is that precisely this role has appealed to the
author. But there is something accidental in every genuine love
affair. The beloved girl surely owns several and far more expensive dresses than the blue-striped, red-checked, etc. in which the
lover perhaps saw her the first time, and yet this dress retains its
own peculiar value for him. When the beloved is dressed up to
go with him to a party—that is, dressed up for others—yes, then
she is dressed in silk etc.; but when she is dressed up perfectly—
that is, for him alone—then she wears that dress.

So it is here also. Truly, no matter how richly the richest
young girl is outfitted with dresses, she still would scarcely be as
richly outfitted as Phister's repertoire is with the most varied and
valuable costumes. But one of them has a purely accidental value
for one spectator, another for another—that is, he is, as it were,
in love with it, and when he must speak he chooses to speak

about this one, or to put it more correctly, not "when he must speak," but—it is for him a pleasure, a joy, a satisfaction to speak about it. Furthermore, he does indeed somewhat understand that basically all falling in love is nevertheless self-love, for there certainly is still some self-love in wanting to get to understand a masterful performance completely, or at least in a way completely different from the way others understand it, and approximately as the artist himself understands it.

But first of all some general comments. Phister's power is: *reflection*. For this reason there is scarcely any other actor on the stage as *diligent* as he is, and not many who even have merely an idea of what *diligence* is. In other words, diligence here, to take it in its pregnant meaning, is: *study*, thoughtfulness, reflection's care for every detail, even the least. It is, to be sure, said generally of every actor that he studies after a fashion; at times there is the complaint that one of them has not studied his role, and at times one of them even offers the excuse that he has not had time to study his role adequately—but how many, indeed, are there who are able to study a role, who have an artistically developed concept and idea of what it means to study a role? Most of them probably study the way Trop "studies,"[43] and therefore it is inconsiderate to reproach them for not having studied their role on a particular occasion, but it is no less remarkable when they themselves at times lament that they have not had the time to study, since Trop himself is an example that the length of time spent on "studying" is not exactly the decisive point. Not so with Phister. Study is essentially seen in his performance even though sometimes a very short time has been allowed to study the role. "Study" is precisely Phister's essential strength; he can use the longest time for studying a role, but he uses even the shortest time so intensively and reflectively that it becomes study. Thus there perhaps is scarcely any actor on our stage who feels to the extent he does the weight of carrying, so to speak, each particular performance forward, precisely because he has so little immediacy and such significant reflection, that is, precisely because the particular performance is in the strictest sense a study, is in each least little detail a thoroughly reflected totality.

IX
B 68
385

But this is also why no other actor on our stage could have as much reason as he to complain over the wretched critic who has nothing to offer but interjections. Even an immediate comedian could very well wish that the critic would intervene as an interpreter and would frequently find what was there to be found even if the artist himself did not know it—but for a reflective comedian who is conscious of every least little factor, his performance lays claim to definitely getting back again what he so definitely gives. The immediate genius himself has a relation to the interjection; but reflection on its own initiative relates to reflection and must require of the critic the tour de force, *si placet* [if you please], of being able to separate every detail in a performance of that kind, analyze each detail, and then put it all together again. In this regard Phister actually suffers under the mediocrity of our situation. Each of his performances is most often a bond, but in such a large denomination of reflection and consciousness that the local critic tries in vain to exchange it, or rather does not even make any attempt; thus the same thing happens to him as an artist as happened to that Englishman who lived in a provincial town and had in his possession a banknote that no one could cash and therefore almost got into a financial predicament.[44]

To say, in regard to reflection and a reflective performance, neither more nor less than "Bravo" or even "Bravissimo" is completely meaningless, is something that can only bore and weary the reflection that is the object of admiration and something that easily becomes a conversation like the one between a Japanese and a Danish sailor that Poul Møller has preserved. The Japanese said: *Tanko-panko*, to which the sailor very appropriately responded: Kiss my a—.[45] Admiration in relation to reflection must be expressed in the language of reflection and not in the language of immediacy. Reflection is this "why?—because"; why is the whole thing structured in this way?—because; why is this little line here?—it is because etc. Everything is consciousness. Admiration is then in turn able to discover and to understand the whole thing: why?—because. In the relation between reflection and reflection (and only like understands like), true admiration is therefore the perfect understanding, neither more

IX
B 68
386

nor less. In a certain sense, then, there is no admiration in the
relation between reflection and reflection. Suppose reflection A
is the one performing and reflection B intervenes as the one admiring. What does this mean? It means that B is trying to show
that he has understood A completely. If he succeeds in this, A
answers, "Fine, it is indeed so; I am well aware of it myself." If
it is a matter of admiration, then it could just as well be the other
way around, that reflection B is able to understand reflection A
totally. But this also cancels itself out; because B might respond
to this, "Fine, it is so; I am well aware of it myself." In other
words, the understanding between reflection and reflection is
released from obligation; there remains nothing incommensurable, the account balances, and for that very reason there is the
infinite remoteness of ideality between reflection and reflection.

So it is in the true relation between reflection and reflection. People who have a little reflection are not aware of this.
They have lost immediacy's beautiful passion to admire. Therefore their little bit of reflection develops a certain constraint in
them; it is this that becomes censorious pettiness and envy. But
this is not the case where there is essential reflection in the admiring reflection; there the relation between the admiring reflection
and the reflection that is its object is the proper relation. There is
nothing of that censorious pettiness, but neither is there any sign
of the pathology of immediate admiration—no heart palpita-
tions, no heightening of the blood pressure, and in the relation
no squeezing of each other's hands either, no gazing into each
other's eyes, no embracing, no genuflecting, no arm-in-arming,
no *gemütlich* [cozy] coagulating or clabbering; the relation is as
infinitely remote as possible, as dignifiedly remote as spirit can be
from spirit; and yet it is a relation between admirers. To immediacy this would seem the most inhuman of all. "Two admirers,"
it would say, "and yet they do not drink *dus*[46] with each other"
etc. No, in the reflective relation between reflection and reflection, this drinking *dus* with each other does not belong; there the
most dignified possible *De* prevails.

People and reviewers ordinarily prefer to become involved
only with admiring the immediate. The immediate or the person
of immediacy does not know which is which, what is good and

IX
B 68
387

what is bad. Furthermore, just because he has no self-awareness, the person of immediacy has a desire to hear this *Bravo, Bravissimo, schwere Noth, Gottes Blitz*! Here this kind of admiration is completely unconstrained; it makes no difference if it mistakenly admires something obtuse, thoughtless, an error in judgment, etc.; the one being admired does not himself know which is which; he is the blindfolded player in blindman's buff, and on the other hand he feels so good when people admire him. On those terms it is easy enough to admire. Not so with the reflective performance and the one who has reflected. The reflective performance is pure consciousness; to admire in this case, therefore, is akin to undergoing an examination: whether one has understood or not, whether one knows anything or not. If one says something obtuse here, a *Bravo* is of no help, and a *Bravo* in the wrong place is promptly registered as obtuseness.

IX
B 68
388

In relation to people, this consciousness is actually a misfortune for every reflective performance and every highly reflective individuality. This consciousness is what people call pride, malice, spite, irony—but immediacy's unconsciousness, which encourages the yowling of admiration, that is good nature, modesty, lovableness.

Scipio
Captain in the Papal Police Force

As far as known, the papal police force is noted for, if nothing else, its splendid uniforms: an almost gala garb with bows and silver trim. According to what I was told, at the time Phister accepted the role, it was his idea to play it exactly in this costume, but it was forbidden. I was also told why Phister even zealously insisted upon it, and this promptly shows his reflection. Scipio is a man who is not drunk, far from it, but nevertheless goes around in a continual state of fogginess, perhaps because, as it says somewhere, it is more economical to maintain it day after day than to get plastered again and again. Phister had correctly understood that the state of being drunk, half-drunk, or the somewhat more dignified state that could be called diplomatic fogginess, makes the best showing—that is, is more comical the more splendid the

uniform is. [47]This is quite correct, because the contradiction is all
the greater. And the greater the contradiction between being
drunk and the man's dignity, his position in society, his clothes,
his costume, or the greater the contradiction between being
drunk and the situation, the moment, the circumstances in
which he is drunk—in short, the greater the contradiction, the
more comic is the drunkenness also. A police officer who is
drunk is comic, but he is still more comic if he is also on duty, not
to mention when, for example, his duty is to clear out a pub
where the people are dead drunk—also the police officer who in
the name of authority orders them to disperse. The comic
emerges all the more strongly the more splendid the uniform is
that he is wearing. The splendid uniform involves a claim, suggests an idea—the drunkenness completely invalidates it by in-
troducing life's squalid side, by turning the underside up. The
more splendid the outer side of the uniform is, the stronger is the
contrast of the underside; and yet one sees both sides at once; one
sees the splendid uniform—and also that the man is drunk.

The idea was entirely right. But the one who has not seen
Phister's Scipio and has merely heard this about his interpretation
would get a conception that would correspond neither to what
the performance is nor to what Phister is as a comedian. He
would almost be prompted to think that Phister had failed in the
role by interpreting it in a much too ordinary way: [*deleted*: a
military man in gala uniform who is half-drunk,] a military man
in full dress [*fuld*] uniform and drunk [*fuld*] in uniform.

When, however, one has seen and sees Phister again, one understands quite correctly that this thought is only a side issue in
relation to the whole interpretation, which lies much deeper in
the comic and is much more concrete.

Captain Scipio is captain in the papal police force—what does
that mean? It means that he is a man who wears a military uniform, a man who advances at the head of the soldiers, who carries
a gun, a man who reviews the military troops, a man [48]who *qua*
military man feels committed to military chivalry, to being amiable, almost dangerous to the opposite sex. This is one side of the
picture. But from the other side—and Captain Scipio has two
sides from which to be seen, which is precisely what constitutes

IX
B 68
389

the deeper level of the comic—Captain Scipio is an ambiguity. IX
B 68
390 From the other side he still is not actually a military man; he is captain in the police force. Seen from this side he is something *à la* district judge, a justice of the peace, a firewarden, a street inspector, etc.—in short, a public official. Indeed, his official position can bring him into anything but military situations; as a police officer he perhaps supervises keeping sewers and gutters freely flowing, apprehends drunks, keeps watch on the old crones who sell on the streets, etc., etc.

What does this mean? It means that there is a contradiction here. Now, it is undoubtedly true that in the situation of actuality a person of culture and character has often resolved this contradiction and made an attractive character out of it. But the contradiction is there, and it is also certain that when a genuine and reflective comedian gets hold of this contradiction and correctly knows how to set at variance these two personae (the military and the civil) in one—but without overdoing it—then the comic effect is priceless.

In a more profound sense this is the comic element in Captain Scipio, and this is what Phister has superbly understood and therefore with a fine sense of the comic plays farcically, inasmuch as he does not forget the contradiction—his futile struggle to maintain a demeanor especially appropriate to his splendid uniform, futile because he continually has one additional incommensurable turn, a bit of the momentum that, in a cab driver's expression, leads one straight to the gutter.[49]

So Scipio is a military man. Not much needs to be done in this regard; this of course is obvious from the uniform and is what at all times immediately presents itself to the spectator. But from the other side Scipio is a civilian. The comic effect is now achieved by having this military person, this splendid uniform, appear in a purely accidental light (incidentally by the man's being half-drunk), mainly by his being more properly a district judge etc. Thus the contradiction is in full swing; at every moment the accidental characteristics of the civilian make the uniform of the military man look ridiculous, or the civilian makes the military man look ridiculous. His manner of walking and standing, his gestures, etc. would perhaps be ludicrous in themselves but are IX
B 68
391 more profoundly comic just because they are somewhat more genuine and somewhat less ludicrous inasmuch as they belong to the civilian. He wears a military uniform but has the civilian businessman's busyness, his accidental movements, his civilian flounce of the whole body, his way of being amiable and dangerous to the opposite sex.

This is the more essentially comic element in Captain Scipio; and this, as here presented in general, will be the basis for the following.

1

CAPTAIN SCIPIO STANDING

Captain S. is a bulky, corpulent man; he has not only an admissible plumpness but is, especially for a military man, inadmissibly potbellied. In connection with a military man, especially when in a splendid uniform, every accidental element promptly produces a comic effect. To be a tall, energetic man, that is as it should be; to be portly, that is not too bad; to be fat, well, to a certain degree that may be all right. But if it goes beyond this certain degree, then it becomes, as something unmilitary, comic for the military man. Such a figure can at most be tolerated in a major of the national guard, who in the stricter sense is not military. And Captain Scipio's stoutness, especially the prominence of his belly, not only goes beyond this certain degree but far beyond what is prescribed. Prince Henry says to the very considerably stouter Falstaff that it is surely impossible for him to see his own knees, to which Falstaff, as is well known, replies: "Well, yes, when I was young I was really thin, but sorrow and worries have blown me up."[50] Whether sorrows and worries have also blown Captain Scipio up I do not decide; but blown up he is in fact, and he certainly cannot see his own knees.[51] He stands before us. This is a military man! The comic has already set a *N.B.* by his figure, but now how is he standing? If the ramrod-straight military posture is called standing cocked or standing fully cocked [*staae paa Heel*], then Scipio is standing half-cocked [*staae paa Halv*]. He stoops over with the upper part of his body and pulls his legs,[52] curved inward, under his prominent belly in this way; his whole figure looks like a bow. He is complaisant, amiable, stooped—take away the uniform and he looks just like a rusticated public official. He removes his shako in order to wipe off the sweat. It so happens that a military man, too, can be sweaty. But as far as Scipio is concerned, one gets the impression that he would become sweaty from walking an eighth of a mile, and he wipes his sweaty brow exactly the way a civilian justice of the peace does. Then, after wiping his sweaty brow, he amiably follows with a motion that uses the hand as a comb to smooth the hair neatly on his half-bald[53] pate.

Well, now, is this a military man? Oh, yes indeed—after all, he is a captain in a splendid uniform. But everything else is civilian; his whole personality, the marks of the extremely diverse functions of his public office, his continual state of being half-tipsy have continually made it impossible to give expression to the military in any way; his bearing is not an approximation to it but a departure from it.[54]

In this posture he carries on a conversation with the "amiable farmer wife"[55] who is to billet him. Again the point is to maintain the duality: the civilian—the military man, with the further additive of spirits in which the two are united. Captain Scipio is amiability and chivalry personified, but he himself is a civilian-military amphibian. A uniform, a splendid uniform, and the feminine essentially go together—that is, the feminine opposite to the splendid uniform is a claim that requires something very specific with regard to bearing etc. If a military man forgot that he was in uniform, standing opposite to a woman would instantly remind him of what the uniform required of him. And Captain Scipio is, after all, a military man. He performs [*præstere*] what he can but not exactly *præstanda* [what ought to be done]. An amiable flirtation involving his whole body in very courteous postures, fiddling with his hands, rumpling his hair, amorous hopping around the "kind lady," etc.—all this can be ludicrous in itself but becomes doubly so because he is wearing this splendid uniform, he, whose figure still mocks the most simple military requirements: belly in and chest out.

IX
B 68
393

2
CAPTAIN SCIPIO WALKING

So Scipio marches in with his detachment, and this is his first appearance. The point is that the actor correctly perceive and convey the duality, the ludicrous ambiguity of military and civilian. How should Captain Scipio make his entrance on the stage? From a military point of view, he would have to enter at the head of the soldiers or walking alongside them. But no, Phister has a better understanding of his art. The soldiers enter first and line up in a row—then comes Captain Scipio. No matter how hastily he comes, the definite impression is that he is following behind. Yet not only this, which is always a properly comic effect in connection with his being in the military. But there is more. As physiology teaches, the human walk is a continuous falling.[56] This is seen especially clearly in Captain Scipio. With the bustling of a civilian justice official, he follows behind—not walking but yet not falling either. He is leaning forward and to one side; thus, as we say, he is walking on the left side of his own r——, walking as if one leg were a couple of inches too short. In this extremely bustling, half-skipping, sideways gait he comes hurrying in—behind. What an incomparable symbol of civilian bustling: to arrive in greatest haste—behind! Now he reviews the line. As we all know, nature has been so chivalrous toward human beings as to excuse them from having a tail. Yet we know from physiology that in the last spinal vertebra there is a faint suggestion of a tail. When Captain Scipio comes on the stage, we are involuntarily tempted to imagine a tail on this figure, and then he would perfectly remind us of a nicked[57] former parade horse but now a hackney that takes it into its head to trot a little.

In this completely civilian bobtailed bustling jog trot, he inspects the line. At this point Phister had the flippant and happy inspiration (which also contributes essentially to the total comic effect of his task: to set the military and the civilian at variance) to have Captain Scipio, with a kind of sudden idiotic notion that he is, after all, a military man, inspect the line with drawn sword—in order to see whether the soldiers are standing abreast in a straight line. Splendid! Even an ordinary home guard major

IX
B 68
394

who is always just a few degrees off course has an incomparably comic effect; the person who is himself off course is clearly most unsuited to correct others, and his efforts are bound to fail even more than the attempt in former times to teach a soldier to stand erect by having him slouch.[58] As we said, a major of that calibre in the home guard has a comic effect, but here the civilian in Captain Scipio produces a completely frenetic effect.

Deleted: The longer one looks at Captain Scipio, the more he evaporates into thin air, or his comic nothingness becomes more and more obvious.

3
THE LORD ONLY KNOWS
WHETHER CAPTAIN SCIPIO ACTUALLY DRINKS OR NOT

In a certain sense it is the easiest thing of all, as any esthetician knows, to represent a drunken man, and therefore every actor is able to do it to a certain degree. In other words, being drunk is an incommensurability; there is no specifically designated posture, behavior, etc. that accurately conveys it; the greatest randomness is possible. On the other hand, it can be very difficult for an esthetician to examine critically the actor representing a drunken man simply because here anything goes. Whereas an actor who can come onstage as a specific character and take a bow in character—a task that could appropriately be used as a test of the would-be actor—is a great rarity in any theater, almost any actor can to a certain degree play the part of a drunken man because the task is so boundlessly undefined and undefinable.

IX
B 68
395

But Captain Scipio is not a drunken man. He is such a man who from the earliest morning hour and at any other time of day—indeed, even if he was called out at midnight—is continually a little tipsy, but no more than that. He can manage his affairs as well as he is usually able to manage them; he does not drink himself drunk, not even when there is opportunity to do so. One may rather say that it has become impossible for him to become drunk; just as the virtuous person reaches a maximum where it is said that he cannot sin, so Captain Scipio has reached the maximum, he cannot get drunk. [*Deleted:* But on the other hand, he

continually staggers the slightest little bit.] We are therefore
never entirely sure that this is his condition, since it may not be
seen immediately, at first glance. Furthermore, Captain Scipio,
who with his many years of experience knows what others can
at most only surmise, is also on his guard to preserve propriety,
dignity, a complaisant and engaging manner; and we may assume
that the Captain (who in his own opinion is a man of the world,
a man who has damned good style, *comportement* [manners], and
subtlety in concealing) has completely deluded himself into
thinking that he is extraordinarily successful in concealing it—
although precisely this, his carefulness to conceal, is what will
betray it.

See, to represent this is a task with a totally different kind of
difficulty; to do this requires a more subtle comedian, a rarity in
any theater. In a certain sense immediacy is nullified; it must
never be directly seen that he is drunk, because he is not that
drunk. The task therefore is a contradiction: to represent (and
here again is a contradiction, because to "represent" is related to
externality) a man who is drunk—and yet is not drunk, a man
who is just a few degrees off course but is enough aware of it
himself both as a civilian and a military man to hide it. The
cunning comic aspect consists in making it manifest *telegraphi-
cally*, in surreptitiously betraying the secret expressly by what the
Captain does to conceal the true situation.

Phister works out the task superbly, and it is indeed a task for
Phister—it is a task of reflection. We do not think that we at any
moment directly see that the Captain is drunk. But we do have
a suspicion; the Lord only knows whether Captain Scipio actually drinks or not. It would surely take a comedian of considerable talent just to comprehend a task such as this, to say nothing
of working it out: a befuddlement kept so totally secret that the
clue, what betrays it, is his very attempt to conceal it.

So, then, Captain Scipio is not drunk, far from it; on the other
hand, he seems to suffer from a kind of fluctuating feverishness,
marked by a slight or dry cough and the blood rising to his head.
Well, it could be the warm weather, or the Captain may have
accidentally overstrained himself etc. But no, it cannot be explained this way; this feverishness seems to stay with him contin-

IX
B 68
396

ually, seems to be something chronic; wherever we meet him and in whatever situation, he seems to be feverish. But Captain Scipio, the only one who knows the true situation, is also the man who continually knows how to conceal it. Therefore the frequent movement of his hand to his head, a fanning with his hand, without our really comprehending why, whether it may not be to fan away a certain vapor that he fears surrounds his head. Therefore the need to take off his shako so often, urbanely to run his fingers through his hair in order to keep the air around his head continually in motion, especially if someone comes close to him. All this he does so that no one will suspect the true reason for his doing it, but everyone may be thrown off the track and be led to think that the Captain—every time they see him— has just come back from a long walk, from some burdensome work, etc., or that he is a great *petitmaitre* [coxcomb].

So, then, Captain Scipio is certainly not a drunken man; and he, the only one who knows his condition, also knows ways of preventing anyone from getting any suspicion of the true situation. For safety's sake he therefore frequently puts his hand to his mouth. What this movement means is not immediately evident; furthermore, the captain reserves to himself the provision of the various interpretations that conceal the true one. If he is speaking with a man, the movement is not to the mouth but from the mouth, a courteous gesture; if he is speaking with a woman, this gesture changes to a complaisant throwing of a kiss with three fingers—and yet the truth is that the movement of the hand to the mouth or in front of the mouth is in order to use the flat of the hand as a valve to conceal and suppress a certain belch that probably would not betray that the captain is drunk—which he is not—but yet could easily betray too much, or that the captain had had too much.

So, then, Captain S. is not drunk, certainly not; he does not stagger, much less fall down—far from it. And the Captain, the only one who knows his condition, is also the man who knows exactly how to conceal it—in such a way that from his very posture one gets, not directly but indirectly, a suspicion about him. We say of a drunken man that his eyes are fixed and rigid; this is not the case with Captain S. His posture, however, has a

IX
B 68
397

certain rigidity that is indeed suspicious; the drunken man staggers and lurches, but the respectable man, who quite secretly
walks with a slight unsteadiness, has precisely this suspicious rigidity in his posture. The captain's walk is a contradiction. Pull-
ing himself and his body together, so to speak, and crooking his
elbows almost like a gentleman dancing, he puts—his best foot
forward, but he gets no further, does not completely carry out
this ceremonious act, cannot perfectly strike the pose he is striving for. As stated, he puts his best foot forward, but, but as he is
"putting the other one ahead of it," in that very same second—
now he has made the step—the total impression is one of a certain unsureness; but then it begins all over again and he puts his
best foot forward. In the second when he stands there on his best
foot, his elbows crooked, graciously bending forward—yes, it is
supremely well done and superbly conceals that he has had a little
too much—he nevertheless cannot possibly remain standing in
this position, and in the next second one has a suspicion, but it
never becomes more than a suspicion, because once again he
takes that position on his best foot. We have a suspicion—the
Lord only knows whether Captain Scipio actually drinks or not.

So, then, Captain Scipio is certainly not drunk. On the other
hand, he is a military man in a splendid uniform; moreover, he
is a police officer; finally, in a certain limited sense he is a man of
the world, conducts himself in good form, and knows how to
conceal his true condition. To represent a character such as this
is a task for a subtle comedian. One can say in advance that it is
a task for Phister; and when one has seen it, we can say: That
is a task for Phister.

4

IN THE SECOND ACT OF THE PLAY CAPTAIN
SCIPIO ACCIDENTALLY IS NO LONGER DRINKING

In the second act of the play, Captain S. is accidentally sober.
What must be noted is that it is by accident; if it had any essentially deeper meaning, that he had stopped drinking for moral
reasons, for example, the comic effect would be missing. The
situation is as follows. Despite all Capt. Scipio's busyness, he still
has not succeeded in apprehending the criminal he has been sent

to arrest. In his zeal he makes a vow not to taste wine or brandy before he succeeds in arresting the guilty man.[59] We have all the more sympathy for him and his pathos-filled lines when, on the occasion of performing an inspection of the house of a hermit who does not drink water but only wine, he bursts out, "What torment to have to inspect the house of a hermit who has vowed to drink nothing but wine when one has oneself vowed to drink nothing but water."[60]

Just because Phister has so superbly played Scipio in the first act, he therefore has also correctly perceived that there is no essential difference at all between Scipio's conduct in the first and second acts. It could seem odd, but still it is quite true: a man can be befuddled because he has had too much to drink but can be in approximately the same condition just because he has had nothing to drink. If someone who has been addicted to the continual use of intoxicating drink without actually being drunk suddenly stops drinking, he is for a time in essentially the same condition because of slackness; indeed, he apparently is almost more intoxicated than when he was drinking. Just by using the customary amount of spirits, a person of this sort almost seems to be completely sober; and when he one day is completely sober, he very likely seems to be almost drunk.

IX
B 68
399

The difference between Captain S. in the first and in the second act, therefore, is simply that in the second act he has a little less of this forced tension; instead a kind of depressed listlessness, a kind of *tristitia* [melancholia] is diffused over his figure. Now for the first time he is more like a drunken man; his walk is unsteady, slouching, his arms hang down loosely, his eyes stare, he staggers, his legs refuse to carry him properly, he no longer has a best foot to strike the least posture—and why? Because now he is sober.

Phister has again understood this correctly, that the wittiness in the task consists in concealing in the first act and only very indirectly letting it be suspected that Scipio is a little bit drunk and in having him in the second act look almost like a drunken man—because he is sober.

This little article is a recollection; it is many years since its author saw *Ludovic*, and it is already a number of years since the play has

been performed.[61] Therefore I am spontaneously tempted to
make a comment. The ordinary drama critics go on the first evening a new play is performed; to see it only this one time is
enough for them to judge the play and each one of the actors—a

IX
B 68
400

Phister, a Rosenkilde, a Nielsen, a Wiehe, a Mrs. Heiberg, a
Mrs. Nielsen, etc.—who at times has spent months and all one's
genius, reflectiveness, and diligence to work out the part.

Not so with this little article. It is not a service to Phister; it has
tried only to reproduce faithfully what he has given us, therefore
what is his own. But it does have the quality of discernment to a
high degree—and Phister surely could lay claim to well-consid-
ered discernment [*deleted:* and surely will also know how to value
it]. This is why it has come into existence. Its author essentially
has tasks quite different from those of drama criticism, which is
entirely outside his sphere. But in such a small country as Denmark, one who perhaps can do it has a duty—and thus it is not
something outside his sphere—to use, while he himself enjoys
and rests, the scantily measured and only rarely granted leisure
time to pay, if possible, a little on the debt to our great dramatic
artists, a debt that only increases continually through the attempts
of the usual newspaper reviews to pay by instalments.

Dec. 1848

Procul[62]

SUPPLEMENT

KEY TO REFERENCES

Marginal references alongside the text are to volume and page [X 100] in *Søren Kierkegaards samlede Vaerker*, I-XIV, edited by A. B. Drachmann, J. L. Heiberg, and H. O. Lange (1 ed., Copenhagen: Gyldendal, 1901–06). The same marginal references are used in Sören Kierkegaard, *Gesammelte Werke*, Abt. 1–36 (Düsseldorf, Cologne: Diederichs Verlag, 1952–69).

References to Kierkegaard's works in English are to this edition, *Kierkegaard's Writings* [*KW*], I-XXVI (Princeton: Princeton University Press, 1978-). Specific references are given by English title and the standard Danish pagination referred to above [*Either/Or*, I, p. 120, *KW* III (*SV* I 100)].

References to the *Papirer* [*Pap*. I A 100; note the differentiating letter A, B, or C, used only in references to the *Papirer*] are to *Søren Kierkegaards Papirer*, I-XI³, edited by P. A. Heiberg, V. Kuhr, and E. Torsting (1 ed., Copenhagen: Gyldendal, 1909–48), and 2 ed., photo-offset with two supplemental volumes, XII-XIII, edited by Niels Thulstrup (Copenhagen: Gyldendal, 1968–70), and with index, XIV-XVI (1975–78), edited by Niels Jørgen Cappelørn. References to the *Papirer* in English [*JP* II 1500], occasionally amended, are to volume and serial number in *Søren Kierkegaard's Journals and Papers*, I-VII, edited and translated by Howard V. Hong and Edna H. Hong, assisted by Gregor Malantschuk, and with index, VII, by Nathaniel Hong and Charles Barker (Bloomington: Indiana University Press, 1967–78).

References to correspondence are to the serial numbers in *Breve og Aktstykker vedrørende Søren Kierkegaard*, I-II, edited by Niels Thulstrup (Copenhagen: Munksgaard, 1953–54), and to the corresponding serial numbers in *Kierkegaard: Letters and Documents*, translated by Henrik Rosenmeier, *Kierkegaard's Writings*, XXV [*Letters*, Letter 100, *KW* XXV].

References to books in Kierkegaard's own library [*ASKB* 100] are based on the serial numbering system of *Auktionsprotokol over*

Søren Kierkegaard's Bogsamling [Auction-catalog of Søren Kierkegaard's Book-collection], edited by H. P. Rohde (Copenhagen: Royal Library, 1967).

In the Supplement, references to page and lines in the text are given as: 100:1–10.

In the notes, internal references to the present volume are given as: p. 100.

Three spaced periods indicate an omission by the editors; five spaced periods indicate a hiatus or fragmentariness in the text.

Christelige Taler

af

S. Kierkegaard.

Kjøbenhavn.

Forlagt af Universitetsboghandler C. A. Reitzel.

Trykt hos Kgl. Hofbogtrykker Bianco Luno.

1848.

Christian Discourses

by

S. Kierkegaard.

———————

Copenhagen.

Published by University Bookseller C. A. Reitzel.

Printed by the Royal Printer Bianco Luno.

1848.

Hedningenes Bekymringer.

Christelige Taler

af

S. Kierkegaard.

Kjøbenhavn.

Forlagt af Universitetsboghandler C. A. Reitzel.

Trykt hos Kgl. Hofbogtrykker Bianco Luno.

1848.

The Cares of the Pagans.

Christian Discourses

by

S. Kierkegaard.

_____

Copenhagen.
Published by University Bookseller C. A. Reitzel.
Printed by Royal Printer Bianco Luno.
1848.

Stemninger i Lidelsers Strid.

Christelige Taler

af

S. Kierkegaard.

> „Jeg vil boie mit Øre til Tanke-
> sprog, og fremsætte mine mørke
> Taler til Harpespil." Pslm. 49, 5.

Kjøbenhavn.

Forlagt af Universitetsboghandler C. A. Reitzel.

Trykt hos Kgl. Hofbogtrykker Bianco Luno.

1848.

States of Mind in the Strife of Suffering.

Christian Discourses

by

S. Kierkegaard.

"I will incline my ear to a proverb;
I will set my dark saying to
the music of the harp." Ps. 49:5.

––––––––––––

Copenhagen.
Published by University Bookseller C. A. Reitzel.
Printed by the Royal Printer Bianco Luno.
1848

Tanker som saare bagfra
— til Opbyggelse.

Christelige Foredrag

af

S. Kierkegaard.

Kjøbenhavn.

Forlagt af Universitetsboghandler C. A. Reitzel.

Trykt hos Kgl. Hofbogtrykker Bianco Luno.

1848.

Thoughts That Wound from Behind

—for Upbuilding.

Christian Addresses

by

S. Kierkegaard.

———————

Copenhagen.
Published by University Bookseller C. A. Reitzel.
Printed by Royal Printer Bianco Luno.
1848.

Taler ved Altergang om Fredagen.

Christelige Taler

af

S. Kierkegaard.

Kjøbenhavn.

Forlagt af Universitetsboghandler C. A. Reitzel.

Trykt hos Kgl. Hofbogtrykker Bianco Luno.

1848.

Discourses at the Communion

on Fridays.

Christian Discourses

by

S. Kierkegaard.

––––––––––

Copenhagen.
Published by University Bookseller C. A. Reitzel.
Printed by Royal Printer Bianco Luno.
1848.

SELECTED ENTRIES FROM
KIERKEGAARD'S JOURNALS AND PAPERS
PERTAINING TO
CHRISTIAN DISCOURSES

The Difference *between a Christian Discourse and a Sermon*

VIII[1]
A 6
6

A Christian discourse deals to a certain extent with doubt—a sermon operates absolutely and solely on the basis of authority, that of Scripture and of Christ's apostles. Therefore, it is neither more nor less than heresy to deal with doubt in a sermon, however well one might be able to deal with it.

VIII[1]
A 6
7

The preface to my "Christian Discourses," therefore, contains the phrase: if a sufferer who is also *going astray in many thoughts.*[1]

A sermon presupposes a pastor (ordination); a Christian discourse can be by a layman.—*JP* I 638 (*Pap.* VIII[1] A 6) *n.d.*, 1847

From final copy; see 3:3:

[*Deleted:* End[2]]
The Cares of the Pagans
Christian [*changed from:* 7] Discourses
by
S. Kierkegaard.
—*Pap.* VIII[2] B 123:4 *n.d.*, 1847–48

From final copy; see 3:4:

S. K.
Deleted: This little book
is dedicated to
"That Single Individual."
—*Pap.* VIII[2] B 123:3 *n.d.*, 1847–48

See 12:

VIII¹
A 430
187

From a Preface

. . . . . That single individual, whom I with joy and gratitude call *my* reader, who honestly and earnestly follows my effort, I will ask not to lose inclination or patience because the work is so VIII¹
A 430
188 arduous. I have not asked this before; but if he has faithfully been forbearing with me so long, then I would like to ask him this once to endure further. —If folly or envy should want to make Copenhagen into a market town and in this market town of Copenhagen make it a crime to be more than ordinarily gifted or extraordinarily industrious: well, I will just pray God to bless me and give me the strength to be able to commit this crime and thank him that up until now that has been granted me. As is well known, there is no power as domineering as obtuseness— naturally, from the standpoint of truth, its dominion is very poorly protected. And there is no power so loathsomely cruel or so loathsome in its being cruel as rabble barbarism, and of course I have really rubbed it the wrong way or hit it on the head— simply in order to do my part to guard and preserve the good spirit in Denmark so that it in turn can protect and benefit and encourage its true children instead of sacrificing them in idolatrous worship to the service of an un-Danish spirit.—*Pap.* VIII¹ A 430 *n.d.*, 1847

From draft; see 12:

Christian Discourses
See journal NB³, p. 30 [*Pap.* VIII¹ A 430]
Preface

That single individual I will directly ask not to lose patience—I have not done this previously—I myself am very well aware of how difficult it must be for a contemporary to be forbearing with me and not grow weary, since I allow neither him nor myself any rest, aware of how difficult it is to get the right impression. I myself am fully aware of this just because I perhaps understand better than anyone that not until I am dead and gone will the time for my books have actually come, the time when they, just as my life, will come into their own and (as the painter says) show up to advantage; as long as I am living, it is part of my task to use almost two-thirds of my energy to confuse, to work against myself and weaken the impression—which is precisely what makes me difficult for the contemporary—*Pap*. VIII^2 B 104 *n.d.*, 1847–48

From sketch, see 7:1–25:

The Gospel for the Fifteenth Sunday after Trinity
In margin: To the typesetter
    as in the service book.
                —*Pap*. VIII^2 B 91:1 *n.d.*, 1847–48

From sketch; see 13:7:

A person needs little in order to live. But if he does not even have this little, his condition in life is: poverty.—*Pap*. VIII^2 B 91:6 *n.d.*, 1847–48

See 18:13–19:28:

The one I portrayed (in the first discourse on the cares of the pagans) as crudely talking about the earnestness of life is not, as one immediately sees, what is called a poor person—indeed, it could never occur to me that such a person would talk that way. No, he is a journalist of sorts, one of those who live, perhaps luxuriously and superfluously, live on writing about—poverty.
                —*JP* V 6120 (*Pap*. VIII^1 A 589) *n.d.*, 1848

From sketch; see 23:25:

When one bird talks to another bird, whatever do they talk about; do you think they talk about what they own? No, the bird does not have . . . . . —*Pap*. VIII^2 B 91:8 *n.d.*, 1847–48

In margin of sketch; see 24:2:

The bird has "the measure in my mouth," as the petty officer said when the woman had no half-pint measure available.[3]—*Pap*. VIII^2 B 91:9 *n.d.*, 1847–48

From sketch; see 29:11–15:

Have you [*essentially the same as Pap.* VIII² B 96, 1–16]. So it
is with the Christian. But God, who here is the owner, has his
own concept of money transactions; he does not speak so much
about 4% or 6% as about something else.—*Pap.* VIII² B 91:10
n.d., 1847–48

From final draft; see 29:11–13:

If you have ever visited the honest merchant—where with
wonder and amazement you see his enormous stock of supplies
and you are already of a mind to express your amazement over
his enormous wealth, if he then says, "This is not mine, it is
entrusted property, it belongs to a friend of mine who is dead"—
is it not true that you then understand that this honest merchant
still is not rich? If you—but of course you would not do it—but
if anyone in the remotest way were to suggest to the merchant
that in view of the fact that his friend was dead and never more
to be seen he could then pass off the whole fortune as his: the
honest person would turn away from such a one in horror and
revulsion, shuddering at the thought of a falsity in *mine* and *yours*.
But if you question the honest person further about that property, what he is doing with it, he will no doubt say that he is
managing it on behalf of the deceased, is doing it in the best way
to make it as profitable as possible. So also with the rich Christian, he is managing it in the best way on behalf of the owner.
—*Pap.* VIII² B 96 *n.d.*, 1847–48

Deleted from final copy; see 54:28:

VIII²
B 123:10
224 Therefore it was also the case in other times, of course more
corrupt and sophisticated, when confidence in one another was
not as great as in these upright and honest times, when they were
not as naive as in these naive times, then it was the case that
people had a rather childish mistrust of these human assurances
that "in one's innermost being one is" etc. As a precaution, then,
one took it a bit seriously (regarding it as by no means the highest

or decisive but rather as a practice for beginners) and actually gave away one's riches (which Christ advises the rich young man to do) and literally became poor; one actually gave up worldly honor and esteem and literally became insulted, scorned, perhaps according to Scripture (Luke 18:32) spat upon; one actually did divest oneself of earthly loftiness and literally became a lowly person—ridiculed by the sagacious Christians for being crazy enough to give no signs of anything, fatuous enough to intimate that one understood Holy Scripture and what it said strictly according to the words, instead of, like the sagacious and enlightened Christians, cleverly pretending it to be nothing, living as pleasurably as any pagan, possessing or aspiring to worldly goods as much as any pagan, and then also being Christians, perhaps even a Christian pastor, and even earning money by this advantageous transaction. In other times—of course more corrupt and more familiar with all sorts of falsehood, deceit, and cunning, when of course trust in one another was lost and people had a great distrust of these human assurances that in one's innermost being etc.—it was the case that when a man or woman gave assurances that there was only one who was the beloved, that one loves only once, it was the case that it was required—of course in view of the corruption of the times—that the outer life also expressed this. But in our simple, honest, upright, naive times, when, just as property security has become so great that it makes no difference whether one locks one's door, so also people's confidence in one another has become the greatest possible. When someone gives assurances of it, we believe him even if his outer life expresses the opposite. He need not even give assurances of it; we believe him just the same; mutual confidence is so great that an assurance actually makes no difference. We all trust one another, that in our innermost beings we etc.; we almost derive our amusement from it—but no, away with jesting when the discourse is about the earnestness of the times—mentally we place honor in the fact that our outer lives express the opposite, because we secretly and mutually know that in our innermost beings we etc.; mentally we smile at that uncertainty and self-distrust that has to call on the help of externality, because we are so very sure of ourselves, sure that in our innermost beings etc.

VIII[2]
B 123:10
225

Well, in any case it is quite convenient and every household must see to having such a convenience.—*Pap.* VIII² B 123:10 *n.d.*, 1847–48

Deleted from margin of sketch; see 72:15:

And the fire of passion is quenched, because to kindle a flame there always must be a draught—but desire and the currents of uncertainty create this very draught that kindles passion to its highest.—*Pap.* VIII² B 91:14 *n.d.*, 1847–48

See 82:35–83:36:

No one can serve two masters. This does not mean only the vacillating, irresolute person who does not quite know which to choose. No, the person who defiantly breaks with God and heaven in order to serve his desires and drives also serves two masters, something no one can do—he has to serve God whether he wants to or not. The situation is not this simple: choose one of the two. The situation is rather this: there is only one to choose if one is actually going to serve only one master, and that is God.—*JP* I 952 (*Pap.* VIII¹ A 359) *n.d.*, 1847

See 91:15:

From "The Cares of the Pagans."

End

VIII¹
A 660
311

Just a word more in conclusion. You struggling one, whoever you are, you who may be carrying the heavy cross of temporal and earthly cares, who are being tested in this difficulty, or you

VIII¹
A 660
312

who for that reason are disquieted and tremble but yet crave comfort, or you who lamentably are going astray but yet crave guidance—you at times, especially in the beginning of each discourse, will perhaps find the presentation to be not sufficiently earnest. Do not, however, make too hasty a judgment; just read, read without worrying, and believe me, what everyone needs first and foremost is to be mollified, to be mollified to and by the smile that is in tears. Not all that is called earnestness is earnestness; there is much that is only a gloomy frame of mind, the ill humor of a worldly worried heart, a bitterness of mind that does not sigh to God but against God and denounces its fate, a foolish and fatuous busyness that busies itself with everything else but the one thing needful,[4] that throughout a long life finds time for everything else but not one single moment for the only thing needful. But to help a person to the smile that mollifies while the tears bring relief, that among other things is the aim of the devotional, the upbuilding address, and it ought to be so. It ought to be able to speak rigorously, it ought to be able to maintain the requirement of the task and to honor the duty, but it also ought to be able to draw the smile. We are not speaking here about the wantonness of shrill laughter, which is an abomination to the wise and is brash presumptuousness to offer to someone who is suffering. No, we are speaking about the smile that is able to do what tears in themselves have a hard time doing—to make the weeping beneficial; this smile that frequently goes unthanked because one thinks it was the tears that helped—alas, just as when one is helped by a child and feels helped but does not bear in mind that the child was the helper. A child, after all, is too inexperienced to be able to help, and a smile is not earnest enough to be able to help. See, it is this smile—which the upbuilding address certainly does not court, since the upbuilding address does not court any smile and needs no one—but it is this smile that the struggling person needs. And the upbuilding address prays to God (truly it does know what it is praying for) that it might be successful in eliciting that smile from him by speaking with him in such a way that he first and foremost is momentarily moved to forget all other bonds [*Baand*] in order to pull the smile-string [*Smilebaand*]. Believe me, precisely this belongs to earnestness; believe me, it is a sure sign that a person is making progress in the eternal and is being matured for eternity if he, the more he suffers (the innocent suffering in which he is being tested, or the suffering he himself incurred as punishment), becomes all the more mollified, all the more enabled by this smile, this smile

VIII¹
A 660
313

through the tears, to endure what he has to endure. Do not think that it is weakness to cry *in this way*.

To take a specific example, imagine an old man who nonetheless has become more vigorous and tough with the years and has the levelheadedness of age. He had gone through much in his life, had been tried in all kinds of earthly adversities; now his life condition was secure, carefree, and as we humans call it, happy. During the adversities no one had seen him cry, nor had anyone ever seen him cry over other people's earthly need; as he used to say, one does not cry over such things, one helps as much as one can. But then it happened one day that as he sat talking with a friend of his youth about this life and its adversities, especially worry about making a living, it so happened that a child who was present innocently broke in with a word in the form of a question, whereupon the old man smiled and promptly began to cry. Now why did this happen, or why this oddity that a word by a child, just when it innocently falls in the midst of an earnest conversation, can produce this effect? It is because the child has no understanding or no intimation at all of the *embittering* that the cares of earthly life can have—but the child does not therefore need to speak senselessly; the child indeed speaks sensibly, but for good reasons entirely leaves out the *embittering*. On such an occasion, therefore, one says, "Yes, my child, what you say is entirely true" and thereby brushes the child aside; one does not wish to pursue this further. Alas, after all, the child has really caused one to be embarrassed, and therefore one seeks to avoid conversing with the roguish little sage who, it is true, does not himself know how ironic he is or how he is that. On account of what the child says, a person involuntarily comes, concentrating on one single impression, to think of all the *embittering* experiences over the many years, things he himself knows but of which the child as yet has no intimation—and yet, after all, what the child says is entirely true. This is the contradiction at which one smiles, but the child touches one. For a moment, with the help of the child's originality, one comes to think quite impartially—yes, almost as if one were in eternity, so impartial and mollified about the pressures of earthly life—therefore one smiles. Is it not strange that

VIII[1]
A 660
314

someone who speaks about what he does not understand at all
goes ahead and says the right thing and then in turn does not
himself understand that he has said the right thing; and is it not
touching that this cryptic sage is a child, that is, something one
once was oneself! Ah, just like a child are those teachers without
a college degree but yet appointed by God—the lily and the
bird!—*Pap*. VIII[1] A 660 *n.d.*, 1847–48

See 93:1, 95:1–4, 106:1–5, 114:1–4:

The Gospel of Sufferings*

No. 2

1. The joy of it that one suffers only once
   but is victorious eternally
   See journal N.B. p. 206
   [*Pap*. VIII[1] A 31–32; pp. 370–71]
2. The joy of it that hardship does not take away
   but procures hope.
   See this book, p. 238
   [*Pap*. VIII[1] A 360–61; p. 372]
3. The joy of it that the poorer one becomes oneself
   the richer one is able to make others.[*]
   —*JP* II 2189 (*Pap*. VIII[1] A 180) *n.d.*, 1847

In margin of Pap. VIII[1] A 180; see 93:1–4:

* Rather: Reassuring and Joyful Thoughts
Christian Discourses
by
S. K.

—*JP* II 2191 (*Pap*. VIII[1] A 182) *n.d.*, 1847

Addition to Pap. VIII[1] A 180; see 115:21–116:9, 119:21–24:

[*] for all worldly possessions (wealth, honor, power, etc.) diminish the possessions of others to the same degree as mine
increase.

Poverty of spirit. the more learned I become, the fewer I
am able to make understand me.
—*JP* II 2193 (*Pap.* VIII¹ A 184) *n.d.*, 1847

In margin of Pap. VIII¹ A 180; see 124:1–4, 134:1–4, 144: 1–4:

4. The joy of it: that the weaker I become the stronger God becomes in me.

5. The joy of it: that what I lose temporally I gain eternally.

6. The joy of it: that it is not the believer who holds the anchor but the anchor of faith that holds the believer. [*Changed to:* that if the believer is not able to hold on to the anchor in spiritual trial, the anchor of faith is able to hold on to the believer.]
—*JP* II 2190 (*Pap.* VIII¹ A 181) *n.d.*, 1847

Addition to Pap. VIII¹ A 181:

See pp. 190 and 191 in this book
[*Pap.* VIII¹ A 300–302, 322–23 (pp. 368–69, 376–77)]
—*JP* II 2192 (*Pap.* VIII¹ A 183) *n.d.*, 1847

See 97:3–5:

See p. 73 in this volume and p. 210
[*Pap.* VIII¹ A 180–83 and 322–23 (pp. 367–68, 376–77)]

*The Gospel of Sufferings, No. 2
VII. The joy of it that it is "for joy" that one does not dare believe the most blessed of all.
You do not believe it—but take courage, because the reason is really only that it is too joyous; take courage, because it is joy that hinders you—is this not joyous?
It is told of the disciples that they did not dare believe for joy.
Luke 24:41.—*JP* II 2194 (*Pap.* VIII¹ A 300) *n.d.*, 1847

In margin of Pap. VIII[1] A 300; *see 93:1–8:*

> * Perhaps better:
> Reassuring Thoughts
> Christian Discourses
> by
> S. K.
> —*Pap.* VIII[1] A 301 *n.d.,* 1847

In margin of Pap. VIII[1] A 300:

. . . . . that whenever you wish you can close your door and speak with God without a middleman, without the tax and burden of superior condescension—is this not blessed—but you do not believe it? Why do you not believe it? Perhaps it is too joyous—but is it nevertheless not joyous? The forgiveness of sins etc.—*JP* II 2195 (*Pap.* VIII[1] A 302) *n.d.,* 1847

From draft; see 93:1–8:

> States of Mind in the Strife of Sufferings
> [*changed from:* States of Mind in the Strife of Suffering
> *changed from:* States of Mind in the Strife]
> Christian Discourses
> by
> S. Kierkegaard
> "I will incline my ear to a proverb;
> I will set my dark saying to the
> music of the harp." Psalm 49:4
> —*Pap.* VIII[2] B 98 *n.d.,* 1847–48

Addition to Pap. VIII[2] B 98; *see 93:8:*

> To an [*changed from:* all] innocent sufferer[s]
> this little book
> is dedicated
> —*Pap.* VIII[2] B 99 *n.d.,* 1847–48

From final copy; see 93:8:

Psalm 49:4

Deleted: To an innocent sufferer

this little book

is dedicated.

—*Pap.* VIII² B 123:12 *n.d.*, 1847–48

Deleted from margin of final copy; see 95:28:

. . . . . just as that liberal enthusiastic Israelite [*changed from:* Jew], who in keeping with the freedom-cry wanted to have the Norwegian constitution introduced into Denmark and incidentally did not know that it turns the Israelites [*changed from:* Jews] out of the country.[5] See, here, we have a difficulty that the wisher had not thought of at all.—*Pap.* VIII² B 123:13 *n.d.*, 1847–48

See 97:6, 27–28:

N.B.

There is something very upbuilding in the thought that what is said of Christ also holds true of all suffering: what he suffered he suffered once.[6] One suffers only once: the victory is eternal. (In a worldly way one hears this talk often enough: Enjoy life— you live only once.)—*JP* IV 4593 (*Pap.* VIII¹ A 31) *n.d.*, 1847

See 96:2, 97:27–98:19, 103:10–104:4:

VIII¹   N.B.
A 32
19   One suffers only once—but is victorious eternally. Insofar as one is victorious, this is also only once. The difference, however,
VIII¹   is that the one time of suffering is momentary (even though the
A 32   moment were seventy years)—but the one time of victory is
20   eternity. The one time of suffering (even though it lasted seventy years) can therefore not be pictured or portrayed in art. Above the altar in Vor Frelsers Church there is a work that presents an angel who holds out to Christ the cup of suffering. The error is

that it lasts too long; a picture always endures for an eternity. It appears interminable; one does not see that the suffering is momentary, as all suffering is according to the concept or in the idea of victory. The victory, however, is eternal; this (insofar as it is not spiritual) can be portrayed, because it endures.

Meanwhile, the first impression of the upbuilding is *terrifying*—if people take time to understand it properly, since in this case to suffer once is like being sick once—that is, for a whole lifetime. But the wisdom and the impatience of this world must not demand that one should be able to comfort the sufferer—at least if one is to speak of the essentially Christian, because the comfort of Christianity begins first of all where human impatience would simply despair. This is how deep the essentially Christian is—*first of all* one must scrupulously try to find the *terrifying* and then scrupulously once again—then one finds the *upbuilding*. Alas, as a rule we try scrupulously in neither the first instance nor the second.—*JP* IV 4594 (*Pap.* VIII[1] A 32) *n.d.*, 1847

In margin of draft; see 101:21–24:

No, the one time of suffering is no time; even if it lasted a whole lifetime and every day was as heavy as a long life: it is still no time. It is able to corrupt the outer person, to corrupt the body, but is not able to corrupt the soul—therefore its one time is still no time[*]. Only sin is a human being's corruption; everything else is to be counted as nothing. But just as there is a chasmic abyss between the rich man in hell and the poor man in heaven, so also there is a chasmic abyss between suffering and the suffering of sin. It is blessed to suffer only once, even if it were for a whole lifetime, but woe to the person who also sinned only once, because eternity will not have understood it in that way. Alas, a person can sin many times. And every time he sins anew, it is a new time—eternity understands this.[**] The sufferer holds fast to eternity and therefore suffers only once, but the person who sins, and every time he sins, breaks with eternity and it becomes a new time.

[*] *In margin:* and let us not lose our way and mock God in this joyful discourse about the heaviest suffering.

[**] *In margin:* Only sin [*changed from:* eternity] has the power to mark a person, so one does not immediately or totally recover from it, perhaps never, in eternity—all temporal suffering is capable of nothing.—*Pap.* VIII^2 B 100:1 *n.d.,* 1847–48

Cf. 106:1–113:24:

> The Correlation of Some Joyful Thoughts
> 4 Discourses
> No. 1
> Hardship gives steadfastness.
> No. 2
> Steadfastness gives experience.
> No. 3
> Experience [gives] hope.
> No. 4
> Hope does not shame.
> —*JP* II 2198 (*Pap.* VIII^1 A 360) *n.d.,* 1847

In margin of Pap. VIII^1 A 360:

> or: The coming into existence of hope.

Perhaps better to be used in one of the discourses in the "Gospel of Sufferings."

> See this book, p. 73, no. 2
> [*Pap.* VIII^1 A 180 (p. 367)]
> —*JP* II 2199 (*Pap.* VIII^1 A 361) *n.d.,* 1847

In margin of draft; see 110:17:

Hardship procures hope. Hardship is in the service of a higher power; hardship is the terrible host with which eternity within a person makes war on temporality in order to win the eternal. It is not a war such as between two forces that can stop for accidental reasons or exhaust their power so that they have to stop; no, eternity can hold out as long as it needs to. Therefore it is a sad

misunderstanding every time the person to whom eternity is laying siege by means of hardship hopes for this or for that—then
the very siege is continued since, after all, hardship procures hope
and therefore wants to go on cutting off the besieged person from
every connection with temporality's [*changed from:* eternity's]
hope.— *Pap.* VIII^2 B 100:2 *n.d.*, 1847–48

From final copy; see 115:21–25:

Changed from: What is it, namely, that can prevent a person
from completely making others rich? It is *either* the nature of
what he possesses (assuming even that he is more willing to give
and to share), the nature of his property, which by its nature
involves his making others poorer in one way or another through
possession of it—that is, it is due to his possessing only the false
riches, the unrighteous mammon; *or* it is due to the manner in
which he possesses the true riches, to his possessing them in a false
way so that as a consequence he possesses only the false riches. All
false riches expressly have the selfish capacity of *begrudging*, to
make others poorer. But in one way or another all false riches are
earthly, worldly riches. The poorer he then becomes in this regard (assuming that he will understand the matter correctly), the
richer he becomes in the true riches, the more he becomes exclusively occupied with and concerned for the true riches. But the
true riches have precisely the blessed quality of *mercy*, so that the
possession essentially in itself, in and by itself, is communication,
so that far from making others poorer the possession in itself
makes others richer. And he will indeed endeavor to increase it,
since he is solely occupied with and concerned for these riches.
Ah, but with regard to the true riches (whose nature is precisely
communication), this increase is neither more nor less than to
communicate—ah, it is not petty-minded as it is with the false
riches, which truly are not increased by being given away.
Therefore: the poorer he becomes, the richer he makes others.
But let us encircle this one and the same joyful thought only
according to a more widely applied criterion.—*Pap.* VIII^2 B
123:14 *n.d.*, 1847–48

From final copy; see 127:18–21:

. . . . . he the Omnipotent One, he who creates out of nothing, and to whom all creation is as nothing, is made into nothing if he stops creating. In this way God is the strongest.—*Pap*. VIII² B 123:15 *n.d.*, 1847–48

In margin of draft; see 137:35:

Only sin is a human being's corruption, is perdition. But we are not speaking of that in these discourses, which address themselves to sufferers in order to alleviate the pain and if possible turn it into joy.—*Pap*. VIII² B 100:3 *n.d.*, 1847–48

From draft; see 141:14:

Suppose it was riches: that is, you lost riches temporally, but you gained riches eternally. That is, you certainly do not get back what you lost—oh, no, it is not such a meager affair as that, it is far richer—what you lost temporally you get again eternally.
—*Pap*. VIII² B 100:4 *n.d.*, 1847–48

From draft; see 144:33:

VIII²
B 100:5
206

How shall I describe this difference between the godly and the merely worldly view? There is a kind of paper called stamped paper—now imagine a child who can read handwriting; the child reads what is written on this paper exactly as the adult does, understands what is written there—but this difference, whether it is paper with a document stamp or not, does not exist for the child. So also with the worldly person's view of life; he struggles and wins, loses, wins and loses again—but it totally escapes him that underneath all this there is something else that should be

VIII²
B 100:5
207

seen. If the powerful emperor at the head of hundreds of thousands of men has invaded another land, has suffered a great defeat—what is the conflict about then? Well, what the conflict is about in the worldly sense you can read in the newspapers, which will scarcely be able to stop writing about it. In comparison with all these journalistic views, what the conflict must be said to be about in the sense of eternity shows up very poorly: the conflict is about this person's soul, about how he will understand this defeat—not in the political sense but in the godly sense.—*Pap.* VIII² B 100:5 *n.d.* 1847–48

See 143:3–149:7:

Inverted Dialectic

VIII¹
A 492
221

Believe that you "gain everything"; then not only do you lose nothing (the theme of VI of "States of Mind in the Strife of Suffering," Part Two of *Christian Discourses*), but the loss itself is a gain, so that losing is not simply losing something, not simply losing nothing, but is a gaining. The everything you lose must be a false everything, since of the everything you win you lose nothing, but the everything you win is the true everything. And losing the false everything is not only not losing anything, is not only losing nothing or losing nothing at all but is a gaining.[*] Completely lose all of the worldly person's understanding of the world and what the world is, lose even the slightest susceptibility to every worldly illusion, become as forgetful in this regard as a weak old man, forget everything as one who has never known it, change yourself in the same way as a person who in a foreign country has lost all facility in his mother tongue and speaks unintelligibly, lose everything in this way—every such loss, if you believe that you gain everything, is a gain. Furthermore, if you lost all understanding of these sham conclusions, all taste for these dubious benefits—if you believe that you win everything, then this loss is also a gain. Therefore, to lose is to gain. Straightforwardly, to lose is to lose; inversely, to lose is to gain.

VIII¹
A 492
222

[*] *In margin:* As the butterfly *gains* by *losing* its cocoon.
                    —*JP* I 760 (*Pap.* VIII¹ A 492) *n.d.*, 1847

Deleted from final copy; see 145:25:

Yes, since the everything you lose is the false everything,[*] every loss of that kind is not only not losing anything, not only losing nothing, but the loss itself is gain; thus you lose not only nothing by losing it, but you gain by losing it; any loss of that kind is in itself gain, just as losing an error, a prejudice, is not only not losing something, not only losing nothing, but is a gaining.

[*] *In margin:* thus you do not merely not lose something by losing it; you lose not merely nothing, but the loss itself is gain.
—*Pap.* VIII² B 123:16 *n.d.*, 1847–48

Deleted from draft; see 148:27:

. . . It is, yes, it is an unequal division that the discourse has only the task of easily running through the thoughts with the speed of thought—while you have the task of holding watch day and night at the post of faith, believing that you gain everything.* But do not be disturbed by the discourse, never mind the discourse; only believe that you gain everything—and every loss is a gain: you not only gain everything and thus lose nothing, but the loss itself is a gain.**

* For it is not the discourse—and even if the one speaking were of all the most worthy of admiration, it is not the discourse—it is not the discourse that can guarantee anything. If you view it this way, everything is confused. It is you who, by believing that you gain everything, must guarantee that the discourse becomes essentially true, not a thought-movement in the air.

** If you also lost all understanding of the ingenious conclusions of the discourse, all interest in this nevertheless ambiguous good—if you believe that you gain everything, this loss also is a gain.—*Pap.* VIII² B 100:6 *n.d.*, 1847–48

See 150:1–159:22:

The joy of it—

> that the more the world goes against us, the less we are delayed along the way in our pilgrimage to heaven.

or

The joy of it—

> that, Christianly understood, adversity is prosperity.

Everything that helps us along the way we are to go is prosperity; but this is exactly what adversity does; ergo, it is prosperity.

See pp. 73, 190, and 191 in this book [*Pap.* VIII^1 A 180–183, 300–302 (pp. 367–68, 368–69)]—*JP* II 2196 (*Pap.* VIII^1 A 322) *n.d.*, 1847

In margin of Pap. VIII^1 A 322:

If a fisherman is to make a good catch, he has to go where the fish are—but the fish swim against the current—then he has to go to that side.—*JP* II 2197 (*Pap.* VIII^1 A 323) *n.d.*, 1847

Bracketed in draft; see 155:5:

. . . . . —that is, if you will believe the truth that adversity leads to the goal (the goal of eternity). But this you must believe. Yet the discourse, even if it cannot give you the belief, can help correct your thought; and you presumably have followed along until now, but let me repeat. The discourse first of all showed what prosperity and adversity are, that prosperity is what leads a person to the goal; next it showed that the goal is the goal of eternity, that any other goal is a false goal; when adversity [*Modgang*] leads you to the goal of eternity (that is, to the goal), then it is really prosperity [*Medgang*].—*Pap.* VIII^2 B 100:7 *n.d.*, 1847–48

From draft; see 161:3–5:

Thoughts that wound from behind—for upbuilding.
[*Deleted:* Christian Discourses]
[*Deleted:* Christian Expositions]
Christian Attack
By
S. K.
—*Pap.* VIII^2 B 101 *n.d.*, 1847–48

See 161:1–246–20:

VIII¹
A 486
216

Some Discourses to Be Written

for Awakening

Thoughts that $^{Attack}_{Wound}$ from Behind—for Upbuilding.[*]

"Watch your step when you go to the house of the Lord" (Ecclesiastes). See one of the earlier journals.[**]

This will be the introduction.

In the following discourses the text is to be chosen in such a way that it appears to be a Gospel text, and is that also, but then comes the stinger.

> No. 1. "What shall we have, we who have left all?" And Christ answers: You will sit on thrones[7] etc.

The satire for us in this question—we who have probably not left anything at all.

> No. 2. All things serve us for good, **when** we love God.[8] When we love God. (The irony.)

> No. 3. There will be the resurrection of the dead, of both the righteous and the unrighteous.[9]

VIII¹
A 486
217

Rejoice, you are not to ask for three demonstrations—it is certain enough that you are immortal—it is absolutely certain—because you must come up for judgment. This is a new argument for immortality.

> No. 4. It is blessed—to be mocked for a good cause. (Rejoice when people speak all sorts of evil about you.)[10]

So rejoice, then—but perhaps there is no one present to whom this discourse applies. You, my listener, rejoice perhaps because you are highly honored, esteemed, and regarded. Yes, then indeed for you it is a meal like the stork's at the fox's house.[11]

The satirical.

"Woe to you if everyone speaks well of you."[12] Here is not appended "and lies"; it is not necessary, since if everyone speaks well of a person, it must be a lie.

No. 5. "We are closer to salvation now than when we became believers."[13]
But are you sure you have become a believer.

No. 6. He (Christ) was believed in the world (I Timothy
3:16).
But this is perhaps merely a bit of historical information.

[*] *In margin:* "An assault by thoughts"
[**] *In margin:* Journal NB[2], pp. 147–48 [*Pap.* VIII[1] A 256
(p. 379)]. Ditto, pp. 242, bottom, and 243, top [*Pap.* VIII[1] A 367
(p. 395)].
— *JP* V 6096 (*Pap.* VIII[1] A 486) *n.d.*, 1847

From draft; see 162:1–6:

The essentially Christian needs no *defense,* [*deleted:* but is the
attacker—if the approach is right] is not . . . —*Pap.* VIII[2] B 102
n.d. 1847–48

See 163:3–4:

Ecclesiastes 5:1: "Watch your step when you go to the house
of the Lord" could very well be used in a sermon as a contrast to
the nondescript mode of preaching concerned primarily with
getting people into church. Take care when entering there. It is
your responsibility if you do not act according to what is
preached. And if the preaching is as it should be, you might
perhaps get an impression that you can never live down, an impression of what God requires of you—self-denial, etc.—therefore take care!—*JP* I 640 (*Pap.* VIII[1] A 256) *n.d.*, 1847

From draft; see 174:7:

. . . . . as we recall the glorious one who suffered the innocent
death of which we say, "That is now long since past." His innocent sacrifice is not past even though the cup of suffering is emptied, is not a past event although it is past, is not a completely past
event although it is eighteen centuries since it happened, and will

VIII[2]
B 103:1
208

not be that even eighteen thousand years from now. He did not,
after all, die a natural death on a sick bed, nor did he die because
of an accident; neither was he attacked and murdered by a few
individuals, nor was it that generation living at the time: it was
humankind—and you also certainly do belong to that. Therefore
you are not an onlooker and spectator at a completely past event,
nor are sympathy and emotion required, as the poet requires, of
you and me—oh, save your sympathy!—*Pap.* VIII² B 103:1 *n.d.*,
1847–48

VIII²
B 103:1
209

From draft; see 184:11:

. . . . . the beloveds! [*deleted:* because one must believe that
they cannot be saved, so true it is that the condition of salvation
is bound to that one whom the beloveds will not accept in
faith.]—*Pap.* VIII² B 103:2 *n.d.*, 1847–48

Deleted from margin of draft; see 195:7:

If your demonstration to him that God is love were carried out
in the most complete and thorough way, so that it would perhaps
arouse people's amazement, would be admired by them as a marvel of penetration and profundity, and that from this it indeed
follows that all things serve us for good—he will ignore the
whole thing as if you were talking to the wind and will repeat:
—yes, *when you* love God.—*Pap.* VIII² B 103:3 *n.d.*, 1847–48

In margin of draft; see 214:3–4:

In Paul it reads: Our salvation is closer now than when we
became believers. Rom. 13:11.—*Pap.* VIII² B 103:4 *n.d.*, 1847–
48

See 222:1–233:7:

In *Christian Discourses*, Part Three, No. 6

This discourse quite properly is constructed in such a way that it
could almost just as well be a discourse about what also has been

interwoven as commentary: Woe to you if everybody speaks well of you. Its polemical aim, therefore, must also be at such an existence: to be along, to be a nobody, to be insignificant, etc. Anyone who has any kind of prominence must expose himself to something—but the numerical, the triumphing number, the crowd, is in the difficult position of being able to avoid all spiritual trials.—*JP* V 6118 (*Pap.* VIII¹ A 576) *n.d.*, 1848

From final copy; see 226:12:

> *Changed from:* not even a comedy
> *Deleted from margin:* not even in a Shrove Monday comedy
> —*Pap.* VIII² B 124:1 *n.d.*, 1847–48

From draft; see 231:22:

> . . . who* are living now.**
> *In margin:* *are living right now, to the misled, corrupted, unchristian, domineering crowd (because the crowd is always misled, corrupt, unchristian, domineering) that now, just *now* is— feared.
> *Deleted from margin:* **thus we actually are in church and not at a comedy—*Pap.* VIII² B 103:5 *n.d.*, 1847–48

Deleted from final copy; see 231:22:

VIII¹
A 564
262

From Thoughts that Wound from Behind for Upbuilding Discourse VI

Just as a child who, about to get a licking, puts a towel under his jacket, unbeknownst to the teacher, so that he will not feel the blows, so, alas, even a preacher of the Law is for good reasons helpful to the congregation by surreptitiously slipping in another figure, who is now punished—to the edification, *contentement* [satisfaction], and enjoyment of the congregation. For good reasons, because in the case of the child there is no danger involved in being the teacher who is to administer the beating; but truly to be a preacher of the Law—yes, here the concept flips over [*slaa om*], because it means not so much to beat [*slaa*] others as to be beaten oneself. The more lickings the preacher of the Law gets, the better he is. Therefore a so-called preacher of the Law does not dare actually to administer a beating, because he knows very well and understands only all too well that those before him are not children, that the others, the ones he is to beat, the moment or those honored, esteemed, and lauded because of their serving the passions of the moment, together with their thousands, are by far, by far the stronger, who will *actually* strike back [*slaa igjen*], perhaps put him to death [*slaa ihjel*], since to be the great preacher of the Law is to be put to death. Therefore the preacher of the Law restricts himself to—beating the pulpit. In this way he achieves his ridiculous purpose, to become the most ridiculous of all monstrosities—a preacher of the Law who is honored and esteemed, greeted with applause!—*JP* I 647 (*Pap.* VIII[1] A 564) *n.d.*, 1848

VIII[1]
A 564
263

Deleted from final copy; see 231:26:

VIII[2]
B 124:4
228

A preacher of the Law, who is the speaker, who shadowboxes and only beats the pulpit, says

In margin: So the speaker shadowboxes and [*deleted:* only beats the lectern (*changed from:* pulpit)] says

—*Pap.* VIII[2] B 124:4 *n.d.*, 1847–48

See 232:30–233:6:

In Part Three of *Christian Discourses*, discourse six, the passage at the end: people whose sole concern is to achieve the *ungodliness* of having everybody everywhere speak well of them. It is altogether correct, precisely because Christianity teaches that this cannot happen to a person except through ungodliness. It is impossible for anyone with an earnest conviction (which everyone, Christianly, ought to have) to achieve this. Therefore, if anyone does achieve it, it is *eo ipso* his ungodliness. Christianity does not have a frivolous idea of what happens to a human being, that, for example, everyone speaks well of him. Christianity says: Such a thing must not happen to you, any more than stealing, whoring, etc. You will not be able to defend yourself by saying that you did not covet it, that you are not responsible—for you are to live as Christianity requires you to live, and then it is *eo ipso* impossible for it to happen to you. If it does happen, then it is *eo ipso* evidence that you are not living as Christianity requires you to live.—*JP* V 6124 (*Pap.* VIII¹ A 596) *n.d.*, 1848

See 232:30–233:6:

Well, the idea of equality will be regarded as an assignment; it has been introduced into the European discussion.

VIII¹
A 598
275

Consequently every one of the older forms of tyranny will now be powerless (emperor, king, nobility, clergy, even money tyranny).

VIII¹
A 598
276

But another form of tyranny is a corollary of equality—fear of people. I have already called attention to this in the last discourse of "The Gospel of Sufferings."[14] I called attention to it again in the third part of *Christian Discourses*, no. 6.

Of all the tyrannies, it is the most dangerous, in part because it is not directly obvious and attention must be called to it.

The communists here at home and in other places fight for human rights. Good, so do I. For that very reason I fight with all my might against the tyranny of the fear of people.

Communism ultimately leads to the tyranny of the fear of people (just see how France at this moment is suffering from it); right here is where Christianity begins.

What communism makes such a big fuss about, Christianity accepts as something that is self-evident, that all people are equal before God, therefore essentially equal. But then Christianity shudders at this abomination that wants to abolish God and create fear of the crowd of people, of the majority, of the people, of the public.—*JP* IV 4131 (*Pap.* VIII¹ A 598) *n.d.*, 1848

Deleted from final copy; see 245:35:

But it is—just because it cannot be done—far less strenuous to be fooled by the trick of wanting to hear at a distance of eighteen hundred years through a human throng of more than fifty [*changed from:* two thousand years] generations.—*Pap.* VIII^2 B 124:5 *n.d.*, 1847–48

From draft; see 247:1–4:

The book is to be dedicated to Bishop Mynster.[15]
                    —*JP* V 6068 (*Pap.* VIII^2 B 116) *n.d.*, 1847–48

From draft:

Preface to Friday discourses.
Addition: used for Note No. 3 in "Three Notes."[16]
                    —*Pap.* VIII^2 B 117 *n.d.*, 1847–48

Addition to Pap. VIII^2 B 117:

To His Excellency
          Right Reverend Bishop Dr. Mynster
                    St. D., DM., a.o.[17]
                    this small book
                    is dedicated
                              in profound veneration.[18]
          —*JP* V 6069 (*Pap.* VIII^2 B 118) *n.d.*, 1847–48

VIII^1
A 414
179   November 20

The fundamental derangement at the root of modern times (which branches out into logic, metaphysics, dogmatics, and the whole of modern life) actually consists in this: that the qualitative chasmic abyss in the difference between God and human beings has been obliterated. Because of this there is in dogmatics (from logic and metaphysics) a depth of blasphemy that paganism never knew (for it knew what blasphemy against God is, but precisely this has been forgotten in our time, this theocentric age) and in ethics a brash unconcern or, more accurately, no ethics at all. The derangement has come about in many ways and has many forms, but mainly as follows. As the crowd intimidates the king, as the public intimidates counselors of state and authors, so the generation will ultimately want to intimidate God, constrain him to give in, become self-important before him, brazenly defiant in their numbers, etc. Thus what we have today, in modern times, is actually not doubt—it is insubordination. It is useless to want to bring religion to the front; it is not even possible to mount the machinery, for the soil is a swamp or a bog. "Of course, we will all be saved" etc. is approximately the refrain. This being the case, what is meant by all this about the consolation of religion!

On this frontier, where smugglers as well as rebels traffic, I have been assigned my place as an insignificant official who by any means, by slyness, by force (that is, spiritual force) must confiscate all illusions and seize those arrogant delusions based on effrontery toward God, unparalleled in either paganism or Judaism, since it is a prodigious fraud, a debasing of the doctrine of the God-man. —As a reward for my work, I must be prepared, of course, to suffer all things from people, for whom it at first can certainly not be agreeable to be torn out of all those grandiloquent delusions in which great numbers of sophists still continually strengthen them.

Humbled and crushed and annihilated, I myself have had to learn as profoundly as anyone will come to learn arduously from me or through me: that a human being is nothing before God. This is what I have to teach, not directly but indirectly. To be able to do that, I must continually go to school to God, who, when necessary, starts me all over again at the beginning to make me understand what I am, what a human being is, before him.

My task is in the service of truth; its essential form is: obedience. Nothing new is to be introduced, but everywhere the springs will be repaired in such a way again that the old, nothing but the old, will be like new again. As long as I live, I will, humanly speaking, have nothing but trouble and will reap ingratitude—but after my death, my work will stand as much as anyone's. As long as I am living, I cannot be acknowledged, for

VIII[1]
A 414
180

only a few are able to understand me, and if people began trying to acknowledge me, I would have to exert all my powers in new mystifications to prevent it.

The only contemporary I have paid any attention to is Mynster. But Mynster cares only about holding office and administering, thinking that this is the truth. He cares nothing about the truth, even if it were suffering right under his eyes. He can only understand that the truth must and shall rule—that it must and shall suffer is beyond his understanding.—*JP* V 6075 (*Pap.* VIII[1] A 414) November 20, 1847

VIII[1]
A 415
180

According to Mynster's view, Christianity is related to the natural man in the same way as horsemanship is related to the horse, as the trained horse to the untrained horse, where it is not a matter of taking away its nature but of improving it. That is, Christianity is a culture; being a Christian is approximately what the natural man in his most blissfully happy moment could wish to be at his best: poised, harmonious perfection in itself and in

VIII[1]
A 415
181

himself consummately prepared virtuosity. But such talk is 100,000 miles removed from the Redeemer who must suffer in the world and who requires the crucifixion of the flesh, all that agony as the birth pangs of salvation, because under the circumstances there is in fact an infinite, a qualitative difference between God and man, and the terror of Christianity is also its blessedness: that God wants to be the teacher and wants the pupil to resemble him. If God is to be the teacher, then the instruction must begin with disrupting the learner (the human being). For the sake of quality, it cannot be otherwise. There is not much use in speaking of God as the teacher and then have the instruction be only a purely human improvement program.

In many ways Mynster himself is the inventor of this confusion of Christianity and culture. But in another sense he has done an extraordinary service and has certainly demonstrated the deep impression from his former days. If there is not to be any conflict between Christianity and the world, if the insignia of battle are not to be carried, if there is to be peace of that sort, then it is really something great to have a figure such as Mynster. He has resolved a most difficult problem. If a debate starts that brings the very concept of "state Church" under discussion, then Mynster's position is dubious—if the concept of state Church is accepted, then Mynster is the master, and it must always be remembered that in judging a man it is an outrageous wrong unceremoniously to delete all the very presuppositions within which a man is to be judged.

Let us pay tribute to Bishop Mynster. I have admired no one, no living person, except Bishop Mynster, and it is always a joy to me to be reminded of my father. His position is such that I see the irregularities very well, more clearly than anyone who has attacked him. But the nature of what I have to say is such that it can very well be said without affecting him at all—*if only he himself does not make a mistake.* There is an ambivalence in his life that cannot be avoided, because the "state Church" is an ambivalence. But now it is very possible to ascribe to him the whole element of awakening within the established order—and then he would once again stand high. If he makes a mistake, if instead of calmly sitting in lofty eminence, holding his scepter, and letting a second lieutenant decide things, he makes the mistake of believing that he should start a battle, then no one can guarantee the results. My corps is just the reinforcement he needs. If he makes a mistake, he will have lost not only my auxiliary-corps— that is of least importance—but he will also have lost his own position.—*JP* V 6076 (*Pap.* VIII^1 A 415) *n.d.*, 1847

VIII^1
A 415
182

But the Friday Discourses[19] cannot be dedicated to Mynster. With my father in mind, I would very much like to do it. It was indeed no ordinary dedication, but at the very moment when I placed a kind of period, if not here then at least in my striving, and in the most solemn way, then to dedicate it to him would be as I desired it, again a concentration of veneration. But it cannot be done. My course through life is too doubtful, with regard to whether I will enjoy honor and esteem or will be insulted and persecuted, for me to be able to dedicate my work to any living person. Furthermore, there are still all-too-significant differences between us. Such a dedication could also in both the one way

VIII^1
A 438
193

and the other wrongly entangle my cause in the circumstances of finitude.—*Pap.* VIII[1] A 438 *n.d.*, 1847

From draft; see 249:1–10:

Discourses at the Communion on Friday

Preface
Of these discourses (which in more essential respects still are not sermons and therefore are not called that either), two (No. 2 and 3) were delivered in Frue Church . . .
Of these discourses (which still lack something doubly essential [*changed from:* more than one essential] in order to be sermons and therefore are not called "sermons" either), two (No. 2 and 3) were delivered in Frue Church . . . . .—*Pap.* VIII[2] B 114 *n.d.*, 1847–48

From draft; see 249:1–8:

Preface[20]

VIII[2]
B 119
219

To the typesetter
to be set in the smallest possible brevier.

Two (No. 2 and 3) of these discourses (which still lack something doubly essential in order to be sermons and therefore are not called "sermons" either) were delivered in Frue Church.

VIII[2]
B 119
220

An authorship that began with *Either/Or* seeks here its decisive place of rest, in the name for which *it* labored, at the foot of the altar, where *I* dedicated myself in resolution.[*] To survey a labor such as this in its totality, to follow it in its step-by-step advance, very few, of course, have the time and opportunity, not to mention the ability and presuppositions. In my opinion it has been successful (something I at no time during the considerable fear and trembling of the work dared say), has succeeded far beyond my expectation, indescribably—for which I thank God indescribably, whose blessing perhaps can be seen by anyone who wants to see, but best, of course, and in quite another sense, by me, who by this blessing have not merely been helped to do what I wanted to do, and to understand what I should understand, but also at times in such a way that not until later did I myself completely understand the rightness of what I was helped to do. Were someone to ask me if I in any way think that I have some special relationship to God, I would answer: No, oh no, oh no! Far from it! There has never lived anyone in Christendom, there is no one, unconditionally no one, who is not unconditionally equally close to God, loved by him. But on the other hand I really do not believe that there are many who have been so occupied as I have been day after day with the blessed undertaking of contemplating that God loves them —and I cannot help it if others disdain the love God lavishes upon them just as richly as on me. So saying, I permit myself and wish to present, as it were, these writings to the small nation whose language I have the honor to write, trusting that it will not be to its discredit that I have written it,[**] willingly forgetting what anyone in the nation may have done against me for which it might be discredited.

VIII²
B 119
221

S. K.

October 1847

[*] *In margin:* When I turn this way, I have nothing further to add, but as I turn to the other side I permit myself, and I wish to present, as it were, these writings to the small nation whose language I have the honor to write . . .

[**] *In margin:* ingratitude for the sympathy and encouragement that may have been shown me. . . . .

—*Pap.* VIII² B 119 October 1847

From draft; see 249:1–10:

In the Preface to Friday Discourses

VIII²
B 122
222

not: [*deleted:* to present] and commend—but only: ***to commend***.

willingly forgetting etc. goes out.[21]

Perhaps add just two words about Christianity as being everything also for a people.

Unable to occupy myself [*deleted:* like those mighty minds and quick intellects,] with what concerns "the many," I have slowly and all the more inwardly occupied myself with what concerns every individual of the people. But perhaps this endeavor does concern the people. Twenty people who are united are an enormous strength. And yet I have not asserted what makes an enormous difference (with regard to strength): that in which they are united. Twelve men united in being Christians have transformed the shape of the world. Therefore there is really only one actual danger for a people in Christendom, that the individuals are not Christians; this danger can become the downfall of a people—any other danger, given this, is in the Christian sense just an opportunity to be victorious. There is only one danger for every person, that of not becoming a Christian, consequently that of not becoming aware of becoming a Christian by not becoming, as a prerequisite, "the single individual";* any other danger, in the Christian sense, is only an [*deleted:* welcome] occasion for becoming victorious in the Christian sense.

*This danger can become his downfall.—*Pap.* VIII^2 B 122 *n.d.*, 1847–48

See 251:3:

Friday Sermon

Text: I have fervently longed to eat this Passover meal with you.

Theme: the truly inward longing to receive Communion.
—*JP* IV 3922 (*Pap.* VIII^1 A 287) *n.d.*, 1847

See 251:30–252:8:

From Friday Discourse No. 1.

On the night when he was betrayed. It is midnight; sleep rests over the city, the populous city is as if dead, everything so quiet, so peaceful in the night. Only treachery, which walks about at night, is sneaking around in the dark; only evil, which turns night into day, is awake as if it were now day; only "the high priests are glad" (Luke 22:5) that the darkness has conquered and may conquer "without any disturbance" (Luke 22:6). In the "great room" he is sitting at supper with the apostles for the last time.

> Was not used—a mistake here, also, since it is evening, not midnight.
>
> Yet it says in John 13:30 that it was night.
>
> —*JP* IV 3924 (*Pap.* VIII¹ A 386) *n.d.*, 1847

From draft; see 251:30–252:8:

See, this is the introduction to the Lord's Supper! How deeply moving! It is the last time he is together with his apostles in this way—ah, but he did not find this out afterward, he knew it beforehand; it is the last time, then follows not only the separation but the suffering. Ah, even if he himself had not said: I have longed with all my heart to eat this Passover Lamb with you, it is implicit in the event itself that it had to be so. Parting from those we love is always hard, but what parting was as hard as this? It is his farewell supper, it is the teacher who is parting from his disciples, and it is this teacher the disciples have recognized as God's only begotten—he is sitting for the last time at supper with them—already betrayed. It was on the night when he was betrayed. The populous city is as if dead, everything is quiet in the night—only evil is awake—only the high priests "are glad" (Luke 22:5). In the "great room" he is sitting at supper with them for the last time. What is going to happen only one person knows—the betrayer, and then one more, the betrayed, who is also present.

In margin: Ah, many a teacher has with heartfelt longing been together with his pupils for the last time, be it life or death that would separate them, but how different it is here! It is the teacher the disciples have recognized as God's only begotten, and only he knows how close at hand is the danger, and what the danger is—of that the disciples have no idea.* Thus all sadness is concentrated in his soul.

*Only he knows who the betrayer is and that the betrayer is present.—*Pap.* VIII² B 105:2 *n.d.*, 1847–48

VIII²
B 105:2
210

VIII²
B 105:2
211

From final draft; see 251:30–252:8:

On the night when he was betrayed! It is midnight; the populous city is as if dead, sleep rests over the city, everything so quiet, so peaceful in the night, only evil is awake—in the dark; only "the high priests are glad"—that the darkness has conquered (Luke 22:5). In the "great room" he is sitting at supper with the apostles for the last time.

In margin: only treachery, which walks about at night, is sneaking around in the dark; only evil, which turns night into day, is awake—as if it were day; only the "high priests are glad" (Luke 22:5) that the darkness has conquered and that there cannot possibly be any disturbance.—*Pap.* VIII² B 106 *n.d.*, 1847–48

From draft; see 255:31:

. . . . . 70,000 fathoms . . . . .
                           —*Pap.* VIII² B 105:3 *n.d.* 1847–48

From draft; see 268:1–274:31:

VIII²
B 108
212

John 10:27. [*In margin:* Friday sermon delivered Aug. 27, '47, in Frue Church.]

VIII²
B 108
213

. . . The false teachers had reversed the relationship; they taught that if one said that the gift with which one could help one's parents was corban, then one did not need to offer it. But Christ reprimands them; he teaches that to make the right application is indeed to offer one's gift.

Oh, do not forget that there where he is, there—in the spiritual sense—is the altar. If this were not so, then you of course would have to remain at the Communion table. If you had a friend from whom you lived apart, but you recollected him faithfully every day—well, yes, it would be the most festive, the most beautiful moment when you saw him again, but if you faithfully recollected him every day, then he would still be with you and you with him.

In margin: The discourse can end with a stanza from Kingo, the

last stanza of the fifth morning sigh.—*Pap.* VIII² B 108 *n.d.*,
1847–48

Addition to Pap. VIII² B 108:

A Christian's life is a divine worship every day, just as today is
divine worship on a weekday.—*Pap.* VIII² B 109 *n.d.*, 1847–48

Addition to Pap. VIII² B 108:

It is not as if everything were settled by your going to the
Communion table on a rare occasion—no, at the Communion
table you learn precisely how to receive Communion.—*Pap.*
VIII² B 110 *n.d.*, 1847–48

See 276:7–278:38:

Text for a Friday Sermon

Our citizenship is in heaven.[22]

VIII¹
A 265
127

. . . . . we are especially aware of this today—for every time these
words are repeated: Our Lord Jesus Christ "on the night when he
was betrayed," the congregation steadily draws still closer around
him, as if the traitor were coming closer again.—*JP* IV 3919
(*Pap.* VIII¹ A 265) *n.d.*, 1847

VIII¹
A 265
128

From draft; see 276:7–278:38:

. . . We should not recall his death as we recall the glorious
one who suffered the innocent death of which we say, "That is
now long since past." We could recall in this way the figures who
surround us here, his apostles[23]—but not him. His death is not
past, although it is eighteen centuries since then; it is not past as
long as the world endures. It was indeed not by accident that he
met his death; it was indeed not some few men who seized him
and killed him; it was indeed not that generation—no, it was
"the human race," and we still are certainly part of it if we are

VIII²
B 112
214

human beings at all, that is, we are not merely spectators and observers at an event, and what the poet demands, fervent sympathy [*Medlidenhed*], is not what is demanded of us—no, we are accomplices [*Medskyldige*].

You have certainly reflected on this yourself, my listeners, so it is not your idea that here in God's house a speaker should more or less eloquently make a deep impression on you, as they say. [*In margin:* You yourself have no doubt brought the deep impression with you.] No, if you, as you call forth the thought of his suffering and death, if you consider yourself to be present as an accomplice, then you do not need the help of eloquence to get an impression of it, especially when you consider that, compared with those contemporaries, it still is like a mitigation for you that you actually are not contemporary with his crucifixion; however vividly you imagine yourself contemporary, it is still only a faint echo. For actuality preaches still better, awakening and penetrating in a completely different way, than all speakers. . . .

But before you partake of this holy meal, the discourse should speak, not about what could distract your attention but about— what could be more appropriate than

about the night when he was betrayed.

Do not, then, let the surroundings distract you, not its beauty, not its splendor, not the art objects, [*]not the almost perfidious, deceitful, fraudulent security in here—let it only be night around you.

On the night when he was betrayed.[**] . . . This night is the turning point. Yet not as in the external world, where the sun pauses and then takes just as long a time to decrease as it did to increase—no, his downfall is speeded up with a dreadful increasing speed. This night is the dividing line; everything is in readiness for the horror—all he needs to do is arise from the table and go out into the night, and then it begins—and just as with the horror of the sudden a storm has darkened the sky in the course of a few moments: so will it be at the peak in one moment. The dreadful upheaval; and yet it is the same, the same people, the same high priests, the same folk: yes, and he, too, is the same, the unchanged one.

VIII²
B 112
215

VIII²
B 112
216

His life is the opposite of their worldly life, which rung by rung ascended in honor, esteem, power, influence, in their continually having more and more people accepting their opinions; he ascends in reverse, rung by rung in the reversed order of precedence, and he now goes through all the ranks from being vilified to being crucified. As truly as he is truth, the truth must suffer this way in the world. At first it seems to please everyone, but the further and further it advances, the more definitely and decisively it has occasion to manifest itself as it truly is, the more and more people fall away from it, until at last it stands utterly alone. Just as the good, from the worldly point of view, is recognized by signs of distinction and by more and more people joining it in admiration, so the truth is recognized by the reverse response; this is its mark of distinction—until it stands alone—and then it is insulted, ridiculed, mocked, and finally crucified. It perhaps pleases the conceited person to see that ascent in worldly ranking; it is upbuilding for the believer to see the reverse movement.

[*] *In margin:* not this, for many people perhaps, even perfidious security in here

[**] *In margin:*   **N.B.**

If this discourse is delivered, the whole introduction would be left out. It would begin immediately after the text. On the night when he was betrayed. Do not let the surroundings distract you, not the solidity of these arches, not the beauty and the splendor, not the art objects, not this, alas, for many people perhaps, even perfidious security in here—let it be only night around you. On the night when he was betrayed. This night is the turning point in his life etc.—*Pap.* VIII^2 B 112 *n.d.*, 1847–48

See 281:3–6:

. . . . . O God, there is so much in the outer world to draw us away from you. That is why we enter into your house, but even here there is at times a security that will deceive us, as if here all danger and terror were far away, here where the greatest danger of all is to be discussed—sin, and the greatest horror—Christ's suffering and death.—*JP* III 3417 (*Pap.* VIII^1 A 367) *n.d.*, 1847

Deleted from draft; see 281:3–6:

> *In text:* So you do it now in remembrance of him.

VIII²
B 113:1
217
> On the night when he was betrayed! Now, however, my devout listeners, here in God's house where all is so quiet and secure
>
> *In margin:* There is so much in the outer world to draw us away from you, O God, and this is why we enter into your house. But in here there is something that so easily deludes us, as if all danger and terror were far away—right here is where we must talk about the greatest danger, *sin*, and about the greatest horror: his suffering and death. Therefore we ask you, our Lord and Savior, to remind us of this in the same way you certainly have reminded them who have come here today to partake of this holy meal: do this, then, in remembrance of him.—*Pap.* VIII² B 113:1 *n.d.*, 1847–48

From draft; see 285:23–24:

> Remember the holy day so that you keep it holy, but also remember Christ's faithfulness so that you do not take it in vain—*Pap.* VIII² B 113:4 *n.d.*, 1847–48

See 289:22–290:29:

> Text for a Friday Sermon
>
> I John 3:20: "Even if our hearts condemn us,
> God is greater than our hearts."
>
> Is it not this that is expressed today: in the confession of sin we all step forward today—and thus we condemn ourselves—but God is greater.—*JP* IV 3920 (*Pap.* VIII¹ A 266) *n.d.*, 1847

From draft; see 290:34–35:

> . . . . . that God is greater than our hearts, indeed, is greater than the heart that condemns itself. [*Deleted:* And even if we warn against extremes of depression in self-condemnation, let us

not wish to debase the greatness of God—either by wanting to make ourselves out to be better than we are, less guilty, or by giving our guilt more trivial names. In so doing we reduce God's greatness, because it is in forgiving; but neither let us insanely want to sin in order that God's greatness can reveal itself all the greater in forgiving.]—*Pap.* VIII^2 B 113:5 *n.d.*, 1847–48

Theme for a Friday Sermon

Luke 24:51. "And it happened, **as he blessed them**, he was parted from them."

It is really about the Ascension, but this is always the way Christ parts from human beings.

—*JP* IV 3917 (*Pap.* VIII^1 A 260) *n.d.*, 1847

From draft; see 299:14–19:

All the deeper is the need for blessing. At the Communion table you yourself are able to do less than nothing; at the Communion table he is—blessing . . . —*Pap.* VIII^2 B 113:6 *n.d.*, 1847–48

From draft; see 299:27–35:

But it is all the more clear that the blessing, that grace is everything here.—*Pap.* VIII^2 B 113:7 *n.d.*, 1847–48

N.B.

Only 7 themes were used for "States of Mind in the Strife of Suffering." Here are three that were set aside.

No. 1. The joy of it—that if the believer is not able to hold on to the anchor in spiritual trial, the anchor is able to hold on to the believer.

See journal NB^2, p. 73
[*Pap.* VIII^1 A 180 (p. 367)]

No. 2. The joyful correlation—that hardship gives steadfast-ness, steadfastness experience, experience hope.*

No. 3. The joy of it—that it is for joy that one does not dare to believe what is most blessed.

See journal NB², p. 238

[Pap. VIII¹ A 360 (p. 372)]

Thus in Acts 12:14 the girl, Rhoda, who was to open the gate for Peter: when she recognized Peter's voice, "in her joy she did not open the gate"—in her joy she let him stand outside.

In margin: They say that misfortunes seldom come singly—the same with joy, it does not come singly.—*JP* II 2200 (*Pap.* VIII¹ A 500) *n.d.*, 1847–48

No preface was written for "States of Mind [*Stemning*] in the Strife of Suffering." If it were to be written, it would be of the following nature. That most valiant of nations in antiquity (the Lacedæmonians) prepared for battle with music—in the same way these are states of mind of triumphant joy that tune one [*stemme*] for the struggle, and far from discouraging [*forstemme*] a person in the struggle will definitely keep him well tuned [*vel-stemt*].—*JP* II 2201 (*Pap.* VIII¹ A 503) *n.d.*, 1848

VIII¹
A 504
227

Instructions for "States of Mind in the
Strife of Suffering"[24]

These discourses are presented in such a way as to be continually tangential to the consciousness of sin and the suffering of sin—sin etc. are another matter: these discourses come to the subject of sin. Because the consolation lyrically rises as high as possible over all earthly need and misery, even the heaviest, the horror of sin, is continually shown. Thus another theme is cunningly concealed in these discourses: sin is the human being's corruption.

VIII¹
A 504
228

In the ordinary sermon this is the confusion: need and adversity are preached together—with sin.

Thus the category for these discourses is different from "The Gospel of Sufferings,"[25] which left the suffering indefinite. Here the distinction is made: the innocent suffering—in order then to approach sin.—*JP* V 6101 (*Pap.* VIII¹ A 504) *n.d.*, 1848

N.B.   N.B.

A new book ought to be written entitled: **Thoughts That Cure Radically, Christian Healing.**

VIII¹
A 558
258

It will deal with the doctrine of the Atonement. First of all it will show that the root of the sickness is sin. It will have two parts. [*Deleted:* Perhaps it is better to have three.

First comes:

VIII¹
A 558
259

(1) Thoughts that wound from behind—for upbuilding. This will be the polemical element, something like "The Cares of the Pagans," but somewhat stronger than that, since Christian discourses should be given in an altogether milder tone.]

(1) [*changed from:* (2)] On the consciousness of sin.

The Sickness unto Death

Christian Discourses

(2) [*changed from:* (3)] **Radical Cure**

[*changed from:* Thoughts That Cure Radically]

Christian Healing

The Atonement

—*JP* V 6110 (*Pap.* VIII¹ A 558) *n.d.*, 1848

I almost went and upset the whole design of *Christian Discourses* and their original purpose by including in them "Thoughts That Wound from Behind for Upbuilding"[26] simply because these discourses were lying there ready. A polemical piece like that belongs there least of all; it will itself be weakened by its surroundings and divert all attention away from the "Friday Discourses."[27] No, my intention is to be as gentle as possible, right after the powerful polemic in *Works of Love*. The Christian discourses are given in this way. Then, too, I may take a journey, and I would like to depart in peace. Finally, the book was getting too large; the smaller, the better I am read.—*JP* V 6111 (*Pap.* VIII¹ A 559) *n.d.*, 1848

VIII¹
A 560
259

No, no, no, no—I did, however, almost fail to appreciate how in Part Three[28] Governance had added what was needed. But I wanted to be a bit sagacious and arrange something myself.

VIII¹
A 560
260

As so often happens, so it happened here, too. I had not thought that the third part, which was written last, should go into *Christian Discourses.** But that is precisely where it belongs. It had not occurred to me, but Governance ordained it in such a way that, sure enough, the little book was ready just when I was about to publish *Christian Discourses*.

Without the third part *Christian Discourses* is much too mild, for me truly not in character; they are mild enough as it is. And how in the world would I get a more felicitous juxtaposition than with the enormous thrust in the third part—and the hidden inwardness in the fourth, simply because it is the Communion on Friday.

The book does not become too large, either; on the contrary, without this third section I would even have been obliged to have it printed in larger type in order to reach a certain number of sheets.

Then, too, without Part Three *Christian Discourses* is too repetitious.

But as said, I wanted to be sagacious. That is not good. In trust and confidence in God I would rather accept from his hand whatever comes than have a comfortable situation if I have sagaciously avoided a potential danger in order to achieve it. No doubt I do need some encouragement. If God will give it to me, I accept it with fervent gratitude. But the embarrassment that would make my heart stand still, the embarrassment that comes over me at the thought that I possibly had let God call but had sagaciously stepped aside—no, this I could not endure. When the devoted teacher looks affectionately at the child and says: Come, now, make a big jump, my little friend, but if you are afraid, if you do not feel like it, well, then, don't do it—what a shame if the child could sadden the teacher by not doing it. So also in a person's relationship to God; he compels no one, he tells one of the dangers in advance, he frightens one through scary imaginings—and then looks at one and says: Just go ahead confidently, my child, but if you are afraid, I will not force you. Truly, there is no more compelling method than this!

At your word, O Lord! When a person does something in this spirit, then, humanly speaking, he is prepared for the worst—but yet, yet I cannot do otherwise. Then he does not expect a happy ending, humanly speaking; he believes that it is possible, that it may happen just the same—but one thing is certain: God will not let him go, God will remain with him in a bold confidence that is worth far more than all the world's beds of roses.

VIII¹
A 560
261

It follows as a matter of course that here again I have considered the possibilities that, if I had initiated a single other person into them, would have immediately prompted him to say: For God's sake, stop. This is why I keep silent. I cannot do otherwise—Amen. Moreover, it could also be very possible that much of what I shudder to think about is a gloomy delusion. Perhaps so. But the pressure of it is just as powerful! And it is still true—what I have always said and taught—that the true action is the inner decision.

But Mynster has touched me by retaining his friendship for me in spite of *Works of Love*. I would so much like to humor him once. I know he would like *Christian Discourses* if it did not have Part Three.[29] But I cannot do it. I would also have liked to dedicate the fourth part to him, but that cannot be done.[30] Perhaps here again it is only a gloomy thought that he would get angry about Part Three; it would even be unfair of him; but in any case I have acted with this pressure upon me also. Oh, the more pressures there are, the clearer it is that one needs God and the clearer it is that one makes decisions trusting in God.—*JP* V 6112 (*Pap.* VIII¹ A 560) *n.d.*, 1848

In margin of Pap. VIII¹ A 560:

[*]Part Three is precisely the weaving of Governance—that it was finished at the right time without my really understanding how it belonged.—*JP* V 6113 (*Pap.* VIII¹ A 561) *n.d.*, 1848

In Tauler's *Nachfolgung des armen Lebens Jesu Christi*,[31] which I am presently reading for my own upbuilding, I find (pt. 2, para. 33, p. 137) a striking similarity to what I have developed in *Christian Discourses* (third part, second discourse[32]). The following is especially excellent: that love prefers to obey counsel rather than commands. Consequently, as I have presented it, renunciation of all things is Christian counsel; Christ desires that you do it but does not command it. Nor does he judge any person who does not do it not to be a Christian.—*JP* II 1844 (*Pap.* VIII[1] A 587) *n.d.*, 1848

The contrast between the third and fourth parts of *Christian Discourses*[33] is as sharp as possible and very intense: first there is something like a temple-cleansing celebration—and then the quiet and most intimate of all worship services—the Communion service on Fridays.—*JP* V 6121 (*Pap.* VIII[1] A 590) *n.d.*, 1848

VIII[1]
A 602
277

March 27, 1848

Once again for a moment I have been concerned about my responsibility in letting *Christian Discourses*, especially Part Three,[34] be published.[*] It is outright dangerous for me to have something written in a completely different situation be read under the current circumstances. But I cannot do otherwise. It is Governance that has arranged it this way for me. I have not plunged myself into any danger. My manuscript was sent in[35] long before this latest event,[36] which no doubt has changed people somewhat. Every word in my discourses is true—nothing is more certain. I have nothing to change. Should I take it back, then, because of personal danger? No, that I dare not do. What I am I am simply and solely by believing in and obeying God.

VIII[1]
A 602
278

The moment I catch myself cravenly fleeing any danger in which he has willed to take me, then I will have escaped the danger all right—but to my own degradation, woe to me—I will collapse into nothing. With God I can endure all things—in God I hope this; without God, nothing.

Perhaps there is considerable hypochondria in my fear, but that makes no difference. God knows how I suffer—but God will also help me, and my cause.

And so I sit here. Out there everything is agitated; the nationality issue inundates everyone; everyone is talking about sacrificing life and blood, is perhaps also willing to do it, but is shored up by the omnipotence of public opinion. And so I sit in a quiet room (no doubt I will soon be in bad repute for indifference to the nation's cause)—I know only one risk, the risk of religiousness. But no one cares about that—and no one has any intimation of what is taking place in me. Well, such is my life. Always misunderstanding. At the point where I suffer, I am misunderstood—and I am hated.—*JP* V 6125 (*Pap.* VIII[1] A 602) March 27, 1848

In margin of JP V 6125 (*Pap.* VIII[1] A 602):

[*]And contrary to my custom for weekdays, I opened Mynster and read my sermon,[37] which I otherwise would have read on Sunday, and it was on Nicodemus.[38] What an admonition against my beating a hasty retreat.—*JP* V 6126 (*Pap.* VIII[1] A 603) *n.d.*, 1848

Perhaps not a soul will read my *Christian Discourses*—perhaps the alarm will be sounded in camp—and I will be the maltreated victim. Perhaps. Oh, it is hard to bear such a possibility.

But in a confused situation, what is letting oneself be put to death on the battlefield, arm in arm with 1000 others, carried away by public opinion, perhaps essentially without one single idea, at most a vague feeling—what is that compared with this slow, consciously prepared advance, always with the possibility of being able to check it?—*Pap.* VIII[1] A 617 *n.d.*, 1848

"Let not the heart in sorrow sin"[39]

IX
A 421
245

Under this title I would like to write a few discourses dealing with the most beautiful and noble, humanly speaking, forms of despair: unhappy love, grief over the death of a beloved, sorrow at not having achieved one's proper place in the world, the forms the "poet" loves and that only Christianity dares to call sin, while the human attitude is that the lives of such people are infinitely more worthwhile than the millions that make up the prosypack.—*JP* VI 6277 (*Pap.* IX A 421) *n.d.*, 1848

IX
A 421
246

"Let not the heart in sorrow sin"[40]

7 Discourses

Here the finest, the, humanly speaking, most lovable forms of despair (which is the "poet's" ultimate) are to be treated—for example, unhappy love, grief over one who is dead, grief over not having achieved one's destiny in life.

Perhaps the 3 or 4 themes left over from "States of Mind in the Strife of Suffering,"[41] which are someplace in a journal [*Pap.* VIII[1] A 500; pp. 397–98], could be combined with these. Each discourse would first of all develop or describe the particular sorrow that it is to treat; then the admonition: Let not the heart in sorrow sin—consider this: and now the theme. For example, about one who is dead—description—let not the heart in sorrow sin—consider this: the joy of it that *at last* and *for a little while*[42] are identical (but this is used lyrically in another piece, "From on High He Will Draw All to Himself"[43]); or consider this: the joy of it that it is for joy that one does not believe the highest etc.[44]

But perhaps (instead of leading backward by means of joyful thoughts) it would be better to concentrate attention constantly on the infinite distinction between sorrow and sin, after having shown explicitly in each discourse how this sorrow is sin, or can become that by a hair's breadth.—*JP* VI 6278 (*Pap.* IX A 498) *n.d.*, 1848

A Direct Word about Myself as an Author[*]

X[6]
B 249
410

From the beginning it was never my thought to be an author for many years, which I could not afford either—and for me it has been in both the one sense and the other seven costly years in which I have been an author in the language that, as I hope and trust, will still not be disgraced by my having the honor to write it. . . .

X[6]
B 249
412

At the end of '47 and in the beginning of '48 I again considered finishing as an author in order to become a rural pastor, which had continually been my desire, to end with *Christian Discourses*, whose last section is "Discourses at the Communion on Fridays," of which two were given in Frue Church—then came the year 1848—for me the richest and most fruitful year, without any comparison, I have experienced as an author. . .

[*]*In margin:* Perhaps the words about Paul by Thomas à Kempis could be used here: He sometimes defended himself lest the weak be offended on account of his silence.[45]—*Pap.* X⁶ B 249 *n.d.*, 1849–51

The Possible Collision with Mynster[46]

X⁴
A 511
330

From the very beginning what Mynster has fought for in opposition to me—often in rather ordinary ways—has been to maintain this view: My proclamation, the Mynsterian approach, is earnestness and wisdom; the Kierkegaardian an odd, perhaps remarkable, but an odd exaggeration.

My position is: I represent a more authentic conception of Christianity than does Mynster.

But I desire nothing less than to attack Mynster, to weaken him. No, just the opposite. A little admission from his side, and everything will be as advantageous as possible for him; no one will see how it all hangs together, something I always have concealed by bowing so deeply to him.

X⁴
A 511
331

From the very beginning I actually have been an alien figure to Mynster (in fact, I myself said so to him the first day: We are completely at variance, something he no doubt instinctively perceived even better than I). I have a kind of passion for the truth and ideas that is utterly foreign to him. In this way I am opposed to him. —Things were still all right with *Concluding Unscientific Postscript,* partly because in the conclusion I personally emphasized him so strongly,[47] partly because Johannes Climacus is a humorist,[48] and thus it was easier for Mynster to maintain that this was only poetic exaggeration, humor, but that his own approach was authentic earnestness and wisdom.

The first part of *Upbuilding Discourses in Various Spirits*[49] irritated him more; but perhaps in appreciation of the postscript to *Concluding Postscript* he let the judgment be: This is an excellent book—especially the last two parts. *Works of Love* offended him. —*Christian Discourses* even more. —And so it mounts. *Practice in Christianity* distressed him very painfully.

Am I out to get Mynster? No, no, I am attached to him with a hypochondriacal passion, the extent of which he has never suspected. [★]But here there is something else that puts pressure on me. I can no longer afford to maintain the battle for the idea that I have represented. Therefore I must make haste. If my future were economically secure so that I knew I was completely able to give myself to the idea, I certainly would bide my time and let Mynster live out his life—oh, it pains me so deeply to have to draw my sword on him. But the economic situation forces me to hurry. Only when I accept an official position can Mynster more easily make his interpretation prevail. He knows that I have financial worries, has known it for several years; I myself told him. Now he is waiting and watching for this to force me to cut back, perhaps even to throw myself into his arms so that he can exploit me and have further proof that his way is the way of wisdom and earnestness.

X⁴
A 511
332

The line about Goldschmidt[50] was fateful. (1) It gives a sad insight into the bad side of Mynster. (2) It provides me with the circumstantial datum against Mynster that I had to have if I were to attack. That everything about him is rather close to the worldly mentality I have perceived for a long time, and therefore I made a division and took his *Sermons*.[51] But this plain fact betrays everything. And it has happened here as generally happens, that I first of all induce someone to provide me with the circumstantial datum I need. (3) It shows that in the sphere of the idea Mynster considers himself impotent. But he has been in an emotional state.

For me the possibility of this collision means that in order to survive I must take a still higher view of Christianity. This is a very serious matter; I have very much to learn and to suffer. —But on the other hand the possibility of this collision signifies that there is a power that works against Mynster. The collision, if it occurs, will occur against my will; it is my economic situation that pressures me to hurry, and Mynster has had it in his power to buy at the most advantageous price what can become extremely dangerous to him if there must be a collision.

He was an old man. Something truer was offered by someone who "in profound veneration"[52] was willing to introduce it in such a way that it appeared to be Mynsterian. He would not have it. True enough, after having enjoyed life as he has, it could be a bitter experience to find out at the end of his life what kind of Christianity it actually was.—*JP* VI 6795 (*Pap.* X⁴ A 511) *n.d.*, 1852

In margin of JP VI 6795 (*Pap.* X⁴ A 511):

[*]Moreover, I remember that the following observations also pressed in on me. (1) If I were completely free of economic concerns, I would have confidence in myself, would know for sure that it was not to spare myself that I kept on avoiding a collision with Mynster. But when I have finite concerns—and in this respect Mynster could in fact be helpful to me—then I would have to suspect myself of possibly sparing myself in order to avoid a collision. (2) I shrink from having Mynster actually help me in a finite way, for in my opinion he has far too much of the worldly mentality that finds it completely all right to secure earthly advantages. (3) If I were to let things go on and did not publish while Mynster is still living what I have written most recently, there would hardly be a person later who would be capable of forming any opposition to me—but then would I not avoid making possible the inspection that could be made if I published it while Mynster is still living.—*JP* VI 6796 (*Pap.* X⁴ A 512) *n.d.*, 1852

X⁴
A 512
333

Fædrelandet.

1848

Abonnementspris i Kjøbenhavn 15 Mk. pr. Qvartal, 5 Mk. pr. Maaned, enkelte Nr. 6 Sk.; udenfor Kjøbenhavn 3 Rbd. pr. Qvartal frit i Huset. Hver Søgne-Aften udgaaer et Numer. Bladets Contoir, store Kjøbmagergade Nr. 54, 2den Sal, er aabent om Formiddagen Kl. 11—1.

9de **Aarg.** **Mandagen den 24. Juli.** **Nr. 188.**

Et Spørgsmaal, der i den nyere Tid har erholdt den fuldstændigste Berettigelse til at stilles ved Siden af ethvert andet, medens det vistnok ogsaa tidligere har været anseet af ethvert oplyst og retsindigt Menneske som særdeles vigtigt, er det, om hvorledes den ringe Arbeiders Kaar kunne forbedres. Det gjælder om denne Sag ligesaavel som om enhver anden, at dens heldige Behandling er betinget af, om man har været i Stand til at tilveiebringe fuldstændig Klarhed med Hensyn til dens hele Beskaffenhed; er denne opnaaet, kan man undgaae Misgreb blot ved at see sig for; men er man nødt til at famle sig frem, naaer man maaskee først Maalet, efter at have gjort mangfoldige Omveie, og maaskee man aldrig naaer det. I Besvarelsen af nærværende Spørgsmaal er der en særegen Anledning til fra alle Sider at beflitte sig paa den størst mulige Klarhed, thi Spørgsmaalet er allerede i sin Behandling andensteds gjort saa forviklet, at den Vanskelighed, som det i og for sig frembyder, derved er bleven betydelig forøget. Det vilde saaledes sikkert være gavnligt, om Enhver, der ved at drøfte dette Spørgsmaal vil anbinde sit til dets heldige Løsning, mere vilde understøtte sine Meninger med Grunde, end dette hidtil har været Tilfældet, og at disse Grunde mere maatte være udledte af vore egne Forholds sande Beskaffenhed, hvorom dog saa Mange udtale sig, efter vor byggede paa Formeninger om Tilstanden af de tilsvarende Forhold i andre Lande, hvorom næsten ingen af os har nogen virkelig velbegrundet Mening. Der er neppe noget Land, der har saameget tilfælles med Danmark, at det endog kun nogenlunde kunde gaae an, at beregne Virkningen af ret gjennemgribende Foranstaltninger hos os efter de vundne Resultater; men de Lande med hvilke man hyppigst har draget Sammenligninger, naar Talen var om Forandringer i vore Arbeidsforhold, England, Frankrig og Tydskland, og hvorfra man har hentet alle Slags Skrækkebilleder, ere i den Henseende saa grundforskjellige fra vort Fødeland, at enhver saadan Sammenstilling er unyttig og urimelig.

Imedens den arbeidende Classe kan deles i Afdelinger, hvis Kaar ere i høieste Grad forskjellige fra hinanden, finder atter ofte en saadan Forskjel Sted i selve de enkelte Afdelinger. Vi ansee det nævnlig for gavnligt, om Enhver vil bidrage hvad han formaaer til at oplyse de herhen hørende Forhold, at man saa snart som muligt kan komme ud af den laumende Uklarhed, hvori man befinder sig med Hensyn til den virkelig stedfindende Tilstand, og vi have villet søge at foranledige Tilveiebringelsen af Oplysninger, der i denne Henseende angaae en af de vigtigste Afdelinger af den arbeidende Classe.

Stammen iblandt Arbeiderne, den Del, hvorom den øvrige Del ligesom grupperer sig, er Haandværkssvendene; de udgjøre et meget stort Antal; deres daglige Syssel egner sig til at danne dem til tænksomme, raske og haardføre Mennesker, og deres pecuniaire Forhold ere i Almindelighed ikke saa slette, at de have tilintetgjort den lykkelige Gemytlighed, der er den bedste Arvelod, som disse Folk have modtaget efter deres Forældre. Enhver, der vil virke for den arbeidende Classes Vel, har her et værdigt Maal for sine Bestræbelser, og i to forskjellige Henseender kan han virke til Bedste for Haandværkssvendstanden: dels kan han betragte denne Stilling som en Overgangstilstand, hvorigjennem Haandværkeren skal vinde sig en friere, selvstændigere og mere fordelagtig Virksomhed; i saa Fald vil han arbeide til, at de Langsbaand løses, som nu gjøre det factisk umuligt for den sædvanlige Svend at blive Mester; dels kan han betragte den som en varig Livsstilling for en stor Del arbeidsomme Folk, der ere tvungne af uheldige Forholds Magt til at blive hvad de ere, og da vil det være ham magtpaaliggende at bidrage Sit til at gjøre dem deres Arbeide taknemligt, forbedre deres Kaar og befrie dem for Næringssorger. I denne Henseende kan der virkes gavnligt paa mange

---

Krisen og en Krise i en Skuespillerindes Liv.

I.

Tanken om det at være Skuespillerinde, det vil da sige af Rang, vækker vistnok hos de Fleste strax Forestillingen om et saa fortryllende og glimrende Vilkaar i Livet, at derover som oftest ganske glemmes Tornene; de utrolig mange Trivialiteter, al den Ubillighed eller dog den Misforstand just i de afgjørende Øieblik, mod hvilke en Skuespillerinde maa have at kæmpe.

Lad os tænke os Forholdet saa gunstigt som muligt; lad os tænke en Skuespillerinde, der er i Besiddelse af Alt hvad der fordres, for ubetinget at være rangerende; lad os tænke, at hun vinder Beundringens Anerkjendelse, og at hun (hvad upaatvivleligt er et stort Held) er heldig ikke nok til at blive Maalet for it eller andet hadefuldt Menneskes Forfølgelse; saa lever hun da hen Aar efter Aar den misundte, den lykkelige Gjenstand for en stadigt vedvarende, anerkjendende Beundring. Det synes vist herligt, det seer ud som var det Noget; men naar man seer nøiere til og seer i hvilken Montsort denne anerkjendende Beundring udredes, seer man lidet fattigt Indbegreb af lurvede Trivialiteter, der i Theaterkritikens Verden constituerer Fondet ad usus publicos (og det er jo af dette Fond at hin stadig anerkjendende Beundring udenligris udredes), saa turde det vel være muligt, at selv dette det heldigste Vilkaar for en Skuespillerinde er tarveligt og fattigt nok. — Er det saa som man siger, at det Noget; men naar man seer meget kostbar og værdifuld, saa er det vist: Bladkritikens Garderobe er rædsom lurvet.

Videre. Den beundrede Kunstnerinde lever da hen Aar efter Aar. Som man i borgerlige Hushholdninger nolagtig veed forud, hvad man hver Dag skal have til Middag, saaledes veed hun nolagtig forud Saisonens Accidenser. 2 à 3 Gange om Ugen bliver hun rost og beundret, indkaldt med Udmærkelse; allerede i Løbet af det første Fjerdingaar vil hun mere end een Gang have gjennemgaaet Bladkritikens Indbegreb af Talemaader og — Vendinger, som de med særligt Eftertryk kunne kaldes, thi de vende i evindk tilbage. 1 à 2 Gange, i gode Aaringer 3 Gange, vil hun blive besunget af it eller andet forulykket Subject eller en vordende Digter; hendes Portrait bliver malet til hver Konstudstilling; hun bliver lithographeret, og er Lykken hende meget gunstig anbringes hendes Portrait endog paa Lommetørklæder og Hattepulle. Og hun, der som Qvinde er een over sit Navn — som en Qvinde, hun veed, at hendes Navn er paa Alles Læber, selv naar de tørre sig om Munden med Lommetørklædet, hun veed, at hun er Gjenstand for Alles beundrende Omtale, ogsaa deres, som i det yderste Vaande af at faae Noget at snakke om. Saaledes lever hun hen Aar efter Aar. Det synes saa herligt, det seer ud som det var Noget, men forsaavidt hun skulde i ædlere Forstand leve af denne Beundringens kostelige Næring, hente Opmuntring fra den, styrkes og opflammes ved den til ny og ny Anstrængelse, forsaavidt dog selv det mest udmærkede Talent, ja især da en Qvinde, i en svagere Time kan see sig mismodet om efter en Yttring af virkelig Paaskjønnelse, saa vil hun, hvad hun naturligvis selv ofte har sandet, i al sandhed Øieblik ret føle, hvor tomt alt Dette er, og hvor uretfærdigt, at hun skulde finde denne byrdefulde Herlighed.

Imidlertid gaaer der da Aar hen, dog i disse Nysgjerrighedens og Utaalmodighedens Tider ikke mange, saa kommer allerede Snakken i Be-

1485   1486

FÆDRELANDET

Subscription price ...

1848

| Vol. 9. | Monday, July 24. | No. 188. |

A question . . . [article calling for clarity in public discussion of the plight of the working class and arguing for a Danish-specific approach]

THE CRISIS AND A CRISIS IN THE

LIFE OF AN ACTRESS

I

The thought of being an actress, that is, one of eminence, no doubt promptly evokes in most people the idea of a situation in life so enchanting and splendid that in the thought of it they often entirely forget the thorns: the incredibly many banalities, all the unfairness, or at least the misunderstanding with which an actress may have to contend especially in the decisive moments.

Let us imagine a situation as propitious as possible; let us imagine an actress who is in the possession of all that is required for being unconditionally eminent. Let us imagine that she receives the recognition of admiration and that she is fortunate enough not to become the target (which is indubitably a tremendous good fortune) of some spiteful person's persecution—so then she goes on living year after year, the envied fortunate object of incessantly continuing appreciative admiration. It seems so glorious, it seems as if it were something; but if one looks more closely and sees the kind of coin in which this appreciative admiration is paid, sees the meager sum of shabby banalities that in the world of theater critics constitutes the fund *ad usus publicos* [for public use] (and it is indeed from this fund that the incessant appreciative admiration is normally paid), it may very well be possible that even this most fortunate situation for an actress is quite shoddy and cheap. —If it is true, as is said, that the wardrobe of the Royal Theater is thought to be very expensive and valuable, it is certain that the wardrobe of the newspaper critics is dreadfully shabby.

Further. The admired artist goes on living year after year. Just as in middle-class households one knows exactly in advance what will be served for dinner each day, so also does she know exactly the season's perquisites in advance. Two or three times a week she will be praised and admired, cited for excellence; already in the course of the first three months, she will more than once have looked through the sum of stock phrases in the newspaper reviews—and turns of speech, as they with special emphasis may be called, since they return again and again. Once or twice, in good years thrice, she will be celebrated by some unsuccessful seedy fellow or would-be poet; her portrait will be painted for every art exhibition; she will be lithographed and, if fortune favors her very much, her portrait will even be printed on handkerchiefs and hat crowns. And she, who as a woman is jealous of her name—as a woman, she knows that her name is on everyone's lips even when they wipe their mouths with the handkerchief; she knows that she is the object of everyone's admiring discussion, also of those who are dying to have something to chatter about. She goes on living like this year after year. It seems so glorious, it seems as if this were something, but insofar as she is to live in the more positive sense on the costly nourishment of this admiration, find encouragement in it, be strengthened and stirred by it to ever new effort, even the most superbly talented person, and especially a woman, in a weaker moment may still look around despondently for an expression of genuine appreciation. Then at such a time she will really feel, something she of course has often sensed herself, how empty all this is and how unfair to envy her this burdensome glory.

Meanwhile, the years go by, yet not many in these times of curiosity and impatience; so there is already gossip going around . . .

SELECTED ENTRIES FROM
KIERKEGAARD'S JOURNALS AND PAPERS
PERTAINING TO
*THE CRISIS AND A CRISIS IN THE LIFE OF
AN ACTRESS* AND ADDENDUM

From final copy of Writing Sampler:

No. 1

The Theater. Last evening Shakespeare's glorious masterpiece, *The School for Scandal*, was performed for the first time.[53] For every connoisseur and admirer of truly classical writing it must be a truly classical joy to participate in such rare artistic enjoyment.[*] It is another question whether it might not have been best for someone with a fond and felicitous hand to have made one or two little changes, at least deleting one or two phrases objectionable to the cultured public. But we have no wish to intrude on the joy but instead in the name of the most honored cultured public wish to thank the theater management for this rare pleasure, while we also take the liberty of suggesting that one of Ifland's[54] plays be staged as soon as possible.

As far as the *performance* is concerned, it was in every way so excellent that one will find it difficult to find its equal outside Copenhagen, at least according to what the reviewer knows of stage performances in other cities. The reviewer recollects having seen the same play performed in Korsør a few years ago, but this performance could by no means match the Royal Theater's.

Unfortunately limited space does not permit us to go into a deep and exhaustive consideration of details; therefore we will be brief. Director Nielsen's[55] performance as Sir Oliver Surface was masterly, far exceeding the performance of Mr. Rasmussen, his predecessor in Korsør. Madame Nielsen's acting was very good; and Phister as Snake acted just splendidly. But Mrs. Heiberg's[**]

mastery beggars all and every description; we would have to copy her whole part if we were to give the reader an idea of the way in which she spoke her lines or of what lines she spoke. But since that would be too lengthy, and furthermore we do not have the play at hand, we will limit ourselves to copying the *Berlingske Tidende*, which so superbly says, "We would have to copy the whole part if we were to give the reader an idea of Wiehe's[56] masterful performance."

VII[2]
B 274:6
323

[*]*In margin:* an enjoyment heightened by the attendance at the performance of His Majesty the King, and His Majesty, Crown Prince Ferdinand.

[**]*ad se ipsum*

It would sound very odd to call her Madame Heiberg instead of Mrs. Heiberg.—*Pap.* VII[2] B 274:6 December 15, 1846

From final copy; see 301:1–2:

The Crisis and a Crisis in the Life of an Actress

Deleted from margin: From the Papers of One Dead[57]
—*Pap.* VIII[2] B 90:1 *n.d.,* 1847

From final copy; see 305:13:

Changed from: outside, there where reviewers and hacks do their stuff, there profanation is at home.—*Pap.* VIII[2] B 90:4 *n.d.,* 1847

Deleted from final copy; see 307:24:

And, as said, an essential esthetician would avoid a task of this kind. With regard to a contemporary, he certainly would be delighted with her excellence and her fortunate qualifications but would say: Let her mature a little, and then her time will surely come. See, this distinguishes the esthetician from the public; he does not at all believe that the sixteenth year is her greatest moment; on the contrary, he believes that her time will come.
—*Pap.* VIII[2] B 90:6 *n.d.,* 1847

Deleted from final copy; see 315:28:

. . . . . at the exclusive circle's aristocratic distance from daily life and the human crowd—*Pap.* VIII² B 90:10 *n.d.*, 1847

Changed in final copy (see 315:29) from:

and then in turn appears impressively before people only on very solemn occasions, they are not spoiled by seeing him.—*Pap.* VIII² B 90:11 *n.d.*, 1847

Deleted from final copy; see 316:13:

. . . . . ; they have never wanted—by means of the concealment and mystification of snobbish life—to serve the truth or to dupe the crowd—*Pap.* VIII² B 90:13 *n.d.*, 1847

Deleted from final copy; see 316:24:

Some years ago a ram was on exhibition on Vesterbro; the price of entry was eight shillings. It was exhibited only in the afternoon; in the morning the same ram grazed in a field out on Gammel Kongevej—there was not a soul who paid any attention to it, but in the afternoon when it cost eight shillings and the exhibition lasted only a few hours—then they gazed at the ram with amazement.[58]—*Pap.* VIII² B 90:14 *n.d.*, 1847

Deleted from final copy; see 317:4:

. . . . . even if he preaches to them only in the figurative sense inasmuch as the people in the church are sitting where they are unable to hear him . . . . . —*Pap.* VIII² B 90:17 *n.d.*, 1847

Deleted from final copy; see 317:11:

. . . . . while the stableman who washes it is not at all amazed.—*Pap.* VIII² B 90:19 *n.d.*, 1847

Changed in final copy (see 317:11) from:

If at the same time as such a silk-padded Chief Court Chaplain and City Chaplain there lives an equally gifted, ordinarily dressed pastor who nevertheless is quite differently gifted, a far better speaker, who on the whole has far greater and essential competence but who simply and without any fuss preaches every Sunday, perhaps even twice, the first one will make history by means of—illusion, and the second one will stand in the shadows by means of—competence. Therefore if the just as unusually talented Theremin, in addition to being Chief Court Chaplain, had seen it as his task to serve the truth in every way and with every self-sacrifice—then he would have taken it upon himself, for example, to preach twice every Sunday for a period of three months (without publicizing that it would only be for this long, for that again would be an incentive).—*Pap.* VIII² B 90:20 *n.d.*, 1847

Changed in final copy (see 317:22–27) from:

By means of the method proposed he surely should be able to do without the armed sextons to make room. Alas, many would have given up hearing him, because if it is nothing but what one can hear twice every Sunday, then there surely is no sensible reason to want to hear it. *Mundus vult decipi* [The world wants to be deceived]. The method would also have helped somebody or other out of an illusion if he thought he was a regular church-goer who went to church every Sunday because he, as someone said to me, went to church every Sunday—when Theremin preached. As we said, *mundus vult decipi*—ergo, every honest person ought to exert all his powers and ingenuity to prevent any deceit that no doubt can bring him worldly advantage but at the same time from the eternal point of view makes him a deceiver. However much the world wishes and the times demand—to be deceived—opportunity makes anyone who avails himself of the opportunity a deceiver, just as we say: opportunity makes the thief. Or if this is not the case, if he is too naive, too ignorant of the world to discover the true facts: then the situation reflects ironically on him, who blissfully and naively thinks he is doing so

VIII²
B 90:23
196

very much for the truth and does not suspect that it is the world's desire to be deceived, the world's craving for illusion that actually makes a fool of him.—*Pap.* VIII^2 B 90:23 *n.d.*, 1847

From final copy:

[*Deleted:* Inter et Inter   John Doe.]
        Summer 1847

                    Inter et Inter

Deleted: The article is even older, but I do not remember exactly.—*Pap.* VIII^2 B 90:26 *n.d.*, 1847

I have been thinking these days of having the little article "The Crisis in the Life of an Actress" printed in *Fædrelandet*. The reasons *for* doing it are the following. There are some minor reasons, but they have persuasive power, and therefore I must first subject them to a critique. I believe I owe it to Mrs. Heiberg, partly also because of the piece about Mme. Nielsen at one time. I would like to poke Heiberg a little again. This way certain things can be said that I otherwise could not say so lightly and conversationally. It would make me happy to humor Giødwad,[59] who has asked for it. And then the main reason that argues for it: I have been occupied now for such a long time exclusively with the religious, and yet people will perhaps try to make out that I have changed, have become earnest (which I was not previously), that the literary attack has made me sanctimonious; in short, they will make my religiousness out to be the sort of thing people turn to in old age. This is a heresy I consider extremely essential to counteract. The nerve in all my work as an author actually is here, that I was essentially religious when I wrote *Either/Or*. Therefore, I have thought that it could be useful in order once again to show the possibility. I regard this as precisely my task, always to be capable of what the vanity and secularmindedness of the world hanker after as supreme, and from which point of view they patronizingly look down on the religious as something for run-down subjects—always to be capable but not essentially to will it. The world, after all, is so insipid that

IX
A 175
84

IX
A 175
85

when it believes that one who proclaims the religious is someone who cannot produce the esthetic it pays no attention to the religious.

This is a very important reason *pro*. But the *contra* speaks. I now have gone so decisively into the essentially Christian, have presented much of it so rigorously and earnestly that no doubt there are some who have been influenced by it. These people might be almost scandalized to hear that I had serialized a piece about an actress. And surely one has a responsibility also to such people.

Allowing the article to be published will mean that perhaps someone will be made aware of the essentially Christian simply by avidly reading that little serialized article. But there may also be the one who is almost offended.

Furthermore, at the moment I have no religious book ready for the printer that could come out at the same time.

Therefore it must not be published. My position is too earnest; a little dialectical mistake could do irreparable harm. An article in a newspaper, particularly about Mrs. Heiberg, creates much more of a sensation than big books.

It is now a matter of faithfulness in serving my cause. There may have been crucial significance in beginning as I began, but not any more. And the article itself is in fact much older.

N.B. This whole matter is interpreted to be conceitedness; it is reflection that wants to make me so extraordinary, instead of placing my confidence in God and being the person I am.

[*A page removed; deleted:* it to Gjødwad—and then I left it alone, and became very sick in the afternoon—ah, I would rather write a folio than publish a page.

But now it must come out whatever happens; I will bitterly regret having remained suspended in reflection.]—*JP* VI 6209 (*Pap.* IX A 175) *n.d.*, 1848

IX
A 178
87 No, no, the little article[60] must be published. I am prey to nothing else than depressive reflection. Lately I have been possessed with the thought that I am going to die soon, and therefore I have continually produced and produced in the hope that it would not be published until after my death. Then the thought of publishing this little article awakens; it appeals to me very

much; Gjødwad[61] joins in at the same time. I hope it is a hint from Governance—and then, my depressive reflection changed what was undeniably a trifle, an innocent matter, a little joy I had wished to have by making a few people happy—my depressive reflection transformed that into something so big that it seemed as if I would create a scandal, as if God might abandon me. It is indolence, depression, nothing more nor less. I have pondered publication of one of the manuscripts already finished. But no, I have the fixed idea that I am going to die, and I coddle myself by shunning the inconvenience and trouble of publishing.

The point is that the subject is too minor, I dare not entreat God's help—but that is wrong. If I remain suspended in reflection, I will lose myself. I will never come out of it. And my relation to Gjødwad, who knows of the article, is a perpetually open sore that will be a fearful drain on me since I actually have nothing with which to counter his requests except a depressive whim.

As far as offense is concerned, let me above all not pass myself off as more religious than I am or be credited with any kind of pietistic excess. Before God I have been able to justify writing it. Well, now I can and must publish it, for I must be honest. Granted that I would not do it again—but it is, after all, an older work. That is why the article is dated: Summer, 1847, and therefore all that troubled doubt is removed.

IX
A 178
88

So in God's name—oh, it is difficult to use God's name in connection with such a minor thing. But it is really a much different issue, that of being true to myself, of having the bold confidence before God to be myself and take everything from his hand.

Perhaps it will turn out in the end just as I began, that I will have joy in having done it.—*JP* VI 6211 (*Pap.* IX A 178) *n.d.*, 1848

Yes, it is certainly true that it was really necessary that there be a little confusion about me. Because I have been a devotional author exclusively for two years, and a very productive one at that, it no doubt has become a habit to think that I have now become earnest. I myself was not far from being pleased to be regarded as the earnest one. That must be prevented. That is direct communication again, and it simply is not earnestness. See, a little article about an actress[62]—it is enough to confuse again if anyone has become lazy and pompous in the habit of thinking that I was the earnest one—perhaps an apostle, something I am a very long way from being.

For the most part I had forgotten this; I had become too depressed to be able to maintain the tension of true self-denial.
                                        —*Pap.* IX A 181 *n.d.*, 1848

Lest it seem odd that I was prompted in any way to publish separately the little article "The Crisis and a Crisis" etc., the pseudonym should be kept, but the thing is to be dedicated to Professor Heiberg.[63]

> To
> Professor J. L. Heiberg
> Denmark's esthetician
> dedicated
> by
> a subordinate esthetician
> the author

God knows that I have always thought well of Heiberg, sticking as always to my first impression. But his treatment of me is not defensible. And even after that time I have still done what could be done to maintain him essentially in a position of honor.—*JP* VI 6218 (*Pap.* IX A 187) *n.d.*, 1848

It was really fortunate that I finally did publish that little article,[64] thereby remaining true to myself to the last, so that my life may not become a detriment rather than a benefit.

If I had died without doing it, I am convinced that in the horrible irresponsible confusing of concepts in our day some would have stepped forward and gabbled something about my being an apostle. Good God, instead of being of benefit for holding the essentially Christian in a position of honor, I would have ruined it. What a charming kinship for the apostle: that a person like me was also an apostle. What a charming fruit of my life to help establish the masterful category: also a kind of apostle and the like. . . . —*JP* VI 6220 (*Pap.* IX A 189) *n.d.*, 1848

It was all right with that little article.[65] The most decisive consequences will come later. But then perhaps the habit of thinking that I have now become earnest will be broken and the thrust will be all the more powerful. Those who live esthetically here at home have no doubt given up reading me, since I "have gone religious and do not write anything but sermon books." Now maybe they will peek into the next book, hoping to find something for them—and perhaps I will get the attention of one or two of them and help him to wound himself.

This explains why the stricter orthodox, Rudelbach[66] also, influence only a small circle, because they have no resources for nipping into the common life of the people. The orthodox write only for and talk only to the orthodox, and that is that. They pay no attention at all to the whole business of a country's calling itself and imagining itself to be Christian, and to the whole business of Christendom.—*JP* VI 6223 (*Pap.* IX A 205) *n.d.*, 1848

Yes, it had to be this way. I have not become a religious author; I was that: simultaneously with *Either/Or* appeared two upbuilding discourses—now after two years of writing only religious books there appears a little article about an actress.

Now there is a moment, a point of rest; by this step I have learned to know myself and very concretely. . . . —*JP* VI 6229 (*Pap.* IX A 216) *n.d.*, 1848

It was a good thing that I published that little article[67] and came under tension. If I had not published it, I would have gone on living in a certain ambiguity about the future use of indirect communication.

Now it is clear to me that henceforth it will be indefensible to use it.

The awakening effect is rooted in God's having given me power to live as a riddle—but not any longer, lest the awakening effect end in being confusing.

IX
A 218
115

The thing to do now is to take over unambiguously the maieutic structure of the past, to step forth definitely and directly in character, as one who has wanted and wants to serve the cause of Christianity.

If I had not published that little article, indirect communication would have continued to hover vaguely before me as a possibility and I would not have had the idea that I dare not use it.

I would not dare to say of myself that I have had a clear panorama of the whole plan of production from the outset; I must rather say, as I have continually acknowledged, that I myself have been brought up and developed in the process of my work, that personally I have become committed more and more to Christianity than I was. Nevertheless this remains fixed, that I began with the deepest religious impression, alas, yes, I who when I began bore the tremendous responsibility for the life of another human being and understood it as God's punishment upon me.—*JP* VI 6231 (*Pap.* IX A 218) *n.d.*, 1848

The thought that I would soon die, the thought in which I have rested, has now been disturbed by the publication of that little article;[68] it would disturb me if this were to be the last thing I publish.

But on the other hand, the thought of dying now was only a depressive notion—how good then that I published that little article. This very thing had to be probed—and the publication of the article served to do this.—*JP* VI 6232 (*Pap.* IX A 219) *n.d.*, 1848

N.B. N.B.

Yes, it was a good thing to publish that little article.[69] I began with *Either/Or* and two upbuilding discourses; now it ends, after the whole upbuilding series—with a little esthetic essay. It expresses: that it was the upbuilding—the religious—that should advance, and that now the esthetic has been traversed; they are inversely related, or it is something of an inverse confrontation, to show that the writer was not an esthetic author who in the course of time grew older and for that reason became religious.

But it is not really to my credit; it is Governance who has held me in rein with the help of an extreme depression and a troubled conscience.

But there still would have been something lacking if the little article had not come out; the illusion would have been established that it was I who essentially had changed over the years, and then a very important point in the whole productivity would have been lost.

It is true I have been educated by this writing, have developed more and more religiously—but in a decisive way I had experienced the pressures that turned me away from the world before I began writing *Either/Or*. Even then my only wish was to do, as decisively as possible, something good to compensate, if possible in another way, for what I personally had committed. That I have developed more and more religiously is seen in my now saying good-bye to the esthetic, because I do not know where I would find the time that I could, would, or would dare fill up with work on esthetic writings. . . . —*JP* VI 6238 (*Pap.* IX A 227) *n.d.*, 1848

IX
A 227
125

Now add the thought of death to the publication of that little article![70] If I were dead without that: indeed, anyone could publish my posthumous papers, and in any case R. Nielsen[71] would be there. But that illusion that I did not become religious until I was older and perhaps by reason of accidental circumstances would still have been possible. But now the dialectical breaks are so clear: *Either/Or* and *Two Upbuilding Discourses*, *Concluding Postscript*, the upbuilding writings of two years, and then a little esthetic treatise.—*Pap.* IX A 228 *n.d.*, 1848

N.B.   N.B.

IX
A 234
131

Yes, so it will be: then a direct explanation of my authorship and what I intend *in toto* [on the whole].

With regard to the decisively Christian, one cannot bear the responsibility in the middle term of one's human reflection.

And just as my whole direction has been toward the restitution of simplicity, an essential part is that what brings it about does not itself in turn use the arts of the maieutic; in a certain sense this is even a contradiction.

The point is that what one intends *in toto* should be said directly and clearly; it is another matter (something that is unavoidable for the person who happens to have superior reflective powers) that one may use it in the particular, but within the direct attesting to what one intends *in toto*. With regard to the essentially Christian, it is also dangerous to hold it *in suspenso* if one does not oneself feel decisively bound by the essentially Christian—however much one served the cause of Christianity, it is an unchristian way to do it, even though useful for a time and relatively justified simply because Christendom has become paganism.

To keep ambiguous what one oneself intends *in toto* is the essentially maieutic. But it is also the daimonic, since it makes a human being into the middle term between God and other persons.

In order to prevent this maieutic ambiguity, direct communication, a testimony once and for all, is crucial. The maieutic is not to be enigmatic in this or that particular matter but is to be enigmatic with regard to the whole. For example, to be enigmatic about whether one is oneself now a Christian or not.

But then the difficulty only recurs, that it not seem as if one had an immediate relationship to God. In that case, the relationship of reflection is far more humble.

Yet all this in which I have become involved is due to the publication of that little article.[72] Without that, I would neither have become so clearly aware of the change that must be made, nor would I have been able to set it forth so decisively. If I had taken that step earlier, it would have been too much in continuity with what preceded and would have been neither the one nor the other.—*Pap.* IX A 234 *n.d.*, 1848

N.B.   N.B.

Strange, strange about that little article[73]—that I had so nearly gone and forgotten myself. When one is overstrained as I was, it is easy to forget momentarily the dialectical outline of a colossal structure such as my authorship. That is why Governance helped me.

Right now the totality is so dialectically right. *Either/Or* and the two upbuilding discourses*—*Concluding Postscript*—for two years only upbuilding discourses and then a little article about an actress. The illusion that I happened to get older and for that reason became a decisively religious author has been made impossible. If I had died beforehand, then the writing I did those two years would have been made ambiguous and the totality unsteady.

In a certain sense, of course, my concern is superfluous when I consider the world of actuality in which I live—since as a matter of fact I have not found many dialecticians.

In margin: *Note. And these two discourses quite properly did not appear at the same time as *Either/Or* but a few months later—just as this little article now.—*JP* VI 6242 (*Pap.* IX A 241) *n.d.*, 1848

IX
A 241
136

How I have suffered because of this relation to R. N.[74] To have him out there in suspense, perhaps even offended, and then to have my responsibility and my fear and trembling—and yet unable to have acted or to act otherwise! And then not to be able to get to see the actual situation because he was out in the country. And then to know that the danger was probably not so great, humanly speaking, but yet before God to have to hold out alone all that time with the most dreadful possibilities! Frightful! And a dying man like me, who was so quiet and calm and reconciled to the thought of death—and now suddenly to suffer and endure so long the torture of not being able to die because I must first see his situation and my responsibility. Frightful!

But then I have also learned indescribably much, one category more. All too depressively and mournfully, I had sought consolation in the thought of death, basically hoping that it would steal a march on me and allow my new books to become posthumous works; then I would be freed from the decision to publish them and freed from going through the latest things. If I had died

IX
A 261
147

before, I actually would have died in an uncertainty, because I
had not definitely understood how I wanted to do it, whether on
the whole direct communication was right, whether it was a
weakness or a strength on my part. I would be dead and removed
from the responsibility of putting into existence such thoughts
that I leave behind in the manuscripts.

Now I have found out what I shall and will do. In a certain
sense God has handled me frightfully, but also in another sense
has given me momentum, clarity, definiteness and insight and
tranquillity that I did not have previously. See, if I were to die
now, my death would not be an escape, because before God I
have understood what I am to do next.

God be praised that I published that article,[75] God be praised
that I kept R. N. in suspense and did not weaken and give him
direct communication; but above all God be praised that God is
to me what he has always been: love. Now I can die tomorrow
and I can go on living—everything is in order.—*Pap.* IX A 261
n.d., 1848

However much reflection I have, in everything I undertake
there is infinitely more that is the bonus of Governance. It is
indescribably helpful to me at all the crucial points. The publication of that little article[76] is another example of it. In reflecting on
it I had earlier seen correctly that its publication could have the
positive effect of banishing an illusion. I was also thinking, however, of almost being able to do it as a trifle. Suddenly I became
really aware of the possibility of the offense it could cause. Then
I became very depressed. I was at my wit's end. Finally I had to
carry out the publishing of it right away in order to save my self.
That I did, trusting in God and putting everything in his hands.
And see, it was absolutely right. It was the question of direct
communication; I had to come to a decision, and for that I had
to be in tension. Now the whole prior authorship is terminated
in the normal dialectical structure, and I gained a category and
momentum. Humanly speaking, it had looked so easy not to
publish that little article, because he who ventures nothing loses
nothing either. Yes, they say, but forget that the one who ven-

tures nothing wins *material* security but loses the most important thing.—*Pap.* IX A 263 *n.d.*, 1848

. . . But my whole life as an author has been a systematically carried out operation—indeed, with perhaps ten times as much sagacity as the sagacious ones have carried out an operation in the opposite direction. I always do things wrong, never at the time of the year when the literary world is in a hubbub, always in big books, never arranged in such a way that it gives the reader opportunity to show off by reading it aloud etc. etc. This carries through to the least trifle. A little theater article about Mrs. Heiberg[77]—yes, it could easily become a firecracker. But as a precautionary measure it comes out in the summer, precisely at the time when no one cares to read articles about the theater. It should have come out at the beginning of the season, should have opened the season—well, thank you very much. On the whole I am as well informed as anyone about the artists—but I scorn using them—indeed, I try to do the very opposite.

Up until now I have always been in the minority, and I *want* to be in the minority, and by the help of God I hope I will succeed in that to my final blessed end—I am far from being so bold as to say (God forbid) that my life resembles Christ's; it would be a satire on him if I were to be honored and esteemed for telling the truth—and he, who was the truth, was crucified.
—*Pap.* IX A 455 *n.d.*, 1848

From draft of Stages:[78]

. . . Just as our young friend now sits there and stares ahead like a stranger among us, like a man who is uncertain whether he should laugh or cry, so also is his speech. If he himself is the welcome guest, his speech is only to be patiently endured; it is both too long and too solemn and with regard to the comic effect is altogether dubious, indeed *anceps* [risqué]. But as host I forbid such things. I would very much like to command you to be as cheerful and jovial as Phister[79] in *Brama og Bajaderen*,[80] but failing that, I will then command you to forget every speech as soon as

V
B 177
302

it is delivered, wash it down like a glass of wine in one gulp, and
be ready to listen to the next one without any aftertalk . . . .
—*Pap.* V B 177:1 *n.d.*, 1844

V
B 177
303

From final copy; see 329:1, 344:22–23:

Phister as Scipio
Final copy
Written at the end of 1848.   Can be signed:
Procul.[81]
—*JP* VI 6292 (*Pap.* IX B 67) *n.d.*, 1848

From draft; see 334:1–18:

This is quite correct; the more prominent and distinguished
the man, the more splendid his *Erscheinung* [appearance], or the
more solemn the occasion, the more ludicrous it is to be drunk
or half-drunk. For example, a half-drunken policeman who on
duty comes into a public place where there is boozing and playing cards—in order to chase them out; to say nothing of a half-
drunken policeman who is himself seized by the watchman and
arrested. The same with the splendid uniform—and a man who
is a bit befuddled.—*Pap.* IX B 70:10 *n.d.*, 1848

From draft; see 334:34–335:3:

. . . . . a man who wears a *port'épée* [sword tassel] and therefore
is shown military honors by the military—a man who *qua* military man feels committed to being amiable, almost dangerous, to
the opposite sex, to show it military gallantry, to speak about his
parol' d'honneur [word of honor] in a military manner. But is this
an actual military man? No, that he is not. He is a captain in the
police force.—*Pap.* IX B 70:12 *n.d.*, 1848

From draft; see 336:30:

. . . . . partly because of his stoutness, which is still not at all
as conspicuous as Falstaff's and which also would be a hindrance

to the mobility that belongs to the role. But partly also for another reason.—*Pap.* IX B 70:18 *n.d.*, 1848

From draft; see 337:1:

. . . . . in under himself. Instead of placing one leg a half step ahead of the other, bent a little at the knee turned outward—he bends his legs backward, bow shaped. His whole form thereby looks like a curve or the letter C.—*Pap.* IX B 70:19 *n.d.*, 1848

From draft; see 337:11:

. . . . . head, in order again in his forward-bending position to be completely complaisant and amiable, yet so insecure in position that, in addition to the contradiction we have pointed out, there is also a continuous suggestion that the drams, if not innumerable yet diverse, could be a hindrance to him, if there were nothing else, in his military posture.

Deleted: In this position he stands conversing with the "amiable farmer wife" with whom he and his detachment are to be billeted.—*Pap.* IX B 70:20 *n.d.*, 1848

In margin; see 337:18:

. . . . . as if a soldier must slouch in order to learn to stand erect.—*Pap.* IX B 70:21 *n.d.*, 1848

From final copy; see 344:23:

If the article about "Scipio" is to be given to *Fædrelandet*, the editor is to state in a note that he has received the manuscript from the author, who was himself not particularly inclined to have it printed because it was written in great haste and he has not reworked it.—*Pap.* IX B 73 *n.d.*, 1848

EDITORIAL APPENDIX

ACKNOWLEDGMENTS

Preparation of manuscripts for *Kierkegaard's Writings* is supported by a genuinely enabling grant from the National Endowment for the Humanities and gifts from the Dronning Margrethes og Prins Henriks Fond, the Danish Ministry of Cultural Affairs, the Augustinus Fond, the Carlsberg Fond, the General Mills Foundation, the Jorck Fond, the Lutheran Brotherhood Foundation, and Gilmore and Charlotte Schjeldahl.

The translators-editors are indebted to Grethe Kjær and Julia Watkin for their knowledgeable observations on crucial concepts and terminology.

Per Lønning, Sophia Scopetéa, and Wim Scholtens, members of the International Advisory Board for *Kierkegaard's Writings*, gave valuable detailed criticism of the manuscript. Jack Schwandt and Julia Watkin helpfully read the manuscript. Kathryn Hong, Regine Prenzel-Guthrie, and Nathaniel Hong, associate editors of *KW*, scrutinized the manuscript. Nathaniel Hong prepared the index. Francesca Lane Rasmus provided systems management and editorial assistance.

Acknowledgment is made to Gyldendals Forlag for permission to absorb notes in *Søren Kierkegaards samlede Værker* and *Søren Kierkegaards Papirer*.

Inclusion in the Supplement of entries from *Søren Kierkegaard's Journals and Papers* is by arrangement with Indiana University Press.

The book collection and the microfilm collection of the Kierkegaard Library, St. Olaf College, have been used in preparation of the text, notes, Supplement, and Editorial Appendix. Gregor Malantschuk's annotated set of *Søren Kierkegaards samlede Værker* was used in the preparation of the text, Supplement, and Editorial Appendix.

The initial manuscript was typed by Dorothy Bolton. Gretchen Oberfranc was compositor of the book. The volume was guided through the press by Marta Nussbaum Steele.

COLLATION OF *CHRISTIAN DISCOURSES*
IN THE DANISH EDITIONS OF
KIERKEGAARD'S COLLECTED WORKS

Vol. X Ed. 1 Pg.	*Vol. X* Ed. 2 Pg.	*Vol. 13* Ed. 3 Pg.	*Vol. X* Ed. 1 Pg.	*Vol. X* Ed. 2 Pg.	*Vol. 13* Ed. 3 Pg.
13	17	13	45	53	43
14	18	15	46	54	44
15	19	15	47	56	45
16	20	16	48	57	46
17	21	17	49	58	47
18	23	18	50	59	48
19	24	20	51	60	49
20	25	20	52	62	51
21	26	21	53	63	51
22	27	22	54	64	52
23	28	23	55	65	53
24	29	24	56	66	54
25	30	25	57	67	55
26	31	26	58	68	56
27	33	27	59	69	57
28	34	28	60	71	58
29	35	29	61	72	59
30	36	29	62	73	60
31	37	30	63	74	61
32	38	31	64	75	62
33	39	32	65	76	62
34	40	33	66	77	63
35	42	34	67	78	64
36	43	35	68	79	65
37	44	36	69	81	66
38	45	37	70	82	67
39	46	38	71	83	68
40	48	39	72	84	69
41	49	40	73	85	70
42	50	41	74	86	71
43	51	41	75	87	71
44	52	42	76	88	72

Vol. X *Ed. 1* *Pg.*	*Vol. X* *Ed. 2* *Pg.*	*Vol. 13* *Ed. 3* *Pg.*	*Vol. X* *Ed. 1* *Pg.*	*Vol. X* *Ed. 2* *Pg.*	*Vol. 13* *Ed. 3* *Pg.*
77	89	73	126	146	118
78	90	74	127	147	119
79	91	75	128	148	120
80	93	76	129	149	121
81	94	77	130	150	121
82	95	78	131	151	122
83	96	79	132	152	123
84	98	81	133	153	124
85	99	81	134	155	125
86	100	82	135	156	126
87	101	83	136	157	127
88	102	84	137	158	128
89	103	85	138	160	130
90	105	86	139	161	130
91	106	87	140	162	131
92	107	88	141	163	132
93	108	89	142	164	133
101	117	95	143	165	134
102	118	95	144	167	135
103	119	96	145	168	136
104	120	97	146	169	137
105	121	98	147	171	139
106	122	99	148	172	139
107	123	100	149	173	140
108	125	101	150	174	141
109	126	102	151	175	142
110	127	103	152	177	144
111	129	105	153	178	144
112	130	105	154	179	145
113	131	106	155	180	146
114	132	107	156	181	147
115	133	108	157	183	148
116	134	109	158	184	149
117	135	110	159	185	150
118	137	111	160	186	151
119	138	112	164	192	156
120	139	112	167	195	157
121	140	113	168	196	157
122	141	114	169	197	158
123	142	115	170	198	159
124	143	116	171	199	160
125	145	117	172	200	161

Vol. X Ed. 1 Pg.	Vol. X Ed. 2 Pg.	Vol. 13 Ed. 3 Pg.	Vol. X Ed. 1 Pg.	Vol. X Ed. 2 Pg.	Vol. 13 Ed. 3 Pg.
173	202	162	215	251	203
174	203	163	216	252	204
175	204	164	217	253	205
176	205	165	218	254	206
177	207	166	219	255	207
178	208	167	220	257	208
179	209	169	221	258	209
180	210	169	222	259	210
181	211	170	223	260	210
182	212	171	224	261	211
183	213	172	225	262	212
184	214	173	226	263	213
185	216	174	227	264	214
186	217	175	228	266	215
187	218	176	229	267	216
188	219	177	230	268	217
189	220	178	231	269	218
190	222	180	232	270	219
191	223	180	233	271	220
192	224	181	234	272	220
193	225	182	235	273	221
194	226	183	236	274	222
195	227	184	237	275	223
196	229	185	238	277	224
197	230	186	239	278	225
198	231	187	240	279	226
199	232	188	241	280	227
200	233	189	242	281	228
201	235	190	243	282	229
202	236	191	244	284	230
203	237	192	251	291	237
204	238	192	255	295	239
205	239	193	256	296	239
206	240	194	257	297	240
207	241	195	258	298	241
208	242	196	259	299	242
209	244	197	260	300	243
210	245	198	261	302	244
211	246	199	262	303	245
212	247	200	263	304	246
213	249	201	264	305	247
214	250	203	267	309	249

Vol. X Ed. 1 Pg.	Vol. X Ed. 2 Pg.	Vol. 13 Ed. 3 Pg.	Vol. X Ed. 1 Pg.	Vol. X Ed. 2 Pg.	Vol. 13 Ed. 3 Pg.
268	310	249	295	337	266
269	311	250	296	338	266
270	312	251	297	339	267
271	313	252	298	340	268
275	317	254	299	341	269
276	318	254	300	342	270
277	319	255	303	347	272
278	320	256	304	348	272
279	321	257	305	349	273
280	322	258	306	350	274
281	324	259	307	351	275
285	327	260	308	352	276
286	327	260	309	353	277
287	329	261	313	357	278
288	330	262	314	358	278
289	331	263	315	359	279
290	332	264	316	360	280
291	333	265	317	361	281

COLLATION OF *THE CRISIS AND*
A CRISIS IN THE LIFE OF AN ACTRESS
IN THE DANISH EDITIONS OF
KIERKEGAARD'S COLLECTED WORKS

Vol. X *Ed. 1* *Pg.*	*Vol. X* *Ed. 2* *Pg.*	*Vol. 14* *Ed. 3* *Pg.*
321	365	210
322	366	210
323	367	105
324	367	105
325	369	106
326	370	107
327	371	108
328	372	109
329	373	110
330	375	111
331	376	112
332	377	113
333	378	114
334	379	115
335	381	116
336	382	117
337	383	118
338	384	119
339	385	120
340	386	121
341	387	122
342	388	122
343	389	123
344	390	124

NOTES

CHRISTIAN DISCOURSES

PART ONE

1. See Supplement, p. 359 (*Pap.* VIII^2 B 123:4; VIII^1 A 6).

2. For an omitted dedication, see Supplement, p. 359 (*Pap.* VIII^2 B 123:3). For an omitted preface, see Supplement, pp. 360–61 (*Pap.* VIII^1 A 430; VIII^2 B 104).

3. Matthew 6:24–34. See Supplement, p. 361 (*Pap.* VIII^2 B 91:1).

4. In the table of contents for Part One, the Introduction [*Indgang*] originally had a counterpart, End [*Udgang*], which was finally deleted. See Supplement, pp. 359, 364–67 (*Pap.* VIII^2 B 123:4; VIII^1 A 660).

5. See Exodus 19:12–13.

6. In the Danish editions of the discourses, the use of capitals and lowercase initial letters in pronouns referring to Christ and God is inconsistent. On the basis of Kierkegaard's changing capitals to lowercase letters in the page proofs of *Practice* (see *Pap.* X^5 B 33b:13), lowercase letters are used in the present translation.

7. See *Letters*, Letter 174, *KW* XXV; *The Lily in the Field and the Bird of the Air*, in *Without Authority*, *KW* XVIII (*SV* XI 41).

8. See Supplement, p. 361 (*Pap.* VIII^2 B 91:6).

9. See John 9:25.

10. Socrates (469–399 B.C.).

11. See Psalm 145:16.

12. See Matthew 4:4.

13. See Matthew 10:29.

14. See John 4:34.

15. St. Arsenius (d. 1267), patriarch of Constantinople, who excommunicated the emperor Michael Palaeologus for putting out the eyes of John, the youthful heir to the throne. See, for example, Abraham à St. Clara, *Sämmtliche Werke*, I-XXII (Passau, Lindau: 1835–54; *ASKB* 294–311), XV, p. 276.

16. See Matthew 6:33.

17. With reference to the remainder of the paragraph, see Supplement, p. 361 (*Pap.* VIII^1 A 589).

18. See Ephesians 2:12.

19. See Matthew 17:27.

20. See John 14:6.

21. See I Timothy 6:9.

Notes to Pages 20–46

22. See Hans Adolph Brorson, *"Jeg gaaer i Fare, hvor jeg gaaer," Psalmer og aandelige Sange*, ed. Jens Albrecht Leonhard Holm (Copenhagen: 1838; *ASKB* 200), 168, stanza 1, p. 513.

23. See Matthew 14:25–31; Mark 6:48.

24. Cf. Matthew 7:15.

25. With reference to the following sentence, see Supplement, p. 361 (*Pap.* VIII² B 91:8).

26. With reference to the following sentence, see Supplement, p. 361 (*Pap.* VIII² B 91:9); *Pap.* IV B 55; *JP* IV 4308 (*Pap.* VII¹ A 235).

27. Cf. Matthew 6:34.

28. Socrates. See, for example Plato, *Apology*, 19 d-20 c; *Meno*, 71 a-b; *Platonis quae exstant opera*, I-XI, ed. Friedrich Ast (Leipzig: 1819–32; *ASKB* 1144–54), VIII, pp. 104–05; IX, pp. 194–97; *The Collected Dialogues of Plato*, ed. Edith Hamilton and Huntington Cairns (Princeton: Princeton University Press, 1963), pp. 6, 354.

29. Cf. I Corinthians 7:29–31.

30. See Luke 12:20.

31. With reference to the remainder of the paragraph, see Supplement, p. 362 (*Pap.* VIII² B 91:10). With reference to the following sentence, see Supplement, p. 362 (*Pap.* VIII² B 96).

32. See Luke 16:1–13.

33. Cf. Proverbs 15:16.

34. Cf. Matthew 6:19–21.

35. See II Corinthians 8:9.

36. Hebrews 13:16.

37. Cf. James 1:17.

38. See Ephesians 2:12.

39. Cf. Luke 10:42.

40. See Matthew 6:21.

41. I Timothy 6:9.

42. The Danish *Spurv* designates any finch (*Fringillidae*), which includes the European house sparrow (*Graa-Spurv, Passer domesticus*) known in America as the English sparrow, and also the yellow bunting or yellowhammer (*Guld-Spurv, Embiriza citrenella*).

43. Cf. Shakespeare, *Hamlet*, III, 1, 56; *William Shakspeare's Tragiske Værker*, I-IX, tr. Peter Foersom and Peter Frederik Wulff (Copenhagen: 1807–25; *ASKB* 1889–96), I, p. 97; *W. Shakspeare's dramatische Werke*, I-VIII, tr. Ernst Ortlepp (Stuttgart: 1838–39; *ASKB* 1874–81), I, p. 289; *Shakspeare's dramatische Werke*, I-XII, tr. August Wilhelm v. Schlegel and Ludwig Tieck (Berlin: 1839–41; *ASKB* 1883–88), VI, p. 63; *The Complete Works of Shakespeare*, ed. George Lyman Kittredge (Boston: Ginn, 1936), p. 1167.

44. See Genesis 1:27.

45. See Homer, *Odyssey*, XI, 582–92; *Homers Odyssee*, I-II, tr. Christian Wilster (Copenhagen: 1837), I, pp. 162–63; *Homer, The Odyssey*, I-II, tr. A. T.

Murray (Loeb, Cambridge: Harvard University Press, 1976–80), I, pp. 427–29:

> "Aye, and I saw Tantalus in violent torment, standing in a pool, and the water came nigh unto his chin. He seemed as one athirst, but could not take and drink; for as often as that old man stooped down, eager to drink, so often would the water be swallowed up and vanish away, and at his feet the black earth would appear, for some god made all dry. And trees, high and leafy, let stream their fruits above his head, pears, and pomegranates, and apple trees with their bright fruit, and sweet figs, and luxuriant olives. But as often as that old man would reach out toward these, to clutch them with his hands, the wind would toss them to the shadowy clouds."

46. Acts 14:16.

47. The Praetorian Guard of the Roman emperor.

48. See Genesis 4:9.

49. See Matthew 6:6.

50. See Acts 10:34; Romans 2:11

51. See Matthew 10:29.

52. The reference is to the prayer for the king in the church service.

53. See Matthew 18:3.

54. See Mark 2:17.

55. See Mark 10:23–25.

56. For continuation of the paragraph, see Supplement, pp. 362–64 (*Pap.* VIII² B 123:10).

57. Geometry.

58. Mr. Vielgeschrey in Ludvig Holberg, *Den Stundesløse*, I, 6, *Den Danske Skue-Plads*, I–VII (Copenhagen: 1788; *ASKB* 1566–67), V, no pagination; *The Fussy Man, Four Plays by Holberg*, tr. Henry Alexander (Princeton: Princeton University Press, 1946), p. 13.

59. See Matthew 6:27.

60. See note 42 above.

61. See Matthew 4:6.

62. See Acts 17:28.

63. See, for example, *Sickness unto Death*, pp. 99, 117, 121, 126, 127, *KW* XIX (*SV* X 210, 227, 231, 235, 237).

64. See "To Need God Is a Human Being's Highest Perfection," *Four Upbuilding Discourses* (1844), in *Eighteen Upbuilding Discourses*, pp. 297–326, *KW* V (*SV* V 81–105).

65. See II Corinthians 12:9.

66. Cf. II Corinthians 12:7.

67. See Matthew 21:33–42; Mark 12:1–9.

68. Genesis 32:22–32.

69. Cf. Matthew 4:5–7.

70. See Acts 8:18–19.

71. See Galatians 6:7.

72. See John 3:36.

73. See Romans 2:9.

74. See II Thessalonians 1:9.

75. Matthew 6:30.

76. See Proverbs 16:32.

77. See Supplement, p. 364 (*Pap.* VIII² B 91:14).

78. Matthew 23:24.

79. Cf. I Timothy 6:6.

80. See Genesis 6:2.

81. The Latin *praesens* means "present" and "powerful."

82. The identity of the church father has not been determined.

83. See Matthew 21:8–11.

84. See Matthew 27:21–23.

85. Cf. I Peter 2:21.

86. Cf. I Peter 5:7.

87. I Corinthians 15:32.

88. See Daniel 5:5.

89. See Luke 23:43.

90. See Hebrews 1:14.

91. See Mark 12:30.

92. With reference to the remainder of the paragraph, see Supplement, p. 364 (*Pap.* VIII¹ A 359).

93. Cf. Matthew 6:24.

94. In English also, the root of "doubt" is "two" (Latin *duo*).

95. See Colossians 3:14.

96. Cf. Genesis 21:12, 22:1–18.

97. See I Thessalonians 5:16,18.

98. See John 14:6.

99. See Philippians 2:8; Hebrews 5:8.

100. Ephesians 1:4; Philippians 2:6–7.

101. I Peter 1:20.

102. See Mark 3:24.

103. See Luke 11:24–26.

104. Sirach 2:12.

105. The nineteenth century Danish Bible has *vankelmodige* [vacillating].

106. See Matthew 5:13; Mark 9:50. For the omitted ending, see Supplement, pp. 364–67 (*Pap.* VIII¹ A 660).

PART TWO

1. See Supplement, pp. 367–70 (*Pap.* VIII¹ A 180, 182, 184, 181, 183, 300–02, 361; VIII² B 98, 99, 123:12).

2. Cf. verse 4 in *The New Oxford Annotated Bible, Revised Standard Edition*

[*RSV*]. For the proposed dedication, see Supplement, pp. 369–70 (*Pap.* VIII² B 99, 123:12).

3. See Supplement, pp. 370–71 (*Pap.* VIII¹ A 31, 32).

4. See Historical Introduction, *Eighteen Discourses*, pp. xiv-xvii, *KW* V.

5. See Supplement, p. 370 (*Pap.* VIII² B 123:13).

6. See Supplement, pp. 370–71 (*Pap.* VIII¹ A 32).

7. Cf. Mark 2:17.

8. See Psalm 51:17.

9. See Supplement, p. 370 (*Pap.* VIII¹ A 31).

10. Cf. Hebrews 9:25,28.

11. With reference to the following two paragraphs, see Supplement, pp. 370–71 (*Pap.* VIII¹ A 32).

12. Cf. Psalm 90:10; Matthew 18:21–22.

13. See Genesis 1:6–7; Job 38:8–11.

14. See Matthew 20:1–16.

15. A cry of the night watchman.

16. Cf. Revelation 7:17, 21:4.

17. With reference to the following paragraph, see Supplement, pp. 371–72 (*Pap.* VIII² B 100:1).

18. Cf. Proverbs 14:34.

19. Cf. Luke 2:35.

20. Cf. Luke 21:18.

21. See Daniel 6:10–24.

22. See Daniel 3:8–27.

23. Cf. Matthew 6:19–20.

24. Cf. Malachi 3:3.

25. Socrates. See Plato, *Republic*, 608 d-611 a; *Platonis quae exstant opera*, I-XI, ed. Friedrich Ast (Leipzig: 1819–32; *ASKB* 1144–54), V, pp. 78–85; *The Collected Dialogues of Plato*, ed. Edith Hamilton and Huntington Cairns (Princeton: Princeton University Press, 1963), pp. 833–36.

26. See Luke 16:19–31.

27. With reference to the following paragraph, see Supplement, pp. 370–71 (*Pap.* VIII¹ A 32).

28. Vor Frelsers Church in Christianshavn.

29. Cf. Luke 22:43.

30. See Matthew 5:11.

31. With reference to the following title, see Supplement, p. 372 (*Pap.* VIII¹ A 360–61).

32. Most Danish dictionaries, if *forhverve* is listed, read "see *erhverve*." The *Ordbog over det Danske Sprog* [*ODS*], ed. Det Danske Sprog- og Litteraturselskab (Copenhagen: Nordisk Forlag, 1919–56), V, col. 545, however, states that Kierkegaard "arbitrarily" distinguishes between them, and as an illustration *ODS* cites *SV* X 115 (p. 110), where both verbs are used and a distinction is drawn.

33. See Psalm 57:8, 108:2.

34. See I Kings 19:11–13.

35. See John 5:5.

36. For continuation of the paragraph, see Supplement, pp. 372–73 (*Pap.* VIII² B 100:2).

37. With reference to the following paragraph, see Supplement, p. 373 (*Pap.* VIII² B 123:14).

38. See Luke 16:9.

39. *Meddele* (*med*, with, + *dele*, divide, share) has come more narrowly to mean "to communicate." In this sense, the term is of great importance in Kierkegaard's writings (see, for example, the drafts of lectures on communication, *JP* I 648–53 [*Pap.* VIII² B 79, 81–85]). On this page the term is used in its root meaning of "division with," "sharing." See the following paragraph for the use of the word in its second meaning.

40. Danish has two words for love: *Elskov* and *Kjerlighed*. *Elskov* is immediate, romantic, dreaming love, as between a man and a woman. *Kjerlighed* is love in a more inclusive and also higher sense. *Elskov* and *Kjerlighed* correspond to "eros" and "agape."

41. Cf., for example, *Two Discourses at the Communion on Fridays*, in *Without Authority*, *KW* XVIII (*SV* XII 267).

42. Cf. Philippians 3:1.

43. See note 39 and *Ordbog over det Danske Sprog*, XIII, col. 1163 and 1165, where the following sentence is cited to illustrate one of the two meanings of *meddele*.

44. See I Corinthians 2:9.

45. See II Corinthians 8:9.

46. See II Corinthians 6:10.

47. Cf. II Corinthians 12:9. See *Four Upbuilding Discourses* (1844), *Eighteen Discourses*, pp. 377–401, *KW* V (*SV* V 149–68).

48. With reference to the remainder of the sentence, see Supplement, p. 374 (*Pap.* VIII² B 123:15).

49. On omnipotence, see *JP* II 1251 (*Pap.* VII¹ A 181).

50. See I John 4:16.

51. See James 2:19

52. See Mark 12:30.

53. See James 4:13–15.

54. See John 4:23–24.

55. Montaigne, *Essays*, II, 5; *Michael Montaigne's Gedanken und Meinungen über allerley Gegenstände*, I-VII, tr. and ed. J. J. Bode (Berlin: 1793–99; *ASKB* 681–87), III, p. 84; *The Essayes of Montaigne*, tr. John Florio (New York: Modern Library, 1933), p. 323: "*Whosoever expects punishment, suffereth the same, and whosoever deserveth it, he doth expect it*"; *JP* III 3634 (*Pap.* VIII¹ A 278).

56. Cf. Mark 8:36.

57. See Supplement, pp. 403–04 (*Pap.* IX A 421, 498). See also *JP* VI 6279, 6280 (*Pap.* IX A 499, 500).

58. See John 6:60.

59. See Acts 8:18–20.

60. See Supplement, p. 374 (*Pap.* VIII² B 100:3).

61. Cf. Matthew 22:30; Mark 12:25.

62. For continuation of the paragraph, see Supplement, p. 374 (*Pap.* VIII² B 100:4).

63. For continuation of the paragraph, see Supplement, pp. 374–75 (*Pap.* VIII² B 100:5).

64. See, for example, *Sickness unto Death*, pp. 26–28, 49–67, *KW* XIX (*SV* XI 140–41, 161–77).

65. Proverbs 7:23.

66. See Supplement, p. 375 (*Pap.* VIII¹ A 492).

67. For continuation of the paragraph, see Supplement, pp. 375–76 (*Pap.* VIII² B 123:16).

68. Attributed to King Francis I of France after the Battle of Pavia in 1525.

69. An allusion to Archimedes. See Plutarch, "Marcellus," 14, *Lives*; *Plutark's Levnetsbeskrivelser*, I-IV, tr. Stephan Tetens (Copenhagen: 1800–11; *ASKB* 1197–1200), III, p. 272; *Plutarch's Lives*, I-XI, tr. Bernadotte Perrin (Loeb, Cambridge: Harvard University Press, 1968–84), V, p. 473: ". . . Archimedes, who was a kinsman and friend of King Hiero, wrote to him that with any given force it was possible to move any given weight; and emboldened, as we are told, by the strength of his demonstration, he declared that, if there were another world, and he could go to it, he could move this."

70. For continuation of the paragraph, see Supplement, p. 376 (*Pap.* VIII² B 100:6).

71. Cf. Supplement, pp. 368, 376–77 (*Pap.* VIII¹ A 300, 322–23).

72. For continuation of the paragraph, see Supplement, p. 377 (*Pap.* VIII² B 100:7).

73. Matthew 6:33. Cf., for example, The Moment *and Late Writings*, *KW* XXIII (*SV* XIV 248–51).

74. See Galatians 6:7.

75. Cf. I Corinthians 3:1–3.

76. The reference is to Ovid (43 B.C.–A.D. 17), Roman poet, and to his poetry written in exile. Kierkegaard had *P. Ovidii Nasonis opera quae exstant*, I-III., ed. Antonius Richter (Leipzig: 1828; *ASKB* 1265).

77. Hans Adolph Brorson, "*I denne søde Juletid*," *Psalmer og aandelige Sange*, ed. Jens Albrecht Leonhard Holm (Copenhagen: 1838; *ASKB* 200), 9, stanza 6, ll. 5–6, p. 28.

PART THREE

1. With reference to the title page, see Supplement, pp. 377–78 (*Pap.* VIII² B 101; VIII¹ A 486).

2. With reference to the following paragraph, see Supplement, p. 379 (*Pap.* VIII² B 102).

3. See Ecclesiastes 5:1; Supplement, p. 379 (*Pap.* VIII¹ A 256).

4. A traditional song by the night watchman.

5. See I Thessalonians 5:3.

6. See Philippians 2:12.

7. See Luke 18:10.

8. See Acts 15:8.

9. Proverbs 20:25.

10. Ecclesiastes 5:2–5.

11. See Genesis 3:8.

12. Danish: *Livslede* (*livs*, of life, + *lede*, disgust, loathing, distaste, nausea), acedia.

13. See John 19:5.

14. For continuation of the paragraph, see Supplement, pp. 379–80 (*Pap.* VIII² B 103:1).

15. See John 6:60.

16. See Psalm 84:10.

17. See Job 1:21.

18. See Luke 9:58.

19. See Matthew 10:37; Luke 14:26.

20. See Matthew 22:37; Mark 12:30; Luke 10:27.

21. For continuation of the paragraph, see Supplement, p. 380 (*Pap.* VIII² B 103:2).

22. See Genesis 2:24.

23. See Luke 9:59–60.

24. See Romans 8:28.

25. Cf., for example, *Fear and Trembling*, pp. 5, 9, 23, 32–33, 88, 121–23, 256–57, *KW* VI (*SV* III 57, 62, 75, 84, 136, 166–68; *Pap.* IV B 94, 76, 95:3,4).

26. Philip of Macedonia to the Spartans. See Plutarch, "Concerning Talkativeness," 511 a, *Moralia*; *Plutarchs moralische Abhandlungen*, I–IX, tr. Johann Friedrich S. Kaltwasser (Frankfurt: 1783–1800; *ASKB* 1192–96), IV, p. 486; *Plutarch's Moralia*, I–XVI, tr. Frank Cole Babbitt et al. (Loeb, Cambridge: Harvard University Press, 1970), VI, p. 445.

27. Cf. I Kings 19:12.

28. Cf. Luke 19:8.

29. Cf. Romans 8:16.

30. See Supplement, p. 380 (*Pap.* VIII² B 103:3).

31. Mark 9:50.

32. See Johann Christoph Friedrich v. Schiller, "*Die Piccolomini*," III, 7 (Thekla's song), *Wallenstein, Schillers sämmtliche Werke*, I–XII (Stuttgart, Tübingen: 1838; *ASKB* 1804–15), IV, p. 145; *Wallenstein*, tr. Charles E. Passage (New York: Ungar, 1958), p. 102.

33. See Acts 24:15; Supplement, pp. 378–79 (*Pap.* VIII¹ A 486).

34. Cf. Acts 23:6–11, 24:15.

35. Danish: *det Venskabelige. Det venskabelige Selskab* (The Friendly Society) was a social club in Copenhagen.

36. See Acts 24:22–25.
37. See Genesis 1:6–8.
38. Cf. Isaiah 34:4; Hebrews 1:12.
39. Philippians 2:12.
40. See Matthew 25:1–12.
41. See Judges 16:21–27.
42. See Romans 13:11; Supplement, p. 380 (*Pap.* VIII² B 103:4).
43. See I Corinthians 9:26.
44. Cf. *JP* II 2240 (*Pap.* I A 1).

45. In the Danish game *Gnavspil*, if the player having the counter with the picture of a house does not want to make an exchange, he says, "Go to the next house." See, for example, *Fear and Trembling*, p. 100, *KW* VI (*SV* III 147); *Philosophical Fragments, or A Fragment of Philosophy*, p. 22, *KW* VII (*SV* IV 191).

46. Socrates (469–399 B.C.). See, for example, Plato, *Apology*, 21 b-23 b; *Platonis quae exstant opera*, I-XI, ed. Friedrich Ast (Leipzig: 1819–32; *ASKB* 1144–54), VIII, pp. 108–13; *The Collected Dialogues of Plato*, ed. Edith Hamilton and Huntington Cairns (Princeton: Princeton University Press, 1963), pp. 7–9.

47. See Cicero, *Tusculan Disputations*, V, 10; *M. Tullii Ciceronis opera omnia*, I-IV and index, ed. Johann August Ernesti (Halle: 1756–57; *ASKB* 1224–29), IV, p. 425; *Cicero Tusculan Disputations*, tr. J. E. King (Loeb, Cambridge: Harvard University Press, 1971), p. 435:

> But from the ancient days down to the time of Socrates, who had listened to Archelaus the pupil of Anaxagoras, philosophy dealt with numbers and movements, with the problem whence all things came, or whither they returned, and zealously inquired into the size of the stars, the spaces that divided them, their courses and all celestial phenomena; Socrates on the other hand was the first to call philosophy down from the heavens and set her in the cities of men and bring her also into their homes and compel her to ask questions about life and morality and things good and evil. . ..

48. Cf. Matthew 5:11–12. With reference to the following discourse, see Supplement, pp. 380–81 (*Pap.* VIII¹ A 576).

49. The Danish *Salighed* means "eternal happiness," "beatitude," "blessedness," "salvation." In the Platonic context of *Fragments* and *Concluding Unscientific Postscript* to *Philosophical Fragments*, "eternal happiness" is fitting. In *Christian Discourses* the context of Matthew 5:1–12 makes "blessedness" more appropriate.

50. See Matthew 5:1–12.
51. See Acts 4:12.
52. See Matthew 5:12.
53. See Luke 17:10.
54. See Romans 2:8.
55. Cf. Acts 14:17.

56. See Kierkegaard's last discourse, *The Changelessness of God*, in *The Moment*, *KW* XXIII (*SV* XIV 277–94).

57. See Psalm 145:16.

58. See Philippians 3:8.

59. See Matthew 18:20.

60. Cf. Philippians 3:10.

61. See Revelation 17:8, 20:15.

62. Cf. Mark 5:2–3; Luke 8:27.

63. With reference to the following phrase, see Supplement, p. 381 (*Pap.* VIII² B 124:1).

64. Cf. Matthew 6:33.

65. The German *Welt* [world] in Danish spelling and with Danish suffix article.

66. See John 1:11.

67. Cf. Matthew 11:7.

68. With reference to the remainder of the sentence, see Supplement, p. 381 (*Pap.* VIII² B 103:5).

69. For continuation of the paragraph, see Supplement, pp. 381–82 (*Pap.* VIII¹ A 564).

70. With reference to the following clause, see Supplement, p. 382 (*Pap.* VIII² B 124:4).

71. With reference to the remainder of the paragraph, see Supplement, pp. 382–83 (*Pap.* VIII¹ A 596, 598).

72. Ulysses. Cf. Homer, *Odyssey*, IX, 364–66; *Homers Odyssee*, tr. Christian Wilster (Copenhagen: 1837), p. 125; *Homer the Odyssey*, I-II, tr. A. T. Murray (Loeb, Cambridge: Harvard University Press, 1976–80), I, p. 329:

> "Cyclops, thou askest me of my glorious name, and I will tell it thee; and do thou give me a stranger's gift, even as thou didst promise. Noman is my name, Noman do they call me—my mother and my father, and all my comrades as well."

73. Gert Westphaler, in Holberg, *Mester Gert Westphaler eller Den meget talende Barbeer*, 7, 8, 18, 24, *Den Danske Skue-Plads*, I-VII (Copenhagen: 1788; *ASKB* 1566–67) I, no pagination; *The Talkative Barber, Seven One-Act Plays by Holberg*, tr. Henry Alexander (Princeton: Princeton University Press, 1950), pp. 24, 28–30, 41–42, 47.

74. See I Corinthians 15:19.

75. Socrates.

76. Alcibiades (c. 450–404 B.C.). See Plato, *Symposium*, 215 d-e; *Platonis quae exstant opera*, I-XI, ed. Friedrich Ast (Leipzig: 1819–32; *ASKB* 1144–54), III, pp. 528–31; *Udvalgte Dialoger af Platon*, I-VIII, tr. Carl Johan Heise (Copenhagen: 1830–59; *ASKB* 1164–67, 1169 [I-VII]), II, pp. 88–89; *The Collected Dialogues of Plato*, ed. Edith Hamilton and Huntington Cairns (Princeton: Princeton University Press, 1963), p. 567:

> But when we listen to you, or to someone else repeating what you've said, even if he puts it ever so badly, and never mind whether the person who's

listening is man, woman, or child, we're absolutely staggered and bewitched. And speaking for myself, gentlemen, if I wasn't afraid you'd tell me I was completely bottled, I'd swear on oath what an extraordinary effect his words have had on me—and still do, if it comes to that. For the moment I hear him speak I am smitten with a kind of sacred rage, worse than any Corybant, and my heart jumps into my mouth and the tears start into my eyes—oh, and not only me, but lots of other men.

77. See, for example, Plato, *Gorgias*, 490 e–491 b; *Opera*, I, pp. 372–73; Heise, III, pp. 111–12; *Dialogues*, p. 273:

CALLICLES: Shoes! You keep talking nonsense.
SOCRATES: Well, if that is not what you mean, here it is perhaps. A farmer for instance who is an expert with good sound knowledge about the soil should have a larger share of seed and use the most seed possible on his own land.
CALLICLES: How you keep saying the same things, Socrates!
SOCRATES: Not only that, Callicles, but about the same matters.
CALLICLES: By heaven, you literally never stop talking about cobblers and fullers and cooks and doctors, as if we were discussing them.
SOCRATES: Then will you not yourself say in what matters a superiority in wisdom and power justly entitles a man to a larger share? Or will you neither put up with my suggestions nor tell me yourself?
CALLICLES: But I have been telling you for a long time. First of all I mean by the more powerful, not cobblers or cooks, but those who are wise in affairs of the state and the best methods of administering it, and not only wise but courageous, being competent to accomplish their intentions and not flagging through weakness of soul.
SOCRATES: You see, my good Callicles, that you do not find the same fault with me as I with you. For you claim that I keep saying the same things, and reproach me with it, but I make the opposite statement of you, that you never say the same things about the same subjects.

78. Cf. I Corinthians 3:19.
79. See notes 27 and 48 above.
80. See Plato, *Phaedo*, 117 a–c; *Opera*, I, pp. 616–17; Heise, I, pp. 122–23; *Dialogues*, p. 97:

At this Crito made a sign to his servant, who was standing near by. The servant went out and after spending a considerable time returned with the man who was to administer the poison. He was carrying it ready-prepared in a cup.
When Socrates saw him he said, Well, my good fellow, you understand these things. What ought I to do?
Just drink it, he said, and then walk about until you feel a weight in your legs, and then lie down. Then it will act of its own accord.

As he spoke he handed the cup to Socrates, who received it quite cheerfully, Echecrates, without a tremor, without any change of color or expression, and said, looking up under his brows with his usual steady gaze, What do you say about pouring a libation from this drink? Is it permitted, or not?

We only prepare what we regard as the normal dose, Socrates, he replied.

I see, said Socrates. But I suppose I am allowed, or rather bound, to pray the gods that my removal from this world to the other may be prosperous. This is my prayer, then, and I hope that it may be granted.

With these words, quite calmly and with no sign of distaste, he drained the cup in one breath.

81. See Supplement, pp. 383–84 (*Pap.* VIII^2 B 124:5).

PART FOUR

1. On the dedication of Part Four, see Supplement, pp. 384–88 (*Pap.* VIII^2 B 116–18; VIII^1 A 414, 415, 438).

2. See Supplement, pp. 388–90 (*Pap.* VIII^2 B 114, 119, 122).

3. Vor Frue Church, the Lutheran cathedral in central Copenhagen.

4. See Supplement, p. 390 (*Pap.* VIII^1 A 287).

5. See, for example, *JP* IV 4409; V 5456 (*Pap.* II A 343; III A 56).

6. For various elements of the prayer, see, for example, Matthew 13:44,46; Philippians 2:13: Colossians 4:5.

7. With reference to the following three sentences, see Supplement, pp. 390–92 (*Pap.* VIII^1 A 386; VIII^2 B 105:2,106).

8. With reference to the remainder of the paragraph, see Supplement, pp. 390–92 (*Pap.* VIII^1 A 386; VIII^2 B 105:2,106).

9. See John 1:29.

10. Matthew 26:30–45; Mark 14:32–41; Luke 22:39–46.

11. See John 3:8.

12. See Acts 14:17.

13. See *Practice in Christianity*, pp. 145–262, *KW* XX (*SV* XII 135–239).

14. See Ecclesiastes 12:2,8.

15. See Supplement, p. 392 (*Pap.* VIII^2 B 105:3).

16. An allusion to Solon and Croesus. See, for example, Herodotus, *History*, I, 32, 34, 86; *Die Geschichten des Herodotos*, I-II, tr. Friedrich Lange (Berlin: 1811–12; *ASKB* 1117), I, pp. 18–19, 20, 49–50; *Herodotus*, I-IV, tr. A. D. Godley (Loeb, Cambridge: Harvard University Press, 1981–82), I, pp. 38–39, 40–41, 108–11:

Thus then, Croesus, the whole of man is but chance. Now if I am to speak of you, I say that I see you very rich and the king of many men. But I cannot yet answer your question, before I hear that you have ended your life well. . . . If then such a man besides all this shall also end his life well, then he is the man whom you seek, and is worthy to be called blest; but we must wait till he be dead, and call him not yet blest, but fortunate.

But after Solon's departure, the divine anger fell heavily on Croesus: as I guess, because he supposed himself to be blest beyond all other men.

So the Persians took Sardis and made Croesus himself prisoner, he having reigned fourteen years and been besieged fourteen days, and, as the oracle foretold, brought his own great empire to an end. Having then taken him they led him to Cyrus. Cyrus had a great pyre built, on which he set Croesus, bound in chains, and twice seven Lydian boys beside him: either his intent was to sacrifice these first-fruits to some one of his gods, or he desired to fulfil a vow, or it may be that, learning that Croesus was a god-fearing man, he set him for this cause on the pyre, because he would fain know if any deity would save him from being burnt alive. It is related then that he did this; but Croesus, as he stood on the pyre, remembered even in his evil plight how divinely inspired was that saying of Solon, that no living man was blest. When this came to his mind, having till now spoken no word, he sighed deeply and groaned, and thrice uttered the name of Solon. Cyrus heard it, and bade his interpreters ask Croesus who was this on whom he called; they came near and asked him; Croesus at first would say nothing in answer, but presently, being compelled, he said, "It is one with whom I would have given much wealth that all sovereigns should hold converse." This was a dark saying to them, and again they questioned him of the words which he spoke. As they were instant, and troubled him, he told them then how Solon, an Athenian, had first come, and how he had seen all his royal state made light of it (saying thus and thus), and how all had happened to Croesus as Solon said, though he spoke with less regard to Croesus than to mankind in general and chiefly those who deemed themselves blest. While Croesus thus told his story, the pyre had already been kindled and the outer parts of it were burning. Then Cyrus, when he heard from the interpreters what Croesus said, repented of his purpose.

17. See Plato, *Gorgias*, 511 d–512 b; *Platonis quae exstant opera*, I–XI, ed. Friedrich Ast (Leipzig: 1819–32; *ASKB* 1144–54), I, pp. 428–31; *Udvalgte Dialoger af Platon*, I–VIII, tr. Carl Johan Heise (Copenhagen: 1830–59; *ASKB* 1164–67, 1169 [I–VII]), III, pp. 164–66; *The Collected Dialogues of Plato*, ed. Edith Hamilton and Huntington Cairns (Princeton: Princeton University Press, 1963), pp. 293–94 (Socrates speaking):

But if this seems to you insignificant, I can tell you of one [art] greater than this, the pilot's art which, like rhetoric, saves not only our lives but also our bodies and our goods from the gravest dangers. And this art is unpretentious and orderly, and does not put on airs or make believe that its accomplishments are astonishing. But, in return for the same results as those achieved by the advocate, if it brings you here safely from Aegina, it asks but two obols, and if from Egypt or the Black Sea, for this mighty service of bringing home safely all that I mentioned just now, oneself and children and goods and womenfolk and disembarking them in the harbor, it asks two drachmas at the most, and the man who possesses this art and achieves these results goes ashore and walks alongside his ship with modest bearing. For I suppose he is capable of reflecting that it is uncertain which of his passengers he has benefited and which he has harmed by not suffering them to be drowned, knowing as he does that those he has landed are in no way better than when they embarked, either in body or in soul. He knows that if anyone afflicted in the body with serious and incurable diseases has escaped drowning the man is wretched for not having died and has received no benefit from him; he therefore reckons that if any man suffers many incurable diseases in the soul, which is so much more precious than the body, for such a man life is not worth while and it will be no benefit to him if he, the pilot, saves him from the sea or from the law court or from any other risk. For he knows it is not better for an evil man to live, for he must needs live ill.

18. Cf. Job 1:13–19.
19. See Revelation 2:10.
20. Cf. Proverbs 14:34.
21. See I John 5:19.
22. See Genesis 4:10.
23. See Hebrews 12:3.
24. See John 19:5.
25. See Luke 23:39–43.
26. See Matthew 27:25.
27. Danish: "*Sorg . . . efter ham [Gud].*" Here *Sorg* is synonymous with *Længsel* (longing). Cf. II Corinthians 7:10; the Danish Bible of the time (Copenhagen: 1830; *ASKB* 7) has "*Bedrøvelse efter Gud,*" and the *Revised Standard Version* has "godly grief." See also *Three Upbuilding Discourses* (1844), *Eighteen Discourses, KW* V, p. 250 (*SV* IV 138); *JP* I 443; IV 3915, p. 53 (*Pap.* II A 360; III C 1, p. 246).
28. See I Corinthians 11:24.
29. See Galatians 2:20.
30. See Genesis 3:19.
31. See Matthew 20:12.
32. See Luke 10:41–42.
33. Cf. Matthew 9:12; Mark 2:17.
34. See note 27 above.
35. The Danish *Bedested* means both a place of prayer (*Bede*) and a place of rest, a provisioning place. Cf. the English *bait, baiting.*
36. In the chancel of Vor Frue Church in Copenhagen, there stands a statue of Christ, with outstretched arms, by the Danish sculptor Bertel Thorvaldsen (1770–1844).
37. See John 13:23,25.

38. See, for example, Hebrews 4:15.

39. See Luke 4:2.

40. See John 19:28.

41. See Matthew 8:20.

42. See Matthew 26:38; Mark 14:34.

43. See Mark 15:34.

44. With reference to the following discourse, see Supplement, pp. 392–93 (*Pap.* VIII^2 B 108).

45. See, for example, *The Changelessness of God*, in *The Moment*, *KW* XXIII (*SV* XIV 277–94).

46. See, for example, Luke 23:43; Hebrews 3:7,13,15.

47. See Matthew 22:5; Luke 14:18–19.

48. Cf. Psalm 139:7–13.

49. See Matthew 7:22–23, 25:12; Luke 13:25–27.

50. Matthew 5:23–24.

51. See Genesis 4:3–5.

52. With reference to the remainder of the discourse, see Supplement, pp. 392–93 (*Pap.* VIII^2 B 108–10).

53. Mount Moriah is the site of the temple in Jerusalem. Gerizim was the holy mountain of the Samaritans. Cf. John 4:21.

54. With reference to the following sentence, see Supplement, p. 393 (*Pap.* VIII^2 B 109).

55. With reference to the following sentence, see Supplement, p. 393 (*Pap.* VIII^2 B 110).

56. See Philippians 1:6.

57. Thomas Kingo, "*Farvel Du hvilesøde Nat*," stanza 5, *Psalmer og aandelige Sange*, ed. Peter Andreas Fenger (Copenhagen: 1827; *ASKB* 203), no. 184, p. 392:

> Strid saa, Du Dag, som aldrig meer
> Mit Ø ie her i Tiden seer,
> Fald hen i Nattens Skygge!
> Jeg strider frem til Himmelrig,
> Min Gud at see evindelig,
> Der paa min Troe skal bygge.

58. Johann Heermann, "*Mind, O Jesu. tidt mit Hjerte*," *Evangelisk-christelig Psalmebog* (Copenhagen: 1845; *ASKB* 197), 147, p. 128.

59. With reference to the following two paragraphs, see Supplement, pp. 393–95 (*Pap.* VIII^1 A 265; VIII^2 B 112).

60. Cf. Luke 10:24.

61. Cf. Luke 10:42.

62. See John 6:15.

63. See Matthew 21:46, 26:5; Mark 14:2; Luke 20:19.

64. Luke 22:7–15.

65. See Matthew 26:55; Luke 22:52, 23:32–33.

66. See John 18:4.

67. See Matthew 26:49; Mark 14:45.

68. See Matthew 27:24.

69. Francis of Assisi. See *JP* I 288; II 1839; V 5492 (*Pap.* II A 276; VIII¹ A 349; III A 93).

70. See Mark 14:27–31.

71. See John 18:37.

72. See Matthew 26:69–75.

73. See Luke 23:34.

74. See Mark 10:45.

75. See Luke 7:38.

76. With reference to the following paragraph, see Supplement, pp. 395–96 (*Pap.* VIII¹ A 367; VIII² B 113:1).

77. See Luke 14:17.

78. For elements of the prayer, see, for example, I John 4:19, 13:1.

79. See Matthew 15:1–20; Mark 4:10–11; 7:1–23.

80. See, for example, Matthew 25:31–46.

81. See Matthew 7:6.

82. Cf. Mark 10:9.

83. With reference to the following two clauses, see Supplement, p. 396 (*Pap.* VIII² B 113:4).

84. See Exodus 20:7.

85. Cf. Matthew 18:21–22.

86. See note 36 above.

87. For elements of the prayer, see Matthew 6:26; Luke 12:6; I Corinthians 13:12.

88. With reference to the following two paragraphs, see Supplement, p. 396 (*Pap.* VIII¹ A 266).

89. See John 8:3–11.

90. See Luke 7:41.

91. With reference to the remainder of the sentence, see Supplement, pp. 396–97 (*Pap.* VIII² B 113:5).

92. See Romans 1:19–20.

93. Genesis 1:31.

94. Matthew 11:6.

95. See Psalm 51:17.

96. See Genesis 32:24–32.

97. See Exodus 20:4.

98. See Romans 3:19.

99. See Matthew 18:12–14; Luke 15:4–7.

100. Cf. Romans 5:10.

101. Cf. John 3:16.

102. See I Corinthians 2:9; *Fragments*, p. 36, *KW* VII (*SV* IV 203); *Sickness unto Death*, pp. 84, 118, *KW* XIX (*SV* XI 195, 228).

103. See Matthew 14:15–21; Mark 6:38–44.

104. Cf. Romans 3:7–8, 6:1–2,15.

105. See Supplement, p. 000 (*Pap.* VIII[1] A 260).

106. Genesis 32:26.

107. See Psalm 127:1.

108. With reference to the following two sentences and the following clause, see Supplement, p. 397 (*Pap.* VIII[2] B 113:6).

109. Attributed to Bias (6 century B.C.), one of the seven sages of Greece. See Diogenes Laertius, *Lives of Eminent Philosophers*, I, 86; *Diogenis Laertii de vitis philosophorum*, I-II (Leipzig: 1833; *ASKB* 1109), I, p. 41; *Diogen Laertses filosofiske Historie*, I-II, tr. Børge Riisbrigh (Copenhagen: 1812; *ASKB* 1110–11), I, p. 38; *Diogenes Laertius*, I-II, tr. R. D. Hicks (Loeb, Cambridge: Harvard University Press, 1979–80), I, p. 89.

110. Cf. Mark 9:36–37; Luke 18:15.

111. See I Corinthians 3:9.

112. With reference to the remainder of the paragraph, see Supplement, p. 397 (*Pap.* VIII[2] B 113:7).

113. Aaron and Hur. See Exodus 17:12.

THE CRISIS AND A CRISIS IN THE LIFE OF
AN ACTRESS AND ADDENDUM

TITLE PAGE AND OVERLEAF

TITLE PAGE. See Supplement, p. 412 (*Pap.* VIII[2] B 90:1).

OVERLEAF. The dedication in a copy of *On My Work as an Author* and the heading in a letter (*Letters*, Letter 283, Dedication 15, *KW* XXV) from Kierkegaard to Luise Heiberg could be regarded as a dedication for *Crisis*:

> To
>
> That fortunate artist
> whose perception and determination were nonetheless
> —fortunately once again!—exactly equal
> to her good fortune,
>
> Mrs. Heiberg
> with admiration
> from
>
> the author.

It is not, not even remotely, my intention with this to persuade you in any way to read a little book that in the final analysis, and perhaps long before then, would probably be boring and exhausting.

No! But somewhere in the book mention is made of a small essay on esthetics by a pseudonymous Inter et Inter, *The Crisis and a Crisis in the Life of an Actress, Fædrelandet* (1848), no. 188–91. If by any chance you happened to notice this article at the time, it would please me if I might tell myself that you, Mrs. Heiberg, were aware that this article belongs among my works, as will be evident from this book. If you did not notice this article at the time, then it is the author's wish that you might find some idle hour that could be filled by reading it. For if you—I request this only for a moment and on behalf of this subject—if you will permit me to say this in all sincerity, that little article has special reference to you. Whether it was read at that time by many or only by a few—if you did not read it, then it is the author's opinion that it has not reached its destination. But on the other hand, if you have read it—if it was then found to be, if not in perfect, yet in happy accord with your thoughts on that subject, then it is the author's opinion that it has indeed reached its destination.

Address:
To Mrs. Heiberg
Added in pencil by J. L. Heiberg: 1851

The above letter was appended to a copy of *On My Work as an Author* that Kierkegaard sent to Luise Heiberg. The letter was printed in *Kjøbenhavnsposten*, 1, January 2, 1856, together with a letter from her husband, poet-critic-philosopher Johan Ludvig Heiberg:

> In *Kjøbenhavnsposten*, no. 301, it has been pointed out that appeal to the utterances of the late Dr. Søren Kierkegaard have recently been made also in matters of dramaturgy. In this connection I will give a supplementary contribution to information about Kierkegaard's dramaturgical views by recalling an essay that he wrote in 1847 and that he had printed a year later as a serial in *Fædrelandet* (188–91, July 24–27, 1848). The occasion for this essay was the resumption of the tragedy *Romeo and Juliet* in the repertoire around New Year's day 1847, when the role of Juliet was played by the same one who had appeared in it nineteen years earlier. When in 1851 Kierkegaard published under his own name a little work with the title *On My Work as an Author*, he acknowledged in it (p. 9 [*SV* XIII 497]) his authorship of the essay, which had originally been anonymous. He included with this work a covering handwritten letter, which is submitted here in copy. Some expressions in the heading refer to categories that he had developed in the essay itself, which certainly deserves to be read anew, if for nothing else, then for the contempt with which it dismisses current incompetent theater criticism in all its esthetic thinness and moral baseness.
>
> Copenhagen, November 30, 1855
>
> J. L. Heiberg

1. A fund or foundation for the support of meritorious artists, writers, scholars, etc.

2. See, for example, *Et Liv. Gjenoplevet i Erindringen*, I–IV, ed. Aage Friis (Copenhagen: Gyldendal, 1944), I, pp. 168–69.

3. Cf. Psalm 149:3.

4. A flattering, uncritically eulogizing character in Ludvig Holberg, *Det Lykkelige Skibbrud*, *Den Danske Skue-Plads*, I-VII (Copenhagen: 1788; *ASKB* 1566–67), IV, no pagination.

5. With reference to the remainder of the sentence, see Supplement, p. 412 (*Pap.* VIII^2 B 90:4).

6. Danish: *det Venskabelige*. *Det Venskabelige Selskab* (The Friendly Society) was a Copenhagen social club.

7. Kierkegaard's unique metaphorical allusion to the extensible sections of a telescope is specifically pointed out in *ODS*, XXV, col. 784. See, for example, *Early Polemical Writings*, *KW* I, p. 69 (*SV* XIII 61); *Stages*, *KW* XI, p. 374 (*SV* VI 349).

8. In Lübeck, Luise Heiberg had "what is called 'good fortune,' a success." Luise Heiberg, *Et Liv*, I, pp. 34–35.

9. See Supplement, p. 412 (*Pap.* VIII^2 B 90:6).

10. See Plutarch, "Caesar," 38, *Lives*; *Plutarchi vitae parallelae*, I-IX, ed. Gottfried Heinrich Schaefer (Leipzig: 1829; *ASKB* 1181–89), VII, pp. 46–47; *Plutarch's Lives*, I-XI, tr. Bernadotte Perrin (Loeb, Cambridge: Harvard University Press, 1968–84), VII, pp. 535–37:

> At Apollonia, since the force which he had with him was not a match for the enemy and the delay of his troops on the other side caused him perplexity and distress, Caesar conceived the dangerous plan of embarking in a twelve-oared boat, without any one's knowledge, and going over to Brundisium, though the sea was encompassed by such large armaments of the enemy. At night, accordingly, after disguising himself in the dress of a slave, he went on board, threw himself down as one of no account, and kept quiet. While the river Aoüs was carrying the boat down towards the sea, the early morning breeze, which at that time usually made the mouth of the river calm by driving back the waves, was quelled by a strong wind which blew from the sea during the night; the river therefore chafed against the inflow of the sea and the opposition of its billows, and was rough, being beaten back with a great din and violent eddies, so that it was impossible for the master of the boat to force his way along. He therefore ordered the sailors to come about in order to retrace his course. But Caesar, perceiving this, disclosed himself, took the master of the boat by the hand, who was terrified at sight of him, and said: "Come, good man, be bold and fear naught; thou carryest Caesar and Caesar's fortune in thy boat." The sailors forgot the storm, and laying to their oars, tried with all alacrity to force their way down the river.

11. Cf., for example, *For Self-Examination*, pp. 19–25, *KW* XXI (*SV* XII 310–14).

12. See John 5:2–9.

13. See Gotthilf Heinrich v. Schubert, *Die Symbolik des Traumes* (Bamberg: 1821; *ASKB* 776), p. 38 (ed. tr.): ". . . voice of nature, the air music on Ceylon, which sings a frightful, merry minuet in the tones of a profoundly plaintive,

heartrending voice." See *The Concept of Irony, with Continual Reference to Socrates*, p. 254, *KW* II (*SV* XIII 329); *Fragments*, p. 108 and note 43, *KW* VII (*SV* IV 269); *Postscript*, p. 333, *KW* XII.1, p. 333 (*SV* VII 287).

14. Cf. *Repetition*, pp. 156–69, *KW* VI (*SV* III 196–207).

15. Christen Niemann Rosenkilde (1786–1861), a Danish actor known especially for his roles in J. L. Heiberg's vaudeville productions at the Royal Theater. See *JP* V 6060 (*Pap.* VIII^1 A 339); *Pap.* VII^1 B 88, p. 290; VIII^2 B 172–74.

16. An allusion to the opera by Gaetano Donizetti; *Regimentets Datter, Det Kongelige Theaters Repertoire*, 121 (1840).

17. Cf. *Fragments*, p. 72, *KW* VII (*SV* IV 235).

18. For continuation of the sentence, see Supplement, p. 413 (*Pap.* VIII^2 B 90:10).

19. With reference to the remainder of the sentence, see Supplement, p. 413 (*Pap.* VIII^2 B 90:11).

20. See Shakespeare, *King Henry the Fourth*, I, III, 2, 39–59; *William Shakspeare's Tragiske Vaerker*, I–IX, tr. Peter Foersom and Peter Frederik Wulff (Copenhagen: 1807–25; *ASKB* 1889–96), III, pp. 108–09; *W. Shakspeare's dramatische Werke*, I–VIII, tr. Ernst Ortlepp (Stuttgart: 1838–39; *ASKB* 1874–81), VI, pp. 195–96; *Shakspeare's dramatische Werke*, I–XII, tr. August Wilhelm v. Schlegel and Ludwig Tieck (Berlin: 1839–41; *ASKB* 1883–88), I, p. 269; *The Complete Works of Shakespeare*, ed. George Lyman Kittredge (Boston: Ginn, 1936), pp. 565–66:

> Had I so lavish of my presence been,
> So common-hackney'd in the eyes of men,
> So stale and cheap to vulgar company,
> Opinion, that did help me to the crown,
> Had still kept loyal to possession
> And left me in reputeless banishment,
> A fellow of no mark nor likelihood.
> By being seldom seen, I could not stir
> But, like a comet, I was wond'red at;
> That men would tell their children, 'This is he!'
> Others would say, 'Where? Which is Bolingbroke?'
> And then I stole all courtesy from heaven,
> And dress'd myself in such humility
> That I did pluck allegiance from men's hearts,
> Loud shouts and salutations from their mouths
> Even in the presence of the crowned King.
> Thus did I keep my person fresh and new,
> My presence, like a robe pontifical,
> Ne'er seen but wond'red at; and so my state,
> Seldom but sumptuous, show'd like a feast
> And won by rareness such solemnity.

21. A game (*Forundringsstolen*; also, but rarely, named *Beundringsstolen*) some-times called the "wonder stool" or "wonder game," in which one person sits blindfolded on a stool in the middle of a circle while another goes around quietly asking others what they wonder about the person who is "it." Upon being told what others had wondered about him, he tries to guess the source in each instance. See, for example, "To Mr. Orla Lehmann," *Early Polemical Writings*, p. 24, *KW* I (*SV* XIII 28); *Fragments*, p. 52, *KW* VII (*SV* IV 219); *Sickness unto Death*, p. 5, *KW* XIX (*SV* XI 117).

22. For continuation of the sentence, see Supplement, p. 413 (*Pap.* VIII² B 90:13).

23. An old saying. See *Irony*, pp. 253–54, *KW* II (*SV* XIII 328); *Stages*, p. 340, *KW* XI (*SV* VI 318); *The Point of View*, *KW* XXII (*SV* XIII 544); *JP* V 5937–38; VI 6680 (*Pap.* VII¹ A 147–48; X³ A 450). See also Augustin Eugène Scribe, [*Puf eller*] *Verden vil bedrages*, tr. Nicolai Christian Levin Abrahams, *Repertoire* (1849); *JP* VI 6395 (*Pap.* X¹ A 320).

24. For continuation of the paragraph, see Supplement, p. 413 (*Pap.* VIII² B 90:14).

25. Dr. Franz Theremin (1780–1846), Court Chaplain, who in his later years restricted his preaching because of illness.

26. For continuation of the sentence, see Supplement, p. 413 (*Pap.* VIII² B 90:17).

27. *Oberhofprædikant*, a Danish word with a German prefix, an allusion to Hans Lassen Martensen, professor of theology, University of Copenhagen, who became Court Chaplain in 1845 and Bishop Mynster's successor in 1854. See *JP* III 6239 (*Pap.* IX A 229): "Furthermore, the article contains a little allusion to Martensen."

28. For continuation of the sentence, see Supplement, p. 413 (*Pap.* VIII² B 90:19).

29. With reference to the following sentence, see Supplement, p. 414 (*Pap.* VIII² B 90:20).

30. From the baptismal liturgy: May God preserve your coming in and your going out. Cf. Psalm 121:8; II Samuel 3:25.

31. With reference to the following sentence, see Supplement, pp. 414–15 (*Pap.* VIII² B 90:23).

32. Cf. Tertullian, *Apology*, 50; *Qu. Sept. Flor. Tertulliani Opera*, I-IV, ed. E. F. Leopold (Leipzig: 1839–41; *ASKB* 147–50), I, 128; *The Ante-Nicene Fathers*, I-X, ed. Alexander Roberts and James Donaldson (Buffalo: Christian Literature Publishing Co., 1885–97), III, p. 55.

33. Cf. Matthew 11:16–17.

34. Hard breathing or pronouncing with a breathing of *h*-sound, as in *hot*, *heaven*, etc.

35. Two brothers in Greek mythology. Prometheus [forethinker (*pro*, "before," + *manthanein*, "learn")] fashioned man from clay, stole fire from the gods and brought it to earth. Epimetheus [afterthinker] was the husband of the

first woman, Pandora, and he allowed her to open the box of human ills and troubles.

36. Danish: *Bølgepige* [wave-maiden], not the more customary *Havfrue* [mermaid]. See *JP* IV 4394 (*Pap.* I A 319), in which Kierkegaard discusses sea nymphs [*Wellenmädchen*] as represented in an etching in Wilhelm Vollmer, *Vollständiges Wörterbuch der Mythologie aller Nationen*, I–II (Stuttgart: 1836; *ASKB* 1942–43), II, plate CXV. For text related to the etching, see I, p. 1537. See also *Irische Elfenmärchen* (Thomas Crofton Croker, *Fairy Legends and Traditions of the South of Ireland*; London: 1825), tr. Grimm Brothers (Leipzig: 1826; *ASKB* 1423), p. 193.

37. The auction catalog (*ASKB*) lists the works (in German) of a number of the English romantic poets (Byron, Shelley, and Young, and also Ossian in Danish) but does not list anything by Wordsworth. Nevertheless, this line and the entire paragraph are reminiscent of the famous statement that poetry "takes its origin from emotion recollected in tranquillity." "Preface to *Lyrical Ballads, with Other Poems*," ed. Paul M. Zall (Lincoln: University of Nebraska Press, 1966), p. 27.

38. See Judge William's discussion of Anna Helene Dorothea Nielsen, an actress contemporary with Luise Heiberg, in *Stages*, pp. 131–32 (*SV* VI 126–27).

39. Archimedes' shout upon discovering, while bathing, the principle of specific gravity. See *Irony*, pp. 291–92, *KW* II (*SV* XIII 362); *Two Ages: The Age of Revolution and the Present Age, A Literary Review*, p. 66, *KW* XIV (*SV* VIII 62).

40. See Historical Introduction, pp. xv–xvi; Supplement, p. 415 (*Pap.* VIII² B 90:26). Mrs. Heiberg played Juliet on January 23, 1847, eighteen years after her latest previous performance (October 1829) of that role.

41. See Supplement, p. 426 (*Pap.* IX B 67).

42. J. H. Vernoy de Saint-Georges, *Ludovic*, tr. Thomas Overskou, *Repertoire*, 61 (1834). The play was staged intermittently 1834–1841 and thereafter only once, June 11, 1846, before Kierkegaard wrote about it.

43. Danish: *stodere* (to stutter, to dodder), a play on *studere* (to study). See J. L. Heiberg, *Recensenten og Dyret*, 3, *Skuespil*, I–VII (Copenhagen: 1833–41; *ASKB* 1553–59), III, pp. 199–207. Trop wants to be a student and in a casual, accidental way goes about preparing for the entrance examination. Indeed, he can produce evidence that he has almost taken the examination.

44. See *Stages*, p. 388, *KW* XI (*SV* VI 362); *JP* V 5738 (*Pap.* V A 52).

45. Poul Martin Møller, "*Optegnelser paa Reisen til China*," *Efterladte Skrifter*, I–III (Copenhagen: 1839–43; *ASKB* 1574–76), III, p. 159.

46. The ritual of pledging friendship (and the use of the familiar second person singular *du* instead of the formal plural *De*). The use of *De* has more or less disappeared in recent years.

47. With reference to the remainder of the paragraph, see Supplement, p. 426 (*Pap.* IX B 70:10).

48. With reference to the remainder of the sentence and the following three sentences, see Supplement, p. 426 (*Pap.* IX B 70:12).

49. See *JP* V 5870 (*Pap.* VII[1] A 1).

50. Shakespeare, *King Henry the Fourth*, I, II, 4, 358–66; Foersom and Wulff, III, pp. 77–78; Ortlepp, VI, pp. 172–73; Schlegel and Tieck, I, p. 249; Kittredge, p. 559:

> *Prince*. Here comes lean Jack; here comes bare-bone. How now, my sweet creature of bombast? How long is't ago, Jack, since thou sawest thine own knee?
>
> *Fal*. My own knee? When I was about thy years, Hal, I was not an eagle's talent in the waist; I could have crept into any alderman's thumb-ring. A plague of sighing and grief! It blows a man up like a bladder.

51. For continuation of the sentence, see Supplement, pp. 426–27 (*Pap.* IX B 70:18).

52. For continuation of the sentence, see Supplement, p. 427 (*Pap.* IX B 70:19).

53. For continuation of the paragraph, see Supplement, p. 427 (*Pap.* IX B 70:20).

54. See Supplement, p. 427 (*Pap.* IX B 70:21).

55. St. Georges, *Ludovic*, I, 6, V, 9, pp. 3, 5. See Supplement, p. 427 (*Pap.* IX B 70:20).

56. See *Either/Or*, II, p. 369, *KW* IV (*Pap.* III B 181:2); *Fragments*, p. 37, *KW* VII (*SV* IV 204); *JP* III 3598 (*Pap.* II A 763).

57. A reference to the practice of making a cut or cuts on the underside of a horse's tail in order to make the horse carry the tail higher.

58. See *JP* I 775 (*Pap.* IV A 150).

59. St. Georges, *Ludovic*, II, 3; *Repertoire*, 61, p. 14.

60. Ibid., II, 15, p. 20.

61. See note 42.

62. See Supplement, p. 427 (*Pap.* IX B 73).

SUPPLEMENT

Christian Discourses

1. "The Gospel of Sufferings," Part Three, *Upbuilding Discourses in Various Spirits*, p. 215, *KW* XV (*SV* VIII 303).

2. See Supplement, pp. 364–67 (*Pap.* VIII[1] A 660).

3. See *JP* IV 4308 (*Pap.* VIII[1] A 235).

4. See Luke 10:41–42.

5. See *Kongeriget Norges Grundlov* (May 19, 1814), (Christiania: May 31, 1814), A, 2, p. 1 (editors' translation): "Furthermore, Jews are excluded from admission to the Kingdom."

6. See Hebrews 7:27, 9:12,26,28, 10:10–14.

7. Matthew 19:27–28.

8. Romans 8:28.

9. Acts 24:15.

10. See Matthew 5:11; Luke 6:22.

11. See Aesop, "The Fox and the Stork"; "*Vulpis et Ciconia*," *Phaedri Augusti Liberti Fabularum Aesopiarum Libri V*, ed. Christian H. Weise (Leipzig: 1828), I, 26, pp. 12–13; *Babrius and Phaedrus*, tr. B. E. Perry (Loeb, Cambridge: Harvard University Press, 1965), pp. 220–23.

12. See Luke 6:26.

13. Romans 13:11.

14. See "The Gospel of Sufferings," *Discourses in Various Spirits*, p. 326–27, *KW* XV (*SV* VIII 402–04).

15. See Historical Introduction, p. xiii.

16. The Preface (*Pap.* VIII^2 B 119) written for Part Four of *Christian Discourses* was not used there. The addition refers to *Point of View*, *KW* XXII (*SV* XIII 599), where Note No. 3 is changed to Note No. 2. See *Pap.* VIII^2 B 121, 190.

17. These letters stand for the Grand Cross, Order of Denmark, and other honors given by the Danish Government for distinguished service to the nation.

18. See *Postscript*, p. [630], *KW* XII.1 (*SV* VII [549]). See Supplement, pp. 386–87 (*Pap.* VIII^1 A 415); *JP* VI 6638, 6639, 6641, 6778 (*Pap.* X^6 B 163, 164, 169; X^4 A 377).

19. Pp. 247–300.

20. Cf. *Two Discourses at the Communion on Fridays*, in *Without Authority*, *KW* XVIII (*SV* XII 267).

21. See Supplement, pp. 388–89 (*Pap.* VIII^2 B 119).

22. See Philippians 3:20.

23. In Vor Frue Church in Copenhagen, there are statues of the twelve apostles by the Danish sculptor Bertel Thorvaldsen (1770–1844).

24. See pp. 93–159.

25. Part Three of *Discourses in Various Spirits*, pp. 213–341, *KW* XV (*SV* VIII 297–416).

26. Pp. 161–246.

27. Pp. 247–300.

28. Pp. 161–246.

29. See Supplement, pp. 405–07 (*Pap.* X^4 A 511).

30. Pp. 247–300. See Supplement, pp. 384, 387–88 (*Pap.* VIII^2 B 116, 117; VIII^1 A 438).

31. Johann Tauler, *Nachfolgung des armen Lebens Christi*, ed. N. Casseder (Frankfurt/M: 1821; *ASKB* 282).

32. Pp. 176–87.

33. Pp. 161–246, 247–300.

34. Pp. 161–246.

35. On March 6, 1848, the manuscript of *Christian Discourses* was delivered to the printer, Bianco Luno. See *Af Søren Kierkegaards Efterladte Papirer*, I-VIII, ed. Hans Peter Barfod and Hermann Gottsched (Copenhagen: 1869–81), III, p. 41.

36. In March 1848, the influence in Denmark of the February Revolution in Paris reached a climax. On the morning of March 21, civic representatives of Copenhagen marched at the head of a crowd of around fifteen thousand and presented their demand for a constitutional monarchy and universal (male) suffrage. The newly crowned King Frederik VII agreed and the peaceful revolution of 1848 was well under way.

On March 18, a German delegation had come to Copenhagen and demanded recognition of the German claims to the Danish duchies Slesvig and Holsten. Their claims were rejected, and on March 24 Prince Friedrich of Augustenburg put himself at the head of a provisional government proclaimed in Kiel. A Danish army subdued the rebels as far as the Eider River. A new national assembly of Germany decided to incorporate Slesvig, and a Prussian army under Wrangel drove the Danes back. On August 26, an armistice was signed in Malmø and the government of the two duchies was entrusted to a commission composed of two Prussians, two Danes, and a fifth member by common consent of the four. From 1848 on, the financial situation of Denmark was precarious and inflation rampant.

37. See note 51 below.

38. See Mynster, "*Christus vil, at vi ganske skulle høre ham til, paa Trinitatis Søndag*" (John 3:1–15), *Prædikener paa alle Søn- og Hellig-Dage i Aaret*, I–II (Copenhagen: 1837; *ASKB* 229–30), II, 38, pp. 51–64.

39. Anon., "*Lad Hjertet i Sorgen ei synde,*" *Tillæg til den evangelisk-christelige Psalmebog* (Copenhagen: 1845), 610, I, p. 51.

40. See note 39 above.

41. Pp. 93–159.

42. See John 16:16–20; *Two Upbuilding Discourses* (1843), *Eighteen Discourses*, pp. 28–29, *KW* V (*SV* III 33–34); *JP* VI 6269 (*Pap.* IX A 379).

43. *Practice in Christianity, KW* XX, pp. 145–262 (*SV* XII 135–239).

44. See Supplement, pp. 368, 369, 397–98 (*Pap.* VIII¹ A 300, 302, 500).

45. Thomas à Kempis, *om Christi Efterfølgelse*, tr. Jens Albrecht Leonhard Holm (Copenhagen: 1848; *ASKB* 273), X, XXVI, p. 131 ("defended [*forsvarede*] himself only by patience and humility . . . he sometimes answered [*svarede*]"); *Of the Imitation of Christ*, tr. anon. (New York: Appleton: 1896), p. 175.

46. See Historical Introduction, p. xiii.

47. See reference to Mynster (pseudonym Kts), *Postscript*, p. [629], *KW* XII.1 (*SV* VII [548]).

48. See ibid., pp. [617–19] (537–39).

49. "An Occasional Discourse," *Discourses in Various Spirits*, pp. 3–154, *KW* XV (*SV* VIII 115–242).

50. Mynster had praised the former editor of *Corsaren* as "one of our most talented writers"; *Yderlige Bidrag til Forhandlingerne om de kirkelige Forhold i Danmark* (Copenhagen: 1851), p. 44. See *JP* VI 6743, 6744 (*Pap.* X⁴ A 167, 168).

51. Michael Pedersen Kierkegaard read Mynster's sermons regularly, and son Søren appreciatively continued this practice. See, for example, *JP* V 6064;

VI 6749 (*Pap*. VIII^1 A 366; X^6 B 173). Twenty-two volumes of Mynster's sermons and other writings are listed in *ASKB*.

52. See Supplement, p. 384 (*Pap*. VIII^2 B 118).

53. Richard Brinsley Butler Sheridan's *School for Scandal* was performed December 14, 1846, and frequently thereafter.

54. August Wilhelm Iffland (1759–1814), actor and director, and a very prolific and popular playwright.

55. Nicolai Peter Nielsen (1795–1860), prominent Danish actor with "director" more as an honorary title than the description of a function.

56. Anton Wilhelm Wiehe (1826–84), who played the role of Charles.

57. Cf. *From the Papers of One Still Living*, in *Early Polemical Writings*, p. 53, *KW* I (*SV* XIII 43).

58. See *Fragments*, p. 21, *KW* VII (*SV* IV 191).

59. Jens Finsteen Gj(i)ødwad (1811–1891), editor of *Fædrelandet* and Kierkegaard's middleman in the publication of the early pseudonymous works.

60. *Crisis in the Life of an Actress*.

61. See note 60 above.

62. See note 61 above.

63. Johan Ludvig Heiberg (1791–1860), leading literary figure and critic of that time and husband of the actress, Johanne Luise Heiberg. The contemplated dedication was not used.

64. See note 61 above.

65. See note 61 above.

66. Andreas Gottlob Rudelbach (1792–1862), scholar, clergyman, and orthodox critic of theological rationalism.

67. See note 61 above.

68. See note 61 above.

69. See note 61 above.

70. See note 61 above.

71. Rasmus Nielsen (1809–1844), professor of philosophy, University of Copenhagen. For a time it seemed as if Nielsen would be allowed to become, in a sense, Kierkegaard's successor. See, for example, *JP* VI 6239, 6246, 6301, 6302, 6341, 6342, 6402–06, 6574 (*Pap*. IX A 229, 258; X^1 A 14, 15, 110, 111, 343; X^6 B 83–86, 121); *Letters*, Letter 257, *KW* XXV.

72. See note 61 above.

73. See note 61 above.

74. See note 72 above.

75. See note 61 above.

76. See note 61 above.

77. See note 61 above.

78. See *Stages*, p. 47, *KW* XI (*SV* VI 49).

79. Joachim Ludvig Phister (1807–1896), noted Danish actor. See *Either/Or*, I, pp. 239, 279, *KW* III (*SV* I 213, 250).

80. Augustin Eugène Scribe, *Brama og Bajaderen*, tr. Thomas Overskou (Copenhagen: 1837).

81. See Virgil, *Aeneid*, VI, 258; *Virgils Aeneide*, tr. Johan Henrik Schønheyder (Copenhagen: 1812); *Virgil*, I–II, tr. Rushton Fairclough (Loeb, Cambridge: Harvard University Press, 1978), I, pp. 524–25: " *'procul o, procul este, profani' conclamat vates, 'totoque absistite luco'* ['Away! away! O unhallowed ones!' shrieks the seer, 'withdrawn from all the grove!']."

See also *Either/Or*, II, pp. 53, 273, *KW* IV (*SV* II 49, 244); *JP* V 5115 (*Pap.* I B 1).

BIBLIOGRAPHICAL NOTE

For general bibliographies of Kierkegaard studies, see:

Jens Himmelstrup, *Søren Kierkegaard International Bibliografi*. Copenhagen: Nyt Nordisk Forlag Arnold Busck, 1962.

Aage Jørgensen, *Søren Kierkegaard-litteratur 1961–1970*. Aarhus: Akademisk Boghandel, 1971. *Søren Kierkegaard-litteratur 1971–1980*. Aarhus: privately published, 1983.

Bruce H. Kirmmse, *Kierkegaard in Golden Age Denmark*. Bloomington: Indiana University Press, 1990.

François H. Lapointe, *Sören Kierkegaard and His Critics: An International Bibliography of Criticism*. Westport, Connecticut: Greenwood Press, 1980.

International Kierkegaard Newsletter, ed. Julia Watkin. Launceton, Tasmania, Australia, 1979–.

Kierkegaard: A Collection of Critical Essays, ed. Josiah Thompson. New York: Doubleday (Anchor Books), 1972.

Kierkegaardiana, XII, 1982; XIII, 1984; XIV, 1988; XVI, 1993; XVII, 1994; XVIII, 1996.

Søren Kierkegaard's Journals and Papers, I, ed. and tr. Howard V. Hong and Edna H. Hong, assisted by Gregor Malantschuk. Bloomington, Indiana: Indiana University Press, 1967.

For topical bibliographies of Kierkegaard studies, see *Søren Kierkegaard's Journals and Papers*, I–IV, 1967–75.

INDEX

Aaron, 455
Abel, 273
Abraham and Isaac, 179
Abraham à St. Clara, 439
absorption: in today, 73
abyss, 102; earthly loftiness as, 57–59; as paganism, 59; and rich and poor man, 371; shriek from, 77
accidental, 323
acedia, 171–72, 446
acting: and diligence, 330; and drunkenness, 339–42
action vs. words, 245
actress: admiration of, 313–14, 317; aging of, 318; debut of, 313; dialectical qualifications, 310; indefinable possession of, 307–09; maturity of, 412; metamorphosis of, 306, 318–24; presence of, 307–09; pressure on, 312; relation to idea, 320; resonance in, 311–12; thirty-first year, 314; voice of, 313; youthfulness of, 307–09
actuality: address to, 231–32; moment of, 232
Adam, 170
address: to actuality, 231–32
admiration, 240–41, 314–15; of actress, 313–14; duplexity of, 130–31; habit of, 318; insipidness of, 303–04, 331, 333; and reflection, 331
age, the: accommodation to, 230; confusing concepts of, 418; demands of, 165, 204, 227; theocentricity of, 384; wisdom of, 67
aging actress, 304–06, 318; prejudice against, 304–06
Alcibiades, 157, 241, 448

aloneness, 257, 265
ambiguity, 193
America, 239
analogy: accounts payable, 185; actor, 53, 56; actor blinded, 73; admiration, 130–31; animal defense weapon, 112; animated conversation, 124–25; arrow in heart, 192; authors, 316; baby's name, 199; beacon, 59; beloved, dressed for, 329; bereaved woman, 136–37; bird singing, 85; blind, 147; blindness, 237; boat, 73–74; book, 75; bubble, 89; building, 255–56; burning at stake, 112; child, 46–47, 53, 56, 84, 374; child excluded, 263; child helping, 365–67; child walking, 286; congratulating caller, 111; cure, 159; dark night, 256; divided kingdom, 87; divining rod and spring, 96; drinking wine, 426; execution, 78; exhausted bird, 79; fair wind, 158; faithfulness between two people, 284–85; fire, 78, 170; fireworks, 206; fisherman, 377; fish/plant relationship, 244–45; former parade horse, 338; fortress, 86–87; fox, 378; fragrant essence, 118; gales and breeze, 109; garment, 208; ghost, 79; gnat and camel, 72; guilty person, 135; help-line, 55; horsemanship, 386; hymn of praise, 85–86; impatient physician, 168; insurance company, 148; kernel of grain, 111–12; leper, 226; lily and bird as children, 62; love, 237; lover's praise, 177; marketplace children, 318;

analogy (*cont.*)

medicine, 96; merchant, 106, 134, 253; military, 76; moth and rust, 102; mourner, 261; murdered actor, 101–02; nature, 255; naughty child, 50; nettles, 158; nighttime sickbed, 164; obedient child, 65; open door, 86; pain of childbirth, 112; painting, 103; parasitic plant, 98–99; parent/ child, 63; party, 81–82; patient blaming physician, 111; perspective in drawing, 135; physician's treatment, 136–37; pirated edition, 64; prisoner, 256; purchase, 88; purified gold, 102; rare plant, 314; reed in the wind, 230; riddle, 256; road and direction, 39–40; rotten wood, 58; royal visit, 315; sailor, 253; sailor's conversation, 331; secret chest, 111; ship adrift, 214; ship reaching goal, 117; ship's boundaries, 219; shipwrecked person, 220, 256; sick, 371; siege, 86–87; Simon, 68; sinking ship, 78; snare, 39–40; soaring bird, 49–50, 82; spelling, 54; steering, 153; stolen goods, 67; storm, 277, 299, 394; subject/king, 63; sun, 272; supernatural, 147; supply, 87; surgeon, 210; Tantalus, 46; teacher punishing child, 381; teacher/pupil, 63, 72–73, 142, 286, 386, 391, 400; theft from beggar, 111; thief, 102; toy tin trumpet, 85; trapdoor, 114; trapped animal, 100; travel, 215; traveler, 106; troll, 71; trombone, 85; two names, 40; two paths, 87; unfruitful tree, 109; unlit candle, 146; vanishing fruit, 46; village, 71; walking on head, 150; water, 98; wife, 210; will-o'-the-wisp, 58; wind, 253; wind and breeze, 192; wolf guarding sheep, 23

angel of Satan, 65
annulled elements, 54
anxiety, 68, 78, 80, 200, 243, 280, 293, 294, 311; of actress, 312; becoming intensity, 312–13; of pagan, 69; in the power of, 66–67; of theater audience, 311; of truth, 170; over unfaithfulness, 284–85
apostle, 235, 292, 359; in these times, 107
apostles, 228, 252, 391, 393
appearances, 315; deceptive, 106; earthly, 207
appreciation, genuine, 304
Archimedes, 148, 324, 445
Arsenius, Saint, 17, 439
artist, 163, 173
Ascension, 296, 397
ascent, downward, 395
assassination, of curiosity, 314
assurance, 363
Atonement, 280, 298–99, 399
atonement, 265
attacker: Christianity as, 162, 202–03, 377
attack from behind, 76, 162, 378
author, 385
authorities, public, 18
authority, xi, 359, 385; divine, 189
awakening, 108, 110, 164, 177, 192, 387, 394
awareness: of God, 64

banalities, 303
baptismal liturgy, 459
bearing, Captain Scipio's. *See* Captain Scipio: posture and bearing
Beatitudes, 222
Beatitudes, Mount of the, 222
becoming something in the world, 183
beginning, 189, 216, 219, 319, 385; return to, 324
behind, attack from, 76, 162, 378